Military Assistance on Request and the Use of Force

Military Assistance on Request and the Use of Force

ERIKA DE WET

Professor of International Law at the Faculty of Law, University of Graz, Austria, and Honorary Professor at the Faculty of Law, University of Bonn, Germany

OXFORD
UNIVERSITY PRESS

OXFORD
UNIVERSITY PRESS

Great Clarendon Street, Oxford, OX2 6DP,
United Kingdom

Oxford University Press is a department of the University of Oxford.
It furthers the University's objective of excellence in research, scholarship,
and education by publishing worldwide. Oxford is a registered trade mark of
Oxford University Press in the UK and in certain other countries

First Edition published in 2020

Impression: 1

Published in the United States of America by Oxford University Press
198 Madison Avenue, New York, NY 10016, United States of America

British Library Cataloguing in Publication Data
Data available

Library of Congress Control Number: 2019954569

ISBN 978–0–19–878440–1

Printed and bound by
CPI Group (UK) Ltd, Croydon, CR0 4YY

Acknowledgements

The research for this monograph was undertaken in my capacity as SARChI Professor of International Constitutional Law at the University of Pretoria, South Africa, and Honorary Professor at the University of Bonn, Germany. It was conceptualized during a fellowship at the Stellenbosch Institute for Advanced Study (STIAS) in 2015. Subsequent research was undertaken with the generous financial support of the South African Research Chairs Initiative of the Department of Science and Technology and National Research Foundation of South Africa (Grant No 98338), as well as scholarships from the German Academic Exchange Service (DAAD) and the Alexander von Humboldt Foundation.

This monograph was preceded by several articles dealing with aspects of military assistance on request. The first was E de Wet, 'The Modern Practice of Intervention by Invitation in Africa and its Implications for the Prohibition of the Use of Force' (2015) 26 European Journal of International Law 979–98. Segments of this article were subsequently integrated into Chapters 2 and 3 of this monograph. The most recent article concerned E de Wet, 'The Role of Democratic Legitimacy in the Recognition of Governments in Africa since the End of the Cold War' (2019) 17 Journal of International Constitutional Law 470–78. This contribution was based on some of the analysis in Chapter 2. I would also like to express my gratitude to Cambridge University Press (CUP) for allowing me to integrate two of my articles previously published with CUP journals into the monograph. These are 'Complicity in the Violations of Human Rights and Humanitarian Law by Incumbent Governments through Direct Military Assistance on Request' (2018) 67 International and Comparative Law Quarterly 287–314, and 'The Invocation of the Right to Self-Defence in Response to Armed Attacks Conducted by Armed Groups: Implications for Attribution' (2019) 32 Leiden Journal of International Law 91–110. While the former article constitutes the basis for Chapter 4 of the monograph, the latter forms the foundation for Chapter 6.

I would like to extend my gratitude to the personnel of the Oliver R Tambo Law Library at the University of Pretoria, the Library of the Peace Palace in The Hague, and the Public International Law Library at the University of Bonn for their invaluable assistance pertaining to the finding of sources. I am particularly indebted to Professor Dr M Matthias Herdegen and his team at the Institute for Public Law (*Institut für Öffentliches Recht*) in the Faculty of Law of the University Bonn, for their sustained support during the past years. Last but not least, I am very grateful to friends and colleagues around the globe (as well as anonymous peer reviewers) for their valuable substantive comments over the years.

Erika de Wet

Contents

List of Abbreviations

ACHPR	African Commission on Human and Peoples' Rights
ACtHPR	African Court of Human and Peoples' Rights
AFISMA	African-led International Support Mission in Mali
AMIB	African Mission in Burundi
AMIS	AU Mission in Sudan
AMISOM	African Union Mission in Somalia
art	article
ASR	Articles on Responsibility of States for Internationally Wrongful Acts
AU	African Union
BSA	Bilateral Security Agreement
CAR	Central African Republic
DAAD	German Academic Exchange Service
DARIO	Draft Articles on the Responsibility of International Organizations
DRC	Democratic Republic of the Congo
EAC	East African Community
ECCAS	Economic Community of Central African States
ECHR	European Convention on Human Rights
ECOMOG	ECOWAS Ceasefire Monitoring Group
ECOWAS	Economic Community of West African States
ECtHR	European Court of Human Rights
EU	European Union
FARC	Revolutionary Armed Forces of Colombia
FARDC	*Forces armées de la République démocratique du Congo*
FSA	Free Syrian Army
GCC	Cooperation Council for the Arab States of the Gulf
HRDDP	Human Rights Due Diligence Policy
IADC	Inter-American Democratic Charter
ICCPR	International Covenant on Civil and Political Rights
ICESCR	International Covenant on Economic, Social and Cultural Rights
ICJ	International Court of Justice
IDI	Institut de Droit International
IGAD	Intergovernmental Authority on Development
ILC	International Law Commission
IS	Islamic State in Iraq and the Levant
ISAF	International Security Assistance Force
KDF	Kenyan Defence Force
KRG	Kurdistan Regional Government
LRA	Lord's Resistance Army

MAES	AU Electoral and Security Assistance Mission
MAPROBU	African Prevention and Protection Mission in Burundi
MINUSMA	Multidimensional Integrated Stabilization Mission in Mali
MNLA	Mouvement National pour la Libération de l'Azawad
MONUC	UN Organization Mission in the Democratic Republic of the Congo
MoU	Memorandum of Understanding
NAM	Non-Aligned Movement
NATO	North Atlantic Treaty Organization
NDS	National Directorate of Security
NGO	non-governmental organization
NIAC	non-international armed conflict
NTC	National Transitional Council
OAS	Organization of American States
OAU	Organization of African Unity
para	paragraph
PKK	Kurdish Workers' Party
RTF	Regional Task Force
SADC	Southern African Development Community
SOC	Syrian Opposition Coalition
SPLA	Sudan People' Liberation Army
SPLM	South Sudan People's Liberation Movement
STIAS	Stellenbosch Institute for Advanced Study
TFG	Transitional Federal Government of Somalia
UK	United Kingdom
UN	United Nations
UNGA	United Nations General Assembly
UNMISS	UN Mission in the Republic of South Sudan
UNOCI	United Nations Operation in Côte d'Ivoire
UNSC	United Nations Security Council
UPDF	Ugandan People's Defence Force
US	United States
VCLT	Vienna Convention on the Law of Treaties
YPG/PYD	Yekîneyên Parastina Gel

1
Introduction

1. Introducing the concept

The analysis undertaken in this monograph is aimed at identifying the legal conditions set by contemporary (post-Cold War) international law for the legal construct of military assistance on request. In so doing, it departs from a definition of military assistance on request that refers to the exercise of forcible measures by the armed forces of a state or those placed at the disposal of an international organization in the territory of another state at the latter's request.[1] The study thus departs from a legal construct that turns on the valid consent of the state in which the forcible measures are to be exercised (the territorial state). As a consequence the terms 'request' and 'consent' can be used interchangeably, as two sides of the same coin.[2] Furthermore, the notion of consent in this study corresponds to the customary international law concept of consent, according to which the exercise of consent by a state is a key manifestation of state sovereignty.[3] By expressing a request for military assistance, a state essentially expresses consent to be bound by an agreement in accordance with which another subject of international law can exercise forcible measures on the requesting state's territory.[4]

[1] The definition was informed by that of the *Institut de Droit International* (IDI), *Resolution on Military Assistance on Request* (8 September 2011), arts 1(a) and 1(b) <http://www.idi-iil.org/idiE/navig_res_chon.html>. However, it also extends beyond this definition, which does not refer to the military assistance that can be rendered by international organizations. For further clarification of the terminology, see section 3.

[2] See IDI (2011 Resolution) (n 1) art 1(b) which refers to a request as the 'free expression of will' of the 'host state's consent'. It stipulates that '"[r]equest" means a request reflecting the free expression of will of the requesting state and its consent to the terms and modalities of the military assistance'. See also *Certain Expenses of the United Nations (article 17, paragraph 2, of the Charter), Advisory Opinion* [1962] ICJ Rep 164. The ICJ used the terms 'request' and 'consent' interchangeably in distinguishing it from 'coercive action'. See also QTT Nguyen, 'Rethinking the Legality of Intervention by Invitation: Toward Neutrality' (2019) [First View] Journal of Conflict and Security Law 4.

[3] See ILC, 'Draft Articles on Responsibility of States for Internationally Wrongful Acts with Commentaries' (2001) II Yearbook of the International Law Commission, UN Doc A/Res/56/83 (12 December 2001). The ILC Commentary to art 20 para (1) described consent as a 'basic international law principle'. See also G Hafner (Rapporteur), 'Final Report: Intervention by Invitation' (2009) 73 Annuaire de l'Institut de droit international 404; G Nolte, *Eingreifen auf Einladung: Zur völkerrechtlichen Zulässigkeit des Einsatzes fremder Truppen im internen Konflikt auf Einladung der Regierung* (Springer 1999) 117; M Byrne, 'Consent and the Use of Force: An Examination of Intervention by Invitation as a Basis for US Drone Strikes in Pakistan, Somalia and Yemen' (2016) 3 Journal on the Use of Force and International Law 101.

[4] Nguyen (n 2) 4.

Contemporary state practice suggests that these agreements can be divided into two broad categories, the first being requests for military assistance by a state to one or more states, while the second concerns requests for military assistance to international organizations (notably in the form of regional and sub-regional organizations).[5] One may further distinguish between ad hoc requests for (or consent to) military assistance in response to a particular situation that has arisen in the territorial state, and *ex ante* consent included in a pro-invasion ('guarantee') treaty clause. The large majority of requests for military assistance in the post-Cold War era have been extended to individual states or groups of states on the basis of ad hoc agreements.[6] Pertinent examples include the French military operation in Mali in 2013, the Ugandan operation in South Sudan from 2014 to 2015, the Russian military presence in Syria since 2015, and the Saudi-led military coalition in Yemen since 2015.[7]

However, in Africa, in particular, requests for military assistance have also been extended to regional or sub-regional organizations on the basis of their treaty frameworks that facilitate ad hoc as well as *ex ante* military assistance to member states. For example, article 4(j) of the Constitutive Act of the African Union (AU) of 2000 enables ad hoc requests for military assistance by a member state of the AU. It explicitly recognizes the right of member states to 'request intervention from the AU in order to restore peace and security'.[8] In addition, article 4(h) of the AU Constitutive Act seems to provide *ex ante* consent to military assistance in specified circumstances. It determines that the AU has the right 'to intervene in a member state pursuant to a decision of the Assembly in respect of grave circumstances, namely: war crimes, genocide and crimes against humanity'.[9] Similarly, article 25 of the Protocol Relating to the Mechanism for Conflict Prevention, Management, Resolution, Peace-Keeping and Security of 1999 of Economic Community of West African States (ECOWAS) at first sight constitutes *ex ante* consent in the form of a pro-invasion clause.[10] It facilitates military intervention by the organization in its member states in situations that range from external (threats of) aggression, to inter-state conflict, situations of serious and massive violations of human rights and the rule of law, as well as the overthrow

[5] For the definitions of an international and regional organization respectively, see section 3.

[6] In fact, in the post-Cold War era military assistance by individual states that were based on *ex ante* consent expressed in pro-invasion treaty clauses hardly ever occurred. For an example of such a treaty clause dating from the Cold War era, see the Treaty of Guarantee of Nicosia of 16 August 1960, 382 UNTS 3, between the United Kingdom, Greece, Turkey, and Cyprus. See also Hafner (n 3).

[7] See Chapter 3, section 4.

[8] Constitutive Act of the African Union of 11 July 2000, 2158 UNTS 3, art 4(j) <http://www.peaceau.org/uploads/au-act-en.pdf>. It confirms 'the right of member states to request intervention from the Union in order to restore peace and security'. See also Chapter 3, section 3.3.

[9] AU Constitutive Act (n 8) art 4(h).

[10] Protocol Relating to the Mechanism for Conflict Prevention, Management, Resolution, Peace-Keeping and Security of 10 December 1999 <https://www.zif-berlin.org/fileadmin/uploads/analyse/dokumente/ECOWAS_Protocol_ConflictPrevention.pdf>. See also Chapter 5, section 2.

or attempted overthrow of a democratically elected government.[11] It also provides for military intervention by the organization during domestic conflicts that threaten to trigger a humanitarian disaster, or that pose a serious threat to peace and security in the sub-region.[12]

A common feature of all the above-mentioned agreements is that the legality of any forcible measures resulting from them hinges on the valid consent expressed by the territorial state.[13] It is a prerequisite for making the forcible measures in question reconcilable with the prohibition of the threat or use of force against the territorial integrity or political independence of a state in article 2(4) of the United Nations (UN) Charter.[14] In the absence of valid consent, the forcible measures would amount to coercive action in violation of article 2(4) of the UN Charter.[15] In such an instance the forcible measures in question would only be permissible if the conditions of the right to individual or collective self-defence in article 51 of the UN Charter have been fulfilled, or where authorized by the United Nations Security Council (UNSC) under Chapter VII and/or VIII of the UN Charter.[16] In this context it is worth noting that in as far as 'regional arrangements or agencies' are concerned,[17] article 53(1) of the UN Charter explicitly affirms that any 'enforcement action' undertaken by them has to be authorized by the UNSC.[18] However, as 'enforcement action' is synonymous with 'coercive action',[19]

[11] ECOWAS Mechanism Protocol (n 10) art 25.

[12] ibid.

[13] As will be illuminated in section 2 following and in particular in Chapter 5, section 5, it remains controversial in scholarship whether *ex ante* consent expressed through a pro-invasion clause needs to be complemented by ad hoc consent at the time that the military assistance takes place.

[14] United Nations, Charter of the United Nations of 24 October 1945 1 UNTS 16 <https://treaties.un.org/doc/source/docs/charter-all-lang.pdf>. Art 2(4) determines that '[a]ll Members shall refrain in their international relations from the threat or use of force against the territorial integrity or political independence of any state, or in any other manner inconsistent with the Purposes of the United Nations'. See also GH Fox, 'Intervention by Invitation' in M Weller (ed), *The Oxford Handbook of the Use of Force in International Law* (OUP 2015) 816; T Ruys and L Ferro, 'Weathering the Storm: Legality and Legal Implications of the Saudi-Led Military Intervention by Invitation' (2016) 65 International and Comparative Law Quarterly 79.

[15] *Certain Expenses* opinion (n 2) 164; PE Harrell, 'Modern-Day "Guarantee Clauses" and the Legal Authority of Multinational Organizations to Authorize the Use of Force' (2008) 33 Yale Journal of International Law 423.

[16] E de Wet, 'The Evolving Role of ECOWAS and SADC in Peace Operations: A Challenge to the Primacy of the United Nation Security Council in Matters of Peace and Security?' (2014) 27 Leiden Journal of International Law 356.

[17] Terms that are broad enough to encompass regional or sub-regional organizations. See section 3 following.

[18] The UN Charter (n 14) art 53(1) determines that '[t]he Security Council shall, where appropriate, utilize such regional arrangements or agencies for enforcement action under its authority. But no enforcement action shall be taken under regional arrangements or by regional agencies without the authorization of the Security Council.' See also generally S Paliwal, 'The Primacy of Regional Organizations in International Peacekeeping: The African Example' (2011) 51 Virginia Journal of International Law 185 ff. See also Harrell (n 15) 422.

[19] See *Certain Expenses* decision (n 2) 164, 177. The ICJ also used the terms 'coercive' and 'enforcement' interchangeably. See also E de Wet, *The Chapter VII Powers of the United Nations Security Council* (Hart Publishing 2004) 32–33; Harrell (n 15) 423.

article 53(1) of the UN Charter would arguably not encompass forcible measures undertaken by regional organizations that are based on the consent of the territorial state.[20] Article 53(1) of the UN Charter, therefore, would not necessarily prevent any consent-based forcible measures by a regional organization in one of its member states.[21]

It is first and foremost in situations where the UNSC actually invokes article 53(1) or any other coercive measures under Chapter VII and/or Chapter VIII of the UN Charter that questions about the permissibility of parallel, consent-based forcible measures would arise.[22] In terms of article 103 of the UN Charter, obligations of member states under the UN Charter takes precedence over conflicting obligations under any other international agreement.[23] Therefore, if the terms of an agreement for military assistance between a regional organization and one of its members states conflict with any prior or subsequent binding UNSC resolution in terms of Chapter VII and/or Chapter VIII of the UN Charter, the agreement would not be enforceable. Moreover, the same reasoning would apply in instances where consent-based forcible measures are executed by individual states. Any agreement between the territorial and assisting state(s) would only be enforceable if and to the extent that it does not conflict with binding obligations under Chapter VII and/or Chapter VIII of the UN Charter. However, where no such resolutions have been adopted, consent expressed by a territorial state to either individual states or a regional organization in relation to forcible measures

[20] De Wet (n 16) 356; Harrell (n 15) 417, 426 ff; SD Murphy, *Humanitarian Intervention: The United Nations in an Evolving World Order* (University of Pennsylvania Press 1996) 342–43.

[21] The 1962 invocation of the Inter-American Treaty of Reciprocal Assistance and Final Act of the Inter American Conference for the Maintenance of Continental Peace and Security of 2 September 1947, 21 UNTS 77, constitutes (somewhat controversial) Cold War state practice in support of this view. During the Cuban missile crisis of that year, the United States *inter alia* relied on a combined reading of art 6, art 8, and art 17 of this treaty to justify the naval blockade ('quarantine') against Cuba. These articles allowed the Consultative Organ of the Organization of American States (OAS) to authorize, by a two-thirds majority, the use of force in situations of intra-continental conflict that endangered the peace on the continent. Accordingly, the OAS adopted a resolution on 23 October 1962 which authorized the use of force for the purpose of enforcing the quarantine. The United States claimed that these measures did not amount to 'enforcement action' in terms of the UN Charter, art 53(1) (n 14). However, from a treaty law perspective the arguments were problematic. The main aim of the quarantine was to block Russian vessels, although Russia (unlike the United States and Cuba) was not a party to the treaty in question. See A Chayes (at the time Legal Advisor in the US State Department), 'The Legal Case for US Action on Cuba' (1962) 47 Department of State Bulletin 763; Q Wright, 'The Cuban Quarantine' (1963) 57 American Journal of International Law 554 ff; Harrell (n 15) 434.

[22] Such an invocation will be preceded by a determination that a situation constitutes a threat to the peace, a breach of the peace, or an act of aggression in terms of the UN Charter (n 14) art 39. In practice, the UNSC does not always explicitly invoke art 53 when authorizing the use of force by a regional 'arrangement'. Instead, it authorizes such measures under Chapter VII of the UN Charter, thereby treating art 53 as an extension of Chapter VII. See C Gray, *International Law and the Use of Force* (4th edn, OUP 2018) 451; De Wet (n 16) 356.

[23] The UN Charter art 103 determines that '[i]n the event of a conflict between the obligations of the Members of the United Nations under the present Charter and their obligations under any other international agreement, their obligations under the present Charter shall prevail'.

on its territory in principle can facilitate the reconciliating of these measures with article 2(4) of the UN Charter.[24]

As far as the reconciliation of the use of force with article 2(4) UN Charter through consent is concerned, two lines of reasoning are identifiable in doctrine. Some authors have argued that it places the forcible measures of the assisting state beyond the scope of the prohibition of the use of force.[25] As a result, there is no intervention 'against' the political independence or territorial integrity of a state. Put differently, military assistance on request would not constitute an 'exception' to the prohibition of the use of force in the proper sense, as the term 'exception' suggests that the type of military action in question would in principle be covered by the prohibition of the use of force.[26] According to another line of argument, the reference to force 'against the territorial integrity or political independence' also covers military assistance on request *unless* it is certain that the request does not undermine the territorial or political independence of the requesting state. The mere fact that the forcible measures were requested by the state does not in and of itself imply that its territorial integrity or political independence was not violated.[27]

For example, military assistance on request which violated the right to self-determination recognized *inter alia* in articles 1(2) and 55 of the Charter would constitute an intervention 'against the political independence' of the requesting state. This in turn would also constitute a violation of article 2(4) of the Charter, regardless of the fact that the military assistance was based on state consent.[28] If interpreted in this manner, permissible military assistance on request is indeed an exception to the prohibition of the use of force. However, regardless of which of these lines of reasoning one prefers, both turn on the assumption that the request for military assistance is underpinned by valid consent. Both interpretations thus allow for military assistance on request that adheres to the requirements for valid consent.

[24] However, see D Wippman, 'Treaty-Based Intervention: Who can Say No' (1995) 62 University of Chicago Law Review 620. He notes that pro-invasion treaty clauses may be interpreted as an attempt to circumvent the UN Charter procedures for centralizing the use of force. Also see Hafner (n 3) 392, who questions whether *ex ante* consent in the form of pro-invasion clauses are reconcilable with the UN Charter (n 14) art 103. As noted in section 2 following, this issue is taken up extensively in Chapter 5.

[25] CJ le Mon, 'Unilateral Intervention by Invitation in Civil Wars: the Effective Control Test Tested' (2003) 35 New York University Journal of International Law and Politics 742; D Wippman, 'Military Intervention, Regional Organizations and Host-state Consent' (1996) 7 Duke Journal of Comparative and International Law 2010; K Bannelier and T Christakis, 'Under the UN Security Council's Watchful Eyes: Military Intervention by Invitation in the Malian Conflict' (2013) 26 Leiden Journal of International Law 860; Harrell (n 15) 429.

[26] See also Ruys and Ferro (n 14) 80, who note that a presumption exists that the use of force on foreign territory with the territorial state's consent generally does not violate international law.

[27] JA Perkins, 'The Right to Counter-Intervention' (1987) 17 Georgia Journal of International and Comparative Law 184–85.

[28] ibid 185–86.

2. Key legal controversies and chapter outline

In scholarship, the controversy concerning the requirements for valid consent centres on the authority entitled to extend a request or invitation for military assistance as well as the type of situations for which such assistance may be requested. A further controversy concerns the permissibility (or impermissibility) of military assistance to states implicated in widespread violations of international humanitarian and human rights law. Questions also arise in relation to what can broadly be determined as formal treaty law requirements applicable to military assistance on request. These notably relate to the specific organ or entity that has the competence to extend the request, the question of whether the consent might have been procured through coercion, as well as whether there are particular temporal requirements that might affect the validity of the consent. Another pertinent issue concerns the relationship between the legal construct of military assistance on request and the right to individual or collective self-defence in article 51 of the UN Charter. Finally, there is also the question of whether (the proliferation of) military assistance on request undermines the notion of collective security underpinning the UN Charter.

The question pertaining to the authority entitled to request military assistance, which will be addressed in Chapter 2, turns on the identification of the authority entitled to act on behalf of a state; that is, the *de jure* government. Particularly controversial is whether the requesting authority needs to enjoy democratic legitimacy and/or be in de facto control of a state's territory. While this question is unlikely to arise in situations where a request is extended by an authority that has effective control over both the territory and state apparatus, it becomes of key importance in situations where the inviting authority fulfils only one of these criteria or even perhaps neither. For example, Russia initially justified its military intervention in the Crimea in March 2014 with the claim that it had been invited by the democratically elected (although by then ousted) Ukrainian President Yanukovych.[29] In The Gambia, newly elected President Barrow requested military assistance from ECOWAS at a time when the incumbent President Jammeh refused to accept the election results and still had control over the state apparatus.[30] At the time of writing, parallel authorities exist in Venezuela, where a majority of states within the Organization of American States (OAS) acknowledged Mr Juan Guaidó as the democratically legitimate interim President of Venezuela. Simultaneously, however, President Maduro remains in control of the state apparatus and is yet to be derecognized as head of state by a majority of states. Under the circumstances it remains uncertain if and to what extent either of them could extend a request for military assistance.[31] An example of an inviting authority which has

[29] See Chapter 2, section 3.3.
[30] See Chapter 2, section 3.2.1.
[31] See Chapter 2, section 3.1.2.

neither been democratically elected nor exercises effective control concerns the Libyan Government of National Accord. This authority, which came about in 2015 through a negotiated settlement, has since its inception been unable to command any meaningful control over the Libyan territory, yet its competence to request military assistance has been acknowledged in UNSC Resolution 2259 (23 December 2015).[32]

A further controversy pertaining to the legal construct of military assistance on request, which is explored in Chapter 3, concerns the type of situation during which such a request may be extended. The debate centres in particular on whether an incumbent government may request (and receive) military assistance during a civil war which, as will be explained in section 3, is nowadays rather referred to as a non-international armed conflict (NIAC). At the heart of the controversy lies the right to self-determination, defined as the right of peoples within an independent state to choose their own political and socio-economic governance without interference from other states.[33] In accordance with one line of reasoning, military assistance to (the incumbent government of) a state during an NIAC would undercut the right of the people(s) within the state to determine their own political future.[34] In a situation where there is open, protracted revolt against an incumbent government to the point where it has lost control over parts of its territory and population, it is no longer 'representative' of the state (and its people) from the perspective of the right to self-determination. Any foreign military assistance provided to the incumbent government under such circumstances would prejudice the outcome of the internal contest for political power and thereby violate the right to self-determination.[35]

This line of reasoning reveals a close connection between the right to self-determination and the prohibition of the use or threat of force in article 2(4) of the UN Charter. It implies that military assistance to an incumbent government that violates the right to self-determination by preventing a state (or its peoples) from

[32] See Chapter 2, section 3.2.2 and Chapter 3, section 4.8.

[33] L Doswald-Beck, 'The Legal Validity of Military Intervention by Invitation of the Government' (1986) 56 British Yearbook of International Law 207; Bannelier and Christakis (n 25) 861; Nolte (n 3) 223, O Corten, *The Law Against War: The Prohibition on the Use of Force in Contemporary International Law* (Hart Publishing 2010) 289. See extensively Chapter 3, section 2.

[34] Le Mon (n 25) 753; Gray (n 22) 85; T Ruys, 'Of Arms and "Non-lethal Assistance": Issues Surrounding Third-state Intervention in the Syrian Civil War' (2014) 13 Chinese Journal of International Law (2014) 39, 43; D Akande, 'Would it be Lawful for European (or Other) States to Provide Arms to the Syrian Opposition?' *EJIL:Talk!* (17 January 2013) para 3 <https://www.ejiltalk.org/would-it-be-lawful-for-european-or-other-states-to-provide-arms-to-the-syrian-opposition/>. See extensively Chapter 3, section 2.

[35] Bannelier and Christakis (n 25) 861; Nolte (n 3) 245–46; Fox (n 14) 827. This reasoning further finds resonance in the IDI (2011) Resolution) (n 1) art 3. It determines that '[m]ilitary assistance is prohibited when it is exercised in violation of the Charter of the United Nations, of the principles of non-intervention, of equal rights and self-determination of peoples and generally accepted standards of human rights and *in particular when its object is to support an established government against its own population*' (emphasis added). See extensively Chapter 3, section 2.

determining its political future independently is also likely to amount to the use of force against the political independence of a state, as prohibited in article 2(4) of the UN Charter.[36] The reasoning further supports the notion that military assistance on request constitutes an exception to the prohibition of the use or threat of force in the sense that any such assistance remains permissible only if it does not violate the territorial integrity or political independence of the territorial state.

However, one of the most (if not the most) heatedly debated questions in scholarship is whether this line of reasoning is indeed a reflection of contemporary customary international law.[37] The uncertainty in this regard can be exemplified by its ambivalent reception within the Institut de Droit International (IDI), which has adopted two resolutions that are of particular relevance to the topic. The first concerned the IDI Resolution adopted in 1975 in Wiesbaden on 'Principles of Non-Intervention in Civil Wars'.[38] Article 2(1) of this resolution determines that '[t]hird states shall refrain from giving assistance to parties to a civil war which is being fought in the territory of another state'.[39] Article 2(a) of the resolution further stipulates that such states shall refrain from 'sending armed forces or military volunteers, instructors or technicians to any party to a civil war'.[40] This attempt at completely banning military assistance on request was a reaction to the political climate of the era, which was characterized by proxy wars of the major powers in countries such as Vietnam.[41] In this context, military assistance on request was regarded as a tool with which major powers could manipulate smaller states and which could easily be abused.[42] Even so, the claim that military assistance to the incumbent government was legally impermissible during a civil war was not unanimously supported within the IDI. In fact, the resolution was adopted with as many members abstaining as those that voted in favour (namely sixteen), while six voted against the resolution. In essence, therefore, only a minority of the IDI members at the time expressed outright support for the resolution.[43]

The differences of opinion within the IDI on the permissibility of military assistance on request during a civil war did not subside with the passage of time. This is

[36] Perkins (n 27) 189; Corten (n 33) 289; M Bennouna, *Le consentement à l'ingérence militaire dans le conflits interne* (Librairie Générale de Droit et de Jurisprudence 1976) 213.

[37] See Chapter 3, section 5.

[38] IDI, 'The Principle of Non-Intervention in Civil Wars' Wiesbaden (1975) http://www.idi iil.org/app/uploads/2017/06/1975_wies_03_en.pdf.

[39] IDI (1975) Resolution (n 38) art 2. See also Hafner (n 3) 365.

[40] IDI (1975 Resolution) art 2(a).

[41] Hafner (n 3) 366.

[42] ibid. See also Nolte (n 3) 314 ff, for an elaboration on the so-called defence treaties which France concluded with former colonies in the wake of decolonization. These agreements facilitated requests for military assistance by the respective African governments to France, for the purpose of upholding external defence as well as the 'internal defence'. However, by the 1970s these treaties were increasingly experienced as a new form of colonialism. Several African states, in an attempt to strengthen their sovereignty, renegotiated the defence treaties in order to remove references to the upholding of 'internal defence'. See also Nguyen (n 2) 13.

[43] Nolte (n 3) 117; Hafner (n 3) 365.

reflected by the fact that the IDI's 2011 resolution on military assistance on request refrained from taking a stand on its permissibility in a civil war.[44] It skirted the issue by limiting the application of the resolution to

> internal disturbances and tensions, such as riots, isolated and sporadic acts of violence and other acts of a similar nature, including acts of terrorism, below the threshold of non-international armed conflict in the sense of Article 1 of Protocol II Additional to the Geneva Conventions relating to the Protection of Victims of Non-International Armed Conflicts of 1977.[45]

It is also noteworthy that the IDI did not in any systematic way engage with state practice when debating and adopting the two resolutions in question.

A further factor that may potentially affect the validity of the consent, which is examined in Chapter 4, concerns the 'international law pedigree' of the territorial (requesting) state. The question notably arises whether third states are prohibited from sending its armed forces to requesting states implicated in widespread violations of international humanitarian and human rights law. If the answer were no, it would essentially imply that the validity of a request by an incumbent government for such military assistance would depend on whether it honoured its international obligations in terms of international humanitarian and human rights law. Article 3 of the IDI 2011 Resolution to some extent has stimulated debate in this regard, by stating that the 'sending of armed forces by one state to another state upon the latter's request' is prohibited if it is in violation of 'generally-accepted standards of human rights'.[46]

This statement may be interpreted as suggesting that it is prohibited under international law to send armed forces where this would result in the aiding or assisting of systematic human rights violations by the requesting state.[47] After all, in these situations the assisting state can potentially incur derivative responsibility for aiding or assisting systematic violations of international humanitarian and human rights law committed by the forces of the requesting state.[48] It is therefore arguable that in order to prevent this from happening, third states must refrain from providing armed forces to incumbent governments implicated in such violations. In the alternative (where such military assistance has already commenced), the assisting state will have to withdraw its armed forces in order to avoid incurring (further) derivative state responsibility for violations of human rights and/or humanitarian law by the requesting state.[49] However, if

44 IDI (1975 Resolution) (n 38) Preamble.
45 IDI (2011 Resolution) (n 1) art 2.
46 ibid art 3.
47 See Chapter 4, section 1.
48 ibid.
49 ibid.

one considers that numerous incidents of military assistance on request since the end of the Cold War originated from incumbent governments with very dubious records in the field of humanitarian and human rights law, the question arises as to whether the claim in article 3 of the IDI actually corresponds to modern state practice and *opinio juris*. Pertinent recent examples include the military assistance to incumbent governments in Afghanistan, Iraq, South Sudan, Syria, and Yemen.[50]

Chapter 5 engages with formal treaty requirements that can affect the validity of the consent underpinning the request for military assistance. In so doing, it analyses the extent to which the general international law rules of treaty law may have been amended by those specifically relating to the use of force. The first question to be explored in this regard concerns the entity or organ within the government that would have the competence to issue and terminate consent on behalf of the requesting (territorial) state. It remains disputed whether anyone but the head of state and/or government would have the competence to request military assistance, given the very intrusive nature of the use of force on the territorial integrity of a state.[51] Second, it needs to be determined what the benchmarks are for freely given consent. As the benchmarks for determining coercion in customary international law are very high, it needs to be determined whether these same benchmarks apply to consent to military assistance.[52] In light of the intrusive nature of forcible measures on a state's territory and the fact that the requesting states tend to be much weaker than the assisting states, it is arguable that the applicable benchmarks for coercion should be lower.[53] A third issue concerns whether consent needs to be expressed explicitly or whether it can be given tacitly; that is, implied by the circumstances. The relevance of the question can be exemplified by the United States' drone strikes in Pakistan since 2004 which (at least for some period) seemed to have been based on tacit consent.[54] The drone strikes in Pakistan further illustrate the fact that similar questions arise regarding the revocation or withdrawal of consent, namely, whether such withdrawal needs to be explicit or can be inferred from the circumstances.[55]

Particularly challenging is the issue of the timing of consent.[56] Under customary international law, consent has to be present at the time of the conduct in question, meaning that it has to be given in advance or at the time the conduct is occurring.[57] This raises the question of the legal implications of *ex post facto* consent, notably for the wrongfulness of the assisting state's conduct at the time of the forcible

[50] See Chapter 4, section 2.
[51] See Chapter 5, section 2.
[52] See Chapter 5, section 3.
[53] ibid.
[54] See Chapter 5, section 4.
[55] ibid.
[56] See Chapter 5, section 5.
[57] ASR (n 3) Commentary to art 20 para (3).

measures.[58] This question *inter alia* arose in The Gambia, where Senegalese troops in January 2017 were reported to have crossed the Gambian border several hours before the newly elected President Barrow had extended his request for military assistance.[59] At the other end of the scale, questions also arise about the need for temporal proximity between the prior consent issued by the requesting state and the actual forcible measures undertaken by the assisting state(s). Specifically, the question arises as to whether the *ex ante* consent in the form of the pro-invasion clauses in article 4(h) of the AU Constitutive Act[60] and article 25 of the ECOWAS Mechanism Protocol[61] would suffice under international law.[62] In view of the impact of the use of force on a state's sovereignty and territorial integrity, there is strong support in scholarship for the position that any *ex ante* consent expressed through bilateral or multilateral pro-invasion clauses has to be supplemented by specific, ad hoc consent by the recognized government at the time of the military presence.[63] Embryonic practice within the AU and ECOWAS, as well as the Southern African Development Community (SADC) supports this view.[64]

Chapter 6 is devoted to exploring the relationship between military assistance on request and the right to individual or collective self-defence in article 51 of the UN Charter.[65] Whereas the former legal construct turns on the presence of valid consent of the territorial state, the latter is triggered when a state falls victim to an armed attack. Despite the different legal criteria underpinning these two legal constructs, forcible measures in territorial states are sometimes justified with reference to both military assistance on request and the right to individual or collective self-defence. For example, Russia and Iran's presence in the Syrian conflict was based on an invitation extended by the Assad regime.[66] The US-led international coalition against the Islamic State (IS), on the other hand, was based on the right to individual or collective self-defence.[67] In Yemen, the Saudi-led coalition against

[58] ASR (n 3) Commentary to art 13 para (1); Island of Palmas (Netherlands/United States of America), UNRIAA [1928] vol II 845.

[59] See Chapter 5, section 5.

[60] ECOWAS Mechanism Protocol (n 10).

[61] ibid.

[62] See Chapter 5, sections 1 and 2.

[63] See IDI (2011 Resolution) (n 1) art 4(3) according to which '[i]f military assistance is based on a treaty, an ad hoc request is required for the specific case'.

[64] See Chapter 5, sections 1, 2, and 3.

[65] UN Charter (n 14) art 51 determines that '[n]othing in the present Charter shall impair the inherent right of individual or collective self-defence if an armed attack occurs against a Member of the United Nations, until the Security Council has taken measures necessary to maintain international peace and security. Measures taken by Members in the exercise of this right of self-defence shall be immediately reported to the Security Council and shall not in any way affect the authority and responsibility of the Security Council under the present Charter to take at any time such action as it deems necessary in order to maintain or restore international peace and security.'

[66] Letter dated 15 October 2015 from the Permanent Representative of the Russian Federation to the United Nations addressed to the President of the Security Council, UN Doc S/2015/792 (15 October 2015) 2.

[67] Letter dated 23 September 2014 from the Permanent Representative of the United states of America to the United Nations addressed to the Secretary-General, UN Doc, S/2014/695 (23 September 2014).

the Houthis invoked self-defence,[68] while the United States was relying on the invitation extended by President Hadi.[69] These examples suggest that the legal constructs of military assistance on request and the right to individual or collective self-defence can serve as parallel grounds for the use of force within the same state. Chapter 6 examines whether this can be the case, as well as whether there may be tensions between the two legal constructs.

In so doing, the analysis places particular emphasis on the increasingly expansive interpretation of the right to individual or collective self-defence and the (potential) implications thereof for the notion of consent that underpins the legal construct of military assistance on request.[70] In this context, two situations in particular come to mind, both potentially affecting the role of the consent to such measures of the state on whose territory the forcible measures are undertaken. The first concerns requests by incumbent governments for military assistance in response to (alleged) prior foreign intervention within the respective state's territory on the side of insurrectional groups. Such support by third states against an incumbent government can, under certain circumstances, amount to an indirect armed attack by a state.[71] Accordingly, the incumbent government can claim a right to receive military assistance from other states on the basis of the right to collective self-defence. If this were to occur, the request for military assistance may constitute a component of the right to collective self-defence, rather than a separate legal basis for the use of force. Moreover, the broader the scope of the type of third state support that would qualify as an indirect armed attack, the more leeway the territorial state and its allies will have to invoke the right to collective self-defence instead of the legal construct of military assistance on request.[72]

Second, states increasingly rely on the right to individual or collective self-defence when retaliating against armed attacks perpetrated by non-state actors located in third states (territorial states), regardless of the extent to which such groups have received assistance from the territorial (or another) state. In these situations, the states invoking self-defence against the non-state actor do not regard the seeking of the consent of the territorial state as decisive for determining the legality of their military operations within the latter's territory.[73] Instead, the question whether such consent was given would be merely one consideration in determining the necessity of the defensive measures in the territory of the state where

[68] Identical Letters dated 26 March 2015 from the Permanent Representative of Qatar to the United Nations addressed to the Secretary-General and the President of the Security Council, Annex, UN Doc S/2015/217 (27 March 2015) 4–5.

[69] See Letter dated 15 October 2016 from the Permanent Representative of the United states of America to the United Nations addressed to the President of the Security Council, UN Doc S/2016/869 (17 October 2016).

[70] See Chapter 6, sections 2 and 3.

[71] ibid.

[72] See Chapter 6, section 4.1.

[73] See Chapter 6, section 4.2.

the non-state actor is located.[74] A pertinent question which thus arises is whether the invocation of the right to self-defence in reaction to an increasing range of purported indirect armed attacks, and its invocation against non-state actors, have the potential to displace or usurp the legal construct of military assistance on request.[75]

Based on the analysis undertaken in Chapter 2 through Chapter 6, Chapter 7 will attempt to draw conclusions on what the customary international law requirements are for valid requests for military assistance. In addition, this concluding chapter will remark on the ambivalent relationship between this legal construct and the notion of collective security embodied in the UN Charter. On the one hand, there is the risk that military assistance provided by individual states or groups of states undermines the notion of the centralization of decisions regarding the use of force with the UNSC. It can further perpetuate the perception of neocolonialism and imperialism that have been associated with military assistance on request ever since the Cold War. On the other hand, clauses such as article 4(j) and potentially article 4(h) of the AU Constitutive Act and article 25 of the ECOWAS Mechanism Protocol suggest that military assistance on request can be deployed as a mechanism for maintaining regional peace and security. Similarly, the UNSC has on occasion endorsed military assistance on request, for example in Libya in UNSC Resolution 2259 (23 December 2015). This in turn suggests that, depending on the context, military assistance on request can be utilized in the interests of international peace and security and could therefore be reconcilable with the notion of collective security underpinning the UN Charter.

3. Methodology, delimitation, and terminology

In attempting to identify the customary international law benchmarks for valid requests for military assistance, the study engages in analytical desk-based research, relying on the traditional sources of international law to be found in article 38(1) of the International Court of Justice (ICJ) Statute.[76] In consequence, it regards customary international law as referring to those rules the existence and content of which are supported by a general practice that is accepted by law (*opinio juris*).[77]

[74] ibid.

[75] See Chapter 6, section 5.

[76] The Statute of the International Court of Justice of 18 April 1946, 33 UNTS 993, art 38(1), determines that '[t]he Court, whose function is to decide in accordance with international law such disputes as are submitted to it, shall apply (a) international conventions, whether general or particular, establishing rules expressly recognized by the contesting states; (b) international custom, as evidence of a general practice accepted as law; (c) the general principles of law recognized by civilized nations; (d) subject to the provisions of Article 59, judicial decisions and the teachings of the most highly qualified publicists of the various nations, as subsidiary means for the determination of rules of law'.

[77] See *inter alia, Jurisdictional Immunities of the state (Germany v Italy)* ICJ Rep [2012] para 55; ILC, 'Conclusions on Identification of Customary International Law' (2018) II Yearbook of the International Law Commission 19 (Conclusion 2).

Some of the questions pertaining to particular characteristics or requirements of a general practice and/or *opinio juris* are addressed in subsequent chapters, where they arise in relation to specific state conduct that can be relevant to the formation of customary international law.[78] In the interests of clarity it should nonetheless already be mentioned that the 'practice' considered includes state practice as well as decisions of international organizations pertaining to military assistance on request.[79] It should further be noted that the decisions of the UNSC and other international organizations are regarded as a form of derived treaty law. This follows from the fact that these decisions are taken on the basis of competencies allocated to the respective organization by means of a treaty. In addition, article 38(1)(d) is broadly understood also to include non-binding international law instruments, such as the draft articles of the International Law Commission and judicial and/or quasi-judicial decisions of international judicial bodies.

The analysis further concentrates on incidents of military assistance on request that have occurred since the end of the Cold War. Up to this point in time this legal construct more often than not was associated with the major powers and former colonial rulers.[80] However, as of the early 1990s, there has been an accumulation of requests for military assistance across regions and involving a diversity of state actors and international organizations. Within a changed political reality, the states requesting and providing military assistance have become increasingly diverse. In addition, new regional organizations such as the AU and ECOWAS regulated military assistance on request in their collective security frameworks. Yet, thus far there has been little comprehensive analysis of the potential legal implications of these developments for customary international law. Scholarly work has mostly been limited to journal articles focusing on specific case studies.[81] The comprehensive monographs on the topic were published either during or shortly after the Cold War, focusing primarily on the major instances of military assistance on request of that era.[82]

By focusing on incidents of military assistance on request since the end of the Cold War, this monograph complements these earlier scholarly works. However,

[78] See eg Chapter 3, section 5 and Chapter 6, section 4. In these sections the question of the relevance of the reaction of third states to certain conduct for determining a general practice and/or *opinio juris* arises.

[79] See ILC (n 77) (Conclusion 4.2). It states that '[i]n certain cases, the practice of international organizations also contributes to the formation, or expression, of rules of customary international law'.

[80] Particularly controversial incidents of this period included the Soviet interventions in Hungary (1956), Czecho-Slovakia (1968), and Afghanistan (1979); the US interventions in the Dominican Republic (1965), Grenada (1983), and Panama (1989); as well as the Belgian-led intervention in Stanleyville (1964). See extensively Nolte (n 3) 79, 261, 268, 271, 273, 282, 289; Doswald-Beck (n 33) 217, 223, 227; Hafner (n 3) 313.

[81] For example, Bannelier and Christakis (n 25); Ruys and Ferro (n 14); C Kreß and B Nußberger, 'Pro-Democratic Intervention in Current International Law: The Case of The Gambia in January 2017' (2017) 4 Journal on the Use of Force in International Law 251.

[82] Nolte (n 3); Doswald-Beck (n 33); Bennouna (n 36).

this does not imply that no reference is made to incidents stemming from the Cold War era. As these events significantly influence(d) the contemporary scholarly debate pertaining to the legality of military assistance on request, examples from the Cold War era are invoked in various chapters to inform the analysis. Furthermore, while not claiming to be exhaustive, the analysis of post-Cold War incidents of military assistance on request does attempt to be comprehensive and representative. It engages with incidents of military assistance across continents and with particular reference to Africa and the Middle East, where most of the modern state and organizational practice is occurring. In so doing, the study also places particular emphasis on military assistance during civil wars (NIACS), given that the permissibility of military assistance in these situations remains one of the most controversial issues in doctrine. As far as the temporal limitations of the study is concerned, it includes incidents relevant to military assistance on request as of 1990 through July 2019. All websites consulted were last visited on 9 December 2019.

The term 'military assistance' in this study refers to forcible measures (whether by land, air, or sea) in the territory of the requesting state, by the armed forces of the assisting state(s) or international organization(s), and under their respective command and control.[83] The study is not concerned with forcible measures undertaken by members of the armed forces of a state or international organization that have been placed under the authority of the requesting state, as a result of which these forces act exclusively for and on behalf of the requesting state.[84] This demarcation, which is informed by the principles of attribution in the Draft Articles on the Responsibility of States for Internationally Wrongful Acts with Commentaries of 2001 (ASR)[85] and the Draft Articles on the Responsibility of International Organizations (DARIO),[86] enables the study to focus on those instances of military assistance on request that has generated the most legal controversy in doctrine.[87] Unless otherwise stated,[88] it furthermore does not concern military assistance in the form of arms and/or other military (support) equipment. The study is thus limited to what can be described as 'direct military assistance'. Also, as the direct military assistance at issue is specifically intended to support the incumbent government of the requesting state, the study does not engage in any systematic

[83] ILC, 'Draft Articles on the Responsibility of International Organizations, with Commentaries' (2011) II Yearbook of the International Law Commission (DARIO). Art 7 determines that '[t]he conduct of an organ of a state or an organ or agent of an international organization that is placed at the disposal of another international organization shall be considered under international law an act of the latter organization if the organization exercises effective control over that conduct'.

[84] See ASR (n 57) art 6. It determines that '[t]he conduct of an organ placed at the disposal of a state by another state shall be considered an act of the former state under international law if the organ is acting in the exercise of elements of the governmental authority of the state at whose disposal it is placed'.

[85] See ASR (n 3) arts 4(1) and 6.

[86] DARIO (n 83) art 7. See also Hafner (n 3) 312–13.

[87] See also Hafner (n 3) 313.

[88] See notably Chapter 4, section 1 and Chapter 3, section 2.

analysis of classic peace-keeping operations. While these operations also require the consent of the territorial state, they further require the peace keepers to conduct themselves in an impartial manner vis-à-vis the parties to the conflict and to use armed force only in self-defence.[89]

Military assistance on request is sometimes also referred to as 'military intervention by invitation'.[90] However, in this monograph the term 'military assistance' is preferred to that of 'military intervention'. This relates to the fact that the term 'intervention' is frequently defined in very broad terms, as well as being associated with coercion.[91] For example, the UN General Assembly's Resolution 2131 (XX) of 21 December 1965 on Inadmissibility of Intervention[92] and Resolution 2625 (XXV) of 24 October 1970 on Friendly Relations[93] *inter alia* referred to intervention as 'armed intervention and all other forms of interference or attempted threats against the personality of the state or against its political, economic and cultural elements'.[94] As the type of forcible measures at issue in this study are, in principle, consent based, the term 'military assistance' seems more appropriate than 'military intervention'. In the same vein, the study rather refers to 'forcible measures' or 'military operation' than 'military intervention'. However, in those instances where the term 'military intervention' is used, this is done without implying that the intervention necessarily is coercive.

In the context of this monograph, the term 'international organization' means 'an organization established by a treaty or other instrument governed by international law and possessing its own international legal personality'.[95] The terms 'regional' and 'sub-regional' organization refer to those international organizations whose membership is composed of countries from a particular geographic (sub)-region and whose collective security frameworks are primarily directed at their own members.[96] This definition has its roots in article 52(1) of the UN Charter, which refers to 'regional arrangements or agencies' that deal with 'matters relating to the maintenance of international peace and security as are appropriate for

[89] UNSG, Supplement to an Agenda for Peace: Position Paper of the Secretary-General on the Occasion of the Fiftieth Anniversary of the United Nations, UN Doc A/50/60-S/1995/1 (3 January 1995) para 33. See also De Wet (n 19) 33; MP Moelle, *The International Responsibility of International Organizations: Co-operation in Peacekeeping Operations* (CUP 2017) 27–28.

[90] See Gray (n 22) 75 ff; Hafner (3) 309.

[91] See Hafner (n 3) 309.

[92] Declaration on the Inadmissibility of Intervention in the Domestic Affairs of the state and the Protection of their Independence and Sovereignty, UN Doc A/RES/2131 (XX) (21 December 1965) para 1.

[93] Declaration on Principles of International Law Friendly Relations and Co-operation among states in Accordance with the Charter of the United Nations, UN Doc A/RES/2625 (XXV) (24 October 1970), Principle 1.

[94] See also R Jennings and A Watts, *Oppenheim's International Law* (OUP 1992) 430. Intervention was defined as 'any dictatorial interference by a state into the affairs of another state for the purpose of maintaining or altering the actual condition of things'. See also Hafner (n 3) 309.

[95] DARIO (n 83) art 2(a).

[96] M O'Connell, 'The UN, NATO, and International Law After Kosovo' (2000) 22 Human Rights Quarterly 66; De Wet (n 16) 456.

regional action'.[97] This article suggests that the composition of a regional organization is premised on a distinctive geographic feature. This can be the (sub)-region from which all the member states come and/or to the geographic area in which the organization will operate.[98] From this article one can further deduce that a regional organization should have the task of taking care of the peaceful settlement of disputes within its own region.[99] In accordance with this reasoning the AU and the OAS would qualify as regional organizations, while ECOWAS and SADC would qualify as sub-regional organizations.

Finally, in light of the controversy regarding the legality of military assistance to incumbent governments in a 'civil war', it is necessary to clarify why this study uses the term interchangeably with that of a NIAC. Historically, the term 'civil war' was often used in relation to situations of belligerence, which was one of three categories used to describe violence within a state, the other two being rebellions and insurgencies.[100] Rebellions were isolated incidents which could be brought under control with limited use of force. Insurgencies implied more sustained violence by the insurgents, coupled with difficulties in suppressing it and an uncertain outcome.[101] For a state of belligerency to be declared there had to be a state of general hostilities, as well as control over and administration of a substantial part of the territory by the opposition forces.[102]

In modern international law the term 'non-international armed conflict' (NIAC) is preferred to 'civil war', ever since the inclusion of the phrase 'armed conflict not of an international character' in Common Article 3 of the 1949 Geneva Conventions on the laws and customs of war.[103] Although the Conventions do not define this phrase, the drafting history indicates that the drafters used the term 'civil war' when referring to the threshold for applicability of Common Article 3.[104]

97 UN Charter (n 14) art 52(1). See also C Walter, *Vereinte Nationen und Regionalorganisationen: Eine Untersuchung zu Kapitel VIII der Satzung der Vereinten Nationen* (Springer 1996) 276–77; De Wet (n 16) 355.

98 Walter (n 97) 356.

99 I Dekker and E Myjer, 'Air Strikes on Bosnian Positions: Is NATO Also Legally the Proper Instrument of the UN?' (1996) 9 Leiden Journal of International Law 413; Walter (n 97) 276; De Wet (n 16) 355.

100 S Sivakumaran, *The Law of Non-International Armed Conflict* (CUP 2012) 9–10; Le Mon (n 25) 746; BR Roth, *Governmental Illegitimacy in International Law* (OUP 1999) 173.

101 Fox (n 14) 822.

102 See extensively Sivakumaran (n 100) 10–11. See also Le Mon (n 25) 746–48; D Fleck, *The Handbook of International Humanitarian Law* (3rd edn, OUP 2013) 581; Fox (n 14) 822; Roth n (3) 175, 177. The relevance of these distinctions for foreign military assistance on the side of the incumbent government was that it was permitted in relation to rebellions, while controversial once the violence escalated into an insurgency. The uncertain outcome combined with some loss of territory questioned the continued capacity of the incumbent government for the purpose of inviting foreign military support. Chapter 3 will illuminate that similar arguments underpin claims that once an incumbent government faces open revolt as a consequence of which it has lost effective control over parts of its population and territory, military assistance to it would violate the right to self-determination.

103 Sivakumaran (n 100) 161. The texts of the four 1949 Geneva Conventions on the laws and customs of war are available at <https://ihl-databases.icrc.org/applic/ihl/ihl.nsf/vwTreaties1949.xsp>.

104 Final Record of the Diplomatic Conference of Geneva of 1949 Vol II-B (1949) 192; Sivakumaran (n 100) 161.

Moreover, the drafting history further indicates that the drafters interpreted the notion of civil war broadly for the purposes of determining the threshold of applicability of Common Article 3. The article operates at the level of internal hostilities that have escalated beyond riots and disturbances into an insurgency and was not to be limited to situations of belligerence.[105] This threshold lower than belligerence was subsequently also confirmed by the Protocol Additional to the Geneva Conventions of 12 August 1949, and Relating to the Protection of Victims of Non-International Armed Conflicts (Additional Protocol II), which excluded internal disturbances such as riots from its application.[106] Subsequent jurisprudence of international criminal tribunals confirmed that the threshold of a NIAC is crossed when the internal hostilities have been of a protracted nature, have reached a certain level of gravity,[107] and where the rebel groups possessed a certain level of organization.[108]

This apparent overlap between the terms 'NIAC' and 'civil war' is also supported by the change in wording that occurred in the 2011 Resolution of the IDI on Military Assistance on Request, compared to its resolution of 1975. While the latter underscored the importance of non-intervention in 'civil wars',[109] the IDI's 2011 Resolution refers to the term 'non-international armed conflict'.[110] Article 2(1) makes the resolution applicable to 'situations of internal disturbances

[105] Sivakumaran (n 100) 161–62.

[106] Protocol Additional to the Geneva Conventions of 12 August 1949, and Relating to the Protection of Victims of Non-International Armed Conflicts (Protocol II), 1125 UNTS 609 <http://www.icrc.org/ihl.nsf/INTRO/475?OpenDocument>. Arts 1(1) and 1(2) determine: '1. This Protocol, which develops and supplements Article 3 common to the Geneva Conventions of 12 August 1949 without modifying its existing conditions of application, shall apply to all armed conflicts ... which take place in the territory of a High Contracting Party between its armed forces and dissident armed forces or other organized armed groups which, under responsible command, exercise such control over a part of its territory as to enable them to carry out sustained and concerted military operations and to implement this Protocol. 2. This Protocol shall not apply to situations of internal disturbances and tensions, such as riots, isolated and sporadic acts of violence and other acts of a similar nature, as not being armed conflicts.' See also ICTY: *Tadic* IT-94-1-T (Trial Judgment, 7 May 1997) para 562; E David, 'International (Non-International) Armed Conflict' in A Clapham and P Gaeta (eds), *The Oxford Handbook of International Law in Armed Conflict* (OUP 2014) 356.

[107] See ICTY: *Tadic* IT-94-1-T (Decision on the Defence Motion for Interlocutory Appeal on Jurisdiction, 2 October 1995) paras 128–34; *Aleksovski* IT-95-14/1 (Trial Judgment, 25 June 1999) para 43; *Jelisić* IT-95-10 (Trial Judgment, 14 December 1999) para 29; David (n 106) 357.

[108] See *inter alia* ICTY: *Limaj and Others* IT-03-66 (Trial Chamber, 30 November 2005) paras 90 ff; ICTR: *Kayishema and Ruzindana* ICTR-95-1-T (Trial Judgment, 21 May 1999) para 174; ICC: *Katanga et Ngudjolo Chui* ICC-01/04-01/07 (Pre-Trial Chamber, Decision on the Confirmation of Charges, 30 September 2008) para 239; David (n 106) 359–61. However, see Fox (n 14) 827 who submits that it remains disputed whether the (restrictive) definition of a NIAC in Additional Protocol II can actually be applied to the term 'civil war'.

[109] IDI (1975 Resolution) (n 38) art 1(1) stipulates: 'For the purposes of this Resolution, the term "civil war" shall apply to any armed conflict, not of an international character, which breaks out in the territory of a state and in which there is opposition between (a) the established government and one or more insurgent movements whose aim is to overthrow the government or the political, economic or social order of the state, or to achieve secession or self-government for any part of that state, or (b) two or more groups which in the absence of any established government contend with one another for the control of the state.'

[110] IDI (2011 Resolution) (n 1) art 2.

and tensions, such as riots, isolated and sporadic acts of violence and other acts of a similar nature, including acts of terrorism, below the threshold of non-international armed conflict in the sense of article 1 of Protocol II Additional to the Geneva Conventions relating to the Protection of Victims of Non-International Armed Conflicts of 1977'.[111] In line with these developments, this study applies the term 'civil war' as being synonymous with that of a NIAC as defined in article 1 of Additional Protocol II.

[111] IDI (2011 Resolution) (n 1) art 2(1).

2

The Authority Entitled to Extend an Invitation for Direct Military Assistance

1. Introduction

The purpose of the current chapter is to determine the authority that is entitled to extend an invitation for direct military assistance by forces of land, air, or sea. In so doing, the chapter departs from the well-established principle in international law that the competence to request either direct military assistance or indirect military assistance (in the form of arms, logistics, or financing) rests with the *de jure* government. This is the authority whose representatives are accepted in international organizations, that accredits ambassadors, can legally enter into treaties, and can legally dispose of the state's assets and natural resources.[1] The current chapter thus turns on identifying the criteria for the recognition of the *de jure* government which, although a unilateral political act, is one of great legal consequence.[2]

Formally the recognition of governments remains the prerogative of states and not of international organizations. The acceptance of credentials of governmental delegations by international organizations, therefore, does not in and of itself amount to its recognition as the *de jure* government.[3] In practice, however, the acceptance of credentials by an organ of an international organization such as the United Nations General Assembly (UNGA) cannot be dissociated from the matter of *de jure* governmental status. It reflects the extent to which the member states accept that a particular authority is entitled to represent the state in question in international relations and incur rights and obligations on its behalf.[4] The practical relevance of the acceptance of credentials by international organizations in this regard has also been enhanced by the fact that states often refrain from explicit

[1] See S Talmon, *Recognition of Governments in International Law: With Particular Reference to Governments in Exile* (OUP 1998) 3 ff. For an analysis of the powers of the *de jure* government, see S Talmon, 'Recognition of the Libyan National Transitional Council' (2011) 15 ASIL Insights <http://www.asil.org/>.

[2] A Schuit, 'Recognition of Governments in International Law and the Recent Conflict in Libya' (2012) 14 International Community Law Review 383. On 384–85, Schuit further notes that due to the unilateral and discretionary nature of recognition, there is neither a duty to recognize a government, nor is there a right to recognition.

[3] Letter dated 8 March 1950 from the Secretary-General to the President of the Security Council Transmitting a Memorandum on the Legal Aspects of the Problem of Representation in the United Nations, UN Doc S/1466 (9 March 1950) 2–23.

[4] B Roth, *Governmental Illegitimacy in International Law* (OUP 2000) 258.

(formal) recognition of governments. Since the 1980s, states increasingly preferred implicit recognition through dealing with governments and entering into diplomatic relations with them.[5] The practice of implicit recognition intensified in particular after the United Kingdom announced that it would no longer engage in recognition but rather would allow its acceptance of a new regime to be implied by the extent of their diplomatic engagement with each other.[6] These developments were inspired by concerns that acts of formal recognition could be interpreted as political approval of the regime rather than a pragmatic acceptance of the actual power relations within a particular state.[7] However, as implicit recognition can make it more difficult to determine the legal status of an authority claiming to be acting on behalf of a state, the acceptance of its credentials by an international organization with broad or even universal membership becomes an important point of reference for determining whether it is the recognized government.

While the bulk of the analysis in this chapter is devoted to assessing the requirements for governmental recognition, section 2 will first revisit the premise that the competence to request direct or indirect military assistance rests exclusively with the *de jure* government. In particular, it will examine whether international law recognizes any exceptions in this regard and, if so, to what extent. Thereafter, section 3 will illuminate the criteria considered for the purpose of governmental recognition. These criteria include in particular the traditional requirement of effective control, as well as that of democratic legitimacy, which has gained prominence since the 1990s. In so doing, the analysis pays particular attention to developments within the Organization of American States (OAS) and the African Union (AU), followed by a comparison with recognition practices in other regions. The emphasis on the OAS and the AU follows from the fact that they represent the regions most affected by unconstitutional (ie undemocratic) changes of government, despite far-reaching institutional reforms aimed at curbing such practices since the end of the twentieth century.

The analysis in section 3 therefore emphasizes the practice in the regions in which there is most frequently a discrepancy between states' explicit, international

[5] See extensively Talmon (n 1) 3 ff; Roth (n 4) 19.

[6] See statement by the Foreign Secretary (Lord Carrington), Hansard, H Vol 408, cols 1121–1122, 28 April 1980: 'The nature of our dealings with regimes which come to power unconstitutionally in the light of our assessment of whether they are able of themselves to exercise effective control of the territory of the state concerned and seem likely to continue to do so.' See also H Charlesworth, 'Democracy and International Law' (2014) 37 Collected Courses of the Hague Academy of International Law 77; Roth (n 4) 137; G Nolte, *Eingreifen auf Einladung: Zur völkerrechtlichen Zulässigkeit des Einsatzes fremder Truppen im internen Konflikt auf Einladung der Regierung* (Springer 1999) 140.

[7] The approach has its roots in the Estrada doctrine of 1930, then introduced by the Mexican Secretary of Foreign Relations, Genaro Estrada. In accordance with his view, pronunciations by third states on the (change of) government of another constituted a violation of sovereignty. See 2 *Boletin Oficial de la Secretaria de Relaciones Exteriores, Estados Unidos Mexicanos*, September 1930, Vol LV No 9, 9, as translated in (1931) 25 American Journal of International Law Supplement 203. See Charlesworth (n 6) 77.

commitments to democratic governance and a 'might is right' approach in practice. In these circumstances, states (within and beyond the respective regions) will be confronted with the issue of whether to recognize either explicitly or implicitly an authority that came into power (or remained in power) through unconstitutional means. This in turn gives an indication regarding whether states give preference to the effective control doctrine or to democratic legitimacy for the purpose of governmental recognition. In other words, it is first and foremost in situations where effective control clashes with explicit international commitments to democratic legitimacy, in which the reactions of other states give the clearest indication which of these doctrines carry the most weight in contemporary international law.

This claim is not intended to deny that the reaction of the (members of the) OAS and the AU to unconstitutional change of government within their respective member states first and foremost gives an indication of their understanding of their own institutional instruments. However, given that these organizations represent almost half of the states within the international community, such reaction also gives some indication of the viability of democratic legitimacy as a pre-condition for governmental recognition in customary international law. Furthermore, the reaction of third states that are not members of the OAS or the AU to unconstitutional change of government within these organizations can give an indication of developments within customary international law. While they are not bound by the respective treaty frameworks of these organizations, such third states are bound by customary international law. Any consistent pattern of non-recognition on their part can be an indication that democratic legitimacy is also evolving into a criterion for recognition under customary international law.[8]

Section 4, the final substantive section of this chapter, draws attention to the fact that once an authority is recognized as the *de jure* government, this triggers a strong presumption of continued *de jure* status. The fact that the *de jure* government would subsequently be confronted with an insurgency, and/or be embroiled in a sustained armed conflict with opposition groups, would not in and of itself lead to a loss of its *de jure* status. However, the section also shows that the bias towards the incumbent government is based on the premise that it actually continues to exist during an armed conflict. In addition, it originated at a time when effective control was the exclusive criterion for governmental recognition. The question thus arises as to whether the presumption of continued recognition has any relevance in situations where the incumbent regime is no longer identifiable. Also, in light of the emergence of democratic legitimacy as a criterion for governmental recognition, it needs to be considered whether this presumption might become

[8] For a discussion of the extent to which the reactions of third states to state practice can amount to *opinio juris*, see Chapter 6, section 3. See also ILC Report of the work of the 68th session UN Doc A/71/10 (2016), Chapter V, Conclusion 9(1) and Commentary to Conclusion 10(1), para (7).

inapplicable if an (authoritarian) incumbent regime is challenged by an authority that claims to be democratically legitimated.

2. The illegality of (direct) military support to opposition groups

The illegality of military support (both direct and indirect) to opposition groups has long since been articulated in various resolutions of the UNGA. Notably, the 1965 UNGA Declaration on the Inadmissibility of Intervention in the Domestic Affairs of States determined that '[n]o states shall organize, assist, foment, finance, incite or tolerate subversive, terrorist or armed activities, directed towards the violent overthrow of the regime of another state'.[9] This statement was reaffirmed in the Friendly Relations Declaration,[10] as well as in the *Nicaragua* decision of the International Court of Justice (ICJ).[11] The ICJ underscored that the prohibition of intervention would become meaningless if opposition groups in a state were (also) permitted to request military intervention.[12] It further confirmed that indirect support in the form of arming and training of opposition groups can amount to a violation of the prohibition of the use of force in international relations.[13]

A narrow exception to this general prohibition of military assistance to the opposition developed in relation to national liberation movements fighting against

[9] Declaration on the Inadmissibility of Intervention in the Domestic Affairs of states and the Protection of their Independence and Sovereignty, UN Doc A/RES/2131 (XX) (21 December 1965) para 2.

[10] Declaration on Principles of International Law concerning Friendly Relations and Co-operation Among States in Accordance with the Charter of the United Nations, UN Doc A/RES/2625 (XXV) (24 October 1970). See elaboration on Principle (c), concerning the duty not to intervene in matters within the domestic jurisdiction of any state, in accordance with the Charter. See also D Akande, 'Would it be Lawful for European (or Other) States to Provide Arms to the Syrian Opposition?' *EJIL:Talk!* (17 January 2013) para 1 http://www.ejiltalk.org/; T Ruys, 'Of Arms and "Non-Lethal Assistance": Issues Surrounding Third-State Intervention in the Syrian Civil War' (2014) 13 Chinese Journal of International Law 32.

[11] See *Military and Paramilitary Activities in and against Nicaragua (Nicaragua v United States)* (Merits) [1986] ICJ Rep 14, para 191. See also *Armed Activities on the Territory of the Congo (Democratic Republic of the Congo v Uganda)* (Judgment) [2005] ICJ Rep 168 para 162.

[12] See *Nicaragua* decision (n 11) para 209: 'Indeed, it is difficult to see what would remain of the principle of non-intervention in international law if intervention, which is already allowable at the request of the government of a state, were also to be allowed at the request of the opposition. This would permit any state to intervene any moment in the internal affairs of another state, whether at the request of the government or at the request of its opposition. Such a situation does not in the Court's view correspond to the present state of international law.' See also GH Fox, 'Intervention by Invitation' in M Weller (ed), *The Oxford Handbook of the Use of Force in International Law* (OUP 2015) 820; C Gray, 'The Limits of Force' (2016) 376 Collected Courses of the Hague Academy of International Law 167.

[13] Although the jurisdiction of the ICJ in the *Nicaragua* decision was concerned with the interpretation and application of the customary prohibition of the use of force and not art 2(4) of the Charter as such, the decision did confirm an overlap in content between the customary rule and art 2(4) of the UN Charter. See *Nicaragua* decision (n 11) paras 188, 195, 228; Gray (n 12) 165.

colonialism, alien domination, and apartheid.[14] In the 1960s and 1970s various UNGA resolutions recognized national liberation movements as the legitimate representatives of their respective peoples in their struggle for self-determination against colonial, alien, or racist rule.[15] These respective liberation movements were thus recognized internationally as the legitimate spokesperson(s) of their peoples in their quest 'freely to determine, without external interference, their political status and to pursue their economic, social and cultural development'.[16] In line with this elevated status, recognized liberation movements *inter alia* gained observer status in various UN bodies.[17] Moreover, several UNGA resolutions further endorsed indirect military support for the national liberation movements in their liberation struggle (ie in the form of weapons, training, or financing).[18] These resolutions were not in themselves binding and were opposed by Western states.[19] Yet, socialist and developing countries consistently supported these resolutions and their foreign assistance to anti-colonial armed struggles in Africa became an open and established practice. In addition, no international body ever claimed that such support was illegal.[20] In light of this extent of third state military support for the liberation

[14] Roth (n 4) 212 ff; D Akande, 'Self Determination and the Syrian Conflict: Recognition of Syrian Opposition as the Sole Legitimate Representative of the Syrian People: What does this Mean and What Implications Does it Have?' *EJIL:Talk!* (6 December 2012) https://www.ejiltalk.org/self-determination-and-the-syrian-conflict-recognition-of-syrian-opposition-as-sole-legitimate-representative-of-the-syrian-people-what-does-this-mean-and-what-implications-does-it-have/.

[15] These included notably notably the Palestinian Liberation Organization (PLO); the African National Congress (ANC); the South-West African People's Organization (SWAPO); and the African Party for the Independence of Guinea and Cape Verde (PAIGC). See eg UN Doc A/RES/37/43 (3 December 1982) para 23 (PLO); UN Doc A/RES/25(227 (6 March 1981) para 4 (SWAPO); UN Doc A/RES/2918 (XXVII) (1972) (PAIGC). See also Akande (n 14); Roth (n 4) 227 ff.

[16] See Friendly Relations Declaration (n 10) Principle (e). See also International Covenant on Civil and Political Rights (adopted 16 December 1966) 999 UNTS 171 (ICCPR) art 1(1), which determines that '[a]ll peoples have the right of self-determination. By virtue of that right they freely determine their political status and freely pursue their economic, social and cultural development.' Similarly, the International Covenant on Economic, Social and Cultural Rights (adopted 16 December 1966) 993 UNTS 3 (ICESCR) art 1(1). The implications of the right to self-determination for military assistance on request is examined in Chapter 3.

[17] See extensively Roth (n 4) 228.

[18] While the Friendly Relations Declaration (n 10) remained vague on the issue, several other resolutions were more explicit. See inter alia UN Doc A/RES/3070 (30 November 1973) para 2, which reaffirmed 'the legitimacy of the peoples' struggle for liberation from colonial and foreign domination and alien subjugation by all available means, including armed struggle'. UN Doc A/RES/35/227 (6 March 1981) para 5 supported the armed struggle of SWAPO, while para 6 explicitly supported material, financial and military assistance to SWAPO.

[19] UN Doc A/RES/3070 (30 November 1973) was passed with ninety-seven votes in favour, five dissents, and twenty-eight abstentions. See UN Doc A/25/PV.111 (6 March 1981) 1914 ff, for criticism expressed by Western states. UN Doc A/RES/35/227 (6 March 1981) was passed by a vote of 114 in favour, no dissents, but 22 abstentions. See Roth (n 4) 2013–214; Akande (n 14).

[20] Roth (n 4) 213, 2015. UN Doc A/RES/3103 (XXVIII) (12 December 1973) characterized armed struggles against colonial, alien and racist regimes as international armed conflicts and attributed combatant status to those engaged in such struggles. The resolution was opposed by most Western states and adopted by a vote of eighty-three in favour, thirteen dissents, and nineteen abstentions. In 1977 this status was also recognized in the Protocol Additional to the Geneva Conventions of 12 August 1949, and Relating to the Protection of Victims in International Armed Conflict (Protocol I) (1977) 16 International Legal Materials 13,91, art 1(4).

movements, as well as the absence of practice condemning such support as illegal, it is fair to conclude that indirect military support to liberation movements constituted an exception to the prohibition of the use of force in international relations.[21]

That being said, the right of liberation movements to receive military support was limited to indirect military assistance. The right of self-determination could not be invoked to justify direct military intervention on the side of the liberation movement. Stated differently, it did not encompass the right of liberation movements to request foreign troops to liberate a territory from colonial, alien, or racist rule.[22] Similarly, liberation movements could not legally invoke the right to self-defence in terms of article 51 of the UN Charter or under customary international law.[23] The notion of 'armed attack' did not include forcible measures by colonial rulers against the people of the specific territory, thereby triggering a right to self-defence that would allow the 'sole representative of the people' to invite foreign troops to curb the aggression of the colonial ruler.[24]

In addition to these limitations attached to the right of liberation movements to receive military support, it is important to note that the right developed in the very particular context of decolonization and the struggle against racist regimes.[25] Outside of this context, states are yet to recognize the right of insurgent groups to receive military support in an armed struggle against the recognized government.[26] This also applies to opposition groups within a state that have been recognized as a separate people entitled to internal self-determination.[27] Moreover, even to the extent that a right to secession by a particular people within a state would be recognized in international law in situations of extreme oppression,[28] this would not encompass the right to military support of an armed struggle.[29]

[21] Roth (n 4) 213; Akande (n 14).

[22] Roth (n 4) 215–16.

[23] For the implications of the right to self-defence, see Chapter 6.

[24] See Roth (n 4) 215, who explained that while the analogy may be tempting, it has no basis in international law.

[25] Roth (n 4) 2010–211; Akande (n 14).

[26] Akande (n 14); A Nollkaemper, 'A Shared Responsibility Trap: Supplying Weapons to the Syrian Opposition' *EJIL:Talk!* (17 June 2013) https://www.ejiltalk.org/a-shared-responsibility-trap-supplying-weapons-to-the-syrian-opposition/.

[27] In accordance with the right to internal self-determination, those communities within a state that qualify as a people in terms of international law have to exercise their right to political, social, and cultural development within the borders of the state in question. See *Reference re Secession of Quebec*, 1998 Can Sup Ct LEXIS 39; Council of European Union, *Independent International Fact-Finding Mission on the Conflict in Georgia Vol II* (2009) 136 http://www.mpil.de/files/pdf4/IIFFMCG_Volume_II1.pdf; see also Chapter 3, section 2.

[28] In *Accordance with International Law of the Unilateral Declaration of Independence in Respect of Kosovo, Advisory Opinion* [2010] ICJ Rep 403 ff, the ICJ circumvented this opinion. For different scholarly opinions on the matter, see *Independent International Fact-Finding Mission on the Conflict in Georgia* (n 27) 138–39. It was also left open in *Reference re Secession of Quebec* (n 27) para 134. See also A Peters, 'Populist International Law? The Suspended Independence and the Normative Value of the Referendum on Catalonia' *EJIL:Talk!* (12 October 2017) https://www.ejiltalk.org/populist-international-law-the-suspended-independence-and-the-normative-value-of-the-referendum-on-catalonia/.

[29] T Ruys and L Ferro, 'Weathering the Storm: Legality and Legal Implications of the Saudi-Led Military Intervention in Yemen' (2016) 15 International and Comparative Law Quarterly 96. See also

This restricted nature of the right to military support to national liberation movements gains particular significance in relation to military support provided to the opposition in the Syrian conflict that broke out in 2011. Since 2013, various Western and Middle-Eastern countries have expressed themselves in favour of military support to the Syrian Opposition Coalition (SOC). For example, in January 2013 the United Kingdom (UK) Foreign Secretary suggested that European Union (EU) countries should consider providing arms to the opposition in Syria.[30] In May 2013 the Council of the European Union opened the door to the supply of arms to the Syrian opposition,[31] although EU member states have remained reluctant to provide equipment beyond body armour and armoured vehicles.[32] The United States Congress in 2014 approved the supply of 'training, equipment, supplies, and sustainment', to so-called appropriately vetted elements of the Syrian opposition.[33] Similarly, Middle-Eastern states such as Saudi Arabia and Qatar have provided the Free Syrian Army (which was regarded as the military wing of the SOC) with arms and funding.[34] The Arab League even went as far as claiming that states have a right to provide all forms of self-defence, including military support, to assist the Syrian people and the Free Army (the military wing of the SOC).[35]

In the period leading up to the endorsement of military support, many countries attributed some form of political legitimacy to the SOC that was reminiscent of the language used vis-à-vis national liberation movements. These

Independent International Fact-Finding Mission on the Conflict in Georgia (n 27) 279. It underscored that the right to self-determination of South Ossetia and Abkhazia did not justify military intervention by Russia.

[30] BBC, 'William Hague Says UK Could Start Arming Syrian Rebels' (10 January 2013) http://www.news.bbc.co.uk; Akande (n 10) para 1.

[31] Council of the EU, 'Council Declaration on Syria' (27 May 2013) http://www.consilium.europa.eu/uedocs/cms_data/docs/pressdata/EN/foraff/137315.pdf.

[32] Ruys (n 10) 15.

[33] HJ Res 124 Sec 149(a)(1)–(a)(3), 19 September 2014 https://www.congress.gov/113/plaws/publ164/PLAW-113publ164.pdf. Ruys (n 10) 16; Gray (n 12) 169; M Hosenball, 'Congress Secretly Approves US Weapons Flow to "Moderate" Syrian Rebels' *Reuters* (27 January 2014) https://www.reuters.com/article/us-usa-syria-rebels/congress-secretly-approves-u-s-weapons-flow-to-moderate-syrian-rebels-idUSBREA0Q1S320140127; P Zengerle and D Lawder 'US Congress Approves Arming Syrian Rebels, Funding Government' *Reuters* (19 September 2014) https://www.reuters.com/article/us-iraq-crisis-congress-vote/u-s-congress-approves-arming-syrian-rebels-funding-government-idUSKBN0HD2P820140919.

[34] Ruys (n 10) 25.

[35] Reuters Staff, 'Summit Says Arab States Have Right to Arm Syria Rebels' *Reuters* (26 March 2013) https://www.reuters.com/article/us-syria-crisis-summit-draft/summit-says-arab-states-have-right-to-arm-syria-rebels-idUSBRE92P0YE20130326. Syria protested against this practice in Identical Letters dated 12 March 2013 from the Permanent Representative of the Syrian Arab Republic to the United Nations Addressed to the Secretary-General and the President of the Security Council 14 March 2013, UN Doc A/67/793–S/2013/151 (14 March 2013) 1–2. In UN Doc S/2014/92 (25 February 2014), Saudi Araba reiterated its assistance to its 'Syrian brethren in their struggle against the terrorism of the Syrian regime'. However, it did not provide any legal justification for this position. See also Gray (n 12) 170.

political endorsements ranged from statements referring to the SOC as the 'sole legitimate representative of the Syrian people' to more qualified acknowledgment, describing the SOC as 'a legitimate representative of the Syrian people'. For example, France recognized the SOC as the 'sole legitimate representative of the Syrian people and thus as the future provisional government of a democratic Syria which paves the way to put an end to Bahar Assad's regime'.[36] The United Kingdom also referred to the SOC as the sole legitimate representative of the Syrian people.[37] States recognizing the SOC as 'the legitimate representative of the people' were issued by the Benelux countries,[38] Turkey,[39] as well as the Gulf Cooperation Council consisting of Saudi Arabia, Bahrain, the United Arab Emirates, Oman, Qatar, and Kuwait.[40] The United States seemed to regard the SOC as one of the legitimate representatives, as opposed to the sole legitimate representative. It referred to the SOC as 'a legitimate representative of the Syrian people'[41] and 'a legitimate representative of the aspirations of the Syrian people'.[42] Similar qualified wording was used by Italy.[43] The European Union was equally

[36] AFP, 'La France reconnaît l'opposition syrienne unifiée comme "seule représentante du people"' *Le Monde* (13 November 2012) http://www.lemonde.fr/proche-orient/article/2012/11/13/la-france-reconnait-l-opposition-syrienne-unifiee-comme-seule-representante-du-peuple_1790027_3218.html; S Talmon, 'Recognition of Opposition Groups as the Legitimate Representative of a People' (2013) 12 Chinese Journal of International Law 221.

[37] I Black, 'UK: Syrian Opposition "sole legitimate representative" of the People' *Guardian* (12 November 2012) https://www.theguardian.com/world/2012/nov/20/uk-syrian-opposition-sole-legitimate-representative-people.

[38] See *inter alia* Benelux Messages at Group of Friends Meeting Marrakech, December (12 December 2012) https://www.google.de/search?client=safariandrls=enandq=Government+of+the+Netherlands,+Benelux+-+messages+at+Group+of+Friends+-+meeting+Marrakech+(12+December+2012)andie=UTF-8andoe=UTF-8andgfe_rd=cranddcr=0andei=r-2jWu32Bcn68Aeq7b64DQ. See also Letter by the Dutch Foreign Minister to the House of Representatives, 'Volkenrechtelijke aspecten sanctieregime Syrië' (4 June 2013) https://zoek.officielebekendmakingen.nl/kst-21501-02-1263.html; Talmon (n 36) 222–23; Ruys (n 10) 36 ff.

[39] Statement by Mr Ahmet Davutoglu, Minister of Foreign Affairs of Turkey, at the 39th Session of the OIC Council of Foreign Ministers, Djibouti (15 November 2012) http://www.mfa.gov.tr/statement-by-mr_-ahmet-davutoglu_-minister-of-foreign-affairs-of-turkey_--at-the-39th-session-of-the-oic-council-of-foreign-m.en.mfa.

[40] BBC, 'Syria Crisis: Gulf States Recognise Syria Opposition' *BBC News* (13 November 2012) http://www.bbc.com/news/world-middle-east-20295857; S Erlanger and R Gladstone, 'France Grants Its Recognition to Syria Rebels' *New York Times* (13 November 2012) http://www.nytimes.com/2012/11/14/world/middleeast/syria-war-developments.html.

[41] MC Toner (Deputy Spokesperson, Office of the Spokesperson), 'Formation of the National Coalition for Syrian Revolutionary and Opposition Forces' Press Statement, Washington DC (11 November 2012) https://2009-2017.state.gov/r/pa/prs/ps/2012/11/200435.htm.

[42] US State Department, Daily Press Briefing, 12 November 2012 and 3 December 2012 https://2009-2017.state.gov/r/pa/prs/dpb/2013/index.htm; 'Obama Recognizes Rebels as "Legitimate Representative" of Syrian People' *NPR* (11 December 2012) https://www.npr.org/sections/thetwo-way/2012/12/11/167008761/obama-recognizes-rebels-as-legitimate-representatives-of-syrian-people; S Arsu and T Arango, 'Turks Grant Recognition to Coalition of Syrians' *New York Times* (12 November 2012) http://www.nytimes.com/2012/11/16/world/middleeast/turkey-recognizes-new-syrian-rebel-group-as-legitimate-leader-of-syria.html; Erlanger and Gladstone (n 38); Talmon (n 36) 223.

[43] See ANSAMED Staff, 'Syria: "Coalition is valid" says Monti' *ANSAmed* (19 November 2012) http://www.ansamed.info/ansamed/en/news/nations/syria/2012/11/19/Syria-coalition-valid-says-Monti_7820520.html. See also Talmon (n 36) 221 ff.

nuanced, referring to the SOC as 'legitimate representatives of the aspirations of the Syrian people'.[44]

The use of the indefinite article 'a' (as opposed to 'the'), the plural ('representatives'), and qualifiers such as 'aspirations' indicated a lack of consensus among states regarding the extent of the representativeness of the SOC.[45] Not all states were convinced that the SOC was speaking on behalf of all (or at least the great majority of) the political, ethnic, religious, and geographical groups.[46] Nonetheless, these references implied a certain political recognition of the SOC by states and a willingness to interact with it.[47] For example, some states permitted the SOC to open offices within their territories and appoint political representatives.[48] Others appointed liaisons to the SOC as its headquarters in Egypt.[49] However, this recognition did not amount to derecognition of the Assad regime as the *de jure* government, nor the recognition of the SOC as the new *de jure* government.[50] This is exemplified by the fact that the Assad government still exercised control of Syrian embassies abroad, including in countries that have recognized the opposition politically.[51] Furthermore, the fact that France referred to the SOC as a 'future provisional government' in and of itself implied that it was not yet recognized as the government.[52]

A pertinent question that arises in this context is whether this qualified political recognition of the SOC would allow it to receive weapons, training, and funding for its armed struggle. As noted earlier, references to the SOC as (a) legitimate representative(s) of the Syrian people is reminiscent of the language used vis-à-vis liberation movements in the 1970s. This language could suggest that the SOC qualified as a national liberation movement and therefore would be entitled to

[44] Council of the European Union, Council Conclusions on Syria, Doc 16392/12 (19 November 2012) http://register.consilium.europa.eu/doc/srv?l=ENandf=ST%2016392%202012%20INIT.

[45] Talmon (n 36) 225, 228.

[46] In relation to the SOC, statements by the United States suggested that political representativeness turned on inclusivity of all political, ethnic, religious, geographic, and gender groups. See US State Department (V Nuland, Spokesperson), *Daily Press* Briefing (8 November 2012) https://2009-2017.state.gov/r/pa/prs/dpb/2012/11/200347.htm. However, at the time of its recognition, more than thirteen armed groups within Syria had rejected the SOC. United Nations Human Rights Council, Independent International Commission of Inquiry on the Syrian Arab Republic, UN Doc A/HRC/22/59 (5 February 2013) para 14. Talmon (n 36) 240–41.

[47] Talmon (n 36) 230.

[48] These included the Netherlands, Britain, France, Hungary, Quatar, Turkey, and the United States. See Talmon (n 36) 243–44.

[49] Talmon (n 36) 244.

[50] Talmon (n 36) 231, 239, 244.

[51] Qatar constituted an exception. In February 2013 it turned over the Syrian Embassy in Doha to the SOC and accepted the appointment of the SOC representative as Syrian ambassador. This effectively amounted to recognizing the SOC as the government of Syria. See Talmon (n 36) 235; R Khalaf and A Fielding-Smith, 'How Qatar Seized Control of the Syrian Revolution' *Financial Times* (17 May 2013) https://www.ft.com/content/f2d9bbc8-bdbc-11e2-890a-00144feab7de. See also K Bannelier-Christakis, 'Military Interventions Against ISIL in Iraq, Syria and Libya, and the Legal Basis of Consent' (2016) 29 Leiden Journal of International Law 762.

[52] See also Nollkaemper (n 26).

indirect military support. However, any such analogy would ignore the fact that the Assad regime, while authoritarian, did not amount to a colonial, alien, or racist regime.[53] Put differently, the SOC was not fighting for independence from colonial rule but instead attempted to overthrow the government of an independent state.[54] Those states politically recognizing the SOC also did not explicitly equate it with national liberation movements, nor did they make any explicit reference to the right to self-determination of the Syrian people.[55]

In essence, therefore, the military support to the SOC in Syria cannot legally be compared to that rendered to national liberation movements.[56] Similarly, the claim of the Arab league that the military support to the SOC would be in line with the right to self-defence ignored the fact that the aggression of the Assad regime towards opposition groups in Syria did not amount to an 'armed attack' in terms of article 51 of the UN Charter.[57] The military support to the SOC for its part amounted to a violation of the customary prohibition of non-intervention, as well as of the prohibition of the use of force under customary international law and article 2(4) of the UN Charter.[58] It further amounted, at least at times, to an (indirect) violation of a UNSC-imposed arms embargo,[59] as elements within the SOC have collaborated with groups designated as terrorist by the UNSC.[60] Moreover, in light of the evolution of the right to self-defence in recent years, such military force could under certain circumstances amount to an armed attack against Syria that is attributable to the states providing military support to insurgent groups. Chapter 6, section 4, elaborates on the evolution of the notion of self-defence in

53 Talmon (n 36) 237.

54 See Akande (n 14); Talmon (n 36) 237.

55 Talmon (n 36) 235, 237.

56 See 'Austrian Position on Arms Embargo' (13 May 2013) https://archive.org/stream/700784-austrian-position-on-arms-embargo/700784-austrian-position-on-arms-embargo_djvu.txt. See also Nollkaemper (n 26); Akande (n 14).

57 In fact, states such as Saudi Arabia contradicted their claim that opposition groups could invoke the right to self-defence when in 2015 they denounced foreign military assistance to the Houthi rebels in Yemen. See Identical Letters dated 26 March 2015 from the Permanent Representative of Qatar to the United Nations addressed to the Secretary-General and the President of the Security Council, Annex, UN Doc S/2015/217 (27 March 2015) 4–5. See also Gray (n 12) 171.

58 See Austrian Position on Arms Embargo (n 56); Talmon (n 36) 232–34; Ruys (n 10) 37; Akande (n 14) para 4; Gray (n 12) 168–69.

59 See UN Doc S/RES/2083 (17 December 2012) paras 1 ff, which imposed extensive sanctions on any individual or entity associated with Al Qaida. Identical Letters dated 13 June 2013 from the Permanent Representative of the Syrian Arab Republic to the United Nations Addressed to the Secretary-General and the President of the Security Council, UN Doc S/2013/348 (17 June 2013) 2. See also Gray (n 12) 169.

60 For example, the Free Syrian Army has worked with Al-Nusrah which was subsequently designated as an Al Qaida affiliate by the UNSC. See *inter alia* UNSC Press Release, UN Doc SC/11010 (30 May 2013); BBC, 'Guide to the Syrian Rebels' *BBC News* (13 December 2013) http://www.bbc.com/news/world-middle-east-24403003. The US Congress made its approval of military assistance to opposition groups dependant on whether they were 'properly vetted' for association with terrorist groups such as Al-Nusrah and IS (see Res 124 Sec 149(e)(1) (n 31)). However, as the composition of the SOC, as well as the future association of units within this coalition with terrorist groups, remained fluid and unpredictable, any attempts at 'proper vetting' were likely to meet with limited success.

recent years, including the relaxation of the principles regulating the attribution of armed attacks by non-state actors to states providing them with military or financial support. Ironically, the very same states that in recent years have been driving an expansive interpretation of the right to self-defence, therefore, will have to consider the reality that their military support for insurgent groups in Syria against the Assad regime may potentially amount to armed attacks that trigger Syria's right to self-defence against those responsible for such attacks.

Politically, the open and sustained military support to the opposition can in part be explained by the manifest loss of credibility of the Assad regime among a broad coalition of states. In this sense, the open military support to insurgent groups is reminiscent of the armed support provided to the Sandinista insurgents in Nicaragua against the Somoza government in the late 1970s.[61] While illegal under international law, the military support to the Sandinistas was openly condoned by states in the region who perceived the *de jure* Nicaraguan government as manifestly unrepresentative of the people it was governing and for its egregious violation of its basic duty of care towards them.[62] In such situations some states are willing to tolerate openly or even applaud indirect military assistance to insurgents, despite the illegality of such actions.[63] However, any such precedent opens the door for states to decide unilaterally and subjectively when to set aside the prohibition on the use of force in international law, thereby risking its complete erosion.[64]

3. Determining the *de jure* government: effective control versus democratic legitimacy

While governmental recognition is a political act, it is not entirely unfettered by legal constraints. Traditionally, the key constraint imposed by customary international law is that of effective control, which served as the point of departure for identifying the recognized *de jure* government of a state.[65] According to this view, the fact that a particular government came into power by military coup, through an uprising of parts of the population, or through civil war was irrelevant for the purpose of recognition.[66] Rather than being concerned with the manner in which governmental power was acquired or exercised, recognition hinged upon

61 See extensively Roth (n 4) 292.
62 ibid 303.
63 ibid 318.
64 See also Roth (n 4) 303.
65 *Tinoco Claims Arbitration (Great Britain v Costa Rica)* 1923 1 RIAA 369; Talmon (n 36) 232; D Akande, 'Recognition of Libyan National Transitional Council as Government of Libya' *EJIL:Talk!* (23 July 2011) http://www.ejiltalk.org/.
66 BR Roth, 'Secessions, *Coups* and the International Rule of Law: Assessing the Decline of the Effective Control Doctrine' (2010) 11 Melbourne Journal of International Law 2; L Doswald-Beck, 'The Legal Validity of Military Intervention by Invitation of the Government' (1986) 56 British Yearbook of International Law 194.

demonstrable and sustainable effective control over the territory.[67] In practice this means that the regime claiming to be the government will usually control most, if not all, of the state's territory. At a minimum it must exercise control of the state machinery; that is, the capital and the state institutions.[68] In addition, effective control requires a certain amount of acquiescence on the part of the civilian population, which has to show an habitual obedience to the regime's authority.[69] The effective control doctrine thus turns on the reaction of the population to an incumbent government and their willingness to adhere to this government's rules.[70] Where such acquiescence in the will of the regime is present, international law assumes the incumbent government as being representative of the state (and its population) as a whole.[71]

This rational underpinned the *Tinoco* arbitration of 1923, which remains the case traditionally cited in support of the effective control doctrine. During a two-year military dictatorship in Costa Rica, following a coup by the Tinoco brothers in 1917, the Tinoco dictatorship *inter alia* granted a petroleum concession to a British company, and also issued special currency notes and bonds.[72] Subsequently, when the former Costa Rican government returned to power, these decisions were all revoked.[73] The United Kingdom then brought a claim on behalf of the British companies that had purchased the concession and currency respectively, arguing that the current Costa Rican government remained bound under international law by the decisions of the Tinoco government, which was the undisputed de facto and *de jure* government at the time of its existence.[74] Costa Rica for its part argued that these acts were invalid, as they were undertaken by a government that came into power in contravention of the country's constitution. In addition, several countries (including the United Kingdom) did not recognize it at the time.[75] The arbitrator (US Chief Justice Taft) rejected the argument that the unconstitutionality of a regime change outweighed effective control for the purpose of determining the recognized government. The evidentiary weight of (non)-recognition in international law depended on whether it related to the ability of a regime to exercise effective control, rather than its irregularity.[76] Stated differently, the decisive issue was not

[67] D Wippman, 'Military Intervention, Regional Organizations and Host-state Consent' (1996) 7 Duke Journal of Comparative and International Law 210; 212; Roth (n 66) 37; Talmon (n 36) 233.

[68] Wippman (n 67) 212; Roth (n 66) 37; Talmon (n 36) 233.

[69] Roth (n 66) 2, 31.

[70] Roth (n 4) 138. See also *Asma Jilali v The Government of Punjab* 1972 PLD SC 139, 179–80 (1972) (Supreme Court of Pakistan) quoted in Roth (n 4) 138.

[71] The reasons for such acceptance or acquiescence are not decisive and often difficult to establish. It need not be based on approval but can also be based on fear or weakness. See Roth (n 4) 140; *Mokotso v King Moshoeshoe II* (Lesotho High Court, 1980) (1982) 90 International Law Reports 427, 519, 140; Wippman (n 67) 212.

[72] *Tinoco* Arbitration (n 65) 75.

[73] ibid 375–76; Charlesworth (n 6) 75.

[74] *Tinoco* Arbitration (n 65) 377.

[75] ibid 377, 380; Charlesworth (n 6) 75.

[76] *Tinoco* Arbitration (n 65) 381; Charlesworth (n 6) 75.

whether the government had been established constitutionally, but whether 'all within its influence recognize its control, and that there is no opposing force assuming to be a government in its place'.[77]

The invocation of the unconstitutionality of the Tinoco regime by Costa Rica is nonetheless an indication that the effective control doctrine has not remained unchallenged. Since the early twentieth century, there have been repeated attempts to elevate normative criteria as preconditions for governmental recognition which, if accepted as part of customary international law, would significantly limit the political discretion of governments in the context of governmental recognition. These included in particular the constitutionality of regime change as personified by a democratic electoral process in accordance with a country's constitution.[78] An early manifestation of these attempts was the Tobar doctrine, embodied by the General Treaty of Peace and Amity of 20 December 1907 between Guatemala, El Salvador, Honduras, Nicaragua, and Costa Rica.[79] In accordance with this doctrine, the state parties *inter alia* undertook to deny recognition to any government in these countries that came to power through a coup or revolution against the incumbent government, as long as the freely elected representatives of the people had not constitutionally reorganized the country.[80] The Tobar doctrine thus constituted an attempt to elevate a procedural notion of democracy that turns on free and fair elections to a requirement for *de jure* governmental recognition. This procedural understanding of democratic legitimacy has since been described as the requirement of 'legitimacy of origin' of governmental power.[81] However, at the time, it did not garner broad support amongst states.[82]

The question of whether normative criteria had to be taken into account when recognizing governmental representatives also surfaced in debates pertaining to the text of UNGA Resolution 396(V) of 14 December 1950.[83] This

[77] *Tinoco* Arbitration (n 65) 381–82; Charlesworth (n 6) 76.

[78] See J d'Aspremont, 'Legitimacy of Governments in The Age of Democracy' (2006) 38 New York University Journal of International Law and Politics 905.

[79] *General Treaty of Peace and Amity of 20 December 1907*, reprinted in 2 American Journal of International Law (Supp) (1908) 219–29; *Additional Convention to the General Treaty of 20 December 1907*, reprinted in 2 American Journal of International Law (Supp) (1908) 229–30. See also Roth (n 4) 146; JB Scott, 'The Central American Peace Conference of 1907', 1 American Journal of International Law (1907) 122 ff.

[80] Art I of the *Additional Convention to the General Treaty* (n 79) 230. See also Roth (n 4) 144. In 1923 these countries further undertook not to recognize elected post-revolutionary governments, headed by revolutionary leaders, their close relatives, or persons holding high military positions in the period leading up to or during the coup. See *General Treaty of Peace and Amity of 7 February 1923*, Art II, reprinted in 17 American Journal of International Law (Supp) (1923) 117–22.

[81] d'Aspremont (n 78) 880, 881.

[82] *Tinoco* Arbitration (n 65), 381–82. In 1934 El Salavador and Costa Rica withdrew from the Tobar inspired treaties. The United States, while not party to these treaties, respected its terms up until 1931. See Roth (n 4) 146.

[83] Recognition by the United Nations of the Representation of a Member State, UN Doc A/RES/396(V) (14 December 1950) https://documents-dds-ny.un.org/doc/RESOLUTION/GEN/NR0/059/94/IMG/NR005994.pdf?OpenElement.

resolution concerned the recognition by the United Nations of the representation of a member state, in instances where 'more than one authority claimed to be the government entitled to represent a member state in the United Nations'.[84] At the time, a British proposal that attempted to elevate effective control as the decisive criterion was rejected.[85] However, an alternative proposal by Cuba, which expressly embraced normative criteria in addition to effective control, was also rejected.[86] In the end the resolution refrained from listing any criteria. It merely stated that whenever the issue of representation became the subject of controversy within the United Nations, it 'should be considered in the light of the Purposes and Principles of the Charter and the circumstances of each case'.[87] This inability to agree on clear criteria for the recognition of government representatives at the United Nations did not at the time prevent the effective control doctrine from remaining the decisive criterion in practice. Yet it indicated sustained attempts by states to link recognition (also) to normative criteria, such as the legitimacy of origin of the governing authority.

The next upsurge in support of taking into account democratic pedigree for the purpose of governmental recognition occurred at the end of the Cold War, as the 1990s witnessed a proliferation of democratic elections, particularly in Central and Eastern European states.[88] Similarly, various inter-state fora adopted declarations in which they determined democracy to be the preferred or even only form of governance.[89] For example, the Charter of Paris for a New Europe of 1990 required its signatories 'to build, consolidate and strengthen democracy as the only system of government of our nations'.[90] It further determined that 'democratic government is based on the will of the people, expressed regularly through free and fair elections'.[91] The Final Warsaw Declaration of the Community of Democracies of 2000, representing 106 states, declared that

[84] ibid para 1; see also Roth (n 4) 258.

[85] UN Doc A/AC.38/L.21/Rev.1 (31 October 1950). See also Roth (n 4) 259 ff. At the time, several states wanted to take normative criteria into consideration when deciding which of the competing Chinese delegations amounted to China's representative at the UN.

[86] These would have included whether the new authority was willing to accept responsibility for carrying out the obligations of the member state under the Charter, as well as the extent to which the authority had been established through internal processes in the member state in question. UN Doc A/AC.38/L.45 (31 October 1950); Roth (n 4) 259–60. See also YL Liang, 'Recognition by the United Nations of the Representation of a Member State: Criteria and Procedure' (1951) 45 American Journal of International Law 695 ff.

[87] Recognition by the United Nations of the Representation of a Member State (n 83) para 1; see also Roth (n 4) 258.

[88] See M Saul, 'From Haiti to Somalia: The Assistance Model and the Paradox of State Reconstruction in International Law' (2009) 11 International Community Law Review 138; Roth (n 66) 2.

[89] See Fox (n 12) 834.

[90] Organization for Security and Co-operation in Europe, *Charter of Paris for a New Europe*, Paris (19–21 November 1990) https://www.osce.org/mc/39516; Charlesworth (n 6) 102.

[91] ibid.

> [t]he will of the people shall be the basis of the authority of government as expressed by exercise of the right and civic duties of citizens to choose their representatives through regular, free and fair elections with universal and equal suffrage, open to multiple parties, conducted by secret ballot, monitored by independent electoral authorities, and free of fraud and intimidation.[92]

These references to democracy all underscored the need for free and fair elections and, by implication, the need for the democratic legitimacy of the origin of governmental power.[93] However, some declarations pertaining to democracy were more ambitious in nature in that they also included substantive elements amongst its benchmarks, such as human rights, the independence of the judiciary, and the rule of law. For example, the Commonwealth Harare Declaration of 1991 identified 'the rule of law and the independence of the judiciary, just and honest government; fundamental human rights, including equal rights and opportunities for all citizens regardless of race, colour, creed or political belief' as benchmarks of democracy.[94] The Biketwa Declaration of 2000 of the Pacific Islands Forum for its part included democracy as one of its guiding principles. It described it as 'reflect[ing] national and local circumstances, including the peaceful transfer of power, the rule of law and the independence of the judiciary, just and honest government'.[95] These notions of democratic legitimacy that turn on substantive benchmarks have been described as legitimacy of exercise of governmental power.[96] On the whole, however, free and fair elections remained the constant, common denominator in international statements relating to democracy, while some also linked the concept to more substantive criteria.[97]

Furthermore, and of particular relevance to this chapter, this new thrust towards democratic governance ignited criticism in scholarship of the effective control doctrine as the basis for governmental recognition. In the wake of the new wave

92 The Community of Democracies, 'Warsaw Declaration: Towards a Community of Democracies' (27 June 2000) http://www.community-democracies.org/app/uploads/2017/02/2000-Warsaw-Declaration-ENG.pdf; Charlesworth (n 6) 106.

93 See also d'Aspremont (n 78) 881, 891.

94 The Commonwealth, Harare Declaration 20 October 1991, art 9 http://thecommonwealth.org/sites/default/files/history-items/documents/Harare%20Commonwealth%20Declaration%201991.pdf; Charlesworth (n 6) 104.

95 See also the Pacific Island Forum, Biketwa Declaration, 28 October 2000 http://www.forumsec.org/pages.cfm/documents/.

96 d'Aspremont (n 78) 881–82, 899.

97 Similarly, in scholarship, free and fair elections constitute the common denominator for the definition of democracy, although it remains debatable whether free and fair elections would be possible in the absence of substantive requirements such as freedom of speech and of assembly. See d'Aspremont (n 78) 882 ff; Charlesworth (n 6) 106, 108; K Nowrot and EW Schabacker, 'The Use of Force to Restore Democracy: International Legal Implications of the ECOWAS Intervention in Sierra Leone' (1998) 14 American University International Law Review 321; T Franck, 'Democracy as a Human Right' in L Henkin and JL Hargrove (eds), *Human Rights: An Agenda for the Next Century* (American Society of International Law 1992) 75; J Vidmar, *Democratic Statehood in International Law: The Emergence of New States in Post-Cold War Practice* (Hart Publishing 2013) 15. See also Fox (n 12).

of democratization, the 'might is right' rationale underpinning this doctrine came under attack by scholars who propagated democratic legitimacy as the appropriate criterion for recognition.[98] State practice in the period immediately following the Cold War seemed to buttress these arguments, in particular in relation to the need for the democratic legitimacy of the origin of governmental power.[99] At the time, the international community rejected the internal overthrow of Haitian President Jean-Bertrand Aristide in 1991 and that of Sierra Leonean President Ahmad Tejan Kabbah in 1997.[100] In both instances the governments had been democratically elected by a very large margin and subsequently took control of the state apparatus, only to be ousted by military coups shortly afterwards. Despite the loss of effective control, both governments continued to be recognized by the international community as the legitimate government.[101]

Also, in both instances these ousted leaders subsequently requested foreign military assistance in order to regain power. Whether the subsequent military interventions indeed were based on these invitations remains disputed. In the case of Haiti the military intervention was also underpinned by United Nations Security Council (UNSC) Resolution 940 of 31 July 1994 which was adopted under Chapter VII of the Charter.[102] In the case of Sierra Leone, the military intervention by the Economic Community of West African States (ECOWAS) at the request of the exiled Kabbah government[103] was subsequently praised by UNSC resolutions, without explicitly authorizing the use of force under Chapter VII of the Charter.[104]

[98] See eg CM Cerna, 'Universal Democracy: An International Legal Right or the Pipe Dream of the West?' (1995) 27 New York University Journal of International Law and Politics 289 ff; GH Fox and G Nolte, 'Intolerant Democracies' (1995) 36 Harvard International Law Journal 1 ff; T Franck, 'The Emerging Right to Democratic Governance' (1992) 86 American Journal of International Law 46 ff; M Reisman, 'Sovereignty and Human Rights in Contemporary International Law' in G Fox and BR Roth (eds), *Democratic Governance and International Law* (CUP 2000) 230 ff; AM Slaughter, *A New World Order* (Princeton University Press 2004); G Fox and BR Roth, *Democratic Governance and International Law* (CUP 2010); S Marks, 'What Has Become of the Emerging Right to Democratic Governance?' (2011) 22 European Journal of International Law (2011) 507 ff.

[99] A similar development could be witnessed in relation to the recognition of states, notably in the practice of European states. This was *inter alia* reflected in the adoption by the (then still) European Community of the Declaration on the Guidelines on the Recognition of New States in Eastern Europe and in the Soviet Union (16 December 1991, reprinted in (1992) 31 International Legal Materials 1486–87. In accordance with these guidelines, the recognition of new states in the region by the European Community depended on whether they respected the rule of law, democracy, and human rights. See also Charlesworth (n 6) 78.

[100] See eg the Preamble to UN Doc S/RES/841 (16 June 1993) regarding Haiti and UN Doc S/RES/1132 (8 October 1997), para 1 regarding Sierra Leone.

[101] Talmon (n 36) 10; Roth (n 66) 37.

[102] UN Doc S/RES/940 (31 July 1994) was finally adopted almost three years after the coup in September 1991; Wippman (n 67) 216; Nowrot and Schabacker (n 97) 397, 399.

[103] See their final Communiqué of the meeting in UN Doc S/1997/499 (27 June 1997) Annex, 3; UN Doc S/1997/695 (8 September 1997) Annex I and Annex 2. See also Nolte (n 6) 426–27; E de Wet, 'The Evolving Role of ECOWAS and the SADC in Peace Operations: A Challenge to the Primacy of the United Nations Security Council in Matters of Peace and Security?' (2014) 27 Leiden Journal of International Law 361–62.

[104] UN Doc S/RES/1162 (17 April 1998) para 2; UN Doc S/RES/1181 (13 July 1998) paras 6, 9; UN Doc S/RES/1260 (20 August 1999) para 3; UN Doc S/RES/1231 (11 March 1999) para 10; UN Doc S/

Even so, some have argued that the ECOWAS intervention in Sierra Leone was a case of *ex post facto* UNSC authorization.[105] Be that as it may, the disputed legal basis of the military interventions in Haiti and Sierra Leone arguably is not decisive for the point at issue, namely that in both instances the democratic legitimacy of origin of the government carried more weight for the purpose of recognition than actual effective control.[106]

Moreover, specifically as far as state and organizational practice is concerned, the OAS and the AU adopted a series of instruments that signalled an attempt to move away from the 'might is right' approach in favour of democratic governance. This raises the question whether the democratic legitimacy of an incumbent authority has become a precondition for recognition as the *de jure* government within these organizations, as well as whether the loss of such pedigree will result in derecognition. If so, what type of democratic pedigree is at issue? Would the initial and continued recognition of an incumbent authority predominantly depend on its legitimacy of origin through free and fair elections? [107] Or does it also depend on whether the incumbent authority respects substantive criteria such as human rights and the independence of the judiciary, which would amount to legitimacy of exercise of governmental power?[108] If the legitimacy of origin constituted a precondition for recognition as the *de jure* government, it would imply that a government that comes about through a military coup may not be recognized. Similarly, a government that has come to power through free and fair elections (and has been recognized accordingly) will face derecognition if it subsequently loses an election but fails to relinquish power to the victorious party.[109] On the other hand, if the legitimacy of exercise of governmental power constituted the benchmark for recognition, a democratically elected government could also be derecognized if it subsequently abolished the independence of the judiciary, or engaged in widespread and systematic human rights violations.[110]

If democratic legitimacy in either of these forms has evolved into a precondition of recognition in the OAS and/ or the AU, the question also arises whether these developments are representative of contemporary customary international

RES/1270 (22 October 1999) para 7; UN Doc S/RES/1289 (7 February 2000) para 2; UN Doc S/PRST/ 1998/5 (26 February 1998). See also De Wet (n 103) 362–63.

[105] T Franck, 'Rethinking Collective Security' in M Schmitt and J Peijc (eds), *International Law and Armed Conflict: Exploring the Faultlines. Essays in Honour of Yoram Dinstein* (Martinus Nijhoff Publishers 2007) 25; see also J Levitt, 'Humanitarian Intervention by Regional Actors in Internal Conflicts: The Case of ECOWAS in Liberia and Sierra Leone' (1998) 12 Temple Journal of International and Comparative Law 369 ff, who suggested various legal bases for the intervention.

[106] UN Doc S/RES/940 (31 July 1994) was finally adopted almost three years after the coup in September 1991; Wippman (n 67) 216; Nowrot and Schabacker (n 97) 397, 399.

[107] d'Aspremont (n 78) 880, 881.

[108] d'Aspremont (n 78) 881, 897.

[109] ibid 881.

[110] ibid 909, 914.

law requirements for recognition. The question would therefore arise whether states in general nowadays regard democratic legitimacy as a precondition for governmental recognition. If so, one would further have to consider whether it exists alongside (in addition to) effective control or, even in place of it, in situations where there is a conflict between the two criteria.

3.1 Institutional reform and practice within the OAS

As far as the OAS is concerned, the linking of governmental recognition to democratic legitimacy of origin was already alluded to in 1979 in a resolution condemning the human rights violations of the Somoza regime in Nicaragua. The resolution *inter alia* described the regime as inhuman and dictatorial and called on the people of Nicaragua to replace the Somoza regime and install a democratic government that reflects the free will of the people of Nicaragua.[111] In the following years, democratization in the region accelerated when military dictatorships handed over authority to civilian government.[112] These developments also sparked institutional changes and in the last decade of the twentieth century, the OAS adopted a series of institutional decisions that introduced the possibility of economic sanctions and suspension from OAS activities if electoral outcomes were not respected.[113] While these sanctions do not in and of themselves amount to non-recognition (or derecognition), they do pave the way for making democratic legitimacy (of origin) a pre-condition for governmental recognition. The fact that states are not willing to engage with an authority within the framework of a regional organization can also be an indication that they also refuse to recognize it as the *de jure* representative of the state at the international level.

The first important institutional development within the OAS in this regard was the Santiago Commitment to Democracy and the Renewal of the Inter-American System, in which the OAS General Assembly attributed special priority to representative democracy as an expression of the legitimate and free manifestation of the will of the people.[114] In addition, Resolution 1080 was adopted in an attempt to curb future military coups in the region. It allowed the OAS General Assembly to call an ad hoc meeting of the Minister of Foreign Affairs or special session of

[111] OAS Doc OEA/Ser.F/II.17, Doc 43/79 (23 June 1979) paras 1 ff; Roth (n 4) 294–95. However, the resolution did not unseat the Somoza government.

[112] CM Cerna, 'Democratic Legitimacy and Respect for Human Rights: The New Gold Standard' (2015) 108 American Journal of International Law Unbound 223.

[113] See the Charter of the Organization of American States (entered into force 13 December 1951) 119 UNTS 3 (1952) art 3(d). It states that the solidarity of the American states and the high aims sought through it require the political organization of those states on the basis of the effective exercise of representative democracy. See also Roth (n 66) 41.

[114] Santiago Commitment to Democracy and the Renewal of the Inter-American System, OAS Doc OEA/SerP/AG Doc 2734/91 (4 June 1991) Preamble [4]; Roth (n 66) 39.

the General Assembly to take appropriate decisions, 'in the event of an irregular interruption of the democratic political institutional process by the democratically elected government in any of the Organizations' member states'.[115]

In a third step, the Protocol of Washington of 1992 amended the OAS Charter in order to allow the General Assembly to suspend, by means of a two-thirds majority, a member state whose democratically constituted government has been overthrown by force.[116] These developments, all of which underscored the importance of the democratic legitimacy of origin of the governmental power, culminated in the Inter-American Democratic Charter of 2001 (IADC). In article 19 of this document, the General Assembly determined that

> an unconstitutional interruption of the democratic order, or an unconstitutional alteration of the constitutional regime that seriously impairs the democratic order in a member state, constitutes, while it persists, an insurmountable obstacle to its government's participation in sessions' of the Organization.[117]

The reference to 'unconstitutional alteration of the constitutional regime that seriously impairs the democratic order' seems to refer to situations that extend beyond interruptions in the form of military coups. It would also include conduct such as self-coups during which the executive abolishes the independence of the judiciary or usurps the powers of parliament.[118] The IADC also provides for collective action if the democratic regime was altered or interrupted. In the case of an unconstitutional interruption, this can include suspension if the OAS General Assembly has determined that diplomatic initiatives to restore democracy have failed.[119] In so doing, the IADC seems to elevate the legitimacy of origin of governmental authority to a requirement for participation in OAS activities.

However, closer scrutiny reveals that the democratic legitimacy of origin of member states (as well as the legitimacy of exercise) remain aspirational goals within the OAS, rather than a binding obligation. First, the IADC was adopted as a resolution of the OAS General Assembly and not a treaty subject to ratification. In addition, the language of article 21 of the IADC does not provide for any automatic suspension once an unconstitutional interruption has been determined. Instead, it remains within the discretion granted to the OAS General Assembly to

115 Representative Democracy, OAS GA Res 1080 (XXI-0/91), OAS Doc OEA/SerP/XXIO2 Doc 2739/91 (5 June 1991); Cerna (n 112) 223; Roth (n 66) 39; Talmon (n 36) 11.

116 OAS, Protocol of Washington of 14 December 1992, OAS Doc OEA/Ser.A/2 Add. 3 (SEPF) (entered into force 25 September 1997) art 1 (amending art 9 of the OAS Charter (n 115)); Roth (n 66) 40.

117 Declaration of Lima: Inter-American Democratic Charter (IADC), OAS GA Res 1 (XXVIII-E/01), OAS Doc OEA/SerP/ AG/Res 1 (XXVIII-E/01) (11 September 2001) art 19; Roth (n 66) 40.

118 See also Cerna (Golden Standard) (n 112) 224. C. Arceneaux and D Pion-Berlin, 'Issues, Threats, and Institutions: Explaining OAS Responses to Democratic Dilemmas in Latin America' (2007) 49 Latin American Politics and Society 4–5.

119 IADC (n 117) arts 20 and 21.

decide whether diplomatic initiatives to restore the democratic order have failed. Moreover, the track record of the OAS in enforcing the democratic legitimacy of origin and exercise of the governments of its member states militates against the conclusion that democratic legitimacy in either form is a pre-condition for participation in OAS activities. Both in the pre-IADC and post-IADC era, the organization has only occasionally reacted forcefully to conduct that amounted to unconstitutional interruptions. It has also remained reluctant to impose sanctions (let alone derecognition) on governments that committed self-coups, thereby forfeiting their legitimacy of exercise of governmental power.

3.2 Practice in the pre-IADC era

The strongest stance of the OAS based on Resolution 1080 followed the (first) coup against President Jean-Bertrand Aristide on 29 September 1991. A call by the OAS Permanent Council the next day for Aristide's return was followed by a resolution of 3 October 1991 that severed diplomatic, financial, economic, and military ties to Haiti until the democratically elected President was restored.[120] The OAS thus gave effect to the principle of democratic legitimacy of origin by continuing to recognize the Aristide government and imposing sanctions on the coup regime. Aristide ultimately returned in 1994, subsequent to the military intervention authorized under Chapter VII of the UN Charter in Resolution 940 of 31 July 1994. In 1996 he stood down because the Constitution barred him from standing for immediate re-election.[121] In May 2000 his party won the parliamentary elections, while Aristide himself won the presidential elections in November of that year. However, after monitoring the May elections, the OAS refused to ratify the result due to irregularities at the polls. Opposition parties also boycotted the November presidential elections in protest to the irregularities during the May elections.[122] The OAS nonetheless recognized Aristide's re-election until his (second) ousting in February 2004. By that time, Haiti was wracked by armed violence related to dissatisfaction with the Aristide presidency. Fearing an armed invasion of the capital by insurgents, he resigned on 29 February 2004 and was escorted from the country by the US Air Force.[123] On this occasion the OAS

[120] OAS, 'Support to the Democratic Government of Haiti' MRE/RES 1/91 (3 October 1991) paras 1 ff, reprinted in (1991) 2 United States Department of State Dispatch760; Arceneaux and Pion-Berlin (n 118) 13.

[121] At the time Aristide unsuccessfully argued that he was entitled to add the three years lost in exile. See O Bowcott, 'Violence and Boycott Mar Haitian Election Campaign' *Guardian* (23 November 2000) https://www.theguardian.com/world/2000/nov/23/owenbowcott.

[122] Bowcott (n 121).

[123] L Polgreen and T Weiner, 'Haiti's President Forced Out; Marines Sent to Keep Order' *New York Times* (29 February 2004) https://www.nytimes.com/2004/02/29/international/americas/haitis-president-forced-out-marines-sent-to-keep.html.

essentially acquiesced in what amounted to a violent overthrow of the Aristide government.[124]

The only other incident in which the OAS acted forcefully in the 1990s concerned the self-coup in Guatemala in 1993. On 29 May 1993 Guatemalan President Jorge Antonio Serrano issued a decree that dissolved Parliament, suspended parts of the Constitution, unseated judges of the high courts, and abolished laws regulation elections and political parties.[125] On the same day the OAS Secretary-General convened a Permanent Council meeting in accordance with Resolution 1080, subsequent to which an ad hoc meeting of the foreign ministers condemned the Guatemalan President's actions. He was also urged to restore all democratic institutions and functions, otherwise risking economic and diplomatic sanctions.[126] The pressure generated by these actions contributed to Serrano losing the support of the military and going into exile in El Salvador.[127]

In all other instances of 'constitutional interruptions' in the pre-IADC era, the reaction of the OAS was much more subdued, stopping short of sanctions or non-recognition of the government in question. In February 1992 and again in November of that year, sections of the Venezuelan armed forces attempted unsuccessful coups against President Carlos Andres Perez. The OAS did not take any concrete action, apart from reaffirming its right to take action in accordance with Resolution 1080.[128] In April 1992 President Alberto Fujimori of Peru engaged in a self-coup by suspending the Constitution, as well as dissolving the country's congress and judicial branch.[129] Invoking Resolution 1080, the OAS condemned the conduct and exerted pressure on Fujimori to reinstate democratic institutions. Fujimori subsequently agreed to hold elections of the Democratic Constituent Congress later that year but merely provided a vague timetable for restoring democratic institutions. This was acquiesced to by the OAS, which described the elections held in November 1992 as an important phase in the process of restoring democracy.[130] At no point did the OAS impose sanctions of its own.[131] Moreover, when the Fujimori regime was accused of large-scale electoral fraud during the 2000 elections, the OAS Permanent Council did not invoke Resolution 1080. This was despite the fact that the OAS observer mission

[124] See also LR Einaudi (Assistant Secretary-General of the OAS), Report on OAS Activities in Connection with Haiti from 11 November 2003 to 10 March 2004 (7 April 2004) http://www.oas.org/en/media_center/speech.asp?sCodigo=04-0070.

[125] Arceneaux and Pion-Berlin (n 118) 14; BS Levitt, 'A Desultory Defense of Democracy: OAS Resolution 1080 and the Inter-American Democratic Charter' (2006) 48 Latin American Politics and Society 104.

[126] Arceneaux and Pion-Berlin (n 118); Levitt (n 125) 104.

[127] Arceneaux and Pion-Berlin (n 118) 14; Levitt (n 125) 104.

[128] Levitt (n 125) 104. He suggests that the lack of OAS action could be explained by the fact that both coup attempts collapsed on their own accord.

[129] Arceneaux and Pion-Berlin (n 118) 16; Levitt (n 125) 103.

[130] Arceneaux and Pion-Berlin (n 118) 16.

[131] Levitt (n 125) 104.

concluded that the elections could not be considered free and fair in terms of international standards.[132]

In Paraguay in 1996, President Juan Carlos Wasmosy, who had been elected to power in 1993, was confronted by a revolt led by a military commander, General Lino Oviedo.[133] When requested by Wasmosy to step down due to interference in the affairs of state, the general threatened a military uprising.[134] The Permanent Council of the AOS condemned General Oviedo's refusal to submit to civilian authority and attempted to call an ad hoc meeting in accordance with Resolution 1080. However, the meeting was never initiated because several members of the Permanent Council were not convinced that the (mere) threat of a military coup constituted an interruption of the constitutional order.[135] The coup threat subsequently imploded due to a lack of support within the military and the broader public. This rapid de-escalation of the situation may also have contributed to the lack of responsiveness of the OAS.[136]

A weak OAS stance also emerged in the wake of electoral fraud in the Dominican Republic in 1994. In May 1994 the incumbent President Balaguer sought re-election for a seventh term. However, soon after the polls closed, charges of electoral fraud emerged. The OAS, supported by domestic groups, demanded a recount of the votes and an investigation into allegations of fraud.[137] The central election committee nonetheless proceeded to declare President Balaguer as the winner on 2 August 1994.[138] The OAS condoned this behaviour by thereafter participating in a negotiated settlement that allowed Balaguer to serve eighteen months as President, after which new elections were called. The OAS never invalidated the elections nor refused to recognize the Balaguer government as a result of the electoral fraud.[139]

In the case of Ecuador, the OAS failed to take action on two occasions of unconstitutional change of government. The first occurred when members of the military 'requested' President Jamil Mahuad on 21 January 2000 to step down in favour of a three-member Junta of National Salvation. At the time Mahuad was facing increasing protests by civil society in reaction to stringent austerity measures.[140] The Junta merely lasted a few hours, but it succeeded in driving Mahuad out of office and out of the country, while Vice-President Gustavo Noboa assumed office.[141] The response of the OAS was limited to expressing its support for Mahuad and democratic institutions in Ecuador, without setting in motion the mechanisms

[132] ibid 109–110.
[133] ibid 105.
[134] ibid 105.
[135] ibid 106.
[136] ibid 105.
[137] Arceneaux and Pion-Berlin (n 118) 17.
[138] ibid.
[139] ibid. In practice, the national Congress allowed permitted Balaguer to add another six months to his presidency.
[140] Levitt (n 125) 107.
[141] ibid 107–108.

of Resolution 1080.[142] The OAS responded equally mildly to the second threat to Ecuadorian constitutional democracy, which occurred after the adoption of the IADC.

3.2.1 Practice in the post-IADC era

The second Ecuadorian constitutional crisis erupted in April 2005. On this occasion the Ecuadorian Congress voted to overthrow President Lutio Gutierez in the wake of mounting public criticism for his Supreme Court purge in December 2004, which occurred with the support of Congress. Subsequently, a newly constituted Supreme Court voided corruption charges against the former President Abdala Bucaram and allowed him to return to Ecuador from exile.[143] In reaction to ensuing public protest, Gutierrez dissolved the Supreme Court and declared a state of emergency, which in turn led to mass protests and his overthrow by Congress. However, this ousting was legally problematic because Congress accused him of abandoning his office, while in fact he was present and conducting official business. In addition, it did not meet the two-thirds majority required for the vote in question.[144] The OAS Permanent Council's response was limited to calling on all sectors to ensure full respect for the democratic order.[145] It did not condemn either the Supreme Court purge or the unconstitutional overthrow of the President, nor did it invoke sanctions.[146]

The responses within the OAS to attempted coups, self-coups, and unfree and unfair elections in Venezuela since 2002 poignantly illustrates the sustained reluctance within the organization to sanction member states whose governments lack legitimacy of origin and/or exercise of governmental power. While a paradigm shift may be occurring since 2019, the overall response of the OAS towards Venezuela can be summarized as mixed, at best. In early 2002 the continued concentration of power in the hands of the executive by then President Hugo Chavez met with increasing public protest and the threat of a military coup.[147] On 11 April 2002 a general of the national guard declared that the Chavez government had abandoned its functions and that the armed forces were in control. The next day the army chief of staff claimed that Chavez had resigned and was in custody.[148] While the OAS Permanent Council condemned the alteration of the constitutional

[142] ibid 108.

[143] Arceneaux and Pion-Berlin (n 118) 18.

[144] ibid 19.

[145] ibid.

[146] ibid. In 2010 the OAS expressed its support for the democratically-elected Correa regime, following protests within the security forces as a result of austerity measures imposed by the government. The Correa government at the time declared a state of emergency, fearing a coup by members within the armed forces. See OAS Doc OEA/Ser.G CP/RES. 977 (1772/10) corr.1 (30 September 2010) para 2; BBC, 'Ecuador declares state of emergency amid "*coup* attempt"' *BBC News* (1 October 2010) https://www.bbc.com/news/world-latin-america-11447519.

[147] Levitt (n 125) 111.

[148] Arceneaux and Pion-Berlin (n 118) 42.

order on 13 April 2002, no punitive measures were recommended.[149] The coup imploded soon afterwards, and it remains uncertain whether the OAS would have acted more forcefully had the coup succeeded.[150]

Fifteen years later, in March 2017, Venezuela underwent a self-coup when the Constitutional Chamber of the Venezuelan Supreme Court abolished the power of the national legislature, granting them to the Constitutional Chamber itself or a body of its choosing.[151] This decision was preceded by a defeat suffered by the party of President Maduro, which lost control over the national legislature during elections in December 2015.[152] At the time voters turned away from the ruling party as the country's economic crisis deepened. However, the decision of the Supreme Court enabled Maduro to undermine the newly constituted legislative branch by concentrating the power in the executive.[153] The OAS Permanent Council condemned the decision of the Supreme Court as an alteration of the constitutional order but limited its measures to diplomatic initiatives.[154]

In May 2018 the OAS General Assembly further determined that the Venezuelan presidential elections that had just taken place lacked legitimacy, for 'not having met the participation of all Venezuelan political actors, and for being carried out without the necessary guarantees for a free, fair, transparent and democratic process'.[155] It also reiterated that an alteration of the constitutional order has occurred.[156] The OAS thus lamented in particular the lack of legitimacy of origin of the Maduro regime. However, when thereafter voting on suspending Venezuela from the OAS, the required two-thirds majority threshold could not be reached.[157] Venezuela for its part had already announced its voluntary withdrawal from the OAS on 27 April 2017, in accordance with a twenty-four-month withdrawal period determined by article 143 of the OAS Charter.[158]

[149] OAS Doc CP/RES.811 (1315/02) (13 April 2002); Arceneaux and Pion-Berlin (n 118) 5–6.

[150] Arceneaux and Pion-Berlin (n 118) 14; Levitt (n 125) 113.

[151] IACHR Press Release, 'IACHR Condemns Supreme Court Rulings and the Alteration of the Constitutional and Democratic Order in Venezuela' (31 March 2017) http://www.oas.org/en/iachr/media_center/preleases/2017/041.asp.

[152] J Watts, 'Venezuela Opposition Allege *Coup* as Supreme Court Seizes Power' *Guardian* (30 March 2017) https://www.theguardian.com/world/2017/mar/30/venezuela-president-nicolas-maduro-national-assembly.

[153] IACHR, Press Release, 'IACHR Condemns Supreme Court Rulings and the Alteration of the Constiutional and Democratic Order in Venezuela' (31 March 2017) http://www.oas.org/en/iachr/media_center/preleases/2017/041.asp; see also Watts (n 155).

[154] OAS Doc, OEA/Ser G CP/RES 1078 (2108/17) (3 April 2017) para 1.

[155] OAS Doc S-032/18 (5 June 2018) para 1 http://www.oas.org/en/media_center/press_release.asp?sCodigo=S-032/18.

[156] OAS Doc S-032/18 (n 155) paras 3 ff; Reuters Staff, 'OAS Calls Extraordinary Assembly to Vote on Suspending Venezuela' *Reuters* (6 June 2018) https://www.reuters.com/article/us-oas-assembly-venezuela/oas-calls-extraordinary-assembly-to-vote-on-suspending-venezuela-idUSKCN1J202X.

[157] There were nineteen votes in favour, four against, and eleven abstentions. Twenty-four votes were required to meet the two-thirds majority threshold. See Reuters Staff, 'OAS Passes Resolution to Begin Process to Suspend Venezuela' *Reuters* (6 June 2018) http://news.trust.org//item/20180606005020-84dom/.

[158] A Illueca, 'The Venezuela Crisis at the Organization of American States: Between Withdrawal and Suspension' *Opinio Juris* (29 May 2017) http://opiniojuris.org/2017/05/29/the-venezuela-crisis-at-

On 10 January 2019, almost three months before Venezuela's withdrawal was supposed to take effect on 27 April 2019 and whilst the humanitarian and economic climate in the country worsened dramatically, a paradigm shift could be observed within a resolution adopted by the OAS Permanent Council. In its Preamble it reaffirmed the right to democracy in article 1 of the IADC, recalled the lack of legitimacy of the May 2018 elections, and underscored the 'constitutional authority of the democratically elected National Assembly'. In its operative part the resolution decided not to recognize the legitimacy of President Maduro's new term as of that day and called for free and fair presidential elections.[159] In so doing, the OAS Permanent Council underscored the lack of the legitimacy of origin of the Maduro presidency (in contrast to that of the Venezuelan National Assembly). In addition, it called on all member states to 'adopt, in accordance with international law and their national legislation, diplomatic, political, economic and financial measures that they consider appropriate, to contribute to the prompt restoration of the democratic order of Venezuela'.[160]

On 23 January 2019, in the wake of this decision, Juan Guaidó, the President of Venezuela's democratically elected National Assembly, declared himself interim President under article 233 of the Constitution of Venezuela and promised to form a transitional government that would pave the way for elections.[161] In accordance with this article, the President of the National Assembly shall take charge of the presidency of the Republic if an elected President becomes permanently unavailable to serve prior to his inauguration. It further determines that new presidential elections shall be held within thirty consecutive days.[162] The appointment of Juan Guaidó as interim President was based on the logic that since the May 2018 elections lacked democratic legitimacy of origin, there was no elected President to assume office when Mr Maduro's first presidential term expired on 10 January 2019.[163] In Venezuela it was controversial whether article 233 was intended to apply

the-organization-of-american-states-between-withdrawal-and-suspension/; Reuters Staff, 'Venezuela to Withdraw from OAS, Denounces Campaign by Washington' *Reuters* (27 April 2017) https://www.reuters.com/article/us-venezuela-oas/venezuela-to-withdraw-from-oas-denounces-campaign-by-washington-idUSKBN17S330.

[159] OAS Doc OEA/Ser GCP/RES.1117 (2200/19) (10 January 2019) paras 1 and 2.

[160] ibid para 3.

[161] R di Carlo (UN Under-Secretary-General for Political and Peacebuilding Affairs) UN Doc S/PV 8452 (26 January 2019) 3.

[162] See Constitution of the Bolivarian Republic of Venezuela, Public Official Gazette No 36860 (30 December 1999) art 322 http://unpan1.un.org/intradoc/groups/public/documents/un-dpadm/unpan042931~1.pdf.

[163] The argument was supported by a decision of the Supreme Court of Venezuela of 29 October 2018, according to which a constitutional vacuum existed. See decision of the Supreme Court of the Bolivarian Republic of Venezuela, 208° y 159°, SP-2018-001 (29 October 2018) 150 ff http://tsjlegitimo.org/wp-content/uploads/2018/11/Sentencia-Definitiva-Exp.-SP-2018-001-final.pdf. However, the judges (appointed by the National Assembly in 2017) had in the same year fled into exile and were provided with office space at the seat of the OAS in Washington DC. See also Deutscher Bundestag, 'Rechtsfragen zur Anerkennung des Interimspräsidenten in Venezuela' WD 2-3000-017/19 (15

to the situation in question and whether Guaidó could be recognized as interim President beyond thirty days.[164] Even so, support for Guaidó and the National Assembly's interpretation of the Venezuelan Constitution came from more than fifty states worldwide that ostensibly recognized him as interim President. These included most members of the OAS (*inter alia* the United States and Canada).[165] In a joint statement, sixteen of these OAS members emphasized the lack of legitimacy of the Maduro regime due to its impairment of free and fair elections and the need for restoring democracy through such elections.[166] In addition, on 9 April 2019 the OAS Permanent Council adopted a resolution by majority vote in which it accepted the National Assembly's designated Permanent Representative, Mr Gustavo Tarré, into the OAS.[167] He presented his credentials to the OAS Secretary-General the following day.[168]

These developments may be interpreted as an attempt by the OAS Permanent Council to sanction the lack of legitimacy of origin of the Maduro regime, manifesting itself in unfree and unfair elections, by calling on member states to derecognize the Maduro regime.[169] If so, it would be the first time that unfree and unfair elections within an OAS member state led to the derecognition of its incumbent government.[170] However, a closer scrutiny reveals that OAS member states

February 2019) 9–10; D Zambrano, 'Guaidó, Not Maduro, Is the *de jure* President of Venezuela' *Lawfare* (1 February 2019) https://www.lawfareblog.com/guaido-not-maduro-de-jure-president-venezuela.

[164] The text of art 233 of the Venezuelan Constitution (n 162) links the notion of 'unavailability' to personal incapacitation in the form of illness or death. Also, the Maduro regime did not accept the authority of the Supreme Court 'in exile'. See Deutscher Bundestag (n 163) 9–10; Zambrano (n 163); C Redaelli, 'Venezuela and the Role of Domestic Constitutional Order in International Law' *Opinio Juris* (23 April 2019) http://opiniojuris.org/2019/04/23/venezuela-and-the-role-of-domestic-constitutional-order-in-international-law/.

[165] See *inter alia* UN Doc S/PV.8452 (26 January 2019) 6 (United States); ibid 6 (United Kingdom); ibid, 7 (Peru); ibid 15 (Germany); ibid 17 (Belgium). Latin American countries that refrained from endorsing Juan Guaidó included Bolivia, Cuba, Dominican Republic, Mexico, Nicaragua, Uruguay, and Suriname. See A Mackinnon, 'Maduro vs Guaidó: A Global Scorecard' *Foreign Policy* (6 February 2019) https://foreignpolicy.com/2019/02/06/maduro-vs-guaido-a-global-scorecard-map-infographic/.

[166] US Mission to the Organization of American states, 'OAS Member States Issue Joint Statement on Venezuela (24 January 2019) https://usoas.usmission.gov/oas-member-states-issue-joint-statement-on-venezuela/. See also the European Parliament Resolution of 31 January 2019 on the Situation in Venezuela, 2019/2543(RSP) (31 January 2019) para 1; C Morello, 'Juan Guaidó, Interim President or Opposition Leader?' *Washington Post* (5 March 2019) https://www.washingtonpost.com/world/national-security/juan-guaido-president-or-opposition-leader/2019/03/05/96a6be42-e89d-4c88-9d9b-d5e0f0eddfa6_story.html?utm_term=.271ac00ea5b5.

[167] OAS Doc OEA/Ser.G, CP/RES 1124 (2217/19) Rev 2 (22 April 2019) para 1. The Resolution received eughteen votes in favour and nine against, while six countries abstained and one was absent. See OAS Press Release, 'Permanent Council Accepts Appointment of Designated Permanent Representative of Venezuela's National Assembly to the OAS, Nr E-019/19 (9 April 2019) http://www.oas.org/en/media_center/press_release.asp?sCodigo=E-019/19.

[168] OAS Press Release, 'New Ambassador of Venezuela Presents Credentials' Nr FNE-96347 (10 April 2019) http://www.oas.org/en/media_center/photonews.asp?sCodigo=FNE-96347.

[169] See S Mantilla-Blanco, 'Rival Governments in Venezuela: Democracy and the Question of Recognition' *Verfassungsblog* (28 January 2019) https://verfassungsblog.de/rival-governments-in-venezuela-democracy-and-the-question-of-recognition/.

[170] Equally remarkable is the fact that this occurred even though Venezuela was not formally suspended from the OAS.

remain divided on whether to derecognize the Maduro regime and acknowledge Juan Guaidó as representing the *de jure* government. First, it remains unclear to what extent all sixteen OAS members that supported the joint statement intended it to have legal consequences rather than to express symbolic, political support. For example, in individual statements Argentina and Chile respectively referred to the Venezuelan National Assembly as the 'sole democratically elected organ' and the 'sole legitimate and democratically elected state power'.[171] This language is reminiscent of the political support expressed (albeit in a different context) to the Syrian Opposition Coalition,[172] which actually stopped short of *de jure* recognition.[173]

Colombia and Brazil, on the other hand, have used language in individual statements that suggests that they do recognize the National Assembly as the *de jure* government. They have respectively expressed support for the National Assembly's 'exercise of all its competences, including those derived from article 233 of the Constitution of the Bolivarian Republic of Venezuela',[174] as well as 'for the National Assembly, democratically elected constitutional institution, at present responsible for the executive power in Venezuela according to the country's legitimate Supreme Court of Justice'.[175] However, despite this language, it remains unclear whether in practice their diplomatic corps have indeed severed ties with the Maduro regime.[176] The United States, on the other hand, has referred to the Venezuelan National Assembly as the 'only legitimate branch of government',[177] as well as attached legal consequences to the act of recognition. These *inter alia* included the accreditation of diplomats appointed by Mr Guaidó and allowed him to control assets held in the Venezuela's name in the United States.[178]

[171] Statements cited in A Gurmendi, 'Recognition of the Venezuelan National Assembly under International Law' *Opinio Juris* (14 January 2019) http://opiniojuris.org/2019/01/14/recognition-of-the-venezuelan-national-assembly-under-international-law/.

[172] As discussed in section 2 earlier.

[173] Gurmendi (n 171). See also F Paddeu and A Gurmendi Dunkelberg 'Recognition of Governments: Legitimacy and Control Six Months after Guaidó' *Opinio Juris* (18 July 2019) https://opiniojuris.org/2019/07/18/recognition-of-governments-legitimacy-and-control-six-months-after-guaido/.

[174] Statement of Colombia cited in Gurmendi (n 171). See also 'Colombia Recognizes Opposition Lawmaker Guaidó as Venezuela's President' *US News* (23 January 2019) https://www.usnews.com/news/world/articles/2019-01-23/colombia-recognizes-opposition-lawmaker-guaido-as-venezuelas-president.

[175] Statement of Brazil cited in Gurmendi (n 171). See also Reuters 'Brazil Recognizes Guaidó as Venezuela's Interim President' Reuters (23 January 2019) https://www.reuters.com/article/venezuela-politics-brazil/brazil-recognizes-guaido-as-venezuelas-interim-president-idUSE6N1TR02H.

[176] Gurmendi (n 171). Paddeu and Gurmendi Dunkelberg (n 173). By mid-July 2019, neither of these countries have transferred government buildings to the diplomatic staff of Guaidó

[177] ibid. See also J Galbraith 'United States Recognizes the Opposition Government in Venezuela and Imposes Sanctions as Tensions Escalate' (2019) 113 American Journal of International Law 601 ff.

[178] Paddeu and Gurmendi Dunkelberg (n 173); SR Anderson, 'What Does It Mean for the United States to Recognize Juan Guaidó as Venezuela's President?' *Lawfare* (1 February 2019) https://www.lawfareblog.com/what-does-it-mean-united-states-recognize-juan-guaidó-venezuelas-president. Canada also seemed to have given full recognition to the Guaidó regime. The Foreign Minister stated that '[w]e recognize and express our full support for the interim presidency of Venezuela assumed by the president of the National Assembly, Juan Guaidó, in compliance with the constitution of Venezuela'. See also A Connolly, 'Canada Will Recognize Juan Guaidó as Venezuela's President, Follows Move

The divisions within the OAS about the legal status of the Guaidó regime are also reflected by the very slim margin with which the OAS Permanent Council passed the resolution accepting Mr Gustavo Tarré as Venezuela's permanent representative. Twelve member states further explicitly expressed concerns about the legality of the resolution, underscoring the fact that it was not within the competence of the Permanent Council to make such a decision.[179] This decision also placed the OAS at odds with the UN, where the Maduro regime still represents Venezuela at the UN organs.[180] In fact, in UNSC debates several countries (including Russia and China) depicted the recognition of Guaidó on the basis of article 233 of the Venezuelan Constitution as an unconstitutional change of government and an interference in the internal affairs of Venezuela.[181] From the perspective of democratic legitimacy this position comes across as counterintuitive, because Mr Guaidó is backed by the only democratically elected organ of state in the country. Nonetheless, it does expose the limited state support also beyond the OAS for elevating democratic legitimacy of origin to a prerequisite for governmental recognition. Similarly, it casts doubt on the willingness of states to regard the absence or loss of such legitimacy as a ground for derecognition.

This also became apparent within the EU, where only nineteen of the twenty-eight members endorsed a statement according to which 'in accordance with the provisions of the Venezuelan Constitution, they acknowledge and support Mr Juan Guaidó, President of the democratically-elected National Assembly, as President and interim of Venezuela, in order for him to call for free, fair and democratic presidential elections'.[182] In addition, a closer scrutiny reveals that not all these

by US to Do the Same' *Global News* (23 January 2019) https://globalnews.ca/news/4878808/trump-venezuela-president-juan-guaido/.

179 Several states (including Venezuela) underscored that it is up to sovereign states to recognize governments (and by extension their representatives) in a bilateral act and not to the OAS Permanent Council. Others (including Mexico) stressed that within the OAS institutional framework, decisions pertaining to representation and membership fell to the Meeting of Consultation of Ministers of Foreign Affairs and the OAS General Assembly. See OAS Doc OEA/Ser.G, CP/RES. 1124 (2217/19) rev 2 (22 April 2019) fn 1 through fn 12. Despite the formal withdrawal of Venezuela from the OAS by 27 April 2019, a delegation of the Guaidó regime attended a meeting of the OAS General Assembly in Medellin, Colombia, 26–28 June 2019. This met with protest with members such as Mexico, Uruguay, and Caribbean countries. Other countries, including Brazil, Argentina, and Paraguay, recognized the delegation. Despite this controversy the Guaidó regime submitted the instrument of ratification regarding the *American Convention on Human Rights ('Pact of San Jose') of 22 November 1969*, 1144 UNTS 123, to the OAS secretariat on 31 July 2019. See also LJ Acosta, 'Uruguay Withdraws from OAS Meeting Over Venezuela Opposition Delegation' *Reuters* (27 June 2019) https://www.reuters.com/article/us-venezuela-politics-oas/uruguay-withdraws-from-oas-meeting-over-venezuela-opposition-delegation-idUSKCN1TS23E.

180 At the time of writing representatives of the Maduro regime *inter alia* took part in UNSC debates. See UN Doc S/PV.8452 (26 January 2019) 25. See also the statement of Mexico in OAS Doc OEA/Ser.G, CP/RES. 1124 (2217/19) rev 2 (22 April 2019) fn 3; See also Paddeu and Gurmendi Dunkelberg (n 173).

181 See UN Doc S/PV.8452 (26 January 2019) 13 (Russia); ibid 16 (China); ibid 8 (South Africa). At 9, Equatorial Guinea also expressed the concern that such regime change would lead to similar destabilization as was the case in Libya subsequent to the adoption and implementation of UN Doc S/RES/1973 (14 March 2011).

182 German Federal Foreign Office, 'Joint Declaration on Venezuela', 'Press Release' (4 February 2019) https://www.auswaertiges-amt.de/en/newsroom/news/eu-declaration-venezuela/2186306. The

countries actually intended this statement to amount to *de jure* recognition. For example, the Netherlands subsequently explicitly stated that such recognition did not have legal implications. Instead, the Dutch government intended to sustain its diplomatic ties with the Maduro regime as that regime was still in effective control over the state apparatus.[183] In fact, at the time of writing most European governments were reluctant to strip the diplomats of the Maduro regime of their credentials and to award diplomatic credentials to the representative of Mr Guaidó.[184] The reluctance within the OAS to derecognize the Venezuelan government for altering the constitutional order through unfree and unfair elections thus also found resonance outside the region. They therefore clearly remained reluctant to derecognize the Maduro regime as the *de jure* government, despite the fact that it has lost its legitimacy of origin through unfree and unfair elections.

In essence, the only instance in which the OAS has thus far suspended a member in accordance with article 21 of the IADC concerned Honduras. On 28 June 2009, democratically elected President Manuel Zeleya was toppled from government by the military with the support of the legislature and the Supreme Court.[185] This occurred after President Zeleya called for a referendum which was aimed at allowing him to amend the Constitution. It was feared that he intended to extend the presidential term of office which was limited by the Constitution (also referred to as 'constitutional coups').[186] Zeleya was succeeded by the President of the National Congress, Roberto Michiletti on the same day.[187] The OAS Permanent Council immediately condemned the coup and demanded the reinstatement of Zeleya, who had fled to Costa Rica. It further determined that no government resulting from the coup would be recognized.[188] On

statement was endorsed by Austria, Belgium Croatia, Czech Republic, Denmark, Estonia, Finland, France, Germany, Hungary, Latvia, Lithuania, Luxembourg, the Netherlands, Poland, Portugal, Spain, Sweden, and the United Kingdom.

183 S Bolk (Minister of Foreign Affairs of the The Netherlands), *Kamerbrief over situatie in Venezuela mbt erkenning van Juan Guadio* BZDOC-1235421577-13 (4 February 2019) https://www.rijksoverheid.nl/documenten/kamerstukken/2019/02/04/kamerbrief-situatie-in-venezuela-over-erkenning-van-juan-guaido. See also J Vidmar, 'Erkenning van Guaidó als Leider Venezuela is Schone Schijn' *NRC Handelsblad* (8 February 2019) https://www.nrc.nl/nieuws/2019/02/08/erkenning-van-guaido-als-leider-venezuela-is-schone-schijn-a3653470.

184 See *inter alia* AFP, 'Bundesregierung Erkennt Guaidó-Gesandten Nicht als Botschafter an' *Frankfurter Allgemeine Zeitung* (27 April 2019) https://www.faz.net/aktuell/politik/ausland/bundesregierung-erkennt-guaido-gesandten-nicht-als-botschafter-an-16110153.html. See also A Faiolo and MJ Lang, 'Maduro vs Guaidó: Venezuela's Dueling Diplomatic Corps in Tug-of-War for Embassies, Access' *Washington Post* (23 April 2019) https://www.washingtonpost.com/world/the_americas/maduro-vs-guaido-venezuelas-dueling-diplomatic-corps-in-tug-of-war-for-embassies-access/2019/04/23/61f0aade-65c9-11e9-a698-2a8f808c9cfb_story.html?noredirect=onandutm_term=.c8dec29583d6.

185 Associated Press, 'Honduras President Arrested in Military Coup' *Guardian* (28 June 2019), available at https://www.theguardian.com/world/2009/jun/28/honduras-coup-president-zelaya

186 N Lakhani, 'Did Hillary Clinton Stand by as Honduras Coup Ushered in Era of Violence?' *Guardian* (31 August 2016), available at https://www.theguardian.com/world/2016/aug/31/hillary-clinton-honduras-violence-manuel-zelaya-berta-caceres.

187 Lakhani (n 186).

188 OAS Doc OEA/Ser.G CP/RES.953 (1700/09) (28 June 2009); Cerna (n 112) 224.

1 July it provided Honduras with an ultimatum of reinstating President Zeleya within seventy-two hours or face suspension.[189] When the de facto regime refused to heed the ultimatum, Honduras was suspended from participating in the OAS.[190] It remained suspended until May 2011 when an agreement was reached between Zeleya and the then President Porfirio Lobo.[191] Zeleya was never reinstated but was allowed to return to Honduras, and democratic elections followed in 2013.[192]

3.3 Institutional reform and practice within the African Union

During its final years of existence the Organisation of African Unity (OAU) adopted three declarations pertaining to democracy, which signalled an attempt to move away from the 'might is right' approach that had plagued the continent in the post-independence period. The first was the Harare Declaration of 1997 in which the OAU Council of Ministers condemned the military coup in Sierra Leone and called for the restoration of the constitutional order.[193] Two years later in Algiers the OAU reiterated its decision that '[m]ember states whose governments came to power through unconstitutional means after the Harare Summit, should restore constitutional legality before the next Summit'. [194] In the Lomé Declaration of 2000 the OAU defined the notion of unconstitutional change of government with reference to four types of situations.[195] These included military coups against a democratically elected government; interventions by mercenaries to replace a democratically elected government; the replacement of democratically elected governments by armed dissident groups and rebel movements; and the refusal by an incumbent government to relinquish power to the winning party after free, fair, and regular

[189] OAS Doc OEA/Ser.P AG/RES.1 (XXXVII-E/09) rev 1 (2 July 2009) para 4; Cerna (n 112) 224.

[190] OAS, 'Suspension of the Right of Honduras to Participate in the Organization of American States' OEA/Ser.p AG/RES.2 (XXXVII-E/09) rev.1 (16 July 2009) para 1; Cerna (n 112) 224.

[191] CNN wire staff, 'Honduran President Signs Deal Allowing Ousted Leader Zelaya's Return' *CNN* (23 May 2011) http://edition.cnn.com/2011/WORLD/americas/05/22/colombia.honduras.ex.president/index.html.

[192] Cerna (n 112) 225.

[193] OAU, Decisions Adopted by the Sixty-Sixth Ordinary Session of the Council of Ministers, CM/Dec.330-363 (LXVI)-C (28–31 May 1997) para (a) https://au.int/sites/default/files/decisions/9622-council_en_28_31_may_1997_council_ministers_sixty_sixth_ordinary_session.pdf. The African Commission on Human and Peoples' Rights has since 1994 consistently condemned coups and the seizure of power by undemodratic means. See *inter alia* its Resolution on the Situation of Human Rights in Africa, ACHPR/Res.14(XVI)94 (25 October–3 November 1994) para 1, https://www.achpr.org/sessions/resolutions?id=446.

[194] OAU, Declarations and Decisions Adopted at the Thirty-Fifth Assembly of the Heads of State and Government, AHG/Dec. 142 (XXXV) (12–14 June 1999) para 1 https://au.int/sites/default/files/decisions/9544-1999_ahg_dec_132-142_xxxv_e.pdf.

[195] OAU, The Declaration on the Framework for an OAU Response to Unconstitutional Changes of Government, AHG/Decl.5 (XXXVI) (10–12 July 2000) (Lomé Declaration) http://www.peaceau.org/uploads/ahg-decl-5-xxxvi-e.pdf.

elections.[196] Essentially these measures were all aimed at protecting the legitimacy of origin of the governing power.

They were subsequently consolidated with the inclusion of article 4(p) in the AU Constitutive Act of 2000, the founding treaty of the AU.[197] This article elevated the condemnation and rejection of an unconstitutional change of government to one of the principles in accordance with which the AU—the successor organization to the OAU—would function.[198] While article 4(p) did not define 'unconstitutional change of government', the AU's understanding of this concept is informed by article 23 of the African Charter on Democracy, Elections and Governance (African Democracy Charter). It was adopted by the AU in 2007,[199] entered into force in 2012, and is currently directly binding on 34 of the fifty-four AU member states.[200] Article 23 of the African Democracy Charter incorporated the Lomé Declaration's definition of unconstitutional change of government, and also added one new benchmark. This concerned '[a]ny amendment or revision of the constitution or legal instruments, which is an infringement on the principles of democratic change of government'.[201] In so doing, article 23(1) attempts to oppose unconstitutional retention of power through measures that undermine free and fair elections or remove presidential term limits.[202] It thus seems to introduce an additional requirement pertaining to the legitimacy of origin of governmental power.

As far as the consequences of an unconstitutional change of government are concerned, article 30 of the AU Constitutive Act determines that '[g]overnments which shall come to power through unconstitutional means shall not be allowed to participate in the activities of the Union'.[203] This suspension clause is also informed by the African Democracy Charter which, in article 25, similarly provides for suspension in case diplomatic initiatives have failed.[204] This article further provides for the possibility of imposing economic sanctions in reaction to an unconstitutional change of government,[205] as well as the non-participation of the perpetrators

[196] The Lomé Declaration (n 195) also suggested procedures for suspension of 'unconstitutional governments' from participation in OAU organs, combined with economic sanctions. See also I Aral, 'Effectiveness of Non-UN Sanctions in Furthering Democracy: The Case of the African Union' (paper on file with author).

[197] Constitutive Act of the African Union of 11 July 2000 (2158 UNTS 3) art 4(p) http://www.peaceau.org/uploads/au-act-en.pdf.

[198] However, art 4(p) does not provide a separate ground for military intervention in an AU member state.

[199] African Charter on Democracy, Elections and Governance of 30 January 2007 (entered into force on 14 February 2012) (African Democracy Charter) art 23 http://archive.ipu.org/idd-E/afr_charter.pdf.

[200] For the most updated list of ratifications, see https://au.int/en/treaties/african-charter-democracy-elections-and-governance.

[201] ibid art 23(4).

[202] SA Dersso, 'Unconstitutional Changes of Government and Unconstitutional Practices in Africa' *African Politics, African Peace* (World Peace Foundation, Paper No 2, June 2016) 3 https://sites.tufts.edu/wpf/files/2017/07/2.-UCG-Dersso-f.pdf.

[203] AU Consitutive Act (n 200) art 30.

[204] African Democracy Charter (n 199) art 25(1).

[205] ibid art 25(7).

of unconstitutional change of government in elections held to restore the democratic order.[206] It is worth noting that the principle that 'perpetrators of coups d'état shall not stand for elections conducted for return to constitutional order' was reaffirmed by the AU Peace and Security Council in 2009 in the so-called Ezulwini guiding principles.[207]

The use of the verb 'shall' in article 30 of the AU Constitutive Act suggests that suspension in case of an unconstitutional change of government is mandatory. However, closer scrutiny reveals that the AU has applied this article with some flexibility. On the one hand it has sanctioned several governmental overthrows as well as incumbent leaders who have refused to relinquish office after electoral defeat, including with non-recognition. On the other hand, it has not acted consistently in this regard. The AU has also been reluctant to sanction unconstitutional retention of power through electoral fraud or the extension of presidential terms.

3.3.1 Practice sanctioning unconstitutional change of government

Subsequent to the adoption of the AU Constitutive Act, the AU at times has sanctioned acts of unconstitutional changes of government in a manner that reinforced the legitimacy of origin of governmental power. For example, military coup regimes that met with suspension from AU activities and/or economic sanctions by the AU included Togo (2005);[208] Guinea (2008);[209] Mauritania (2008);[210] Madagascar (2009);[211] and Burkina Faso (2015).[212] In the case of Egypt, the AU's

[206] ibid art 25(4). This article also determines that such perpetrators may not hold any position of responsibility in the political institutions of their states.

[207] AUPSC, Ezulwini Framework for the Enhancement of the Implementation of Measures of the African Union in situations of Unconstitutional Changes of Government in Africa (17–19 December 2009) para 4 (iv) http://www.peaceau.org/en/article/ezulwini-framework-for-the-enhancement-of-the-implementation-of-measures-of-the-african-union-in-situations-of-unconstitutional-changes-of-government-in-africa-ezulwini-kingdom-of-swaziland-17-19-december-2009. Para 4(ii) and para 4(iii) of these guidelines also proposed individual criminal responsibility for perpetrators of unconstitutional change of government. This proposal culminated in the inclusion of the crime of unconstitutional change of government in art 28(E) of the Protocol on the Amendments to the Protocol on the Statute of the African Court of Justice and Human Rights of 27 June 2014 https://au.int/ar/treaties/protocol-amendments-protocol-statute-african-court-justice-and-human-rights. This protocol has, however, not yet attracted any ratifications.

[208] AUPSC, Communiqué of the 25th Meeting, PSC/PR/Comm (XXV) (25 February 2005) paras 3, 4 http://www.peaceau.org/uploads/communiqueeng-25th.pdf.

[209] AUPSC, Press Statement, 20th Meeting, PSC/PR/BR.1 (CCVI) (15 October 2009) http://www.peaceau.org/uploads/presscommunique.pdf. AUPSC, AUPSC Communiqué of the 164th meeting, PSC/PR/Comm(CLXIV) (24 December 2008) para 2 http://www.peaceau.org/uploads/communiquerepguineaeng.pdf; Associated Press, 'Guinea: Sanctions From African Union *New York Times* (29 December 2008) https://www.nytimes.com/2008/12/30/world/africa/30briefs-SANCTIONSFRO_BRF.html.

[210] See AUPSC, Communiqué of the 163rd Meeting, PSC/MIN/Comm.3 (CLXIII) (20 December 2008) para 9 http://www.peaceau.org/uploads/communiquemauritaniaeng.pdf.

[211] AUPSC, Communiqué of the 181st Meeting, PSC/PR/COMM (CLXXXI) (20 March 2009) para 4 https://reliefweb.int/report/madagascar/madagascar-communiqué-181st-meeting-peace-and-security-council.

[212] AUPSC, Communiqué of the 554th Meeting, PSC/PR/COMM/3 (DXLIV) (18 September 2015) paras 11, 12 http://www.peaceau.org/uploads/psc-544-comm-burkina-faso-18-9-2015.pdf. Furthermore, when President Bozize of the Central African Republic (CAR) was overthrown by Seleka

reaction was more ambivalent. It softened an initial tough stance on democratic legitimacy of origin, subsequent to the ousting of the democratically elected President Morsi by the military in 2013.[213] The fact that President Morsi was facing extensive popular protest at the time of his removal and that millions of Egyptians demanded his resignation did not deter the AU from classifying the forceful overthrow as an unconstitutional change of government and suspending the coup government from AU activities.[214] However, when in May 2014 the military leader Sisi, who ousted President Morsi, stood for and won the presidential elections (with a voter turn-out below 50 per cent),[215] the AU lifted Egypt's suspension.[216] In so doing, the AU acted contrary to its own guiding principles as it condoned the participation of a coup perpetrator in elections conducted to return to constitutional order. The AU essentially conceded as much by justifying Egypt's readmission with the need to remain engaged with the country.[217] Simultaneously it noted that this should not set a precedent for the participation of coup perpetrators in such elections in future.[218]

As far as sanctioning incumbent leaders who have refused to relinquish power after electoral defeat is concerned, the AU has shown some resolve. In 2007 Mr Abdallah Sambi won the presidential elections in the Comoros. However, Mohammed Bacar, who had ruled the island of Anjouan since 2001, refused to relinquish power. Subsequent to organizing an illegal election of which he declared himself the winner, Bacar announced the independence of Anjouan from the Union of the Comoros.[219] The AU responded by adopting a range of targeted

rebels in 2013, the AU suspended the rebel government from its activities, as well as imposed targeted sanctions on the rebel leaders. Subsequently the designation by the National Transitional Council of Catherine Samba-Panza as Transitional Head of State in January 2014 was welcomed by the international community. See AUPSC, Communiqué of the 363rd meeting, PSC/PR/COMM(CCCLXIII) (25 March 2013) paras 6ff http://www.peaceau.org/uploads/psc-com-363.car.pdf; UN Doc S/RES/2149 (10 April 2014) para 1.

[213] AUPSC, Communiqué of the 384th Meeting, PSC/PR/COMM (CCCLXXXIV) (5 July 2013) para 6 http://www.peaceau.org/uploads/psc-384-com-egypt-05-07-2013.pdf.

[214] AUPSC, Communiqué of the 384th Meeting, PSC/PR/COMM (CCCLXXXIV) (5 July 2013) para 6 http://www.peaceau.org/uploads/psc-384-com-egypt-05-07-2013.pdf. See Z Yihdego, 'Democracy, Peoples' Uprising and Unconstitutional Change of Government in Egypt: The African Union Principles and Responses' *EJILTalk*! (8 July 2013) https://www.ejiltalk.org/author/zyihdego/.

[215] P Kingsley, 'Abdel Fatah al-Sisi Sweeps to Victory in Egyptian Presidential Election' *Guardian* (29 May 2019) https://www.theguardian.com/world/2014/may/29/abdel-fatah-al-sisi-sweeps-victory-egyptian-election.

[216] AUPSC, Communiqué of the 442th Meeting PSC/PR/COMM.2 (CDXLII) (17 June 2014) para 8 http://www.peaceau.org/uploads/psc-com-442-egypt-17-06-2014.pdf.

[217] ibid para 7(ii)

[218] ibid para 8. Earlier that year the AUPSC formally acknowledged that factors such as mismanagent, systematic violations of human rights, and manipulation of the constitution can result in popular uprisings. However, it simultaneously underscored that the people had to express its will against oppressive regimes peacefully and condemned any attempt to seize power by force. See AUPSC, Press Statement of the 432nd meeting PSC/PR/BR.(CDXXXII) (29 April 2014) http://www.peaceau.org/uploads/ps-432-psc-29-4-2014.pdf.

[219] P Williams, 'The African Union's Peace Operations: A Comparative Analysis' in F Söderbaum and R Tavares (eds), *Regional Organisations in African Security* (Routledge 2011) 38.

sanctions against the Anjouanese leaders.[220] Moreover, in 2008 the AU measures culminated in a military intervention in Anjouan that facilitated an interim leader for the island and a rerun of the island's presidential elections.[221] As will be illuminated in Chapter 3, section 3, this military operation occurred at the request of the recognized government of the Comoros and constituted the AU's first robust intervention in a member state.[222] While the refusal by Bacar to relinquish power affected only one island of the Comoros, the AU's reaction nonetheless reflected a determination to enforce the country's election results.

Moreover, the AU has recently also derecognized incumbent presidents that refused to relinquish power in the wake of electoral defeat. This first occurred in Côte d'Ivoire in 2010 and thereafter in The Gambia in 2017. In both situations the AU acted in tandem with the Economic Community of West African States (ECOWAS) and the United Nations Security Council (UNSC). In Côte d'Ivoire, Alassane Quattara won the democratic elections that were monitored by the UN against incumbent Laurent Gbagbo on 28 November 2010. When the latter nonetheless refused to leave office, the AU, which recognized Mr Quattara as the President-elect, in December 2010 suspended Côte d'Ivoire from AU activities.[223] A similar step was taken by ECOWAS a few days prior.[224] The UNSC followed by recognizing the election outcome and Mr Qattara as President-elect under Chapter VII of the UN Charter.[225] Subsequently, in Resolution 1975 of 30 March 2011, the UNSC authorized the United Nations Operation in Côte d'Ivoire (UNOCI) to use all necessary means to protect civilians under imminent threat of physical violence, and expressed its support for the French troops supporting UNOCI.[226] In the wake of this resolution UNOCI and French forces struck Gbagbo's compound which facilitated his capture by the forces of President Quattara in April 2011.[227] The Chapter VII authorized enforcement action in Côte d'Ivoire thus facilitated a regime change in line with the outcome of the election results of November 2010.

[220] AUPSC, Communiqué of the 111th Meeting, PSC/PR/Comm (XCV) (10 October 2007) paras 5 ff http://www.peaceau.org/uploads/communiquy-95-eng.pdf.

[221] Report of the Chairperson of the Commission on the Situation in the Comoros Since the 10th Ordinary Session of the Assembly of the African Union held in Addis Ababa from 31 January–2 February 2008, PSC/PR/2 (CXXIV) (30 April 2008) paras 13, 15–21 http://archives.au.int/bitstream/handle/123456789/2229/2008_124_R1E.pdf?sequence=1andisAllowed=y.

[222] AUPSC, Communiqué of the 124th Meeting, PSC/PR/Comm (CXXIV) (30 April 2008) paras 3, 17 http://www.peaceau.org/uploads/communiquecomoreseng.pdf.

[223] AUPSC, Communiqué of the 252nd meeting, PSC/PR/COMM.1 (CCLII) (9 December 2010) paras 3, 4 http://www.peaceau.org/uploads/communiquy-of-the-252nd.pdf.

[224] ECOWAS Authority of the Heads of State of Government, Final Communiqué of the Extraordinary Session on Côte d'Ivoire, ECW/CEG/ABJ/EXT/FR./Rev 2 (7 December 2010) paras 7 ff http://www.ecowas.int/wp-content/uploads/2015/02/2010-7-december-Extra.pdf.

[225] UN Doc S/RES/1962 (20 December 2010) para 1.

[226] UN Doc S/RES/1975 (11 March 2015) paras 6, 7; Fox (n 12) 836.

[227] See D Tladi, 'Security Council, the Use of Force and Regime Change: Libya and Côte d'Ivoire' (2012) 37 South African Yearbook of International Law 41 ff; Fox (n 12) 836. See also Chapter 3, section 2.

This in turn enabled Mr Quattara to take control of the state institutions, following which he was sworn in as President in May 2011.[228]

In The Gambia in 2016, the incumbent President Yahyah Jammeh also refused to relinquish power, subsequent to losing the elections held in late November 2016 to Adama Barrow.[229] On 2 December 2016 the country's Independent Electoral Commission declared Mr Barrow the winner of the elections held the previous day. This result was rather ironic, as there were concerns about the extent to which free and fair elections would be possible, in light of the incumbent President's control over the media and the intimidation of voters.[230] As a consequence, ECOWAS was unwilling to participate in election monitoring, while EU election observers were not allowed to enter the country.[231] In the end, the impartial election monitoring was conducted by a small AU contingent.[232] The somewhat unexpected results nonetheless were initially accepted by outgoing President Jammeh. However, a week later he withdrew his recognition after the Independent Electoral Commission had announced corrections to the initial results, although he also indicated that these did not have any effect on the outcome.[233] Subsequently, on 13 December 2016 the Independent Electoral Commission was taken over by the Gambian armed forces, and on 18 January 2017 Parliament (in which Mr Jammeh still held a majority) extended his term for three months beyond his formal mandate. This ostensibly was to give the country's Constitutional Court the opportunity to decide on the consequences of the irregularities in the electoral process.[234]

This domestic contestation of the constitutionality of the Gambian election results did not prevent the international recognition of Mr Barrow as the head of state. By 17 December 2016 the ECOWAS Heads of State and Government had adopted a communiqué in which they decided to uphold the results of the elections

[228] BBC, 'Ivory Coast: Alassane Ouattara Sworn in as President' *BBC News* (6 May 2011) http://www.bbc.com/news/world-africa-13306858. See also Fox (n 12) 836–37.

[229] ECOWAS Authority of Heads of State and Government, Final Communiqué of the 50th Ordinary Session (17 December 2016) paras 34 ff http://www.ecowas.int/wp-content/uploads/2016/12/Communiqu%C3%A9-Final_50th-Summit_Abuja_Dec-16_Eng.pdf. See also Chapter 3, section 2.

[230] BBC, Gambia: ECOWAS Observers Boycott "unfair poll"' *BBC News* (11 November 2016) https://www.bbc.com/news/world-africa-15851706. See also O Corten, 'Intervention by Invitation: The Expanding Role of the UN Security Council' 4 Max Planck Trialogues on the Law of Peace and War (forthcoming in 2019, on file with author) 53.

[231] African News Agency, 'ECOWAS to Boycott Gambia's Presidential Elections' *The Citizen* (30 November 2016) https://citizen.co.za/news/news-africa/1361893/ecowas-to-boycott-gambias-presidential-elections/; A Rahman and A Shaban, 'Gambia Says EU Cannot Observe December 1 Presidential Polls' *Africanews* (19 November 2016) https://www.africanews.com/2016/11/19/gambia-says-eu-cannot-observe-december-1-presidential-polls/.

[232] R MacLean and E Graham-Harrison, 'The Gambia Bans International Calls and Internet as Voters Go to Polls' *Guardian* (1 December 2016) https://www.theguardian.com/world/2016/dec/01/the-gambia-bans-international-calls-and-internet-as-voters-go-to-polls; Corten (n 230) 53.

[233] ECOWAS Authority of Heads of State and Government, Final Communiqué, 50th Ordinary Session (n 229) para 34.

[234] C Kreß and B Nußberger, 'Pro-Democratic Intervention in Current International Law: The Case of The Gambia in January 2017 (2017) 4 Journal on the Use of Force and International Law 240.

of 1 December 2016.[235] This decision was endorsed by the AU on 13 January 2017.[236] The AU further underscored its support for the outcome of the presidential elections, and declared that as of 19 January 2017, outgoing President Yahya Jammeh would cease to be recognized by it as The Gambia's legitimate President.[237] On 19 January 2016, Mr Adama Barrow was sworn in as President in the Gambian Embassy in Senegal. In his inaugural address, he made a special appeal to ECOWAS, the AU, and in particular the UNSC to 'support the government and peoples of The Gambia in enforcing their will, restore their sovereignty and constitutional legitimacy'.[238] As will be explored in more detail in Chapter 3, section 2, this invitation constituted the most plausible basis for the ECOWAS troops that crossed the border of The Gambia, following the inaugural speech of President Barrow. While the UNSC also recognized Mr Barrow as President a few hours after having been sworn in[239] and expressed support for ECOWAS in its 'commitment to ensure, by political means first, the respect of the will of the people of The Gambia',[240] it did not authorize enforcement measures under Chapter VII of the UN Charter.[241]

For purposes of the current chapter it is important to stress that President Barrow was recognized internationally on the basis of having won the presidential elections. At the time, he was still outside the country and did not have any control over territory or state institutions.[242] It is also worth noting that ECOWAS, the AU, and the UNSC paid little attention to the fact that incumbent President Jammeh was contesting the validity of the election before the country's Constitutional Court, subsequent to which the Gambian Parliament (which was still under his control) extended Mr Jammeh's mandate for ninety days beyond its formal mandate.[243] Similarly, it remains uncertain whether the inaugural ceremony at the Gambian Embassy in Senegal was in accordance with the Gambian Constitution.[244] Despite these potential formal irregularities in terms of domestic

[235] During this period ECOWAS undertook various high-level delegations to The Gambia aimed at ensuring a peaceful transfer of power to President-elect Barrow. ECOWAS Authority of Heads of State and Government, Final Communiqué of the 50th Ordinary Session (n 229) paras 36, 38(a), 38(h).

[236] AUPSC, Communiqué, 647th meeting, PSC/PR/COMM (DCXLVII) (13 January 2017) para 3 https://data2.unhcr.org/en/documents/download/53007.

[237] ibid para 5.

[238] 'Inaugural Address of Adama Barrow, President of the Republic of The Gambia' *The Fatunetwork* (20 January 2017) http://fatunetwork.net/inaugural-address-adama-barrow-president-republic-gambia/. See also R Maclean, 'Troops Enter The Gambia after Adama Barrow Is Inaugurated in Senegal' *Guardian* (19 January 2017) https://www.theguardian.com/world/2017/jan/19/new-gambian-leader-adama-barrow-sworn-in-at-ceremony-in-senegal.

[239] UN Doc S/RES/2337 (19 January 2017) paras 1, 5.

[240] ibid para 6.

[241] Kreß and Nußberger (n 234) 243; C Gray, International Law and the Use of Force (4th edn, OUP 2018) 67.

[242] Kreß and Nußberger (n 234) 249; Maclean (n 238); T Cocks and E Farge, 'West African Military Halt Gambia Operation, Issue Jammeh Deadline' *Reuters* (20 January 2017) http://af.reuters.com/article/idAFKBN1540NA.

[243] See also Kreß and Nußsberger (n 234) 240, 248.

[244] ibid 248.

law, ECOWAS, the AU, and the UNSC appeared to accept the election victory of Mr Barrow at face value. This may in part have been due to a shared consensus that had the elections been entirely free and fair from intimidation and manipulation by the incumbent President Jammeh, Mr Barrow would have won by an even larger margin. His clear democratic legitimacy in terms of electoral support thus was not doubted internationally and seemed to have outweighed concerns about domestic procedural irregularities.

3.3.2 Practice condoning unconstitutional change of government

From the above analysis one may conclude that the AU has given some effect to the prohibition of unconstitutional changes of government contained in article 4(p) of the AU Constitutive Act. At times, the sanctions have also resulted in the withholding of recognition or derecognition. In so doing, the AU has elevated the importance of the legitimacy of origin of governmental power on the continent. However, a closer scrutiny of AU practice reveals that the organization has not been consistent in this regard. In addition, it has hardly attached any weight to the legitimacy of exercise of governmental power. To begin with, at the time of the AU's creation in 2000, several member states were represented by recognized governments that had previously come about through coups. Two poignant examples at the time included Libya and Sudan. Furthermore, the AU (and sub-regional organizations) from time to time continues to tolerate new coup regimes or accepts their integration in subsequent transitional arrangements. In some instances, it has even remained unwilling to acknowledge that a coup has taken place. The AU (and sub-regional organizations) has on occasion also acquiesced in the replacement of governments by rebel groups and has condoned the unconstitutional retention of power through unfree or unfair elections, or the extension of presidential terms.

When the democratically elected government in São Tomé and Príncipe was toppled during a military coup in July 2003, the AU strongly condemned the coup but did not suspend the country from AU activities.[245] Inconsistencies also plagued responses within Africa and beyond to the respective coups in Guinea-Bissau (at the time a party to the African Democracy Charter) and Mali in 2012. While the AU condemned the coup and suspended Guinea-Bissau from its activities,[246] ECOWAS supported a process of cooperation with the coup government aimed at restoring democracy, despite its condemnation of the coup.[247]

[245] This could perhaps be explained by the fact that the constitutional order was restored within a few weeks, including the return of the elected President. See AUPSC, Communiqué of the 93rd Ordinary Session at Ambassadorial Level of the Central Organ of the Mechanism for Conflict Prevention, Management and Resolution, Central Organ/MEC/AMB/COMM (XCIII) (24 July 2003) paras 1 ff http://www.peaceau.org/uploads/240703com.pdf.

[246] See *inter alia* AUPSC, Communiqué of the 318th Meeting at the Level of Heads of State and Government, PSC/PR/COMM (CCCXVIII) (17 April 2012) paras 3 ff http://www.peaceau.org/en/.

[247] Institute for Security Studies, (2013) 45 Peace and Security Report 8–9; see also Extraordinary Summit of the Authority of the ECOWAS Heads of State and Government, Final Communiqué

Democratic presidential and democratic elections were ultimately held in 2014.[248] In the case of Mali, the AU suspended the country from AU activities after the military coup on 22 March 2012 against President Amadou Touré.[249] However, the junta responsible for the military *coup* was subsequently accommodated in the transitional government that took office in August 2012.[250] This government was swiftly recognized by the AU and the UN also endorsed its request for military assistance by France, due to the deterioration of the security situation in the north of Mali.[251]

In November 2017 the AU also condoned the military coup in Zimbabwe, resulting in the resignation of President Robert Mugabe.[252] The military takeover was sparked on 14 November 2017 by the firing of the Vice-President, after which the military placed President Mugabe under house arrest. Widespread protests followed, demanding Mr Mugabe's resignation. This only occurred on 21 November 2017, when he was faced with the choice of resignation or impeachment by Parliament.[253] On 24 November 2017 Mr Emmerson Mnangagwa (a former Vice-President to Mr Mugabe) was sworn in as President and gave assurances that elections planned for 2018 would proceed.[254] Neither the AU nor the Southern African Development Community (SADC) condemned the coup, nor in fact did any state seem eager to refer to the military takeover as a coup. The AU instead chose to praise President Mugabe for stepping down, recognizing that the Zimbabwean

(3 May 2012) paras 19 ff https://reliefweb.int/sites/reliefweb.int/files/resources/comfinal04052012.pdf. The UNSC for its part condemned the *coup* in Guinea-Bissau in UN Doc S/RES/2048 (18 May 2012) paras 1, 4. See also EU, Conclusions of the Council on Guinea-Bissau, Brussels, 9010/12 (23 May 2012) paras 1 ff http://register.consilium.europa.eu/doc/srv?l=ENandf=ST%209010%20 2012%20INIT.

[248] BBC, 'Guinea-Bissau Votes for New President and Parliament' *BBC News* (13 April 2104) https://www.bbc.com/news/world-africa-27005788.

[249] AUPSC, Communiqué of 315th Meeting, PSC/PR/COMM (CCCXV) (23 March 2015) para 9 http://www.peaceau.org/uploads/psc-comm-mali-23-03-2012-eng.pdf.

[250] See Extraordinary Summit of the ECOWAS Heads of State and Government, Final Communiqué (26 April 2012) paras 9 ff http://documentation.ecowas.int/; Institute for Security Studies, 'ECOWAS Peace and Security Report Series, Mali: Making Peace While Preparing for War (1 October 2012) 2 https://issafrica.s3.amazonaws.com/site/uploads/ECOWAS1-ENG.pdf.

[251] See AUPSC, 332nd Meeting, Communiqué, PSC/PR/COMM (CCCXXXII) (4 September 2012) para 3 http://www.peaceau.org/uploads/psc.332.com.mali.pdf. Elections were ultimately held in August 2013 and President Ibrahim Keita was elected President. See Reuters Staff, 'Mali Dismisses Candidates for Fraud in Elections' *Reuters* (1 January 2014) http://www.reuters.com/article/2014/01/01/us-mali-elections-idUSBREA000KK20140101.

[252] AFP, 'Timeline: How Zimbabwe's "*coup*" Unfolded' *Guardian* (21 November 2017) https://mg.co.za/article/2017-11-21-timeline-how-zimbabwes-coup-unfolded. Similarly, 'Statement by the Executive Secretary of SADC Following the Resignation of President Robert Mugabe' (24 November 2017) http://www.sadc.int/news-events/news/statement-executive-secretary-sadc-following-resignation-president-robert-mugabe/.

[253] AFP (n 252).

[254] AFP, 'From Exile to Election: Emmerson Mnangagwa's Timeline to Victory' *Guardian* (3 August 2018) https://www.theguardian.com/world/2018/aug/03/emmerson-mnangagwa-zimbabwe-timeline-to-victory.

people had expressed their will that there should be a peaceful transfer of power in a manner that secured the democratic future of their country.[255]

The AU thereby chose to ignore the fact that the will of the people was not expressed by means of elections and that the threat of impeachment by Parliament was facilitated (or rather coerced) by the unconstitutional use of force.[256] Ironically, the AU and the SADC also condoned the unconstitutional behaviour of President Mugabe while still in power. Notably, neither of these organizations took action against the President in 2002, when elections were overshadowed by large-scale violence and intimidation.[257]

As recently as April 2019 Africa had witnessed another coup, when in Sudan the Defence Minister establishment a two-year transitional military government and suspended the country's Constitution.[258] On 15 April 2019 the AU Peace and Security Council demanded the handing over of power to a transitional civilian-led government within fifteen days, or otherwise face automatic suspension from participation in AU activities.[259] When this demand had not been fulfilled by 30 April 2019, Sudan was initially given an extension of sixty days, in acknowledgment of 'gradual progress' made towards an agreement in this regard.[260] However, subsequent to a paramilitary crackdown on protests in Khartoum in early June 2019 that left more than 120 people dead, the AU suspended Sudan from its activities 'until the effective establishment of a civilian-led Transitional Authority'.[261]

[255] Statement of the Chairperson of the Commission of the African Union on the Situation in Zimbabwe (21 November 2017) http://www.peaceau.org/uploads/auc-statement-zimbabwe-21nov2017english.pdf.

[256] P Roessler, 'How AU Got It Wrong on Zimbabwe' *Al Jazeera* (8 December 2017) https://www.news24.com/Africa/Zimbabwe/how-au-got-it-wrong-on-zimbabwe-20171208. Subsequent to the presidential elections held on 30 July 2019, Mr Mnangagwa was declared winner by the national electoral commission, despite claims of fraud and intimidation of voters by the opposition and EU election observers. H Mohamed, 'Zimbabwe Election: Emmerson Mnangagwa Declared Winner' *Al Jazeera News* (3 August 2018) https://www.aljazeera.com/news/2018/08/zimbabwe-election-emmerson-mnangagwa-declared-winner-180802214534796.html.

[257] SADC Parliamentary Forum Election Observation Mission, 'Zimbabwe Presidential Elections 9–10 March 2002 Statement (13 March 2002) http://archive.kubatana.net/docs/demgg/crisis_cwealth_apr_030410_appdx.pdf. However, at the time Zimbabwe had been suspended by the Commonwealth. See The Commonwealth, 'Zimbabwe is Suspended From the Councils of the Commonwealth' (2002) http://thecommonwealth.org/history-of-the-commonwealth/zimbabwe-suspended-councils-commonwealth. Other countries that faced (temporary) suspension from the Commonwealth in the wake of military coups included Nigeria (1995), Pakistan (1999, 2007), and Fiji (2000, 2009). See http://www.commonwealthofnations.org/commonwealth/commonwealth-membership/withdrawals-and-suspension/. See also Charlesworth (n 6) 81, 104.

[258] M Osman and M Bearak, 'Sudan's Omar Hassan al-Bashir Is Ousted by Military After 30 Years in Power' *Washington Post* (11 April 2019) https://www.washingtonpost.com/world/africa/sudans-military-expected-to-announce-overthrow-of-president-following-months-of-popular-protests/2019/04/11/bedcc28e-5c2b-11e9-842d-7d3ed7eb3957_story.html?utm_term=.841d6b8fa73c.

[259] AUPSC, Communiqué of the 804th Meeting, PSC/PR/COMM (DCCCXL) (15 April 2019) paras 5(a), 5(c).

[260] AUPSC, Communiqué of the 846th Meeting, PSC/PR/COMM (DCCCXLVI) (30 April 2019) paras 4, 5.

[261] AUPSC, Communiqué of the 854th Meeting, PSC/PR/COMM (DCCCXLIV) (6 June 2019) para 12 http://www.peaceau.org/uploads/psc.854.comm.sudan.6.6.19.pdf; J Burke, 'African Union

In August 2019 negotiations were concluded regarding the establishment of a three-year transitional government which, although civilian-led, also included military leaders. Shortly afterwards the AU's suspension of Sudan was lifted.[262] The AU's acceptance of power-sharing between civilians and elements of the coup government reflects that legitimacy of origin and exercise had to be balanced with governmental stability and effective control.

In the case of Libya, the AU was confronted with the replacement of a recognized government by rebel groups, after the popular revolt against the Qaddafi regime culminated in UNSC Resolution 1973 of 17 March 2011 and a North Atlantic Treaty Organization (NATO) military intervention. Despite disagreement within the AU about the extent to which regime change had been foreseen by Resolution 1973 (2011),[263] it subsequently did recognize the National Transitional Council of Libya (NTC) as the legitimate government of Libya. In a statement in October 2011 the AU—while underscoring the uniqueness of the situation in Libya and the exceptional circumstances surrounding it—authorized the NTC to occupy the seat of Libya in the AU and its organs.[264] Outside of the AU the NTC was already recognized as the legitimate governing authority by thirty-two countries (including the United Kingdom and the United States) on 15 July 2011.[265] The UN accepted the credentials of the NTC on 16 September 2011 (which was almost a month before the AU).[266]

The fact that the NTC came to power through a violent overthrow as opposed to democratic elections prevented neither the AU nor the thirty-two states forming part

Suspends Sudan Over Violence Against Protesters' *Guardian* (6 June 2019) https://www.theguardian.com/world/2019/jun/06/sudan-african-union-suspension-military-rulers.

262 AUPSC, Communiqué of the 875th Meeting PSC/PR/COMM. (DCCCLXXV) (6 September 2019) para 4 http://www.peaceau.org/uploads/eng.875.psc.communique.sudan.6.9.2019.pdf; see also BBC 'Sudan Crisis: Military and Opposition Agree Power-Sharing Deal' *BBC News* (5 July 2019) https://www.bbc.com/news/world-africa-48878009; Agency Staff, 'African Union Lifts Suspension of Sudan after Announcement of New Cabinet', *Business Day* (7 September 2019) https://www.businesslive.co.za/bd/world/africa/2019-09-07-african-union-lifts-suspension-of-sudan-after-announcement-of-new-cabinet/.

263 See *inter alia* South Africa's criticism of NATO's interpretation of its mandate in G Ulfstein, 'The Legality of the NATO Bombing in Libya' (2013) 62 International and Comparative Law Quarterly 167.

264 AUPSC, Communiqué of the 297th Meeting, PSC/PR/COMM/2 (CCXCVII) (20 October 2011) para 4 http://www.peaceau.org/uploads/297thpsccommuniqueen.pdf.

265 These countries also took the unusual step of explicitly derecognizing the Qaddafi regime. However, this could be seen as a logical consequences of the fact that they interpreted the military mandate foreseen in UN Doc S/RES/1973 (17 March 2011) as authorizing regime change. See the joint statement on behalf of the United States, Britain and France by B Obama, D Cameron, and N Sarkozy, 'Libya's Pathway to Peace' *New York Times* (14 April 2011) http://www.nytimes.com/2011/04/15/opinion/15iht-edlibya15.html?_r=0. For an overview of the different opinions of states, see Ulfstein (n 270) 165 ff. See Fourth Meeting of the Libya Contact Group,' Chair's Statement' (15 July 2011) para 4 http://www.mfa.gov.tr/fourth-meeting-of-the-libya-contact-group-chair_s-statement_-15-july-2011_-istanbul.en.mfa. See also S Talmon, 'De-Recognition of Colonel Qaddafi as Head of State of Libya?' (2011) 60 International and Comparative Law Quarterly 759 ff.

266 UN Doc A/RES/66/1 A (16 September 2011).

of the Libya Contact Group from recognizing it as the legitimate government of Libya. In the case of the AU the recognition took place at a time when the NTC was in effective control of most of the territory, a fact which may have contributed to the AU's acquiescence in the NTC's status as the recognized government. When recognizing the NTC three months earlier, the US Legal Adviser to the US State Department also claimed that this was due to the effective control exercised by the NTC.[267] He underscored that '[i]nternational law focuses on the question of recognition and recognition tends to follow facts on the ground, particularly control over territory'.[268]

Subsequent to its recognition, the NTC announced the formation of an interim government headed by Prime Minister El-Keib on 22 November 2011.[269] Following elections on 7 June 2012 with a 62 per cent turnout, the NTC handed over its functions to the democratically elected General National Congress on 8 August 2012, after which the NTC was dissolved.[270] Unfortunately, the hold of the elected government over the capital and large parts of the country rapidly deteriorated. In 2014 the General National Congress was replaced by a new parliament, following elections in June 2014, which elected Mr Abdullah al-Thinni as Prime Minister in September of that year. At the time of his confirmation, Mr Al-Thinni had already left Tripoli for Tobruk as his government had no control over the capital.[271]

By 17 December 2015, this government was replaced by a nine-member Presidency Council of the Government of National Accord, headed by the Prime Minister-designate, Fayiz al-Sarraj.[272] The Government of National Accord did not result from democratic elections. Instead, it was the product of a negotiated settlement spearheaded by the UN and culminating in the Libyan Political Agreement of 17 December 2015 in Skhirat, Morocco (Agreement). The Government of National Accord was welcomed by the AU,[273] as well as the

[267] However, doubts have been expressed as to whether the NTC had been in effective control at the time of its recognition by the thirty-two states forming part of the Libya Contact Group. Talmon (n 36) 233; Akande (n 65). This point is taken up again below in section 4.

[268] US Senate, Committee on Foreign Relations, Libya and War Powers, Hearing, S Hrg 112-189, 28 June 2011 39 https://fas.org/irp/congress/2011_hr/libya.pdf. An older example of premature recognition constitutes recognition of the new republican government in Yemen in 1962, subsequent to the coup against the monarchy. When both royalist and republic factions presented their credentials at the UN, the UNGA voted in favour of the new republican regime. This was despite the fact that the royalists, although ejected from the capital, remained engaged in resistance with a strong presence in the country. See UN Doc UN/RES/1871 (XVII) (20 December 1962). See also Roth (n 4) 274.

[269] Report of the Secretary-General on the United Nations Support Mission in Libya, UN Doc S/2012/129 (1 March 2012) para 5.

[270] Report of the Secretary-General on the United Nations Support Mission in Libya, UN Doc S/2012/675 (30 August 2012) paras 2, 3, 9.

[271] Report of the Secretary-General on the United Nations Support Mission to Libya, UN Doc S/2015/144 (26 February 2015) para 7.

[272] Report of the Secretary-General on the United Nations Support Mission in Libya, UN Doc S/2016/182 (25 February 2016) para 3.

[273] AU Commission, Press Release: The Chairperson of the AU Commission Welcomes the Formation of a Government of National Accord (GNA) in Libya (19 January 2016) http://www.peaceau.org/uploads/aucpr-libya-19-1-2016.pdf.

UNSC which in Resolution 2259 of 23 December 2015 described it as the sole legitimate government of Libya.[274] While not adopted under Chapter VII of the UN Charter, the unanimous support within the UNSC for the resolution reflected strong international political backing of the Government of National Accord.[275]

Finally, it is worth mentioning that in 2015 the AU also tolerated unconstitutional retention of power when President Pierre Nkurunziza of Burundi won re-election to a third term, despite a constitutional two-term limit.[276] The decision to run for a third term sparked political violence and a failed coup attempt in May 2015.[277] The run-up to the election was also marred by intimidation and the elections were boycotted by several opposition parties.[278] The AU as well as the East African Community (EAC) criticized the violence and climate of fear and called for a postponement of the presidential elections in order to facilitate dialogue between rivalling parties.[279] However, subsequent to the presidential elections that proceeded in July 2015, the AU Peace and Security Council was concerned neither with the lack legitimacy of origin of the Nkurunziza government, nor with its lack of legitimacy of exercise of governmental power. It merely 'took note of the recent parliamentary and presidential elections', while calling for an inclusive dialogue that would lead to the formation of a government of national unity.[280] A subsequent decision to adopt targeted sanctions, including travel bans and asset freezes against those Burundians who contributed to the violence, was not implemented by states.[281] It is also worth noting that in 2015 an attempt within ECOWAS to ban constitutional amendments aimed at

[274] UN Doc S/RES/2259 (23 December 2015) para 3.

[275] See also UN Doc S/PV.7598 (23 December 2015) 2 (United Kingdom); ibid 5 (Spain).

[276] According to the Burundian Constitution, Presidents can only serve two terms. When seized with the matter, the Burundian Constitutional Court concluded that the President could seek a third term. It was argued that the first term should not be taken into calculation, as he was elected by popular vote, but appointed by Parliament. However, the Vice-President of the Court claimed that the judges had been pressured to come to this decision. See BBC Staff, 'Burundi Court Backs President Nkurunziza on Third Term' *BBC News* (5 May 2015) http://www.bbc.com/news/world-africa-32588658. See also J Bedzigiu and N Alusala (Institute for Security Studies) 'Central African Report. The AU and the ICGLR in Burundi' (9 September 2016) 2 https://issafrica.s3.amazonaws.com/site/uploads/car9-1.pdf.

[277] See Bedzigiu and Alusala (n 276) 2 ff.

[278] J Hatcher, 'Burundi's President Pierre Nkurunziza Wins Third Term in Disputed Election' *Guardian* (24 July 2015) https://www.theguardian.com/world/2015/jul/24/burundi-pierre-nkurunziza-wins-third-term-disputed-election.

[279] AUPSC Communiqué of the 523rd Meeting, PSC/PR/COMM (DXXIII) (9 July 2015) para 5(a) http://www.peaceau.org/uploads/psc-523-comm-burundi-9-7-2015-1-.pdf; AUPSC, Report of the Chairperson of the Commission on the Situation in Burundi, PSC/AHG/3(DXV) (4 June 2015) paras 3 ff http://www.peaceau.org/uploads/psc-515-rpt-burundi-13-06-2015.pdf.

[280] AUPSC, Press Statement, PSC/BR/COMM.(DXXXI) (6 August 2015) http://www.peaceau.org/uploads/pr.531st-psc-burundi-6-08-2015.pdf. See also Bedzigiu and Alusala (n 276) 4.

[281] AUPSC Communiqué, 551st Meeting, PSC/PR/COMM (DLI) (17 October 2015) para 12 http://www.peaceau.org/uploads/psc.551.burundi.17.10.2015.pdf; Bedzigiu and Alusala (n 276) 5. Similarly, the AU did not follow through on a decision to invoke art 4(h) of the AU Constitutive Act (n 197), as will be illuminated in Chapter 5, section 5.1.

removing presidential term limits failed,[282] due to resistance among states in the region.[283]

3.4 Placing the implications of the OAS and AU practice in a global perspective

The above analysis of the institutional developments and practice within the OAS and AU leads to the conclusion that democratic legitimacy—in the narrow sense of legitimacy of origin—is indeed one factor that is taken into account when recognizing a new government, or continuing to recognize a former government that had been ousted by a coup.[284] This may particularly be the case where a sitting President refuses to accept electoral defeat or where those exercising a coup against a democratically elected government are politically isolated in and outside the region. In such situations the legitimacy of origin of the newly elected or recently ousted government can effectively compensate for its lack of effective control over territory, as a result of which it will (continue to) be recognized as the *de jure* government. An illustrative example is that of The Gambia in 2017, where the newly elected President was recognized as head of state before he had taken control of any state territory or institutions. In this instance the election results were monitored by only a handful of AU election observers and the results were also domestically contested. Yet, due to the political isolation of the incumbent President, the AU (along with ECOWAS and the UNSC) accepted the electoral victory of the rival candidate at face value.

Even so, the legal impact of this precedent, coupled with that of instances where organizations such as the OAS and AU have suspended coup governments from their respective activities and even refused to recognize them, should not be overestimated. The above analysis has also illustrated that coups within OAS and AU member states are at times still tolerated within these organizations as well as by other states. Moreover, the OAS and the AU as well as states beyond these regions remain reluctant to derecognize member states that retain power through unconstitutional means such as unfree and unfair elections, or that have lost their legitimacy of exercise of governmental power through self-coups. This is exemplified by the divided and at times

[282] Since 2014 the removal of the presidential term limit was attempted *inter alia* in Burkina Faso, the Congo and (successfully) in Rwanda. See J Steyn Kotze, 'Africa Faces a New Threat to Democracy: The "Constitutional *coup*" ' *The Conversation* (8 February 2017) http://theconversation.com/africa-faces-a-new-threat-to-democracy-the-constitutional-coup-72011. See generally CM Fombad, 'Constitutional Reforms and Constitutionalism in Africa: Reflections on Some Current Challenges and Future Prospects' (2011) 59 Buffalo Law Review 1007 ff.

[283] See also K Camara, 'Here's How African Leaders Stage "Constitutional *Coups*": They Tweak the Constitution to Stay in Power' *Washington Post* (16 September 2016) https://www.washingtonpost.com/news/monkey-cage/wp/2016/09/16/heres-how-african-leaders-stage-constitutional-coups-they-tweak-the-constitution-to-stay-in-power/?utm_term=.e17dfce95b34. See also Steyn Kotze (n 282).

[284] Nolte (n 6) 161.

ambivalent reaction within and beyond the OAS towards the 2019 Maduro/Guaidó saga in Venezuela. It seems that in these situations, states prefer to sustain the *de jure* governmental status of the authority that is in effective control, regardless of its legitimacy of origin or exercise. This has been poignantly illustrated by the mere symbolic recognition of Mr Guaidó by the majority of EU countries.[285]

In summary therefore the practice within the OAS and the AU suggests that extensive discretion remains as to whether coups or other manifestations of unconstitutional change of government should result in sanctions potentially culminating in non-recognition or derecognition. The institutional (treaty) measures adopted within the OAS and AU for the purpose of countering unconstitutional changes of government or alterations to the constitutional order are in practice interpreted as guiding principles rather than binding obligations. The extent to which they will be decisive will depend on the factual and political context of each case.

Outside of Latin America and Africa, a lingering reluctance amongst states to regard democratic legitimacy as a *sine qua non* for governmental recognition can also be observed. Even within the Council of Europe, which has a democratic pedigree that dates back to 1949, some inconsistencies can be observed. While the Statute of the Council of Europe does not explicitly refer to democracy, it is considered as interlinked with the rule of law and human rights to which member states commit themselves in article 3 of the Statute.[286] As a result, Greece withdrew in 1969 and Turkey was suspended in 1981, subsequent to the military coups in the respective countries.[287] In the wake of democratic elections held in central and eastern European countries after the break-up of the Soviet Union, the membership of the Council of Europe expanded to forty-seven states. While (attempted) military overthrows have been a rare occurrence since,[288] the organization has not consistently enforced other manifestations of a lack of democratic legitimacy of origin, nor of exercise of governmental power. A poignant recent example was the decision in June 2019 to restore Russia's voting rights, which was suspended in 2014 due to its annexation of the Crimea.[289] This restoration took place at a time when free and fair elections within Russia occurred only in name.[290] Other salient

[285] See Gurmendi (n 171) who noted that 'Maduro is an illegitimate President, but a President nonetheless; and the National Assembly is a democratically elected organ, but not the government'.

[286] Statute of the Council of Europe of 5 May 1949 (entered into force 3 August 1949), ETS No 001 https://www.coe.int/en/web/conventions/full-list/-/conventions/treaty/001.

[287] See *inter alia* Council of Europe (Committee of Ministers) (12 December 1969) CM (69) PV 4, 20; Council of Europe (Parliamentary Assembly) (14 May 1981) Order 398 (1981).

[288] The most prominent of which was the failed military coup attempt in Turkey in July 2016. See H Barkey 'One Year Later, The Turkish Coup Attempt Remains Shrouded in Mystery' *Washington Post* (14 July 2017) https://www.washingtonpost.com/news/democracy-post/wp/2017/07/14/one-year-later-the-turkish-coup-attempt-remains-shrouded-in-mystery/.

[289] PACE, 'Challenge, on substantive grounds, of the still unratified credentials of the parliamentary delegation of the Russian Federation' Res 2292 (26 June 2019) http://assembly.coe.int/nw/xml/XRef/Xref-XML2HTML-en.asp?fileid=28049&lang=en.

[290] G Bogush 'Voting in Russia: Please do Don't Call it Elections' *Verfassungsblog* (25 September 2019) https://verfassungsblog.de/voting-in-russia-please-dont-call-it-elections/. Russia's voting rights in the Parliamentary Assembly were also briefly suspended in 2000 due to its conduct in Chechnya. See

examples at the time of writing included Hungary, Poland, and Turkey, all of which were experiencing a systematic erosion of democratic legitimacy of exercise, *inter alia* through measures that undermined the separation of powers and judicial independence.[291] Yet, no limitation of voting rights or suspension was imposed. Moreover, at no point was derecognition of the respective incumbent authorities contemplated.[292]

As far as the UN is concerned, section 3 above has already indicated that democratic legitimacy (of origin) is not a formal requirement for accreditation of government representatives. The fact that a prominent member of the UNSC remains committed to an authoritarian one party regime also suggests that this position is not likely to change in practice in the near future. Incidents in which the UNSC refuses to recognize authorities that acquire (or retain) governmental power through unconstitutional means, as in the case of Côte d'Ivoire and The Gambia,[293] are therefore likely to remain the exception rather than the rule. This can *inter alia* be illustrated by the fact that no similar consequences resulted from the military coups in Egypt in 2013,[294] Thailand in May 2014,[295] or Zimbabwe in 2017. Neither

PACE, Recommendation 1456 (2000) of the Parliamentary Assembly of the Council of Europe on the Conflict in the Chechen Republic (Implementation by Russia of Recommendation 1444 (6 April 2000).

[291] PACE (Monitoring Committee), *The progress of the Assembly's monitoring procedure (January–December 2017) and the periodic review of the honouring of obligations by Estonia, Greece, Hungary and Ireland* Doc 14450 Part 4 (HU) (8 January 2019) paras 114 ff http://semantic-pace.net/tools/pdf.aspx?doc=aHR0cDovL2Fzc2VtYmx5LmNvZS5pbnQvbncveG1sL1hSZWYvWDJILURXLWV4dHIuYXNwP2ZpbGVpZD0yNDMwMiZsYW5nPUVO&xsl=aHR0cDovL3NlbWFudGljcGFjZS5uZXQvWHNsdC9QZGYvWFJlZi1XRC1BVC1YTUwyUERGLnhzbA==&xsltparams=ZmlsZWlkPTI0MzAy; D Mijatovic (Commissioner for Human Rights of the Council of Europe), Report Following her Visit to Poland from 11 to 15 March 2019 CommDH(2019)17 (28 June 2019) 5 ff https://rm.coe.int/2nd-quarterly-activity-report-2019-by-dunja-mijatovic-council-of-europ/16809718f1; ibid. The worsening situation of opposition politicians in Turkey: what can be done to protect their fundamental rights in a Council of Europe member State? Doc 14812 (22 January 2019) paras 8 ff http://semantic-pace.net/tools/pdf.aspx?doc=aHR0cDovL2Fzc2VtYmx5LmNvZS5pbnQvbncveG1sL1hSZWYvWDJILURXLWV4dHIuYXNwP2ZpbGVpZD0yNTM0OSZsYW5nPUVO&xsl=aHR0cDovL3NlbWFudGljcGFjZS5uZXQvWHNsdC9QZGYvWFJlZi1XRC1BVC1YTUwyUERGLnhzbA==&xsltparams=ZmlsZWlkPTI1MzQ5.

[292] Also within the European Union it remains uncertain whether the procedures initiated against Hungary and Poland for violations of foundational values including democracy and the rule of law will ultimately result in any sanction. See European Parliament, Report on a proposal calling on the Council to determine, pursuant to Article 7(1) of the Treaty on European Union, the existence of a clear risk of a serious breach by Hungary of the values on which the Union is founded A8-0250/2018 (4 July 2019); European Commission, Press Release: Rule of Law: European Commission launches infringement procedure to protect judges in Poland from political control (3 April 2019) https://europa.eu/rapid/press-release_IP-19-1957_en.htm.

[293] See section 3.3.1

[294] States outside the AU, including the United States and members of the European Union, remained reluctant to call the ousting of Morsi a coup. See BBC Staff, 'World Reaction to the Ousting of Egypt's Mohammed Morsi' *BBC* (4 July 2013) http://www.bbc.com/news/world-middle-east-23175379. In October 2015 Egypt (represented by the Sisi government) was elected by the UNGA to serve on the UNSC for a two-year period. See UN Doc A/70/PV.33 (15 October 2015) 3.

[295] States within and beyond Asia maintained bilateral relations with the military dictatorship, despite formal criticism of the coup by the United States and some Western states. M Ichihara, J-W Koo, N Sahoo, and T Pongsudhirak, 'Asian Democracies and Thailand's Military Takeover' *Carnegie Rising Democracies Network* (13 October 2015) https://carnegieendowment.org/2015/

did the (attempted) derecognition of the Maduro regime in Venezuela by the OAS Permanent Council lead to its disaccreditation within the UN. Also, as mentioned in section 3.3.2, the UN accredited the NTC in Libya that came about through violent overthrow.

Another example, particularly interesting in the context of this chapter, concerns the reaction within the UN to the developments in the Crimea in 2014. At the time, Russia initially justified its military intervention in the Crimea in March 2014 with the argument that it had been requested by the democratically elected (but by then ousted) Ukrainian President Yanukovych to restore order in the Crimea.[296] Russia presented a letter to this effect to the UNSC, signed by Mr Yanukovych and dated 1 March 2014.[297] At this point in time, Mr Yanukovych's own parliament had already voted to remove him from power on 22 February 2014. However, this vote appeared to be unconstitutional as it did not confirm to the two-thirds majority requirement contained in the Ukrainian Constitution.[298] As a consequence, the legitimacy of origin of his successor was open to question. Even so, no fewer than 100 states subsequently supported UNGA Resolution 262 of 27 March 2014 not to recognize the altered territorial status of the Crimea. Only eleven states (including Russia) voted against the resolution, while fifty-eight states abstained.[299] It is arguable that a resolution which was explicitly supported by more than half of the membership of the UN, while explicitly having been rejected by merely eleven states, can be interpreted as an implicit rejection of Mr Yanukovych's claim that due to him being democratically elected, he still represented the *de jure* government of the Ukraine.[300] After all, had Mr Yanukovych still been regarded as the head of state, an invitation to Russia to intervene militarily in the Crimea would not have resulted in a disruption or alteration of the territorial integrity and status of the Ukraine.[301]

10/13/asian-democracies-and-thailand-s-military-takeover-pub-61553. See also QTT Nguyen, 'Rethinking the Legality of Intervention by Invitation: Toward Neutrality' (2019) (First View) Journal of Conflict and Security Law 32.

[296] UN Doc S/PV.7125 (3 March 2014) 2 (Russia). See also Z Vermeer, 'Intervention With the Consent of a Deposed (but Legitimate) Government? Playing the Sierra Leone Card' *EJILTalk*! (6 March 2014) https://www.ejiltalk.org/intervention-with-the-consent-of-a-deposed-but-legitimate-government-playing-the-sierra-leone-card/; N Krisch, 'Crimea and the Limits of International Law' *EJILTalk*! (10 March 2014) https://www.ejiltalk.org/crimea-and-the-limits-of-international-law/; D Wisehart, 'The Crisis in the Ukraine and the Prohibition of the Use of Force: A Legal Basis for Russia's Intervention?' *EJILTalk*! (4 March 2014) https://www.ejiltalk.org/the-crisis-in-ukraine-and-the-prohibition-of-the-use-of-force-a-legal-basis-for-russias-intervention/.

[297] UN Doc S/PV.7125 (3 March 2014) 2 (Russia).

[298] Vermeer (n 296); Ruys and Ferro (n 29) 83.

[299] UN Doc A/RES/68/262 (27 March 2014).

[300] See Vermeer (n 296) 61. UN Doc A/RES/68//262 (27 March 2014) para 6; see also GH Fox, 'Ukraine Insta-Symposium: Intervention in the Ukraine by Invitation' *Opinio Juris* (10 March 2014) http://opiniojuris.org/2014/03/10/ukraine-insta-symposium-intervention-ukraine-invitation/.

[301] See Ruys and Ferro (n 29) 84, who underscore the fact that Mr Yanokovich had clearly lost effective control over the country and no longer had the authority to invite foreign military assistance. See also UN Doc S/PV.7125 (3 March 2014) 7 (United Kingdom).

All in all, state and organizational practice across regions remains too inconsistent and ambivalent to support the conclusion that democratic legitimacy—even in the narrow sense of legitimacy of origin—is a pre-condition for governmental recognition under customary international law. This is (somewhat cynically) illustrated by the fact that some of the very same states that derecognized the Maduro regime in Venezuela for lacking democratic legitimacy of origin overlooked the lack of such legitimacy of the NTC in Libya, as well as of the successor to Mr Yanukovych in the Ukraine, when recognizing it as the *de jure* government.

Finally, the developments in Libya subsequent to the recognition of the NTC, culminating in the Government of National Accord, indicate that in situations of internal turmoil, governmental recognition is sometimes neither determined by effective control nor democratic legitimacy in the form of elections. Instead, it is the product of a negotiated settlement under the auspices of one or more international (including regional) organizations in an attempt to terminate the conflict.[302] In these instances effective control, to the extent that it is achieved, comes after governmental recognition rather than preceding it. Similarly, democratic legitimacy through elections is achieved only where this is foreseen in the transitional agreement and after the coming into being of the transitional government.[303] Stated differently, the recognition of these negotiated governments is not so much based on their actual effective control and/or democratic legitimacy (of origin) as on the aspirations of the international community that effective control and free and fair elections will result from a negotiated government that includes all or most parties to the conflict.

Notable examples in Africa and beyond include the Afghanistan Interim Authority that was negotiated in December 2001 under the auspices of the UN;[304] the 2004 Iraqi Interim Government that was formed with the assistance of the UN;[305] the 2004 Transitional Federal Government of Somalia which was mediated by the Intergovernmental Authority on Development (IGAD);[306] the 2012 Interim Government in Mali which was mediated under the auspices of ECOWAS;[307] and the 2013 National Transitional Council in the Central African Republic that came

302 See also Nolte (n 6) 159.

303 Nolte (n 6) 159 notes that these negotiated agreements usually foresee the transfer of power to a democratically-elected government. They also tend to be broadly representative by including all or most parties to the conflict.

304 Agreement on Provisional Arrangements in Afghanistan Pending the Re-Establishment of Permanent Government Institutions of 5 December 2001 (Bonn Agreement) UN Doc S/2001/1154 (5 December 2001).

305 UNSG, Report of the Secretary-General Pursuant to Paragraph 24 of Resolution 1483 (2003) and Paragraph 12 of Resolution 1511 (2003) S/2004/625 (5 August 2004) para 26.

306 UNSG, Report of the Secretary-General on the Situation in Somalia UN Doc S/2004/804 (8 October 2004) paras 2 ff.

307 See Extraordinary Summit of the ECOWAS Heads of State and Government, Final Communiqué (26 April 2012) paras 9 ff; Report of the Secretary-General on the Situation in Mali UN Doc S/2012/894 (28 November 2012) para 7.

into being through mediation efforts, including the AU and Economic Community of Central African states (ECCAS).[308] Chapter 3, section 4, will illustrate that neither the lack of effective control by these interim governments nor their lack of democratic legitimacy (of origin) has prevented them from requesting and receiving direct military assistance.

4. The continued *de jure* status of governments once recognized

Once an authority is recognized as the *de jure* government, this triggers a strong presumption of continued *de jure* status. This presumption has its origins in situations where an incumbent government in effective control subsequently loses control over parts of the territory and population in the wake of internal conflict.[309] In these circumstances the incumbent government continues to be recognized as the *de jure* government, until it becomes clear that it no longer is resisting the attempts to overthrow it.[310] During the Cold War this presumption of continued recognition manifested itself *inter alia* in situations where incumbent African governments of former British and French colonies were subjected to coups by mutinous troops.[311] The initial loss of control over the territory (including the capital and state institutions) did not automatically terminate the *de jure* status of the recognized government.[312]

This was illustrated by the fact that third states by and large continued to recognize the right of the ousted governments to request military assistance from former colonial powers, in order to facilitate their reinstatement.[313] For the most part the reinstatement of these ousted regimes occurred relatively swiftly and their interruption of effective control remained brief.[314] However, Chapter 3, section 4 will illustrate that state practice also extends the presumption of continued de jure status where incumbent governments have suffered extensive and protracted loss of control over territory and sections of the population (such as Syria and Yemen). The presumption further applies to transitional governments that have limited control over territory and/or state institutions (eg Mali and Central African Republic) or that have even acquired such control only after several years (eg Somalia).[315]

[308] UN Doc S/RES/2149 (10 April 2014) para 1.
[309] Wippman (n 67) 214; Roth (n 4) 138.
[310] Nolte (n 6) 147; see also Ruys and Ferro (n 29) 82.
[311] Nowrot and Schabacker (n 97) 390.
[312] See also Ruys and Ferro (n 29) 85.
[313] Nowrot and Schabacker (n 97) 390.
[314] ibid.
[315] However, see Nolte (n 6) 160–61, who submits that transitional governments that are unable to contain the military conflict risk being derecognized and merely treated as another party to the conflict.

A consequence (or rather the flipside) of the strong presumption of continued *de jure* status of the incumbent government is that it should be given the benefit of the doubt in cases of competing claims for governmental recognition. The recognition of an opposition group as the new *de jure* government is to be considered only where it is very evident that it has taken charge of the state apparatus without facing any more meaningful resistance from the incumbent government.[316] Any *de jure* recognition of rival groups prior to this point is likely to amount to premature recognition and a violation of the principle of non-intervention in the internal affairs of another state.[317] In fact, in the case of Libya the early recognition of the NTC by the thirty-two members of the Libya Contact Group has been criticized as premature and, therefore, constituting an illegal interference in the affairs of another state.[318] As far as the current Libyan Government of National Accord is concerned, its continued recognition has been assured through its endorsement in UNSC Resolution 2259 of 23 December 2015 which determined the Government of National Accord to be the sole legitimate government of Libya.[319] Even though this resolution was not adopted under Chapter VII of the UN Carter, it carries significant political weight as it was unanimously adopted. As a result, it is unlikely that any new government will be recognized (prematurely) by states, unless or until the UNSC has withdrawn support for the current Government of National Accord.

This bias towards the incumbent government is motivated by the need for stability in international relations.[320] If the incumbent government were derecognized due to internal conflict and before the competing forces have gained control in a manner that commanded acquiescence of the population, the state would effectively be left without a government with which the international community can engage.[321] The swift recognition of opposition groups as the *de jure* government could also serve as an incentive for insurgent groups elsewhere, with destabilizing effects for other states. In addition, states are reluctant to set a precedent through (de)-recognition that could subsequently be used against themselves.[322] That being said, the traditional bias towards the incumbent government is based on the premise that it actually continues to exist during an armed conflict. In addition, it originated at a time when effective control was the undisputed criterion for governmental recognition. This raises the question of whether the presumption of continued recognition remains applicable in situations where the incumbent government has imploded. It further raises the

[316] Nolte (n 6) 147.
[317] Roth (n 4) 182.
[318] See Talmon (n 36) 233; Akande (n 65).
[319] UN Doc S/RES/2259 (23 December 2015) para 3.
[320] Nolte (n 6) 148.
[321] ibid 148–49.
[322] ibid 149.

question of whether the presumption is applicable in situations where the *de jure* governmental status of the incumbent regime is challenged by an authority that claims to be democratically legitimated.

The situation in Somalia in 1991/1992 serves to illustrate that it is possible for an incumbent government to disintegrate entirely. At the time there was a complete collapse of state structures as a result of which no incumbent government could be identified. As a result, the presumption of continued recognition was not applicable in this instance. Moreover, the situation was further complicated by the fact that no rival party or coalition of rival parties could claim to be in effective control over the state apparatus.[323] This meant that it also was not possible at the time to recognize a new *de jure* government. Somalia thus was left without any authority that could represent the state internationally, including consenting to any form of assistance, whether military assistance or otherwise.[324] This was an important consideration when the UNSC decided to authorize military measures in Somalia under Chapter VII of the UN Charter.[325] Parallel attempts to establish an interim government through a political settlement under the auspices of the UN and regional organizations continued. This finally bore sustainable fruit with the emergence of the Transitional Federal Government in 2004.[326]

The continued existence of the incumbent government can also be at issue where the revolution comes from within the government itself. In such a situation it can become difficult to identify the entity that constitutes the incumbent government, as a result of which the presumption of continued recognition would be of little use for the purpose of determining the *de jure* government. An older example illustrating this point concerns that of the Congolese government which collapsed very soon after the country's independence in June 1960. Thereafter, President Joseph Kasavubu (the head of state) and Prime Minister Patrice Lumumba (the head of government) both claimed to represent the incumbent government.[327] In the ensuing conflict, the Kasavubu regime supported by the military dominated the capital, while Lumumba's forces controlled other parts of the country. The United Nations Credential Committee and the United Nations General Assembly

[323] ibid 156.

[324] ibid 151.

[325] See Letter dated 29 November 1992 from the Secretary-General addressed to the President of the Security Council, UN Doc S/24868 (30 November 1992) 3. The UNSG, referring to the collapse of the state structures in Somalia at the time, noted that there was no government in Somalia that could request forcible intervention. See also UN Doc S/RES/794 (3 December 1992) para 10; Nolte (n 6) 151.

[326] See Chapter 3, section 4.3.

[327] President Kasavubu for his part dismissed Prime Minister Lumumba on 5 September 1960 on the basis of national legislation. Prime Minister Lumumba responded by dismissing President Kasavubu, a decision that was subsequently backed by the Congolese Parliament. President Kasavubu then declared the Parliament's action unconstitutional, and on 14 September 1960 authorized the chief of the military, Mobuto, to disperse parliament temporarily. See Letter dated 16 November 1960 to the Secretary-General from the President of the Republic of the Congo (Leopoldville), UN Doc A/4577 (17 November 1960) 1 ff; Roth (n 4) 268 ff.

subsequently accepted the credentials presented by the Kasavubu delegation,[328] thereby seating the Kasavubu regime as the representative of the Congo at the UN.[329] The acceptance of the Kasavubu regime was controversial in as far as it occurred amidst an ongoing internal conflict in which there was significant ambivalence regarding the identity of the incumbent government.[330] In such a situation, it is arguable that until such time as one side has clearly gained effective control over most of the territory and state apparatus, or a transitional government is negotiated by means of a negotiated settlement, the state would effectively be without a *de jure* government that can incur rights and obligations on its behalf.[331]

Finally, the emergence of democratic legitimacy (of origin) as a criterion for governmental recognition can also in certain circumstances render inapplicable the presumption of continued recognition. This would particularly be the case where the competing entity claiming to constitute the *de jure* government has won elections against the incumbent regime and the election results have been widely endorsed by states through international (including regional) organizations. A case in point would be The Gambia, where the newly elected President was recognized as such by ECOWAS, the AU, and the UNSC, despite the fact that the incumbent President was still contesting the election results and retained effective control (by refusing to leave office). More uncertain would be situations where an incumbent regime retains effective control through unfair and unfree elections. As indicated above in section 3, on the whole states have remained reluctant to derecognize incumbent regimes solely on this basis. The derecognition of the Maduro regime in combination with the recognition of Mr Guaidó as interim President by some countries remains a controversial exception and has been described by some as premature.[332] Given the divided reaction of states in this regard combined with

[328] See debate in UNGA Credentials Committee, Credentials of Representatives of the Republic of the Congo (Leopoldville), UN Doc A/4578 (17 November 1960) paras 8 ff. See also UNGA Res 1498 (XV) (22 November 1960); Roth (n 4) 271–72.

[329] Roth (n 4) 271–72.

[330] The matter was also complicated by the fact that Kasavubu and Lumumba, in the period before their government collapsed, had requested the UN for military assistance. As the restoration of law and order in collaboration with the Congolese government was central to the UN mission, it needed to be determined which Congolese forces were operating in the service of the recognized government and which forces were seeking to subvert it. See UN Doc S/4382 (12 July 1960); UN Doc S/RES/143 (1960) (8-0-3); Roth (n 4) 268–70, 274.

[331] A similar example from the Cold War era concerns the overthrow of the government of the Dominican Republic in April 1965. Subsequently, two opposing forces in the form of the 'Constitutional Government' and the 'Government of National Reconstruction' emerged and both claimed to represent the Dominican state. In May 1965 both authorities approached the UN for the purpose of accreditation. The UNSG noted that it was unclear which of the two contenders constituted the government (UN Doc S/PV.1207 (13 May 1965) paras 14 ff). The UNSC subsequently gave an audience to representatives of both authorities, but without accepting either as the official representative of the Dominican Republic (S/PV.1212 (19 May 1965) paras 211 ff). The situation was resolved only by September of that year, when the Government of National Reconstruction gained effective control with controversial military assistance of the United States. See O Corten, *The Law Against War: The Prohibition on the Use of Force in Contemporary International Law* (Hart Publishing 2010) 278 ff.

[332] See *Deutscher Bundestag* (n 163) 11.

the strength of the presumption of continued recognition, it is arguable that the presumption remains applicable vis-à-vis incumbent governments that retain effective control through unfair and unfree elections.

Moreover, the divergent reaction of states to the developments in Venezuela underscores the potential destabilizing effect of the derecognition of an incumbent regime on the basis of an emerging criterion whose application in the case in question is not clearly supported by a large majority of states, including all major powers. At the time of writing, Venezuela was represented by two parallel regimes, both of which claimed to be the *de jure* government. This in turn implies that both these regimes could potentially direct a request for military assistance to those states recognizing them. If this were to happen, it could result in a Cold War-style proxy conflict, with destabilizing effects for the region as a whole.[333] In essence, therefore, a decision not to apply the presumption of continued recognition to an incumbent government due to its lack of democratic legitimacy (of origin) should not be taken lightly. In the absence of a broad consensus within the state in question and among third states about the need for the incumbent regime to step down, as well as about who should take its place, any such decision risks being very destabilizing.

5. Conclusion

In the post-Cold War era, the extension of an invitation for direct military assistance remains the exclusive prerogative of the recognized, *de jure* government. Military assistance to opposition groups, whether direct or indirect, constitutes a violation of the principle of non-intervention, as well as the prohibition of the use of force. The only exception in this regard includes indirect military assistance to liberation movements in the decolonization context. For the purposes of determining the authority that can claim to be the *de jure* government, the effective control doctrine remains the point of departure, but will not necessarily be decisive. Since the end of the Cold War the democratic legitimacy doctrine, as personified by free and fair elections (ie legitimacy of origin), has also gained significance. Practice, in particular in the Americas and Africa, indicates that in times of internal turmoil, the democratic pedigree of a particular authority, rather than its effective control, has on occasion been decisive for determining *de jure* governmental status.

[333] In fact, in March, 100 Russian soldiers arrived in the country at the request of the Maduro regime, ostensibly to assist with the maintenance of aircraft and training. Earlier that year, the United States for its part had indicated that a military solution (in support of Mr Guaidó) could not be excluded. See A Roth, 'Russian Military Arrive in Venezuela to Discuss "Training And Strategy"' *Guardian* (25 March 2019) https://www.theguardian.com/world/2019/mar/25/russian-military-officials-arrive-in-venezuela-to-discuss-training-and-strategy; Anderson (n 168); T O'Conner, 'Will US Attack Venezuela? Trump "Made it Very Clear … All Options Are on the Table", Says John Bolton' *Newsweek* (28 January 2019) https://www.newsweek.com/us-attack-venezuela-trump-military-news-1308418.

However, these practices have not been consistent and it would be premature to claim that democratic legitimacy of origin has replaced effective control as the point of departure for determining the *de jure* government. Also, the proliferation of internationally recognized interim governments that came about through negotiated settlements suggests that in conflict situations both effective control and democratic legitimacy of origin at times remain aspirational criteria for governmental recognition. In these situations the recognition of the interim authority as the *de jure* government is based on the hope that a government in which all major parties to the conflict is represented may ultimately yield the stability required for effective control and the holding of free and fair elections.

Once recognized as the *de jure* government, international law attaches a strong presumption of continued recognition to the incumbent government. This implies that also in instances of internal turmoil in which the incumbent government may have lost control over parts of its territory, it retains the competence to incur rights and obligations on behalf of the state. While the presumption of continued recognition may not be of use in situations where the incumbent regime is no longer identifiable, or may under circumstances be outweighed by principles of democratic legitimacy of origin, it remains strong on the whole. A pertinent question which arises in the context of military assistance on request, is whether the presumption of continued *de jure* recognition implies that the incumbent government retains all the competencies usually associated with such recognition. In particular, the question arises whether it can still request direct military assistance, once it has lost control over parts of its territory and population. As will become clear in Chapter 3, the answer to this question turns on the implications of the right to self-determination for military assistance on request.

3
Direct Military Assistance on Request During Civil Wars

1. Introduction

The previous chapter drew attention to the fact that once recognized as the *de jure* government, a strong presumption of continued recognition is triggered. Where the incumbent government subsequently finds itself in internal turmoil, this will not in and of itself result in its derecognition. It would therefore still be able to represent the state in international relations and incur rights and obligations on its behalf. However, a separate question that arises is whether a *de jure* government that is facing internal revolt is (still) permitted to exercise all the competencies that are associated with *de jure* governments in peace time. In the context of military assistance on request it is often argued that this is not necessarily the case. In particular, the *de jure* government's right to invite direct foreign military assistance would exist only as long as the level of internal violence has not crossed the threshold of a civil war.[1] The purpose of this chapter is to test this claim which, since the second half of the twentieth century, has become inextricably linked with the right to self-determination in as far as it concerns the right of peoples within an independent state to determine their own government with no outside interference.[2]

The chapter in particular will examine whether the right to self-determination in international law prevents military intervention on the side of the recognized government during a civil war. In so doing, the analysis uses the terms 'civil war' and 'non-international armed conflict' (NIAC) interchangeably.[3] Section 2 analyses the doctrinal debate pertaining to this right. This analysis, however, does not attempt to examine all aspects of this highly complex and controversial legal construct.

[1] See United Kingdom Foreign Policy Document No 148, Part II.7 (1986) 57 British Yearbook of International Law 616; CJ le Mon, 'Unilateral Intervention by Invitation in Civil Wars: The Effective Control Test Tested' (2003) 35 New York University Journal of International Law and Politics 753; C Gray, *International Law and the Use of Force* (4th edn, OUP 2018) 85; T Ruys, 'Of Arms and "Non-lethal Assistance"—Issues Surrounding Third-State Intervention in the Syrian Civil War' (2014) 13 Chinese Journal of International Law 39, 43; D Akande, 'Would it be Lawful for European (or Other) States to Provide Arms to the Syrian Opposition?' *EJIL:Talk!* (17 January 2013) para 3 <https://www.ejiltalk.org/would-it-be-lawful-for-european-or-other-states-to-provide-arms-to-the-syrian-opposition/>.

[2] L Doswald-Beck, 'The Legal Validity of Military Intervention by Invitation of the Government' (1986) 56 207; K Bannelier and T Christakis, 'Under the UN Security Council's Watchful Eyes: Military Intervention by Invitation in the Malian Conflict' (2013) 26 Leiden Journal of International Law 861.

[3] As explained in Chapter 1, section 3.

Instead, it focuses on those aspects of the right to self-determination that potentially pose a legal barrier to forcible military assistance on request during a civil war. Thereafter, the chapter examines whether the doctrinal arguments underpinning a prohibition against direct military assistance on request during a NIAC find support in a post-Cold War state and organizational practice. This analysis focuses specifically on ad hoc requests for military assistance, with a particular emphasis on those that occurred in situations in which the conflict in the requesting state had escalated into a NIAC.[4] In particular, section 3 gives an overview of forcible assistance by international (including regional) organizations, while section 4 provides a similar overview regarding forcible assistance rendered by individual (coalitions of) states.

Finally, section 5 explores the implications of state and organizational practice (including the reaction of third states thereto) for the claim that military assistance to the recognized government is prohibited during a civil war/NIAC. A pertinent question arising in this context is whether state and organizational practice to recognized governments during a NIAC could be explained by purposive exceptions in the form of the counter-terrorism exception and counter-intervention.[5]

2. The doctrinal debate

It is well recognized that the right to self-determination acknowledges the right of colonial peoples to independence.[6] In addition, there is wide support in doctrine for the position that the right to self-determination entitles the peoples within an independent state to choose their own political and socio-economic governance without interference by other states.[7] This view has been informed by the United Nations General Assembly (UNGA) Declaration on the Inadmissibility

[4] The legal implications of *ex ante* consent in particular regional arrangements containing pro-invasion treaty clauses are assessed in Chapter 5 section 5.1 through section 5.3.

[5] T Ruys and L Ferro, 'Weathering the Storm: Legality and Legal Implications of the Saudi-Led Military Intervention in Yemen' (2016) 65 International and Comparative Law Quarterly 88; K Bannelier-Christakis, 'Military Interventions Against ISIL in Iraq, Syria and Libya, and the Legal Basis of Consent' (2016) 29 Leiden Journal of International Law 748.

[6] *Western Sahara* (Advisory Opinion) [1975] ICJ Rep para 55; see *Legal Consequences of the Separation of the Chagos Archipelago from Mauritius in 1965* (Advisory Opinion) [2019] ICJ paras 154 ff https://www.icj-cij.org/files/case-related/169/169-20190225-01-00-EN.pdf. See generally J Vidmar, *Democratic Statehood in International Law: The Emergence of New States in Post-Cold War Practice* (Hart Publishing 2013) 169 ff; V Sarantini, 'Pro-Democratic Intervention, Invitation, or "Responsibility to Protect"? Challenges to International Law from the "Arab Spring"' in C Panara and G Wilson (eds), *The Arab Spring: New Patterns for Democracy and International Law* (Brill 2013) 192; G Nolte, *Eingreifen auf Einladung: Zur völkerrechtlichen Zulässigkeit des Einsatzes fremder Truppen im internen Konflikt auf Einladung der Regierung* (Springer 1999) 223.

[7] Doswald-Beck (n 2) 207; Bannelier and Christakis (n 2) 861; Nolte (n 6) 223, O Corten, *The Law Against War: The Prohibition on the Use of Force in Contemporary International Law* (Hart Publishing 2010) 289.

of Intervention,[8] which was subsequently concretized by UNGA Resolution 2625 (1970) on Friendly Relations[9] and which has acquired customary international law status.[10] Whereas the Declaration on the Inadmissibility of Intervention refers to the rights of states to determine their political and socio-economic system without external interference,[11] the Friendly Relations Resolution describes the right to self-determination as the right of 'peoples'.[12] This textual difference has found its way into the doctrinal debate, with some authors regarding the right to self-determination as vesting in the state itself, while others view it as vesting within the people(s) of a state. However, closer scrutiny reveals that both interpretations of self-determination have the same consequences for military assistance on request of the incumbent government. Both imply a so-called negative equality principle;[13] that is, an obligation to refrain from military assistance to an incumbent government during a civil war (NIAC).[14]

In line with the state-oriented interpretation of the right to self-determination, the right vests in the *state* as an abstract entity (consisting of a population and territory). It is this abstract entity rather than the people(s) within a state that has to choose a specific form of governance without outside interference.[15] This in turn implies that the right to self-determination and the customary right to non-intervention are two sides of the same coin, as both concern the right of states to make choices about their political, economic, social, and cultural system without external interference.[16] A logical consequence of this reasoning is that the right

[8] UN Doc A/RES/2131 (XX) (21 December 1965) para 5 determines that '[e]very state has an inalienable right to choose its political, economic, social and cultural systems, without interference in any form by another state'.

[9] UN Doc A/RES/2625 (XXV) (24 October 1970) Principle (e) commences by stating: 'By virtue of the principle of equal rights and self-determination of peoples enshrined in the Charter of the United Nations, all peoples have the right freely to determine, without external interference, their political status and to pursue their economic, social and cultural development, and every state has the duty to respect this right in accordance with the provisions of the Charter.'

[10] The customary status of the UNGA Resolution on Friendly Relations (n 9) has been confirmed in the *Military and Paramilitary Activities in an Against Nicaragua (Nicaragua v United states)* (Merits) [1986] ICJ Rep 14, para 191 and *Armed Activities on the Territory of the Congo (Democratic Republic of the Congo v Uganda)* (Judgment) [2005] ICJ Rep 168 para 162. See also Gray (n 1) 76; Le Mon (n 1) 753. Nolte (n 6) 223 described this principle as the point of departure of the right to self-determination. See also T Christakis and K Bannelier, '*Volenti non fit injuria*? Les effets du consentement à l'intervention militaire' (2004) 50 Annuaire Français de Droit International 113 ff.

[11] UNGA Declaration on the Inadmissibility of Intervention (n 8) para 5.

[12] UNGA Resolution on Friendly Relations (n 9).

[13] GH Fox, 'Intervention by Invitation' in M Weller (ed), *The Oxford Handbook of the Use of Force in International Law* (OUP 2015) 827.

[14] United Kingdom Foreign Policy Document No 148 (n 1) para II. 7, 616.

[15] Doswald-Beck (n 2) 207–08; Ruys and Ferro (n 5) 87; SA Dersso, 'The Jurisprudence of the African Commission on Human and Peoples' Rights with Respect to Peoples' Rights' (2006) 6 African Human Rights Law Journal 362.

[16] The customary right of states to determine their own political and socio-economic system without interference was further confirmed in in the *Nicaragua* decision (n 10) paras 202, 2015. See also Nolte (n 6) 212 who noted that that the Friendly Relations Resolution was initially intended as a concretization of the right to non-intervention; Dersso (n 15) 362.

to self-determination does not require the government that represents the state on the international level to come about through free and fair elections.[17] Instead, the government can also arise through a violent overthrow, including a civil war (NIAC). Decisive is the fact that the hostilities aimed at overthrowing the established regime must be decided without external interference, as such interference would violate the right of non-intervention.[18] This logic finds implicit support in Principle (a) of the Friendly Relations Resolution, which elaborates on the obligation of states to refrain from the use of force against the territorial integrity or political independence of another state. It explicitly refers to the duty of every state to 'refrain from organizing, instigating, assisting or participating in acts of civil strife or terrorist acts in another state ... when the acts referred to in the present paragraph involve a threat or use of force'.[19] While the term 'civil strife' is not necessarily identical to civil war, it arguably would be broad enough to include a civil war, given the explicit connection in the Friendly Relations Resolution between 'civil strife' and the use of force.[20]

An alternative line of reasoning emphasizes that the right to self-determination vests in the people(s) of a state. This view has gained ground especially since the codification of self-determination as a human right in article 1 of both the United Nations (UN) International Covenant on Civil and Political Rights of 1966 (ICCPR)[21] and the UN International Covenant on Economic, Social and Cultural Rights of 1966 (ICESCR),[22] as well as article 20 of the African Charter on Human and Peoples' Rights.[23] A reading of these articles together with the paragraph of the Friendly Relations Resolution, which is dedicated to self-determination,[24] suggests that the reference to 'peoples' in these treaties first and foremost concerns the

[17] See in particular Doswald-Beck (n 2) 203.

[18] Doswald-Beck (n 2) 207; JA Perkins, 'The Right to Counter-Intervention' (1987) 17 Georgia Journal of International and Comparative Law 186.

[19] UNGA Resolution on Friendly Relations (n 9) para 1.

[20] See also the Declaration on the Inadmissibility of Intervention, UNGA Res 375 (IV) (6 December 1949) art 4, which affirms the duty of every state to refrain from fermenting 'civil strife' in the territory of another state; Gray (n 1) 75–76.

[21] The International Covenant on Civil and Political Rights (adopted 16 December 1966) 999 UNTS 171 (ICCPR) art 1(1) determines that '[a]ll peoples have the right of self-determination. By virtue of that right they freely determine their political status and freely pursue their economic, social and cultural development.' See extensively Vidmar (n 6) 143 ff.

[22] International Covenant on Economic, Social and Cultural Rights (adopted 16 December 1966) 993 UNTS 3 (ICESCR) art 1(1). See also UNGA Resolution on Friendly Relations (n 9); see also Opinion of Advocate General Wathelet, Case No C-266/6, *Western Sahara Campaign UK, The Queen v Commissioners for Her Majesty's Revenue and Customs, Secretary of state for Environment, Food and Rural Affairs* (10 January 2018) paras 99 ff http://eur-lex.europa.eu/legal-content/EN/TXT/?uri=CELEX:62016CC0266.

[23] The African Charter on Human and Peoples' Rights (African Charter) (Nairobi, 27 June 1981, 21 ILM 58) is the only regional human rights treaty that guarantees the right to self-determination. Art 20(1) of the Charter determines that '[a]ll peoples shall have the right to existence. They shall have the unquestionable and inalienable right to self- determination. They shall freely determine their political status and shall pursue their economic and social development according to the policy they have freely chosen.'

[24] UNGA Resolution on Friendly Relations (n 9).

people of the state as a whole.[25] The relevant paragraph in the Friendly Relations Resolution emphasizes the fact that this right has to be exercised with due regard to the territorial integrity and political unity of the state in question. In so doing, it explicitly links compliance with the right to self-determination to the existence of 'a government representing the *whole people belonging to the territory* without distinction as to race, creed or colour'.[26]

This understanding of 'people', as such, is accepted among states.[27] More controversial (among states and authors alike) is the question of whether the people of a state can be sub-divided into legally distinct communities that qualify as 'peoples'. This debate turns on whether the subjects of peoples' rights in international law are (also) the different groups or inhabitants within the state who, on account of historical, traditional, racial, ethnic, cultural, linguistic, ideological, geographical, or economic identities and affinities, have come to form a separate identity.[28] However, for the purposes of the current chapter this ongoing debate about the existence of 'peoples within peoples' is not decisive. Of importance is the fact that a right to self-determination that vests in the people, at a very minimum, provides those belonging to the territory of a state as a whole with a right to choose their own political dispensation without external interference.

This in turn raises the question of whether international law provides benchmarks for determining how this choice is to take place. The Friendly Relations Resolution for its part indicates that the government must be 'representative' of the

25 Nolte (n 6) 250; Dersso (n 15) 361–62.

26 According to the elaboration of Principle (e) of the UNGA Resolution on Friendly Relations (n 9): 'Nothing in the foregoing paragraphs shall be construed as authorizing or encouraging any action which would dismember or impair, totally or in part, the territorial integrity or political unity of sovereign and independent states conducting themselves in compliance with the principle of equal rights and self-determination of peoples as described above and thus possessed of a government representing the whole people belonging to the territory without distinction as to race, creed or colour' (emphasis added).

27 It *inter alia* finds textual resonance in art 23(2)(b) of the African Charter (n 23) which determines that for the strengthening of peace, solidarity, and friendly relations, state parties have to ensure that 'their territories shall not be used as a basis for subversive or terrorist activities against *the people of any other state party*'.

28 See *Reference re Secession of Quebec* 1998 Can Sup Ct LEXIS 39. On the African continent, the African Commission on Human and Peoples' Rights (ACHPR) and the African Court of Human and Peoples' Rights (ACtHPR) have expressed their support for a differentiated definition of peoples, despite continued scepticism among African states. See eg ACtHPR, *African Commission of Human and Peoples' Rights v Republic of Kenya*, Appl No 6/2012, Judgment (26 May 2017) paras 103–12; ACHPR, *Katangese Peoples' Congress v Zaire* (2000) AHRLR 72 (ACHPR 1995) paras 3 ff; ACHPR, *Legal Resources Foundation v Zambia* (2001) AHRLR 84 (ACHPR 2001) para 73; ACHPR, *Centre for Minority Rights Development and Others v Kenya* (2009) AHRLR 75 (ACHPR 2009) para 151; ACHPR, *Sudan Human Rights Organisation and Another v Sudan* (2009) AHRLR 153 (ACHPR 2009); ACHPR, *Gunme and Others v Cameroon* (2009) AHRLR 9 (ACHPR 2009) paras 171, 189 ff; *Advisory Opinion of the African Commission on Human and Peoples' Rights on the United Nations Declaration on the Rights of Indigenous Peoples*, 41st Ordinary Session (16–30 May 2007) paras 27, 220 http://www.achpr.org/files/special-mechanisms/indigenous-populations/un_advisory_opinion_idp_eng.pdf; Draft Aide-Memoire: United Nations Declaration on the Right of Indigenous People (New York, 9 November 2006) paras 2.2, 3.1–3.2 http://www.ipacc.org.za/en/2007/15-aide-memoire/file.html.

people within the state, but without elaborating on what this means.[29] However, if one recalls that only a recognized *de jure* governments may represent the (people of a) state in international relations, it is arguable that the benchmarks for representativeness are likely to overlap with those pertaining to recognition.[30] As illuminated in Chapter 2, the most prominent criterion in this regard is not (yet) whether the government has come about through democratic elections, although such elections have on occasion been decisive for international recognition.[31] Instead, it remains effective control, understood as the acquiescence by the population in the authority exercised by the incumbent government.[32]

As far as the right to self-determination is concerned, 'representativeness' of the state (and its people) is also equated with acquiescence by the population in the authority of the incumbent government. Some scholars regard the extent of the acquiescence required by the right to self-determination to be more comprehensive than that required for continued *de jure* recognition. A *de jure* government is no longer 'representative' of the state (and its people) from the perspective of the right to self-determination where it faces open revolt to the point where it has lost control over parts of its population and territory.[33] Specifically, such a government would lack the level of representativeness required to invite foreign military assistance in such a situation. Any foreign military assistance provided to it under such circumstances would coerce the outcome of the internal contest for political power and thereby violate the right to self-determination.[34] Consequently, while the *de jure* status of a recognized government in principle continues when it becomes embroiled in a civil war (NIAC), the scope of its competencies—in particular in as far as it concerns the invitation of foreign military assistance—is curbed by the right to self-determination.[35]

At this juncture, it transpires that there are key similarities in the reasoning of those regarding the right to self-determination as vesting in the people(s) versus those regarding it as vesting in the state as an abstract entity. Both lines of reasoning appear to hinge on the acquiescence in the authority exercised by the incumbent government. Only as long as such acquiescence exists would foreign

[29] Bannelier-Christakis (n 5) 746.

[30] See also S Nenadic, 'Lawfulness of New Zealand's Military Deployment to Iraq: Intervention by Invitation Tested' (2014) 12 New Zealand Yearbook of International Law 10.

[31] See Chapter 2, section 3.1 through section 3.3.

[32] See Chapter 2 section 3.1 through section 3.3.

[33] Le Mon (n 1) 746; Nolte (n 6) 246.

[34] Bannelier and Christakis (n 2) 861; Nolte (n 6) 245–46; Fox (n 13) 827. This reasoning further finds resonance in Institut de Droit International (IDI), Resolution on Military Assistance on Request (8 September 2011) art 3 http://www.idi-iil.org/idiE/navig_res_chon.html. It links the violation of *inter alia* the right to self-determination to military assistance to a government 'against its own people'. It determines that '[m]ilitary assistance is prohibited when it is exercised in violation of the Charter of the United Nations, of the principles of non-intervention, of equal rights and self-determination of peoples and generally accepted standards of human rights and *in particular when its object is to support an established government against its own population*' (emphasis added).

[35] Ruys and Ferro (n 5) 88.

military intervention on the side of the government not threaten the political independence of the (people of the) state and remain reconcilable with the right to self-determination. This in turn suggests that both interpretations can support the conclusion that a violation of the right to self-determination through foreign military assistance during a civil war (NIAC) simultaneously results in a violation of the prohibition of the use of force.[36] After all, a military intervention that violates the right to self-determination by preventing a state (or its peoples) from determining its political future independently is likely to amount to the use of force against the political independence of a state, as prohibited in article 2(4) of the UN Charter and customary international law.[37] This close relationship between the right to self-determination and the prohibition of the use of force is also alluded to in the Friendly Relations Resolution. When elaborating on the prohibition of the use of force against the territorial integrity or political independence of another state, the Resolution underscores the duty of states to refrain from 'any forcible action which deprives peoples ... of their right to self-determination and freedom and independence'.[38]

In summary, therefore, there are powerful doctrinal arguments underpinning the position that the right to self-determination would prevent incumbent governments embroiled in a civil war/NIAC from relying on foreign military assistance to decide the conflict in their favour. Yet, while these arguments may seem conceptually convincing, they are fraught with practical challenges. First, determining in practice when hostilities within a state have escalated beyond mere internal disturbances into a NIAC remains highly challenging. Governments embroiled in violent hostilities have persistently been unwilling to admit that the threshold of a NIAC had been crossed, due to a reluctance to legitimize opposition forces.[39] Similarly, third states are often also reluctant to acknowledge the existence of a NIAC.[40] As a result, the threshold for triggering the restraining consequences of the right to self-determination vis-à-vis the incumbent government is very high. Moreover, even if the existence of a NIAC is acknowledged by the affected and/or third states, this does not necessarily imply that that the population as a whole (or even a significant majority) indeed is revolting against the incumbent government.[41] Stated differently, the mere fact that a group has the capacity to engage in sustained hostilities against the government or even

[36] Perkins (n 18) 189.

[37] ibid; Corten (n 7) 289; M Bennouna, *Le consentement à l'ingérence militaire dans le conflits interne* (Librairie Générale de Droit et de Jurisprudence 1974) 213.

[38] UNGA Resolution on Friendly Relations (n 9).

[39] Gray (n 1) 85; Fox (n 13) 827.

[40] Gray (n 1) 85; Ruys (n 1) 44.

[41] D Akande and Z Vermeer, 'The Airstrikes against Islamic State in Iraq and the Alleged Prohibition on Military Assistance to Governments in Civil Wars' *EJIL: Talk!* (2 February 2015) http://www.ejiltalk.org/the-airstrikes-against-islamic-state-in-iraq-and-the-alleged-prohibition-on-military assistance-to-governments-in-civil-wars/. See also Y Dinstein, *War, Aggression and Self-Defence* (5th edn, CUP 2011) 119, Nolte (n 6) 246; Nenadic (n 30) 10.

control parts of the state's territory need not be a reflection of the fact that the population is no longer acquiescing in the authority of the incumbent government.[42] Whether this is the case and whether the incumbent government has thus become 'unrepresentative' for the purposes of self-determination will depend on the facts of each case.

It is also worth noting that on the few occasions on which the International Court of Justice (ICJ) has referred to the right of the government to request foreign military assistance, it has not made mention of any potentially limiting effect of the right to self-determination in this regard. In the *Nicaragua* decision, the ICJ stated that while military intervention on request of the opposition is prohibited, it is allowed when occurring on the invitation of the recognized government. The ICJ made this statement in an unqualified manner: it did not give any indication that the right of the recognized government to invite military support would be curtailed during a NIAC.[43] Furthermore, in the decision *Armed Activities on the Territory of the Congo (Democratic Republic of the Congo v Uganda)* the ICJ acknowledged that an intervention in a civil war had occurred.[44] The military presence of Uganda on the invitation of the Democratic Republic of the Congo (DRC) thus occurred in a context that crossed the threshold of a NIAC. Yet, the ICJ regarded the consent (during the time that it actually existed) as a valid and sufficient basis for the Ugandan presence.[45]

The reasoning of the ICJ in these cases, combined with the practical challenges in determining the existence of a NIAC, already suggests that the so-called negative equality principle may not be as well-established in international law as proclaimed in doctrine. In order to determine whether this indeed is the case, one needs to measure the doctrinal arguments against state and organizational practice. What follows is an analysis of situations since the end of the Cold War, in which international organizations (including regional organizations) or individual states have responded to ad hoc requests for direct military assistance by recognized governments. As indicated in the introduction to this chapter, section 3 gives an overview of forcible assistance by international organizations, whereas section 4 provides a similar overview regarding forcible assistance rendered by individual

[42] Akande and Vermeer n (41); Dinstein) (n 41) 119; B Nußberger, 'Military Strikes in Yemen in 2015: Intervention by Invitation and Self-Defence in the Course of Yemen's "Model Transitional Process"' (2017) 4 Journal on the Use of Force and International Law 146.

[43] *Nicaragua* decision (n 10) paras 206, 246. However, some authors caution against reading too much into this statement, as it was not directly addressing the issue of a government receiving military assistance against a purely internal insurgency. See Perkins (n 18) 195.

[44] *Armed Activities* decision (n 10) para 165.

[45] *Armed Activities* decision (n 10) 92, paras 42–45, 46 ff. The ICJ's main concern with the Ugandan intervention was that Uganda overstepped the boundaries of the consent given by the DRC. Uganda remained present in the DRC after the consent had been withdrawn. See G Nolte, 'The Resolution of the *Institut de Droit International* on Military Assistance on Request' (2012) 45 Revue Belge de Droit International 261; see also L Visser, 'Russia's Intervention in Syria' *EJIL: Talk!* (25 November 2015) https://www.ejiltalk.org/russias-intervention-in-syria/.

(coalitions of) states. Thereafter section 5 assesses the implications of this practice for the negative equality principle.

3. Forcible assistance on request by international organizations

Direct military assistance based on ad hoc requests from states to international organizations since the end of the Cold War occurred mainly in Africa.[46] These operations took place under the auspices of African regional economic communities, namely, the Southern African Development Community (SADC) and the Economic Community of West African States (ECOWAS), as well as the African Union (AU). As will be reflected below, not all the military operations were based on the legal construct of military assistance on request. Some were backed by United Nations Security Council (UNSC) resolutions under Chapter VII of the UN Charter, while others were based either on the right to individual or collective self-defence or resembled classic peace-keeping operations.[47]

3.1 SADC

The SADC's competence to intervene in internal conflicts has been formally included in article 11(2) of the Protocol on Politics, Defence and Security Co-operation of 14 August 2001.[48] However, the organization in practice already

[46] During the early 1990s the Commonwealth of Independent States (CIS) engaged in operations comparable to classic peace-keeping in the Caucasus. In 1993 peace-keeping troops were sent to Tajikistan under the auspices of the CIS. See Letter Dated 20 October 1993 from the Permanent Representative of the Russian Federation to the United Nations Addressed to the Secretary-General, UN Doc S/26610 (21 October 1993) including annexes. Similarly, the CIS provided a peace-keeping force in Abkhazia (Georgia) in 1994. See UN Doc S/1994/583 (17 May 1994) Annex 1. The Tajikistan peace-keeping operation had to be distinguished from the Declaration of the Inviolability of the Frontiers that was adopted by Kazakhstan, Kyrgyzstan, the Russian Federation, and Tajikistan. This agreement, which was aimed at securing the Tajik–Afghan border, was based on the right to individual or collective self-defence. See Letter Dated 10 August 1993 from the Permanent Missions of Kazakhstan, Kyrgyzstan, the Russian Federation and Tajikistan to the United Nations addressed to the Secretary-General, UN Doc A/48/304-S/26290 (11 August 1993) including annexes. See extensively Nolte (n 6) 452 ff. See also QTT Nguyen, 'Rethinking the Legality of Intervention by Invitation: Toward Neutrality' (2019) (First View) Journal of Conflict and Security Law 26–27; Gray (n 1) 439 ff.

[47] The ICJ endorsed the concept of classic peace-keeping based on consent, impartiality and the limitation of the use of force to self-defence in *Certain expenses of the United Nations* (Article 17, paragraph 2 of the Charter), Advisory Opinion, [1962] ICJ Rep, 151 at 164 ff. See also Chapter 1, section 3.

[48] SADC's competence to assist in resolving intra-state conflicts was formally included in art 11(2) of the Protocol on Politics, Defence and Security Co-operation of 14 August 2001 http://www.sadc.int/files/3613/5292/8367/Protocol_on_Politics_Defence_and_Security20001.pdf arts 3–9. It *inter alia* granted the organization jurisdiction over intra-state conflicts concerning large-scale violence between sections of the population or between the state and sections of the population including genocide, ethnic cleansing and gross violations of human rights; a military *coup* or other threat to the legitimate authority of a state; and a condition of civil war or insurgency. The details of the SADC security framework are elaborated on in Chapter 5, section 5.3.

intervened in member states in 1998 and, after the adoption of the 2001 Protocol, only once in 2017. In 1998 troops from Angola, Namibia, and Zimbabwe (all SADC members) intervened in the conflict in the DRC. At the time of intervention there was no formal authorization by SADC to intervene. The three countries themselves argued that they were relying on collective self-defence in support of President Kabila, who requested assistance against Congolese Tutsi rebels supported by Uganda and Rwanda.[49] Subsequently, in September 1998 the SADC member states adopted a joint declaration that commended the troop-providing countries for assisting the government and the people of the DRC. Despite this formal gesture, the exact legal basis for the military intervention remained disputed within the organization and seemed to have constituted an example of the exercise of collective self-defence[50] rather than military assistance on request.[51] From a political perspective, the wisdom of the operation was questionable as neither the military intervention nor parallel efforts by SADC to broker a ceasefire managed to put a halt to the conflict in the eastern DRC.[52]

In the same year, political turmoil erupted in Lesotho subsequent to an election victory by the ruling party. Opposition parties rejected the results, due to dissatisfaction with the first-past-the-post electoral system that facilitated the large victory. As a result of the fear for a *coup d'état*, the Lesotho government in September 1998 requested assistance from SADC member states.[53] The military intervention by troops from Botswana, South Africa, and Zimbabwe was carried out under the auspices of SADC and at the request of the Lesotho government and succeeded in restoring order.[54] While the intervention was politically controversial and perceived as a trade-off between member states pursuing their national interests,[55]

[49] In 1999 Angola, Namibia, Zimbabwe and the DRC concluded a defence pact. See M Schoeman and M Muller, 'Southern African Development Community as Regional Peacekeeper: Myth or Reality' in F Söderbaum and R Tavares (eds), *Regional Organizations in African Security* (Routledge 2010) 113–14.

[50] The relationship between military assistance on request and the right to individual or collective self-defence is discussed in Chapter 6.

[51] See E de Wet, 'The Evolving Role of ECOWAS and the SADC in Peace Operations: A Challenge to the Primacy of the United Nations Security Council in Matters of Peace and Security?' (2014) 27 Leiden Journal of International Law 367; Schoeman and Muller (n 49) 113; F Söderbaum and B Hettne, 'Regional Security in a Global Perspective' in U Engel and J Gomes Porto (eds), *Africa's New Peace and Security Architecture* (Routledge 2011) 25; J Sarkin, 'The Role of the United Nations, the African Union and Africa's Sub-Regional Organisations in Dealing with Africa's Human Rights Problems: Connecting Humanitarian Intervention and the Responsibility to Protect' (2009) 53 Journal of African Law 28.

[52] Global and Inclusive Agreement on Transition in the DR Congo: Inter-Congolese Dialogue—Political Negotiations on the Peace Process and on Transition in the DRC of 16 December 2002 http://reliefweb.int/node/410903; De Wet (n 51) 367.

[53] A van der Vleuten and A Ribeiro Hoffmann, 'Explaining the Enforcement of Democracy by Regional Organizations: Comparing EU, Mercosur and SADC' (2010) 3 Journal of Common Market Studies 752; De Wet (n 51) 368.

[54] Sarkin (n 51) 28; Schoeman and Muller (n 49) 116; De Wet (n 51) 368.

[55] For example, South Africa's motives for the intervention was questioned, as it appeared to be driven by concern for the future of the Lesotho Highlands water scheme which was crucial to providing water to South Africa's most densely populated province (Gauteng). See Schoeman and Muller (n 49) 112; De Wet (n 51) 368.

the right of the Lesotho government to request military assistance under the circumstances was not disputed.[56] At the time the military intervention took place, the political turmoil was restricted in nature and could arguably be classified as a rebellion, rather than an insurgency or NIAC.

Almost twenty years later, in November 2017 SADC again deployed a 258-strong force in Lesotho at the request of the Lesotho government. This followed the breakdown of the rule of law in the wake of the assassination of a commander of the defence force.[57] The SADC force consisted of soldiers, police officers, intelligence officers, and civilians, with an initial mandate of six months. Its purpose was to work with the government of Lesotho, which came to power through elections in June 2017, to create the secure and stable environment necessary for implementing a series of political and judicial reforms.[58] These reforms *inter alia* included the depoliticization of the military, whose meddling in political affairs had been destabilizing the country for many decades.[59] The AU for its part underscored that the SADC mission was

> in line with the United Nations (UN) Charter, Chapter VI, the Protocol Relating to the Establishment of the Peace and Security Council of the AU and the relevant provisions contained in the SADC Treaty, Protocol on Politics, Defence and Security Cooperation, including the Memorandum of Understanding (MoU) establishing the SADC Standby Brigade of 2007.[60]

Neither the AU nor the SADC specified the exact articles in these treaties on which the invitation by the government was based, although the consent of the Lesotho government to the mission was emphasized in press briefings.[61] In this context it is worth noting that article 11(3)(d) of the SADC Protocol on Politics, Defence and Security Co-operation of 14 August 2001 explicitly makes any enforcement action dependent on UNSC authorization in terms of article 53 of the

[56] Schoeman and Muller (n 49) 116; Van der Vleuten and Ribeiro Hoffmann (n 53) 752.

[57] SADC Secretariat, 'SADC Secretariat Briefs African Union Peace and Security Council on the Contingent Force Deployed in Lesotho' (25 January 2018) https://www.sadc.int/news-events/news/sadc-secretariat-briefs-african-union-peace-and-security-council-contingent-force-deployment-lesotho/. See also the Director of the Organ on Politics, Defence and Security Affairs (Jorge Cardoso), 'The Official Launch Ceremony of the SADC Preventive Mission in the Kingdom of Lesotho, Maseru, Kingdom of Lesotho' (2 December 2017) http://www.sadc.int/files/7315/1223/1520/REMARKS_.pdf.

[58] The force members originated from Angola, Malawi, Namibia, South Africa, Tanzania, Zambia, and Zimbabwe; SADC Secretariat (n 57).

[59] P Fabricius, 'Lesotho: Seven-Nation SADC Force Deployed to "Establish Secure, Stable Environment" in Mountain Kingdom' *Daily Maverick* (3 December 2017) https://www.dailymaverick.co.za/article/2017-12-03-lesotho-seven-nation-sadc-force-deployed-to-establish-secure-stable-environment-in-mountain-kingdom/.

[60] AUPSC, Communiqué of 748th Meeting, PSC/AHG/COM.(DCCXLIX) (27 January 2018) para 3 http://www.peaceau.org/uploads/psc.summit.749.com.ahg.terrorism.27.01.2018.pdf.

[61] SADC Secretariat (n 57).

UN Charter. While no UNSC resolution was adopted in relation to the Lesotho crisis,[62] the consent of the government was not disputed. In addition, the SADC mission (as was the case in 1998) occurred in a context that arguably had not yet escalated beyond that of a riot.

3.2 ECOWAS

As far as ECOWAS is concerned, it had already committed itself to collaboration in matters of internal conflict in the revised Treaty of ECOWAS of 1993[63] and implemented this commitment through a Protocol in 1999.[64] Even so, the legal basis of the ECOWAS military operations in its member states differed from operation to operation. Chapter 2 already noted that in the case of Sierra Leone in 1997, it remains disputed whether the forcible measures were underpinned by UNSC resolutions or humanitarian considerations (rather than military assistance on request).[65] Similar uncertainties pertain to the ECOWAS military operation in Liberia in August 1990. While the forcible measures were not preceded by any UNSC resolution, some scholars have regarded them as having been authorized by the UNSC in an *ex post facto* manner.[66] Others have either claimed that these forcible measures were requested by the then still internationally recognized President Doe,[67] or that humanitarian considerations constituted the legal

[62] See Protocol on Politics, Defence and Security Co-operation of 14 August 2001 (n 48) art 11(3)(d): 'The Summit shall resort to enforcement action only as a matter of last resort and, in accordance with Article 53 of the United Nations Charter, only with the authorization of the United Nations Security Council.' See also Chapter 5, section 5.3.

[63] See Economic Community of West African States (ECOWAS) Revised Treaty of 24 July 1993 art 58(2) http://www.ecowas.int/wp-content/uploads/2015/01/Revised-treaty.pdf. This article committed member states to cooperate with ECOWAS in establishing and strengthening appropriate mechanisms for the timely prevention and resolution of intra-state and inter-state conflicts.

[64] Protocol Relating to the Mechanism for Conflict Prevention, Management, Resolution, Peace-Keeping and Security of 10 December 1999 art 3, art 10(c), arts 21 and 22 https://www.zif-berlin.org/fileadmin/uploads/analyse/dokumente/ECOWAS_Protocol_ConflictPrevention.pdf. This Protocol established an elaborate regional peace and security mechanism, including peace-keeping forces that could also be deployed in instances of internal conflict. The details of the ECOWAS security framework, including the extent to which it provides for *ex ante* consent (in the form of pro-invasion treaty clauses) are discussed in Chapter 5, section 5.2.

[65] See Chapter 2, section 3. See also E de Wet, 'Reinterpreting Exceptions to the Use of Force in the Interest of Security: Forcible Intervention by Invitation and the Demise of the Negative Equality Principle' (2017) 111 American Journal of International Law Unbound 307; Gray (n 1) 439 ff.

[66] See UN Doc S/22133 (22 January 1991) and UN Doc S/23886 (7 May 1992). In these statements the President of the UNSC 'recognized' the ECOMOG action. See also I Österdahl, 'The Continued Relevance of Collective Security Under the UN: The Security Council, Regional Organizations and the General Assembly' (1999) 10 Finnish Yearbook of International Law 57; Gray (n 1) 428 ff.

[67] At the time, President Doe requested military assistance stating: 'It would seem most expedient at this time to introduce an ECOWAS peace-keeping force into Liberia to forestall increasing terror and tension and to assure a peaceful transitional environment.' See Letter Addressed by President Samuel K Doe to the Chairman and Members of the Ministerial Meeting of ECOWAS Standing Mediation Committee, Doc No 39 (14 July 1990) in M Weller (ed), *Regional Peace-Keeping and International Enforcement: The Liberian Crisis* (CUP 1994) 61. See also Nolte (n 6) 634.

basis.[68] As a result, neither Liberia nor Sierra Leone would constitute a convincing example of military assistance on request.

Furthermore, the ECOWAS operation in Guinea-Bissau in 1998 for its part also would not amount to serve this purpose. It resembled a classic peace-keeping mission aimed at maintaining peace between the different sides in an impartial manner rather than forcible military assistance at the request (and on the side) of the recognized government. This follows from the fact that the deployment of troops along the border between Guinea-Bissau and Senegal, in the wake of a threat of a mutiny against President Bernardo Vieira in 1998, was undertaken with the express consent of both President Viera and the leader of the mutiny.[69]

The military involvement of ECOWAS in Côte d'Ivoire between 2002 and 2011 commenced at the request of an incumbent government that had lost control over significant parts of its territory and population. Subsequent to a mutiny by soldiers in Abidjan in September 2002 and rebel groups seizing control of the north of the country, ECOWAS deployed its first mission in Côte d'Ivoire in October 2002. However, while the operation occurred at the request of the then incumbent President Laurent Gbagbo, it more resembled a peace-keeping mission.[70] Before the initiation of the ECOWAS peace-keeping operation, France reportedly rejected a request by the government of Côte d'Ivoire to provide military assistance on the basis of a defence agreement between the two countries, for lack of sufficient proof of external aggression.[71] At the time, the French Minister of Foreign Affairs stated in the French senate that while France supported the protection of French nationals, the unity of Côte d'Ivoire, and the security of the region, it was at pains not to interfere in Côte d'Ivoire's internal affairs.[72]

Shortly afterwards, with the adoption of UNSC Resolution 1464 of 4 February 2003, the legal basis of the operation changed. In this resolution the UNSC welcomed the deployment of ECOWAS as well as French troops in Côte d'Ivoire, and

[68] At the time of the Liberian intervention, ECOWAS expressed grave concern about the humanitarian situation in the country. See ECOWAS Standing Mediation Committee, Banjul, Republic of Gambia, Final Communiqué of the First Session, Doc No 54 (7 August 1990) in Weller (n 67) 72. See also J Levitt, 'Humanitarian Intervention by Regional Actors in Internal Conflicts: The Case of ECOWAS in Liberia and Sierra Leone' (1998) 12 Temple Journal of International and Comparative Law 342 ff.

[69] The ECOMOG troops were deployed subsequent to UN Doc S/RES/1216 (21 December 1998) paras 3, 4, 6. However, this resolution was not adopted under Chapter VII of the UN Charter. ECOMOG also could not prevent President Vieira from being forced from power in May 1999 and was withdrawn shortly afterwards. See also S Paliwal, 'The Primacy of Regional Organisations in International Peacekeeping: the African Example' (2011) 51 Virginia Journal of International Law 211; C Obi, 'Economic Community of West African States on the Ground: Comparing Peacekeeping in Liberia, Sierra Leone, Guinea Bissau, and Côte d'Ivoire' in Söderbaum and Tavares (n 49) 60.

[70] See UN Doc S/RES/1464 (4 February 2003) Preamble. See Corten (n 7) 307.

[71] See Corten (n 7) 307; Christakis and Bannelier (n 10) 129.

[72] X de Villepin, Statement in French Senate (2 October 2002) https://www.senat.fr/commission/etr/etrg021005.html; see also Christakis and Bannelier (n 10) 129.

authorized them under Chapters VII and VIII of the UN Charter to guarantee the security and freedom of movement of their personnel in order to ensure the protection of civilians.[73] As of this point, the legal basis for the presence of ECOWAS (and French) forces first and foremost were UNSC resolutions. By February 2004, the UNSC had established the United Nations Operation in Côte d'Ivoire (UNOCI) under Chapter VII of the UN Charter, which coexisted alongside the French forces and whose mandate was extended and refined continuously between 2004 and 2011.[74] This expansion of the mandate culminated in regime change in March 2011, after Mr Gbagbo had refused to hand over power following President Quattara's electoral victory in November 2010.[75]

The military presence of ECOWAS in The Gambia in January 2017 occurred at the request of the newly elected and sworn-in President Adama Barrow, after the previous incumbent, Mr Yahyah Jammeh, had refused to hand over power.[76] As indicated in Chapter 2, the victory of the newly elected President Barrow was unexpected (and was contested by the previous incumbent on formal grounds).[77] However, this did not prevent the international recognition of Mr Barrow as head of state. By 17 December 2016 the ECOWAS Heads of State and Government had adopted a Communiqué in which they *inter alia* decided to uphold the results of the elections of 1 December 2016 and 'to take all necessary measures to strictly enforce the results of the 1st December 2016 elections'.[78] By 19 January 2017 the AU for its part had endorsed the ECOWAS decision and had ceased to recognize President Jammeh as President.[79] On the same day, Mr Barrow was sworn in as President in the Gambian Embassy in Senegal. In his inaugural address, he made a special appeal to ECOWAS, the AU, and in particular the UNSC to 'support the

[73] UN Doc S/RES/1464 (4 February 2003) Preamble and paras 8, 9. See also A Orakhelashvili, 'The Legal Framework of Peace Operations by Regional Organisations (2007) 11 Journal of International Peacekeeping 133; D Zounmenou and R Loua, 'Confronting Complex Political Crises in West Africa: An Analysis of ECOWAS Response to Niger and Côte d'Ivoire' (2011) 230 Institute for Security Studies (ISS) Paper 10 http://www.iss.co.za; Obi (n 69) 61.

[74] The combined efforts of ECOWAS and the French troops were complemented by the establishment of the United Nations Mission in Côte d'Ivoire (MINUCI) in UN Doc S/RES/1479 (13 May 2003) para 2. This mission was subsequently replaced by the United Nations Operation in Côte d'Ivoire (UNOCI), with the adoption of UN Doc S/RES/1528 (27 February 2004) under Chapter VII of the UN Charter. The result was the integration of MINUCI and ECOMICI in a hybrid force (UNOCI) which co-existed alongside the French forces. See extensively De Wet (n 51) 364.

[75] See Chapter 2, section 3.2.1.

[76] See extensively C Kreß and B Nußberger, 'Pro-Democratic Intervention in Current International Law: The Case of The Gambia in January 2017' 4 Journal on the Use of Force and International Law 239 ff.

[77] See Chapter 2, section 3.2.1.

[78] During this period ECOWAS undertook various high-level delegations to The Gambia aimed at ensuring a peaceful transfer of power to President-elect Barrow. See ECOWAS Authority of Heads of State and Government, Final Communiqué, 50th Ordinary Session (17 December 2016) paras 36, 38(a), 38(h) http://www.ecowas.int/wp-content/uploads/2016/12/Communiqu%C3%A9-Final_50th-Summit_Abuja_Dec-16_Eng.pdf.

[79] AUPSC, Communiqué of the 647th Meeting, PSC/PR/COMM (DCXLVII) (13 January 2017) para 5 http://www.peaceau.org/uploads/647.psc.comm.gambia.13.01.2017-1.pdf.

government and peoples of The Gambia in enforcing their will, restore their sovereignty and constitutional legitimacy'.[80]

A few hours after having been sworn in and making the appeal for enforcement, the UNSC adopted Resolution 2337 of 17 January 2017. The Resolution endorsed the ECOWAS and AU decision to recognize President Barrow and to cease recognizing outgoing President Jammeh as of 19 January 2017.[81] It further expressed its full support for ECOWAS in its 'commitment to ensure, by political means first, the respect of the will of the people of The Gambia as expressed in the results of 1st December elections'.[82] While this reference to 'political means first' implies that force could be used as a last resort, it is important to note that this resolution was not adopted under Chapter VII of the UN Charter.[83] This factor, combined with the timing of the Resolution (a few hours after the inauguration of President Barrow and his explicit request for enforcement action) suggests that his invitation for military assistance constituted the legal basis of the ECOWAS military presence.[84]

This conclusion is further supported by the fact that the ECOWAS troops from Nigeria and Senegal that had assembled at the Gambian border officially only moved into The Gambia after the inauguration of President Barrow and his official request for support.[85] According to some press reports, Senegalese troops had already unintentionally crossed the border soon after midnight on 19 January 2017, due to unfamiliarity with the terrain.[86] While this admittedly raises concerns about the legal basis for the presence of foreign troops in the hours before the invitation was extended, the fact remains that the ECOWAS member states only deliberately moved their forces across the Gambian border after having received the invitation from Mr Barrow. This in turn underscores the fact that this request for military assistance was the intended legal basis of their military presence.[87]

[80] 'Inaugural Address of A Barrow, President of the Republic of The Gambia' *Fatunetwork* (20 January 2017) http://fatunetwork.net/inaugural-address-adama-barrow-president-republic-gambia/. See also R Maclean, 'Troops Enter The Gambia After Adama Barrow is Inaugurated in Senegal' *Guardian* (19 January 2017) https://www.theguardian.com/world/2017/jan/19/new-gambian-leader-adama-barrow-sworn-in-at-ceremony-in-senegal.

[81] UN Doc S/RES/2337 (19 January 2017) paras 1, 5.

[82] UN Doc S/RES/ 2337 (19 January 2017) para 6.

[83] UN Doc S/PV.7866 (19 January 2017) 23 (Uruguay); ibid 3 (Bolivia); ibid 6 (Egypt); ibid 7 (Sweden). See also Gray (n 1) 67, 450. According to press reports, both Russia and the United Kingdom confirmed that President Barrow was entitled to request military assistance, if negotiations proved unsuccessful. See EM Lederer 'UN Adopts Resolution Backing Gambia's New President Barrow' *AP News* (19 January 2019) https://apnews.com/44fe8d11a7134ad084794fb450c95556. See also Kreß and Nußberger (n 76) 242–43.

[84] Kreß and Nußberger (n 76) 244.

[85] MacLean (n 80); T Cocks and E Farge, 'West African Military Halt Gambia Operation, Issue Jammeh Deadline' *Reuters* (20 January 2017) http://af.reuters.com/article/idAFKBN1540NA.

[86] See Kreß and Nußberger (n 76) 241; D Searcey, 'Why Democracy Prevailed in Gambia' *New York Times* (30 January 2017) <https://www.nytimes.com/2017/01/30/world/africa/gambia-barrow-democracy-africa.html>.

[87] Had the Senegalese troops indeed crossed the border before President Barrow had extended his invitation, he could subsequently have acquiesced in their presence within a reasonable time through a lack of protest. Thereby he would have lost the right to invoke state responsibility for the violation of The Gambia's territorial integrity and the prohibition of the use of force, resulting from the Senegalese

A day after the ECOWAS troops had entered The Gambia on 19 January 2017, the military operations were halted in order to attempt final mediation efforts by regional leaders. On 21 January 2017 Mr Jammeh conceded defeat and left The Gambia, allowing a peaceful transfer of power to President Barrow.[88] In essence, therefore, the request for military assistance by President Barrow occurred at a time when he had not yet had any control over the state apparatus, population or territory. Instead, the purpose of the ECOWAS troop presence was to enable the taking of such control, fortunately within a context which had remained largely peaceful.[89]

3.3 AU

The African Union's mandate to assist forcibly in response to an ad hoc request by a member state is contained in article 4(j) of the Constitutive Act of the AU of 2000. This article confirms '[t]he right of member states to request intervention from the Union in order to restore peace and security'.[90] This article has (albeit implicitly) formed the basis for military operations ranging from classic peace-keeping operations to more robust military assistance to incumbent governments.

The AU's first military operation, in Burundi in 2003, resembled classic peace-keeping rather than forcible measures at the request and on the side of the recognized government.[91] In 2003 the African Mission in Burundi (AMIB) consisted of troops from Ethiopia, Mozambique, and South Africa. This mission was aimed at brokering a settlement to Burundi's long-running civil war.[92] It was sparked by a

presence before he had extended the request for military assistance. See ILC, Draft Articles on Responsibility of States for Internationally Wrongful Acts with Commentaries' (2001) II Yearbook of the International Law Commission; UN Doc A/Res/56/83 (12 December 2001), Commentary to Art 45 (para 6 and para 11). See also Chapter 5, section 5.1.

[88] 'Krise Entschärft. Ex-Präsident Jammeh hat Gambia Verlassen' *Frankfurter Allgemeine Zeitung* (21 January 2017) http://www.faz.net/aktuell/politik/ausland/krise-entschaerft-ex-praesident-jammeh-hat-gambia-verlassen-14720114.html; Maclean (n 80); Cocks and Farge (n 85).

[89] See Also UN Doc S/RES/2337 (19 January 2019) Preamble.

[90] Constitutive Act of the African Union of 11 July 2000 (2158 UNTS 3) art 4(j) http://www.peaceau.org/uploads/au-act-en.pdf. This article is to be distinguished from art 4(h) of the AU Constitutive Act, which establishes the right of the AU 'to intervene in a member state pursuant to a decision of the Assembly in respect of grave circumstances, namely: war crimes, genocide and crimes against humanity'. The extent to which this article amounts to *ex ante* consent (in the form of a pro-invasion treaty clause) is discussed in Chapter 5, section 5.1.

[91] For a discussion of the AU' failed attempt to invoke art 4(h) of the AU Constitutive Act (n 90) in Burundi in 2015, in the wake of widespread violence after President Nkurunziza had announced his seeking of a third term of office, see Chapter 5, section 5.1.

[92] This mission was preceded by a contingent of 750 South African troops, sent at the request of the Burundian government in order to protect Hutu politicians who had returned to the country, as well as to train a local protection force. See P Williams, 'The African Union's Peace Operations: A Comparative Analysis' in Söderbaum and (n 49) 30–31.

coup in 1993 and came into being subsequent to a peace agreement in December 2002 between the transitional government and the rebel Forces for the Defence of Democracy.[93] The AU Mission in Sudan (AMIS), which was created in response to the conflict in Darfur (Sudan), also resembled a peace-keeping force. AMIS was formally created by a Communiqué of the AU Peace and Security Council at its seventeenth meeting in October 2004.[94] AMIS enjoyed the consent of the government of Sudan and was charged with monitoring the ceasefire agreement in place between the government and opposition forces, protecting civilians, and returning internally displaced persons to their homes.[95] It was also endorsed by the UN in Resolution 1574 of 19 November 2004, but without investing AMIS with any enforcement power under Chapter VII or VIII of the UN Charter.[96]

The AU military operation in the Comoros in 2008 constituted the first robust intervention at the bequest of a recognized government. Subsequent to the election of Abdallah Sambi as President of the Comoros in 2007, tensions rose as Mohammed Bacar (who had ruled the island of Anjouan since 2001) refused to relinquish power. Bacar organized an illegal election on the island of which he declared himself the winner and announced the independence of Anjouan from the Union of the Comoros.[97] In response, the AU Peace and Security Council in 2008 amended the mandate of the AU Electoral and Security Assistance Mission (MAES), which the AU had created in May 2007 to support and monitor the election process.[98]

The amended mandate authorized a direct invasion of Anjouan, the installation of an interim leader for the island, and plans to resume or rerun the Anjouan presidential elections on the island.[99] The military operation was undertaken with the consent and at the request of the recognized government of the Comoros.[100] It was spearheaded by Tanzania and Sudan and with logistical support from Libya and

[93] Williams (n 92) 31. The mission's mandate included monitoring the ceasefire agreements; securing identified assembly and disengagement areas; ensuring safe passage for the parties during planned movements to designated assembly areas; facilitating and providing technical assistance to the disarmament and reintegration process; and facilitating the delivery of the humanitarian assistance and providing VIP protection for designated returning leaders. See Communiqué of the 91st Ordinary Session of the Central Organ of the Mechanism for Conflict Prevention, Management and Resolution at Ambassadorial Level, Central Organ/MEC/AMB/Comm (XCI) (2 April 2003) para 5 http://www.peaceau.org/uploads/comapr03.pdf; Paliwal (n 69) 201.

[94] AUPSC, Communiqué of 17th Meeting, PSC/PR/Comm (XVII) (20 October 2004) para 4 http://www.peaceau.org/uploads/communiqueeng-17th.pdf.

[95] ibid para 7.

[96] UN Doc S/RES/1574 (19 November 2004) para 13; Paliwal (n 69) 199.

[97] Williams (n 92) 38.

[98] ibid.

[99] Report of the Chairperson of the Commission on the Situation in the Comoros Since the 10th Ordinary Session of the Assembly of the African Union held in Addis Ababa from 31 January–2 February 2008, PSC/PR/2 (CXXIV) (30 April 2008) paras 13, 15–21 http://archives.au.int/bitstream/handle/123456789/2229/2008_124_R1E.pdf?sequence=1andisAllowed=y.

[100] AUPSC, Communiqué of the 124th Meeting, PSC/PR/Comm (CXXIV) (30 April 2008) paras 3, 17 http://www.peaceau.org/uploads/communiquecomoreseng.pdf.

France, but without any formal UN involvement. Militarily the operation was easy to enforce as the crisis was limited to an island that was small and weak.[101] It would therefore seem that article 4(j) of the AU Constitutive Act was the most likely basis for the intervention, albeit implicitly, as the legal basis was not explicitly articulated in any of the AU Communiqués.[102]

At the time of writing, the AU's only other robust military operations on request were undertaken in the context of its 2011 Regional Cooperation Initiative for the Elimination of the Lord's Resistance Army (LRA) (Initiative). By the time of the adoption of the Initiative, the AU had classified the LRA as a terrorist organization.[103] Over a period of thirty years this organized armed group has been held responsible for more than 100,000 deaths and thousands of rapes, abductions, and mutilations as well as the widespread use of child soldiers.[104] The purpose of the Initiative was to strengthen the capability of the countries in the region that had been affected by the atrocities of the LRA. It included a military component in the form of the Regional Task Forces (RTF)[105] that comprised approximately 5,000 troops from the affected countries, namely, Uganda, Central African Republic (CAR), DRC, and South Sudan.[106] The European Union (EU) and the United States have also provided financial and logistical support.[107] The RTF became operational in March 2012 and has since made some inroads in the activities of the LRA. These included the destruction of some of its camps in the CAR and the DRC and fighting capacity.[108] However, the grave security situation in countries such as

[101] De Wet (n 51) 327; Williams (n 92) 39.

[102] See also A Ferreira-Snyman, 'Intervention with Specific Reference to the Relationship Between the United Nations Security Council and the African Union' (2010) 63 Comparative and International Law Journal of Southern Africa 157. She suggested that the rejection of unconstitutional changes of government in art 4(p) of the AU Constitutive Act (n 90) may have constituted the basis, although this is not formulated as a separate ground for intervention in the AU Constitutive Act.

[103] AUPSC, Communiqué of the 299th Meeting, PSC/PR/COMMM (CCXCIX) (22 November 2011) paras 5, 10 http://www.peaceau.org/uploads/psc.436.com.rca.lra.23.05.2014.pdf; AUPSC, Communiqué of the 455th Meeting, Report of the Chairperson of the Commission on Terrorism and Violent Extremism in Africa PSC/AHG/2(CDLV) (2 September 2014) (n 103) para 60 http://www.peaceau.org/uploads/psc-rpt-terrorism-nairobi-2-09-2014.pdf.

[104] P Fabricius, 'The LRA Rising Again?' Institute for Security Studies (ISS) (6 July 2016) https://issafrica.org/iss-today/the-lra-rising-again.

[105] The other two components included a Joint Coordination Mechanism, chaired by the AU Commissioner for Peace and Security and comprising the Ministers of Defence of the affected countries; and a Headquarters for the RTF, including a Joint Operations Centre, staffed with officers seconded by the affected countries. Report of the Chairperson of the Commission on Terrorism and Violent Extremism in Africa (n 103) para 60.

[106] In 2016 Sudan also expressed its readiness to join the initiative. See AU PSC, Communiqué of the 601st Meeting, PSC/PR/COMM (DCI) (30 May 2016) para 8 http://www.peaceau.org/uploads/psc-601-comm-lra-30-5-2016.pdf. See also Report of the Chairperson of the Commission on Terrorism and Violent Extremism in Africa (n 103) para 60.

[107] European Commission, Press Release, 'New EU Support to Increase Security in the Central African Region' (27 March 2014) http://europa.eu/rapid/press-release_IP-14-322_en.htm; A Arieff, L Ploch Blanchard, and TF Husted, 'The Lord's Resistance Army: The US Response' Congressional Research Service Report R42094 (28 September 2015) 9 ff https://fas.org/sgp/crs/row/R42094.pdf.

[108] See Report of the Chairperson of the Commission on Terrorism and Violent Extremism in Africa (n 103) para 61; UN Doc S/PRST/2013/18 (25 November 2013) 1–2.

the CAR and South Sudan, as well as the limited capacity of the RTF, have limited its ability to eradicate the LRA.[109]

The AU Communiqués do not refer explicitly to any legal basis for the RTF mandate. The UNSC for its part has consistently commended the Initiative and the work of the RTF in various presidential statements.[110] However, none of these were adopted under Chapter VII of the UN Charter. In light of the fact that the operation has been conducted with the consent of the affected states, it is likely that article 4(j) of the Constitutive Act of the AU constituted the implicit basis for this military operation. Furthermore, it seems that this consent has not been affected by the ousting of the CAR's former President Bozize in a coup on 24 March 2013.[111] In April 2013 a National Transitional Council came into being through international mediation efforts,[112] which in January 2014 designated Ms Catherine Samba-Panza as a transitional head of state.[113] She was succeeded by Faustin Archange Touadéra as President following elections in February 2016.[114]

The period following the coup and leading up to the elections was marked by violence between sectarian militias that left thousands dead and almost half a million people displaced.[115] The fact that the AU has consistently extended the mandate of the Initiative despite these developments suggests that the new CAR governments had neither withdrawn their support for the Initiative, nor did the protracted hostilities in the CAR affect the validity of the consent of their recognized governments to forcible interventions by the RTF.[116] The same applies to that

[109] UN Doc S/PRST/2015/12 (11 June 2015); Fabricius (n 104).

[110] UN Doc S/PRST/2012/18 (29 June 2012); UN Doc S/PRST/2013/240 (22 April 2013); UN Doc S/PRST/2013/18 (25 November 2013); UN Doc S/PRST/2015/12 (11 June 2015).

[111] Report of the Secretary-General on the situation in the Central African Republic, UN Doc S/2013/261 (3 May 2013) para 6. Subsequently, in the first week of April 2013, the then South African President Zuma withdrew 200 South African troops that were based in the CAR. In accordance with an oral agreement between Zuma and former President Bozize, the South African troops had to provide training to government troops and security. See BBC, 'South African Troops to Withdraw from CAR' *BBC News* (4 April 2013) https://www.bbc.com/news/world-africa-22025593.

[112] Report of the Secretary-General on the Situation in the Central African Republic, UN Doc S/2013/261 (3 May 2013) para 12.

[113] UNSG Press Release, 'Secretary-General Welcomes Election of Catherine Samba Panza in Central African Republic as Head of State of Transition, Chance to Put Process Back on Track' UN Doc SG/SM/15597-AFR/2798, (20 January 2014) https://www.un.org/press/en/2014/sgsm15597.doc.htm.

[114] Report of the Secretary-General on the Situation in the Central African Republic, UN Doc 2016/305 (1 April 2016) para 8.

[115] UN Doc S/PRST/2014/28 (18 December 2014) 1; UN Doc S/PRST/2015/17 (20 October 2015) 1; 'Central African Republic: Touadera Wins Election' *Al Jazeera* (21 February 2016) http://www.aljazeera.com/news/2016/02/central-african-republic-touadera-wins-election-160221044730048.html.

[116] The AU Peace and Security Council has consistently extended the mandate of the Initiative. See eg AUPSC, Communiqué of the 601st Meeting, PSC/PR/COMM (DCI) (30 May 2016) para 8 http://www.peaceau.org/uploads/psc-601-comm-lra-30-5-2016.pdf; AUPSC, Communiqué of the 436th Meeting PSC/PR/COMM/1 (CDXXXVI) (23 May 2014) para 10 http://www.peaceau.org/uploads/psc.436.press-statement-terrorism.-nigeria.-23.05.2014.pdf; AUPSC, Communiqué of the 508th Meeting PSC/PR/COMM (DVIII) (18 May 2015) para 11 http://www.peaceau.org/uploads/psc-com-508-lra-18-05-2015.pdf.

of the government of South Sudan, which (as will be discussed below) degenerated into civil war as of December 2013.[117] In fact, these AU interventions against the LRA in the CAR, DRC, and South Sudan thus far constitute the only instances in which (sub)-regional organizations in Africa have relied on the legal construct of military assistance on request as a basis for intervening in situations that qualified as NIACs.[118] In all the other above-mentioned instances the forcible measures based on consent tended to take the form of traditional peace-keeping operations, or occurred on the side of recognized governments in situations which had not (yet) amounted to NIACs. This was notably the case during the interventions by SADC in Lesotho, ECOWAS in Côte d'Ivoire and The Gambia, as well as the AU intervention in the Comoros. As a result, the question whether the recognized government's request for military assistance constituted a violation of the negative equality principle did not arise. The subsequent analysis will reveal that this forms a clear contrast with the forcible measures undertaken by individual (coalitions of) states at the request of recognized governments since the end of the Cold War.

4. Forcible military assistance on request by (coalitions of) individual states

A decade into the twenty-first century, direct military assistance by (coalitions of) individual states on the invitation of recognized governments proliferated in Africa and the Middle East.[119] Some of these forcible measures were of limited scope and duration and/or in conflicts that at the time had not yet escalated into NIACs. These notably included France's military assistance to a number of former African colonies such as Chad (1990 and 1992), Gabon (1990), Zaire (1991 and 1993), Djibouti (1991 and 1992), Togo (1991), and CAR (1996 and 1997).[120] A pertinent

[117] See section 4.

[118] The legal basis for the intervention by certain SADC states in the DRC remains ambivalent, as it was also justified with the right to collective self-defence.

[119] A request for military assistance from south-east Europe, which attracted very little attention at the time, concerned that of the government of Bosnia and Herzegovina to Croatia. On 24 June 1995 several thousands of Croatian soldiers crossed the border to Bosnia with the consent of the Bosnian government. Within days they won control over parts of western Bosnia from the Bosnian Serbs. With the exception of the former Federal Republic of Yugoslavia, hardly any state reacted. On one of the rare occasions that the presence of the Croatian troops in Bosnia was addressed in the UNSC on 10 August 1995, Croatia stated that support for a friendly government at its request was in accordance with the UN Charter. The military operation was preceded by the Declaration on Implementation of the Washington Agreement, Joint Defence Against Serb Aggression and Achievement of a Political Solution in Accordance with the Efforts of the International Community of 22 June 1995 (Split Agreement). See Letter Dated 7 August 1995 from the Secretary-General Addressed to the President of the Security Council, UN Doc S/1995/666 (7 August 1995); UN Doc S/PV.3563 (10 August 1995) 3 (Croatia); Nolte (n 6) 539 ff.

[120] In 1990 French President Mitterrand claimed that while France would provide support to befriended African countries against external aggression and protect its own nationals, it would not involve itself in internal conflicts. See statement cited in Christakis and Bannelier (n 10) 129. Yet, in Rwanda the French presence lasted for two years from 1991 to 1993 and the extent to which France

example in the Middle East is Bahrain, where troops from Saudi Arabia and the United Arab Emirates entered briefly in 2011 in order to suppress the protests by the Shiite majority against the Sunni monarchy.[121]

However, several other conflicts were of a protracted nature that had long since escalated into NIACs. At the time of writing, these included (in chronological order) Afghanistan, Somalia, Mali, South Sudan, Iraq, Yemen, Syria, and Libya. It is important to note that in Afghanistan, Somalia, Iraq, Yemen, and Syria the forcible interventions were not based exclusively on the legal construct of military assistance on request. Instead, some states (also) justified their forcible action in these countries with the right to individual or collective self-defence. The subsequent paragraphs will explore only the extent to which military assistance on request served as a justification for these forcible interventions. The extent to which the right to self-defence can be relied on to justify forcible intervention in a third state is illuminated in Chapter 6.

4.1 Afghanistan

The US military operations in Afghanistan since 2001 have been based on a mixture of self-defence and consent by the recognized government. Several weeks after the adoption of Resolution 1368 of 12 September 2001, the United States commenced Operation Enduring Freedom by launching air attacks in the territory of Afghanistan on the basis of the right to individual self-defence.[122] Subsequent to the overthrow of the Taliban in late 2001, an Afghan Interim Authority led by Hamid Karzai was negotiated in December 2001 under the auspices of the UN.[123] In October 2004 Karzai was elected as President which he remained until

actively participated in the fighting between the then Hutu government and the Tutsi rebels remains disputed. See also Nolte (n 6) 334 ff, 348, 355; I Österdahl, *La France Dans l'Afrique de l'Apres-Guerre Froide Interventions et Justifications* (Nordiska, Afrikainstitutet 1997) 5 ff.

[121] These troops operated under the authority of the Gulf Cooperation Council (consisting of Bahrain, Kuwait, Oman, Qatar, Saudi Arabia, and the United Arab Emirates). See E Bronner and M Slackman, 'Saudi Troops Enter Bahrain to Help Put Down Unrest' *New York Times* (11 March 2014) http://www.nytimes.com/2011/03/15/world/middleeast/15bahrain.html. See also C Gray, 'The Limits of Force' (2016) 367 Collective Courses of The Hague Academy of International Law 175.

[122] UN Doc S/RES/1368 (12 September 2001). Following the initiation of military action, the United States and the United Kingdom reported to the UNSC, invoking the right of individual and collective self-defence. See Letter Dated 7 October 2001 from the Permanent Representative of the United States of America to the United Nations Addressed to the President of the Security Council, UN Doc S/2001/946 (7 October 2001) and Letter Dated 7 October 2001 from the Chargé d'Affaires of the Permanent Mission of the United Kingdom of Great Britain and Northern Ireland to the United Nations addressed to the President of the Security Council, UN Doc S/2001/947 (7 October 2001). See also Chapter 6, section 2.

[123] Agreement on Provisional Arrangements in Afghanistan Pending the Re-Establishment of Permanent Government Institutions of 5 December 2001 (Bonn Agreement), UN Doc S/2001/1154 (5 December 2001).

September 2014.[124] Once the Afghan Interim Authority came into power, it requested the US military to remain in Afghanistan in order to fight the Taliban and Al Qaida, thereby complementing the legal basis of the US military operations by consent.[125] Parallel to this presence, the UNSC also adopted Resolution 1386 of 20 December 2001, which authorized member states to use all necessary means to maintain security in Kabul and its surrounding areas.[126] Follow-up UNSC resolutions saw the creation of the International Security Assistance Force (ISAF) under Chapter VII of the UN Charter, which operated under the command of the North Atlantic Treaty Organization (NATO) from August 2003 until its termination in December 2014. The primary objective of ISAF was to enable the Afghan security forces to provide effective security across the country.[127]

In the course of Mr Karzai's term, his dissatisfaction with the US military presence in Afghanistan grew, and towards the end of his term he refused to sign a long-term security arrangement with the United States that had been in the making for some time.[128] However, his successor, President Ashraf Ghani, signed the Bilateral Security Agreement (BSA) with the United States on 30 September 2014.[129] The BSA regulated a long-term US military presence (at least until 2024) aimed at enhancing the capacity of the Afghan security forces, countering terrorism, as well as contributing to regional and international peace and stability.[130] The BSA was adopted at a time that the withdrawal of ISAF left a security vacuum and the Afghan government faced escalating offensives by the Taliban, which was controlling up to a third of the country.[131] The BSA also explicitly determined that unless otherwise mutually agreed, US forces would not conduct combat operations in Afghanistan.[132] However, in the face of an increasing number of Taliban offensives and an expanding Islamic State in Iraq and the Levant (IS) presence in Afghanistan throughout 2015 and 2016,[133] the Afghan and US governments agreed to an

[124] Afghan Government, 'Institute of the Study of War http://www.understandingwar.org/afghan-government.

[125] TS Purdum, 'In Flash of an Afghan Cape, a World Star Is Born' *New York Times* (30 January 2002) http://www.nytimes.com/2002/01/30/world/a-nation-challenged-diplomacy-in-flash-of-an-afghan-cape-a-world-star-is-born.html.

[126] UN Doc S/RES/1386 (20 December 2001) paras 1, 4.

[127] NATO, 'ISAF's Mission in Afghanistan (2001–2014) (Archived)' (1 September 2015) <http://www.nato.int/cps/en/natohq/topics_69366.htm>.

[128] D Walsh and A Ahmed, 'Mending Alliance, US and Afghanistan Sign Long-Term Security Agreement' *New York Times* (30 September 2014) https://www.nytimes.com/2014/10/01/world/asia/afghanistan-and-us-sign-bilateral-security-agreement.html?_r=0.

[129] Security and Defence Cooperation Agreement Between the Islamic Republic of Afghanistan and the United States of America of 30 September 2014 (Bilateral Security Agreement/BSA) https://www.state.gov/documents/organization/244487.pdf. For an overview of the protracted elections that took place in Afghanistan in 2014, see Report of the Secretary-General, The Situation in Afghanistan and Its Implications for International Peace and Security UN Doc A/69/540–S/2014/656 (9 September 2014) paras 4 ff.

[130] Bilateral Security Agreement (n 129) art 2.1.

[131] Walsh and Ahmed (n 128).

[132] Bilateral Security Agreement (n 129) para 2.1.

[133] In 2015 the Taliban temporarily captured Kunduz city as well as sixteen district centres mainly in the north. Control over 25% of the district centres in the country remained contested. There was also

intensification of US air strikes against Taliban and IS targets.[134] The instability in the country was further exacerbated by growing tensions within the Afghan government and from political opposition groups.[135]

4.2 Iraq

In the case of Iraq, the US and coalition forces had been present in Iraq since 2003, following their invasion and occupation of the country in March 2013.[136] The invasion was not authorized by the UNSC, which only authorized the presence of the occupation powers (referred to as the Coalition Provisional Authority) in Iraq and their administration of the territory *ex nunc* under Chapter VII of the UN Charter in UNSC Resolution 1483 of 2 May 2003.[137] In October of the same year, the UNSC also authorized under Chapter VII of the UN Charter the presence of a multinational force under unified command which could take all necessary measures to contribute to the maintenance of security and stability in Iraq.[138] The presence of this multinational force was extended on an annual basis until 31 December 2008.[139] Resolution 1483 (2003) also called for the restoration of representative governance in which the Iraqi people determined their own political future.[140] This first resulted in the establishment of a Governing Council in July 2003 under the auspices of the Coalition Provisional Authority.[141] On 28 June 2004 an Interim Government of Iraq was formed with the assistance of the UN, to which the Coalition Provisional Authority transferred sovereign powers.[142] In December 2005 Iraq held parliamentary elections that resulted in the formation of a new government and the election of Jawad al-Maliki as Prime Minister in May 2006.[143]

an escalation of confrontations between Afghan forces and anti-government forces including IS. See Report of the Secretary-General, The Situation in Afghanistan and Its Implications for International Peace and Security, UN Doc A/70/601–S/2015/942 (10 December 2015) paras 13 ff.

134 See also Report of the Secretary-General, The Situation in Afghanistan and Its Implications for International Peace and Security, UN Doc A/71/616–S/2016/768 (7 September 2016) para 19; D Walsh and A Ahmed, 'US Air Strikes Spike as Afghans Struggle Against Taliban, Islamic State' *Reuters* (26 October 2016) http://www.reuters.com/article/us-afghanistan-airstrikes-idUSKCN12Q0FH.

135 UN Doc A/71/616–S/2016/768 (7 September 2016) para 3.

136 G Bruno, 'US Security Agreements and Iraq' *Council on Foreign Relations* (23 December 2008) http://www.cfr.org/iraq/us-security-agreements-iraq/p16448.

137 UN Doc S/RES/1483 (2 May 2003) para 4.

138 UN Doc S/RES/1511 (16 October 2003) para 13.

139 The last extension was granted in UN Doc/ S/RES/1790 (18 December 2007) para 1.

140 UN Doc S/RES/1483 (22 May 2003) para 4.

141 Report of the Secretary-General Pursuant to Paragraph 24 of Security Council Resolution 1483 (2003) UN Doc S/2003/715 (17 July 2003) para 24.

142 Report of the Secretary-General Pursuant to Paragraph 24 of Resolution 1483 (2003) and Paragraph 12 of Resolution 1511 (2003) UN Doc S/2004/625 (5 August 2004) para 26; Report of the Secretary-General Pursuant to Paragraph 30 of Resolution 1546 (2004) UN Doc S/2004/710 (3 September 2004) paras 3 ff.

143 Report of the Secretary-General Pursuant to Paragraph 30 of Resolution 1546 (2004) UN Doc S/2006/360 (2 June 2006) paras 3, 8; Bruno (n 136).

By early 2008 it was clear that the Maliki government did not wish to extend the UNSC-authorized multinational force in Iraq beyond 2008.[144] Instead, it entered into an agreement with the United States that allowed for the latter's military to remain in Iraq until 31 December 2011,[145] *inter alia* for the purpose of fighting 'al-Qaeda and other terrorist groups, outlaw groups, and remnants of the former regime'.[146] Subsequent to the expiration of this agreement and the withdrawal of US troops by December 2011,[147] the security situation in Iraq deteriorated in the wake of the growing presence of IS.[148] The instability escalated as of 2012 and in the course of 2014, not long after country-wide elections had been held on 30 April, IS had taken control of key cities and infrastructure in the north-western and north-central parts of Iraq.[149] The UNSC described the situation as a large-scale offensive aimed at destabilizing the country.[150] In the wake of these developments, the Iraqi government requested US and other Western allies for military support, including air strikes.[151]

Responding to this call, a US-led coalition on 8 August 2014 commenced air strikes against IS in Iraq. The (then) President Obama underscored that this action was taken at the request of the Iraqi government and in order to help forces in Iraq to counter IS.[152] This statement was in broad terms, as were statements by other Western members of the military coalition. For example, the United Kingdom stated that '[i]nternational law is equally clear that th[e] prohibition [on the use of force in international relations] does not apply to the use of military force by one

[144] Report of the Secretary-General Pursuant to Paragraph 6 of Resolution 1770 (2007) UN Doc S/2008/19 (14 January 2007) para 6.

[145] Agreement Between the United States of America and the Republic of Iraq on the Withdrawal of United States Forces from Iraq and the Organization of Their Activities During Their Temporary Presence in Iraq of 17 November 2008 (Status of Forces Agreement) para 24(1) https://www.state.gov/documents/organization/122074.pdf. See also the Strategic Framework Agreement for a Relationship of Friendship and Cooperation Between the United States of America and the Republic of Iraq of 17 November 2017 http://www.usf-iraq.com/wp-content/uploads/2012/12/security-agreement-2.pdf.

[146] Status of Forces Agreement (n 145) paras 4(1), 4(2).

[147] J Logan, 'Last US Troops Leave Iraq, Ending War' *Reuters* (18 December 2011) http://www.reuters.com/article/us-iraq-withdrawal-idUSTRE7BH03320111218.

[148] Third Report of the Secretary-General Submitted Pursuant to Paragraph 6 of Resolution 2110 (2013) UN Doc S/2014/485 (11 July 2014) paras 2, 11 ff.

[149] Letter Dated 25 June 2014 from the Permanent Representative of Iraq to the United Nations Addressed to the Secretary-General UN Doc S/2014/440 (25 June 2014).

[150] UN Doc S/RES/2169 (30 July 2014); Annex to the Letter Dated 20 December 2014 from the Permanent Representative of Iraq to the United Nations, Addressed to the President of the Security Council UN Doc S/2014/691 (22 September 2014) 2; Ruys and Ferro (n 5) 91; Bannelier-Christakis (n 5) 750.

[151] Letter Dated 25 June 2014 from the Permanent Representative of Iraq to the United Nations Addressed to the Secretary-General UN Doc S/2014/440 (n 135); Letter dated 20 September 2014 from the Permanent Representative of Iraq to the United Nations addressed to the President of the Security Council UN Doc S/2014/691 (22 September 2014). At the time, twenty-six states had already committed themselves to support for the coalition against IS.

[152] The White House, 'Statement of the President' (7 August 2014) www.whithouse.gov/the-press-office/2014/08/07/statement-president; Bannelier-Christakis (n 5) 751.

state on the territory of another if the territorial state so requests or consents'.[153] Similarly, broad legal justifications were issued by Australia and France.[154] The Canadian Foreign Minister for his part emphasized the legality as well as political legitimacy of the military assistance by noting that the request for military assistance had come from the democratically elected government of Iraq.[155] As will be elaborated in Chapter 6, several members of the US-led coalition have subsequently (especially since 2015) also based their military operations against IS in Iraq on the right to individual or collective self-defence.[156] No state has thus far challenged the validity of US-led air strikes against IS in Iraq.[157]

4.3 Somalia

Subsequent to the collapse of state structures in Somalia in 1992, numerous attempts to create an interim government through a settlement ultimately resulted in the 2004 Transitional Federal Government of Somalia (TFG), which was mediated by the Intergovernmental Authority on Development (IGAD).[158] The TFG originally operated from Nairobi in Kenya and commenced relocation to Somalia in March 2005. During this time the TFG was characterized by divisions concerning *inter alia* the seat of the government and security issues.[159] In January 2007 the

[153] (United Kingdom) Prime Minister's Office, 'Summary of the Government Legal Position on Military Action in Iraq Against ISIL' *Policy Paper* (25 September 2015) https://www.gov.uk/government/publications/military-action-in-iraq-against-isil-government-legal-position/summary-of-the-government-legal-position-on-military-action-in-iraq-against-isil.

[154] T Abbott (Australian Prime Minister), 'Interview with F Kelly' *ABC Radio National* 16 September 2014) http://pmtranscripts.pmc.gov.au/release/transcript-23831; JY le Drian (French Minister of Defence), 'Déclaration du Gouvernement sur l'Intervention des Forces Armées en Irak et Débat sur Cette Déclaration' Assemblée nationale, XIVe législature, Troisième session extraordinaire de 2013–2014 (24 September 2014) 3 http://www.assemblee-nationale.fr/14/cri/2013-2014-extra3/20143001.asp.

[155] J Baird (Canadian Minister of Foreign Affairs), House of Commons Debates, Official Report (Hansard), Vol 147 (6 October 2014) 8257 http://www.parl.gc.ca/HousePublications/Publication.aspx?Language=EandMode=1andParl=41andSes=2andDocId=6717243. See also Akande and Vermeer (n 41).

[156] See Chapter 6, section 2.

[157] However, Iraq has persistently protested against Turkish incursions beyond the Turkish border into Iraq as part of Turkish offensives against the Kurdistan Worker's Party (PKK), which Turkey claimed Iraq was harbouring. Iraq underscored the fact that in its battle against IS all foreign military engagement in Iraq had to occur in accordance with express Iraqi consent and in line with bilateral or multilateral agreements to this effect. In relation to Turkey's presence, no such consent existed. See *inter alia* Annex to the Letter Dated 11 December 2015 from the Permanent Representative of Iraq to the United Nations Addressed to the President of the Security Council UN Doc S/2015/963 (15 December 2015); Annex to Identical Letters Dated 17 October 2016 from the Permanent Representative of Iraq to the United Nations Addressed to the Secretary-General and the President of the Security Council UN Doc S/2016/870 (19 October 2016). The extent to which Turkey has justified these incursions on the basis of self-defence will be considered in Chapter 6, section 2.

[158] Report of the Secretary-General on the Situation in Somalia UN Doc S/2004/804 (8 October 2004) paras 2 ff.

[159] Report of the Secretary-General on the Situation in Somalia UN Doc S/2005/89 (18 February 2005) para 7; Report of the Secretary-General on the Situation in Somalia, UN Doc S/2005/392 (16

AU established the African Union Mission in Somalia (AMISOM) in order to protect the TFG and its institutions.[160] AMISOM was also endorsed by the UNSC in Resolution 1744 of 21 February 2007, which authorized the mission under Chapter VII of the UN Charter to take all necessary measures as appropriate to carry out its mandate.[161] The AMISOM mandate has been continuously extended and modified, also after elections were finally held in the country in September 2012.[162]

However, from 16 October 2011 and February 2012—and parallel to the existence of AMISOM—Kenya engaged in military operations against al-Shabaab in Somalia with the consent of the TFG. On 17 October 2011 Kenya informed the UNSC that 'with the concurrence of the Transitional Federal Government of Somalia', Kenya had been 'compelled to take robust, targeted measures to protect and preserve the integrity of Kenya and the efficacy of the national economy and to secure peace and security in the face of the al-Shabaab terrorist militia attacks emanating from Somalia'.[163] A day later the two countries adopted a Joint Communiqué according to which al-Shabaab posed a threat to both and they agreed to collaborate, also through military operations, to stamp out al-Shabaab and pursue armed elements that attacked and threatened both countries.[164] In line

June 2005) paras 2 ff; Report of the Secretary-General on the Situation in Somalia UN Doc S/2005/642 (11 October 2005) paras 2 ff; Report of the Secretary-General on the Situation in Somalia UN Doc S/2006/122 (21 February 2006) paras 3 ff.

[160] AUPSC, Communiqué of the 69th Meeting, PSC/PR/Comm (LXIL) (19 January 2007) http://www.peaceau.org/uploads/communiqueeng-69th.pdf. AMISOM replaced the protection and training mission (IGASOM) which was endorsed under Chapter VII of the UN Charter in UN Doc S/RES/1725 (6 December 2006) para 3. This resolution mandated the Intergovernmental Authority for Development (IGAD) and member states of the AU to establish a force that was responsible *inter alia* for monitoring the dialogue between the Transitional Federal Institutions and the Union of Islamic Courts; ensuring free movement and safe passage of all those involved in the dialogue process; maintaining and monitoring security in Baidoa; providing protection for members of the Transitional Federal Institutions and Government as well as their key infrastructure; and providing training for the Transitional Federal Institutions' security forces.

[161] UN Doc S/RES/1744 (20 February 2007) Preamble, paras 4, 12; Paliwal (n 69) 204.

[162] See http://amisom-au.org/key-documents/united-nations-security-council-resolutions/ for relevant UNSC and AU decisions pertaining to the AMISOM mandate. Somalia's transitional process ended in 2012 with the selection of a federal parliament by 135 traditional elders in August 2012. They subsequently selected Hassan Sheikh Mohamud as President. See Report of the Secretary-General on Somalia UN Doc S/2013/69 (31 January 2013) paras 2 ff. See also D Smith, 'Somalia Chooses New Leader in Presidential Elections' *Guardian* (10 September 2012) https://www.theguardian.com/world/2012/sep/10/somalia-chooses-new-president-elections.

[163] Letter Dated 17 October 2011 from the Permanent Representative of Kenya to the United Nations Addressed to the President of the Security Council UN Doc S/2011/646 (18 October 2011).

[164] Joint Communiqué Issued at the Conclusion of a Meeting Between the Government of Kenya and the Transitional Federal Government of Somalia of 18 October 2011, paras 1, 2 http://graphics8.nytimes.com/packages/pdf/world/joint-communique-kenya-somalia.pdf. According to some reports, the initial reaction within the government to the Kenyan forcible measures were somewhat contradictory, casting doubt on the depth of its consent. While the Prime Minister reportedly supported the forcible measures, the President expressed objections to it. However, this did not result in a formal protest at the UNSC level or a revocation of the Joint Communiqué. See E Lieblich, *International Law and Civil Wars. Intervention and Consent* (Routledge 2013) 16; J Kron, 'Kenyan Offensive Is Not Welcome, Somalia's President Says' *New York Times* (24 October 2011) https://www.nytimes.com/2011/10/25/world/africa/grenade-attack-on-kenyan-bar-raises-fear-of-widening-conflict.html.

with this agreement, the Kenyan Defence Force (KDF) pursued insurgents within Somalia.[165]

While the letter to the UNSC underscored the consent of Somalia, it also referred to the security risk that al-Shabaab posed also to Kenya (as did the Joint Communiqué). The Kenyan forcible measures, therefore, seemed to have been based both on the legal construct of military assistance on request as well as the right to individual or collective self-defence. These military operations against al-Shabaab were further complemented by US air strikes. As in the case of Kenya, the United States seemed to justify the forcible measures both with reference to requests by the Somali government, as well as the right to individual or collective self-defence.[166] While emphasizing that the air strikes occurred with the consent of the Somali government,[167] the United States also noted that al-Shabaab increasingly constituted a threat to itself and neighbouring countries.[168]

On 22 February 2012 UNSC Resolution 2036 was adopted, resulting in the integration of the Kenyan military operations in AMISOM under Chapter VII of the UN Charter.[169] In its Preamble this resolution condemned all attacks by armed opposition groups, and notably by al-Shabaab on AMISOM, UN personnel, and civilians, stressing that they constituted a terrorist threat to Somalia and the international community. It further welcomed the integration of the Kenyan forces into AMISOM and, acting under Chapter VII of the UN Charter, decided that AMISOM may take all necessary measures as appropriate in the sectors where it was deployed and in coordination with the Somali security forces to reduce the threat posed by al-Shabaab and other armed opposition groups.[170]

Subsequent to the adoption of this Resolution, the KDF has launched air strikes in pursuit of al-Shabaab at regular intervals, as well as undertaken joint military operations with AMISOM and Somalian and Ethiopian forces aimed at expelling al-Shabaab from its strongholds in Somalia.[171] While these operations were

[165] See African Union Mission to Somalia (AMISOM) http://amisom-au.org/kenya-kdf/.

[166] See also M Byrne, 'Consent and The Use of Force: An Examination of "Intervention by Invitation" as a Basis for US Drone Strikes in Pakistan, Somalia and Yemen' (2016) 3 Journal of the Use of Force in International Law 116.

[167] In May 2011 the Somali Minister of Defence expressed support for the air strikes. R Young Pelton, 'Enter the Drones' *Somalia Report* (7 June 2011) http://piracyreport.com/index.php/writer/139/Robert_Young_Pelton. In early 2013 the Somali government requested more military assistance from the United States, resulting in closer cooperation between the two countries. See J Rogin, 'Somali President Asks for More American Help' *Foreign Policy* (18 January 2013) http://foreignpolicy.com/2013/01/18/somali-president-asks-for-more-american-help/.

[168] G Jaffe and K de Young, 'US Drone Targets Two Leaders of Somali Group Allied With al-Qaeda' *Washington Post* (29 May 2011) https://www.washingtonpost.com/national/national-security/us-drones-target-two-leaders-of-somali-group-allied-with-al-qaeda/2011/06/29/AGJFxZrH_story.html?utm_term=.12f5c59ff3da.

[169] See African Union Mission to Somalia (AMISOM) http://amisom-au.org/kenya-kdf/.

[170] UN Doc S/RES/2036 (22 February 2017) para 1.

[171] See *inter alia* Report of the Secretary-General on Somalia UN Doc S/2013/709 (2 December 2013) para 13; Report of the Secretary-General on Somalia UN Doc S/2014/699 (25 September 2014) para 20; Report of the Secretary-General on Somalia UN Doc S/2015/702 (11 September 2015) para 12; 'Kenyan Air Force Jets Carry Out Airstrikes in Somalia' *Shabellanews* (30 June 2016)

undertaken in cooperation with the Somali government, their legal basis since the adoption of UNSC Resolution 2036 (2012) first and foremost is UNSC authority under Chapter VII of the UN Charter.[172] The US air strikes against al-Shabaab have continued alongside these UNSC-authorized operations and have systematically intensified since 2013.[173] The United States has consistently justified these military actions with reference to the consent of the Somali government, as well as with reference to the right to individual or collective self-defence.[174]

4.4 South Sudan

In South Sudan the People's Liberation Movement (SPLM) were voted into power in 2010 during democratic elections in the period leading up to the country's independence in July 2011.[175] Barely two years later, in December 2013, the long-standing rivalry between South Sudan President Salva Kiir Mayardit and his Vice-President, Riek Machar, reached a tipping point, when violence broke out in Juba and immediately spread to Jonglei, Unity, and Upper Nile states.[176]

http://www.shabellenews.com/2016/06/kdf-launches-more-airstrikes-on-al-shabaab-bases/; M Som, 'Kenya Sends More KDF Troops to Somalia' *AllAfrica* (25 January 2016) http://allafrica.com/stories/201601250155.html.

172 Some of the Kenyan operations have gone awry, resulting in civilian casualties, loss of homes, livestock, water, and well houses, which in 2016 provoked a rebuke from the Somali authorities. See Report of the Secretary-General on Somalia UN Doc S/2016/430 (9 May 2016) paras 50–51; A Abdirahman, 'Somalia Calls on Kenya to Halt Airstrikes Against Civilians' *Horseed* (1 February 2016) https://horseedmedia.net/2016/02/01/somalia-calls-on-kenya-to-halt-airstrikes-against-civilians/ . The two countries nonetheless continue to cooperate closely in the fight against Al-Shabaab, as reflected by a Joint Communiqué adopted in June 2016 in which appreciation was expressed for the role Kenya and AMISOM played in stabilizing Somalia and promoting peace in the country. See the (Kenyan) Presidency, Joint Communiqué of the Republic of Kenya and Federal Republic of Somalia of 8 June 2016 http://www.president.go.ke/2016/06/08/joint-communique-of-the-republic-of-kenya-and-federal-republic-of-somalia/.

173 Rogin (n 167): Byrne (n 166) 116.

174 L Martinez, 'Inside the US Military's Mission in Somalia' *ABC News* (5 May 2017) http://abcnews.go.com/International/inside-us-militarys-mission-somalia/story?id=47239816; L Martinez, 'US Military Now Authorized to Conduct Offensive Airstrikes in Somalia' *ABC News* (30 March 2017) http://abcnews.go.com/Politics/usmilitary-now-authorized-conduct-offensive-airstrikes-somalia/story?id=46475314; T Gibbons-Neff, 'US Acknowledges Airstrike in Somalia Caused Civilian Deaths' *The New York Times* (5 April 2019) https://www.nytimes.com/2019/04/05/us/politics/us-civilians-somalia-airstrikes.html.

175 Report of the Secretary-General on South Sudan UN Doc S/2011/678 (2 November 2011) paras 3 ff.

176 For a detailed overview of the outbreak of the conflict and its development, see Report of the Secretary General on South Sudan UN Doc S/2014/158 (6 March 2014) paras 1 ff. See also Report of the Secretary-General on South Sudan UN Doc S/2014/708 (30 September 2014) paras 1 ff; Report of the Secretary-General on South Sudan UN Doc S/2014/821 (18 November 2014) paras 1 ff; Report of the Secretary-General on South Sudan (covering the period from 12 August to 25 October 2016) UN Doc S/2016/950 (10 November 2016) paras 1 ff. See also F Nicolaisen, T Heggli Sagmo, and O Rolandsen, 'South Sudan—Ugandan Relations. The Cost of Peace' African Centre for the Constructive Resolution of Disputes (ACCORD) (23 December 2015) http://www.accord.org.za/conflict-trends/south-sudan-uganda-relations/.

On 19 December 2013 Mr Machar announced to the press that he had appealed to SPLM and the Sudan People' Liberation Army (SPLA) to remove the President from office.[177] Two days later he announced a rebellion against the government, and by February 2014 he had formed a resistance group to fight the government. These armed opposition forces became known as the Sudan People's Liberation Movement/Army in Opposition (SPLM/A in Opposition).[178]

Almost from the outset of the conflict, the Government of South Sudan invited the Ugandan People's Defence Force (UPDF) to intervene on its side.[179] The responsibilities of the UPDF included the securing of the Juba airport and the evacuation of Ugandan nationals.[180] However, their mandate also encompassed the halting of rebel advances in and around Bor, the capital of Jonglei, including aerial bombardments in January 2014. Thereafter the UPDF was redeployed to train South Sudanese forces and to protect Juba airport and the road to Bor.[181] The UPDF troops remained in South Sudan until after the conclusion of the Agreement on the Resolution of the Conflict in the Republic of South Sudan of 17 August 2015 (Agreement).[182] One of the conditions of this Agreement was that allied forces had to withdraw within forty-five days, and in September 2015 Uganda announced that the withdrawal of its troops would be completed by 10 October 2015.[183] The Ugandan intervention was tacitly condoned by neighbouring countries as well as the UNSC, which did not address the intervention in any of its resolutions pertaining to the South Sudanese conflict.[184]

Following the signing on 17 August 2015 in Addis Ababa of the Agreement on the Resolution of the Conflict in the Republic of South Sudan, the parties declared a permanent ceasefire which came into effect on 29 August 2015.[185] However,

177 Report of the Secretary-General on South Sudan UN Doc S/2014/158 (6 March 2014) para 8.

178 ibid.

179 President Museveni of Uganda sent troops across the border at the invitation of President Salva Kiir shortly after fighting broke out between forces loyal to President Kiir and rebels in December 2013. The countries signed a Status of Forces Agreement between the Government of the Republic of Uganda and the Government of the Republic of South Sudan of 10 January 2014 www.sudantribune.com/IMG/pdf/status_of_forces_agreement-2.pdf. The Ugandan Parliament also adopted a motion approving the sending of troops to South Sudan at the request of the latter's government. See Motion for a Resolution of Parliament to Authorize his Excellency the President of the Republic of Uganda do Deploy Uganda People's Defence Forces to the Republic of Southern Sudan in Accordance with Article 210 of the Constitution and Section 40 of Uganda Peoples' Defence Forces Act, 2005 of 14 January 2014 http://www.parliament.go.ug/new/index.php/documents-and-reports/daily-hansard.

180 Nicolaisen, Heggli Sagmo, and Rolandsen (n 176).

181 ibid.

182 The Agreement on the Resolution of the Conflict in the Republic of South Sudan of 17 August 2015 http://www.gurtong.net/LinkClick.aspx?fileticket=CytVwytJdyM%3Dandtabid=124. This Agreement was steered by the Intergovernmental Authority on Development (IGAD) and signed by the two warring parties and another breakaway SPLM faction, the G10. See Nicolaisen, Heggli Sagmo, and Rolandsen (n 176).

183 The Agreement (n 164) paras. 1.4–1.5; UN Doc S/2015/902 (23 November 2015) para 3. See also Nicolaisen, Heggli Sagmo, and Rolandsen (n 176).

184 Nicolaisen, Heggli Sagmo, and Rolandsen (n 176).

185 Report of the Secretary-General on South Sudan UN Doc S/2015/902 (23 November 2015) paras 2 ff.

this ceasefire has on numerous occasions been broken.[186] In August 2016, amidst ongoing fighting, the UNSC decided under Chapter VII of the UN Charter and with the support of the AU that the UN Mission in the Republic of South Sudan (UNMISS) should be strengthened by a Regional Protection Force in an attempt to improve the security situation within and around Juba.[187]

4.5 Mali (and the Sahel region)

The French intervention in Mali in January 2013 resulted from an invitation by the Mali interim government, in the wake of a *coup d'état*, as well as the takeover of the northern part of the country by the Mouvement National pour la Libération de l'Azawad (MNLA) that threatened the territorial integrity of the country. While the unity of the country had for some time been under threat due to tensions between various rivalling groups, a *coup d'état* on 22 March 2012 against President Amadou Touré brought the country to the brink of collapse.[188] The coup, which was driven by dissatisfied soldiers from the north who fell victim to armed groups in the area, accelerated the takeover of the northern part of the state by the MNLA.[189] In the wake of the coup ECOWAS mediated the crisis and signed a framework agreement with the military junta that resulted in appointing Dioncounda Traoré as interim President on 12 April 2012.[190]

By 20 December 2012 the UNSC also authorized the deployment of an African-led International Support Mission in Mali (AFISMA) under Chapter VII of the UN Charter to take all necessary measures to support the Malian authorities *inter alia* in recovering the areas in the north of its territory under the control of terrorist, extremist, and armed groups.[191] However, as the deployment of AFISMA incurred

[186] Special Report of the Secretary-General on the Review of the Mandate of the United Nations Mission in South Sudan UN Doc S/2016/951 (10 November 2016) paras 14 ff; S Jones, 'UN Report: South Sudan Allowed Soldiers to Rape Civilians in Civil War' *Guardian* (11 March 2016) https://www.theguardian.com/global-development/2016/mar/11/south-sudans-soldiers-allowed-to-rape-civilians-civil-war-says-un-government-torture. See also UN Doc S/RES/2206 (3 March 2015) Preamble; UN Doc S/RES/2223 (28 May 2015) paras 22 ff; UN Doc S/RES/2252 (15 December 2015) para 25; UN Doc S/RES/2327 (16 December 2016) paras 22 ff.

[187] The Regional Task Force was to be integrated within UNMISS and had to report to the UNMISS Force Commander. See UN Doc S/RES/2304 (12 August 2016) para 8; AUOSC, Communiqué of the 626th Meeting, PSC/AHG/COMM.(DCXXVI) (19 September 2016) paras 9–10 http://www.peaceau.org/uploads/psc-626-comm-south-sudan-19-9-2016-eng.pdf. The UNMISS mandate has been extended *inter alia* in S/RES/2327 (16 December 2016) paras 5 ff; S/23/92 (14 December 2017) paras 1 ff; S/RES/2406 (15 March 2018) paras 5 ff; S/RES/2459 (15 March 2019) paras 5 ff.

[188] AUPSC, Communiqué of 315th Meeting, PSC/PR/COMM (CCCXV) (23 March 2015) para 9 http://www.peaceau.org/uploads/psc-comm-mali-23-03-2012-eng.pdf.

[189] Report of the Secretary-General on the Situation in Mali UN Doc S/2012/894 (28 November 2012) paras 5, 6.

[190] ibid para 7. Elections were ultimately only held in August 2013, subsequent to the intervention by the French, and President Ibrahim Keita was elected President. See Reuters Staff, 'Mali Dismisses Candidates for Fraud in Elections' *Reuters* (1 January 2014) http://www.reuters.com/article/2014/01/01/us-mali-elections-idUSBREA000KK20140101.

[191] UNSC Res 2085 (20 December 2012) para 9(b).

delays related to logistical challenges and the security situation in the north worsened with the fall of the city of Konna, the Malian government requested military assistance from France to restore the country's territorial integrity.[192] In its official letter of 11 January 2013 sent to the UNSC, France stated that its intervention was in response to a request for assistance from the interim President of the Republic of Mali, Mr Dioncoundra Traoré. It noted that Mali was facing terrorist elements from the north that were threatening the territorial integrity and the very existence of the state and the security of its population.[193]

The United States supported the intervention, emphasizing the consensus about the gravity of the situation and the right of the Malian authorities to seek 'what assistance they can receive'.[194] Similarly, ECOWAS endorsed the decision of the UNSC to authorize a military intervention in Mali and thanked the French government for its initiatives to support Mali.[195] In addition, in its follow-up Resolution 2100 of 13 April 2013, the UNSC welcomed the French action in the Preamble. This Resolution also provided a Chapter VII authorization for future military action in Mali by the UN Multidimensional Integrated Stabilization Mission in Mali (MINUSMA) as well as the French forces, where their assistance was requested by the UN Secretary-General in case of a grave and imminent threat.[196]

However, parallel to this support for MINUSMA, France remained militarily active in the Sahel region on the basis of a counter-terrorism agreement with the Group of Five for the Sahel (Burkina Faso, Mali, Mauritania, Niger, and Chad), known as Operation Barkhane.[197] The UNSC has subsequently welcomed the establishment of a joint action by the Group of Five in the Sahel, as well as the continued French action at the request of Mali to deter the terrorist threat in the north of the country.[198] In February 2019 France deployed aeroplanes from Operation

[192] Report of the Secretary-General on the Situation in Mali UN Doc S/2013/189 (26 March 2013) paras 3, 4, 44 ff.

[193] Identical Letters Dated 11 January 2013 from the Permanent Representative of France to the United Nations addressed to the Secretary-General and the President of the Security Council UN Doc S/2013/17 (14 January 2013); see also Bannelier and Christakis (n 2) 859.

[194] SE Rice, 'Remarks at a Press Gaggle Following UN Security Council Consultations on Mali' (10 January 2013) https://2009-2017-usun.state.gov/remarks/5641; Bannelier and Kristakis (n 2) 859.

[195] Statement of the President of ECOWAS Commission on the Situation in Mali (12 January 2013) http://www.news/ecowas.int/presseshow.php?nb=006andlang=enandannee2013; Bannelier and Christakis (n 2) 869.

[196] UN Doc S/RES/2100 (13 April 2013) paras 16–18; see also Bannelier and Christakis (n 2) 867–68. The mandate of MINUSMA has since been extended in *inter alia* S/RES/2164 (25 June 2014) paras 11 ff; S/RES/2227 (29 June 2015) paras 12 ff; S/RES/2295 (29 June 2016) paras 14 ff; S/RES/2364 (29 June 2017) paras 15 ff; S/RES/2423 (28 June 2018) paras 24 ff.

[197] French Ministry of Defence, *Opération Barkhane* (14 February 2019) 3–4 https://www.defense.gouv.fr/operations/barkhane/dossier-de-presentation/operation-barkhane. This operation may be interpreted as a response to UNSC in S/RES/2100 (13 April 2013) para 29, which '[u]rges Sahel and Maghreb states to enhance interregional cooperation and coordination in order to develop inclusive and effective strategies to combat in a comprehensive and integrated manner the activities of terrorist groups'.

[198] See S/RES/2227 (29 June 2015) Preamble, paras 28, 29; S/RES/2295 (29 June 2016) Preamble, paras 42, 43; S/RES/2364 (29 June 2017) Preamble, paras 42, 43; S/RES/2423 (28 June 2018) Preamble, para 48.

Barkhane in airstrikes in Northern Chad against rebels who were advancing to the capital in order to topple the government of President Idriss Déby.[199] In so doing, the French government underscored that France acted 'in response to a request from Chadian authorities'.[200] During a parliamentary debate on 12 February 2019, the French Foreign Minister further stated that 'France intervened militarily to prevent a *coup d'état*'.[201] France for its part therefore did not—as it did in the case of Côte d'Ivoire in 2002—display concern about potentially intervening in the Chadian domestic affairs for fighting rebel groups opposing the government. While members of Chadian civil society and analysts have questioned the propriety of such conduct,[202] condemnation by other states or international organizations is yet to be forthcoming.

4.6 Yemen

In Yemen the internationally recognized President Abdo Rabbo Mansour Hadi was elected President in 2012.[203] Subsequent to his election, he came under increasing pressure from the Houthi militia in the north-west part of the country who systematically captured territory.[204] On 24 March 2015 the increasingly destabilizing impact of the Houthi insurrection resulted in a request by President Hadi for military assistance, addressed to the Cooperation Council for the Arab States of the Gulf (GCC) and the League of Arab States.[205] By the time this invitation was extended, President Hadi's government had fled to Aden from the capital Sana'a, which had fallen to the Houthis in September 2014.[206] In early 2015 President Hadi and members of his cabinet collectively resigned, after having been placed under house arrest. On 6 February 2015 the Houthis released a constitutional declaration

[199] A Nossiter, 'Can France Ever Leave Africa? Airstrikes in Chad Raise an Old Question' *New York Times* (14 February 2019) https://www.nytimes.com/2019/02/14/world/africa/france-airstrikes-chad.html. See P Fabricius and L Louw-Vaudran 'The Recent Air Strike Recalls an Era of Open Interference in the Internal Politics of African countries' *Daily Maverick* (22 February 2019) https://www.dailymaverick.co.za/article/2019-02-22-was-frances-military-intervention-in-chad-a-regression/.

[200] 'Rebel Incursion Exposes Chad's Weaknesses' *International Crisis Group* (13 February 2019) https://www.crisisgroup.org/africa/central-africa/chad/au-tchad-lincursion-des-rebelles-devoile-les-fragilites-du-pouvoir.

[201] ibid.

[202] Fabricius and Louw-Vaudran (n 199).

[203] L Kasinof, 'Yemen's Election Ensures Leader's Exit' *New York Times* (21 February 2012) http://www.nytimes.com/2012/02/22/world/middleeast/yemen-votes-to-remove-ali-abdullah-saleh.html.

[204] Final Report of the Panel of Experts on Yemen Established Pursuant to Security Council Committee Resolution 2140 (2014) UN Doc S/2015/125 (20 February 2015) para 32.

[205] Statement Issued by the Kingdom of Saudi Arabia, the United Arab Emirates, the Kingdom of Bahrain, the State of Quarter and the State of Kuwait, Enclosure to Annex of Identical Letters Dated 26 March 2015 from the Permanent Representative of Qatar to the United Nations Addressed to the Secretary-General and the President of the Security Council UN Doc S/2015/217 (27 March 2015) 5. See also UN Doc S/PV.7426 (14 April 2015) 7 (Yemen); UN Doc S/RES/2216 (14 April 2015) Preamble.

[206] Final Report of the Panel of Experts on Yemen (n 204) paras 130 ff; Ruys and Ferro (n 5) 64, 92.

which dissolved parliament and established a five-member Presidential Council and a Supreme Revolutionary Committee.[207] A week later President Hadi escaped from house arrest and fled to Aden. He released a statement rescinding his resignation and declared Aden the temporary capital.[208] The UNSC condemned the Houthi dissolution of parliament and their taking over of governmental institutions in Resolution 2201 of 15 February 2015.[209] Subsequently, in April 2015 the UNSC also expressed its support for the legitimacy of President Hadi, while once again condemning actions taken by the Houthi militias.[210]

After extending the invitation for military support against the Houthi insurrection on 24 March 2014,[211] President Hadi fled to Saudi Arabia in the face of advancing Houthi forces. On 26 March 2015 an intensive aerial campaign led by Saudi Arabia (Operation Decisive Storm), the objective of which was 'limited to defending and protecting the legitimate government of Yemen and preventing its collapse to the Houthis'.[212] Saudi Arabia, the United Arab Emirates, Bahrain, Qatar, and Kuwait also submitted a joint letter to the UNSC in which they referred to the request for assistance by President Hadi 'in every form'.[213] This letter further referred to the right to self-defence in article 51 of the United Nations Charter, as did the request of President Hadi himself.[214] The United States and Canada issued statements claiming that the operation had been undertaken to defend Saudi Arabia's border and to protect Yemen's legitimate government at the request of the Yemini President.[215] The legal justification of the military intervention, therefore, was based on military assistance on request as well as the right to self-defence.

[207] Saudi–US Relations Information Service, 'Statement by Saudi Ambassador Al-Jubeir on Military Operations in Yemen (Transcript)' (26 March 2015) http://susris.com/2015/03/26/statement-by-saudi-ambassador-al-jubeir-on-military-operations-in-yemen-transcript/. The UNSC subsequently demanded the return of the Houthis to the negotiating table and the release of all individuals under house arrest, as well as the withdrawal of their forces from government and security institutions. See UN Doc S/RES/2201 (15 February 2015) Preamble, paras 1 ff; Ruys and Ferro (n 5) 64.

[208] Ruys and Ferro (n 5) 64.

[209] UN Doc S/RES/2201 (15 February 2015) paras 1 ff.

[210] UN Doc S/RES/2216 (16 April 2015) Preamble and para 1. See also UN Doc S/PRST/2015/8 (22 March 2015).

[211] M Nichols, 'UPDATE 1-Yemen Asks UN to Back Military Action by "Willing Countries"' *Reuters* (24 March 2015) http://uk.reuters.com/article/yemen-security-un-idUKL2N0WQ29620150324.

[212] Saudi–US Relations Information Service (n 182); Ruys and Ferro (n 5) 62, 64–65.

[213] Statement Issued by the Kingdom of Saudi Arabia, the United Arab Emirates, the Kingdom of Bahrain, the State of Quarter and the State of Kuwait, Enclosure to Annex of Identical Letters Dated 26 March 2015 From the Permanent Representative of Qatar to the United Nations Addressed to the Secretary-General and the President of the Security Council, UN Doc S/2015/217 (27 March 2015) 5.

[214] ibid 4. Similarly, the statement by UN Doc S/PV.7426 (14 April 2015) 7 (Yemen) determines that '[t]he President was forced, in the context of his constitutional prerogative, to ask his brothers and friends to protect the Yemeni people and the territorial integrity of Yemen, in keeping with Article 51 of the Charter of the United Nations'.

[215] The White House, 'Statement by NSC Spokesperson Bernadette Meehan on the Situation in Yemen' (25 March 2015) https://obamawhitehouse.archives.gov/the-press-office/2015/03/25/statement-nsc-spokesperson-bernadette-meehan-situation-yemen; Government of Canada, Department of Foreign Affairs, Trade and Development, 'Minister Nicholson Concerned by Crisis in Yemen' (27 March 2015) http://news.gc.ca/web/article-en.do?nid=956649; Ruys and Ferro (n 5) 67–68.

The aerial campaign against the Houthi rebels in Yemen received military support from various states in and outside the region. For example, Egypt, Sudan, and Senegal committed to providing ground troops, while Somalia consented to the use of its air space, ports and territory by the coalition. The United Kingdom and the United States for their part offered logistical and intelligence support.[216] Somalia also consented to the use of territory, air space, and ports for coalition purposes.[217] Opposition to Operation Decisive Storm was expressed by Iran who condemned the aerial attacks as being in 'flagrant defiance of the most basic principles of international law, flouting the purposes and principles of the Charter of the United Nations, in particular the obligation to refrain from the threat or use of force in international relations'.[218]

In April 2015 Russia was reported as saying that the aerial attacks were illegal.[219] However, in the UNSC debates pertaining to UNSC Resolution 2216 of 14 April 2015, which was adopted almost three weeks after the aerial campaign had been launched, Russia did not actually claim that the aerial attacks were in violation of international law. It justified its abstention from voting for the Resolution (which received affirmative votes from all other fourteen UNSC members) with political considerations, namely, that the Resolution did not require all parties to the conflict to halt fire and begin peace talks.[220] In its Preamble, Resolution 2216 (2015) took note of Yemen's request for military support addressed to the GCC and League of Arab States, as well as of the letter of the five Gulf states to the UNSC dated 26 March.[221] While it did not express support for these actions, it also did not condemn them. It is also worth noting that the Saudi-led coalition has received widespread criticism for the manner in which it has conducted the air campaign, including violations of international human law.[222] However, as indicated above, no state, with the exception of Iran, claimed that the intervention on behalf of the Hadi government was as such in contravention of international law.

On 21 April 2015 Operation Decisive Storm was replaced by Operation Renewal of Hope. While this operation introduced a political process for the stabilization

[216] The White House (Bernadette Meehan statement) (n 215); United Kingdom Parliament, 'Saudi Arabia: Yemen: Written question—HL1125' (14 July 2015) http://www.parliament.uk/business/publications/written-questions-answers-statements/written-question/Lords/2015-07-06/HL1125; Ruys and Ferro (n 5) 65.

[217] Ruys and Ferro (n 5) 65.

[218] Annex to the Letter Dated 17 April 2015 from the Permanent Representative of the Islamic Republic of Iran to the United Nations Addressed to the Security Council UN Doc S/2015/263 (17 April 2015). See also Iran's statement about aggression against Yemen in UN Doc S/PV.7527 (30 September 2015) 82 (Iran); Ruys and Ferro (n 5) 68.

[219] 'Saudi-Led Coalition Operation in Yemen Has No Legal Foundation—Lavrov' *Sputnik News* (6 April 2015) https://sputniknews.com/world/201504061020533752/; see also Ruys and Ferro (n 5) 69.

[220] UN Doc S/PV.7426 (14 April 2015) 2 (Russia); see also Ruys and Ferro (n 5) 70.

[221] UN Doc S/RES/ 2216 (14 April 2015); see also Ruys and Ferro (n 5) 69–70.

[222] Final Report of the Panel of Experts on Yemen (n 204) paras 119 and 126 ff; European Parliament, Resolution on the Situation in Yemen (2015/2760(RSP) (9 July 2015) (AB B(EP)1-B(EP) 6). See also Chapter 4, section 2.

of Yemen, it also continued the aerial attacks on Houthi strongholds.[223] Despite the extensive support that the recognized government based in Riyadh received from the Saudi-led coalition, the Houthis continued to consolidate their control over the state apparatus, *inter alia* by forming a Houthi–Saleh political alliance in 2016.[224] By January 2017 the Houthis continued to control the capital and municipality of Sana'a, as well as 27 per cent of the surface area of Yemen, comprising more than 80 per cent of the total population before the conflict.[225] Thereafter and throughout the first months of 2019, the Houthis maintained their grip on Sana'a and the surrounding region, while the Saudi-led coalition also continued its aerial campaign.[226] In addition, terrorist groups such as Al Qaida had gained control over parts of the south of the country.[227]

4.7 Syria

In February 2011 the government of Bashar al Assad, who succeeded his father, Hafez al Assad, in 2000, was confronted with protests concerning rural poverty, corruption, freedom of expression, democratic rights, and the release of political prisoners.[228] By mid-March 2011, the protests had extended to include demands for far-reaching socio-economic and legal reforms. Violent responses by state forces were met with continuing protests and increasing violent responses by the Syrian armed forces, which consistently claimed to be the target of (foreign-funded) armed gangs and terrorists.[229] The civil unrest systematically spiralled into a NIAC in which government forces and allies were pitted against various non-state actors, characterized by fragmentation and infighting.[230] The anti-government forces included the so-called Free Syrian Army (FSA), the military wing of the Syrian Opposition Coalition (SOC), as well as several radical Islamic

[223] DA Weinberg, 'Understanding Operation "Renewal of Hope in Yemen"' *Al Arabiya English* (22 April 2015) http://english.alarabiya.net/en/perspective/analysis/2015/04/22/Understanding-the-Saudi-led-Operation-Restore-Hope in-Yemen.html; Ruys and Ferro (n 5) 65.

[224] Final report of the Panel of Experts on Yemen (n 204) para 15.

[225] They also controlled the Sana'a airport, and strengthened their hold over intelligence and security agencies. Until September 2016 the Houthis further controlled the central bank, at which point the President moved the bank to Aden and appointed a new governor. Final Report of the Panel of Experts on Yemen (n 204) paras 13, 16, 18, 19, 51 ff.

[226] BBC, 'Yemen Crisis: Who is Fighting Whom?' *BBC News* (21 March 2019) http://www.bbc.com/news/world-middle-east-29319423.

[227] See also UN Doc S/RES/2456 (26 February 2019), Preamble. In December 2018 the Hadi government and Houthi representatives agreed to a ceasefire in relation to the governorate of Hudaydah and the ports of Hudaydah, Salif, and Ra's Isa. See Report of the Secretary-General on Status of Implementation of Security Council Resolution 2451 (2018) UN Doc S/2018/1173 (28 December 2019) paras 1 ff.

[228] UN Human Rights Council, First Report of the Independent International Commission of Inquiry on the Syrian Arab Republic UN Doc A/HRC/S-27/2/Add.1 (23 November 2011) paras 14, 27.

[229] UN Doc A/HRC/S-27/2/Add.1 (23 November 2011) (n 228) paras 27–30.

[230] UN Human Rights Council, Report of the Independent International Commission of Inquiry on the Syrian Arab Republic UN Doc A/HR/C/21/50 (16 August 2012) paras 21 ff.

armed groups, notably the al-Nusrah Front linked with Al Qaida and IS.[231] At an early stage the conflict became internationalized on all sides. For example, in the course of 2013 Russia announced the shipment of military materials to the Syrian government, while the EU allowed a ban on weapon deliveries to the FSA to lapse.[232] Saudi Arabia and Qatar, as well as the US Congress, approved the arming and funding to anti-government forces in August 2013.[233]

As of August 2014, as the influence of IS and its control over parts of Syria continued to grow, a US-led coalition of Western states, allied Gulf states, and Turkey has been engaging in airstrikes against IS in Syria. These states have consistently justified their actions with the right to individual or collective self-defence against IS.[234] However, Russia, Iraq, and Iran have coordinated their operations against IS with the Syrian government by setting up a 'joint information centre' in Baghdad.[235] Since 30 September 2015 Russia has been engaged in airstrikes as well as ground offences in support of the Syrian government, directed against IS as well as other anti-government forces.[236] Similarly, Iran has reportedly sent up to 3,000 troops to Syria in support of the Assad regime.[237] Both Russia and Iran have justified their military presence in Syria with a request from President Assad to assist in combating IS and other terrorist groups in Syria.[238]

These military actions were criticized by Western states and international organizations, to the extent that they were also directed at so-called moderate rebels that were not designated by the UNSC as terrorist groups.[239] However, these criticisms

[231] UN Doc A/HR/C/21/50 (16 August 2012) (n 230) paras 27 ff; UN Human Rights Council, Report of the Independent International Commission of Inquiry on the Syrian Arab Republic UN Doc A/HRC/23/58 (18 July 2013) paras 28–29. Human Rights Council, Report of the Independent International Commission of Inquiry on the Syrian Arab Republic UN Doc A/HRC/25/65 (12 February 2014) para 16.

[232] The Lebanese Hizbullah also publicly stated that it was intervening in the conflict on the side of the government, and Russia announced the shipment of military materials to the Assad regime. See UN Doc A/HRC/23/58 (18 July 2013) (n 205) paras 14, 16.

[233] Ruys (n 1) 25. See also Chapter 2, section 2.

[234] See Letter Dated 23 September 2014 from the Permanent Representative of the United States of America to the United Nations Addressed to the Secretary-General UN Doc, S/2014/695 (23 September 2014). See also Chapter 6, section 2.

[235] UN Human Rights Council, Report of the Independent International Commission of Inquiry on the Syrian Arab Republic UN Doc A/HRC/31/68 (Advanced Edited Version) (11 February 2016) paras 19, 28.

[236] UN Doc A/HRC/31/68 (Advanced Edited Version) (11 February 2016) (n 235) paras 19, 28. See also Human Rights Council, '"They came to destroy": ISIS Crimes Against the Yazidis' UN Doc A HRC/32/CRP.2 (15 June 2016) para 191; S Rosenberrg, 'Syria War: Putin's Russian Mission Accomplished' *BBC News* (13 December 2017) http://www.bbc.com/news/world-europe-42330551.

[237] Bannelier-Christakis (n 5) 760.

[238] Letter Dated 15 October 2015 from the Permanent Representative of the Russian Federation to the United Nations Addressed to the President of the Security Council UN Doc S/2015/792 (15 October 2015) 2; H Rohani, 'La Lutte Contre le Terrorisme Doit Être la Base de Tout en Syrie' *Le Monde* (29 January 2016) http://www.lemonde.fr/international/article/2016/01/29/hassan-rohani-la-lutte-contre-le-terrorisme-doit-etre-la-base-de-tout-en-syrie_4855748_3210.html. See also Bannelier-Christakis (n 5) 760–61.

[239] As underscored by O Corten, 'L'Intervention de la Russie en Syrie: Que Reste-t-il du Principe de Non-Intervention dans les Guerres Civiles?' (2018) 4 Questions of International Law para 2.2 http://

did not explicitly state that Russia's attacks on moderate rebel groups would violate the negative equality principle and, therefore, would be illegal.[240] Instead, the criticism was first and foremost of a political nature, claiming that the Russian military measures undermined a political settlement. For example, the Council of the EU stated that Russian military attacks that extended beyond IS and other UN-designated terrorist groups risked the prolonging of the conflict, undermining a political process, and aggravating the humanitarian situation.[241]

The same political and humanitarian concerns were expressed by the UNGA in 2018, when calling for an immediate cessation of all attacks against the Syrian 'moderate opposition'. It underscored that 'such attacks benefit so-called ISIL-Da'esh and other terrorist groups, such as al-Nusrah Front, and contribute to a further deterioration of the humanitarian situation'.[242] Similarly, the Foreign Minister of the United Kingdom submitted that the fact that most of the Russian airstrikes were aimed at opposition groups other than IS bolstered the Assad regime and undermined international efforts to end the conflict in Syria.[243] In addition, the United Kingdom and the United States have accused Russia of direct violations of international humanitarian law, as well as aiding and assisting such violations by the Syrian government.[244] Even so, all these statements stopped short of stating that the military presence of Russia in Syria at the request of the Assad regime as such was illegal under international law.

4.8 Libya

In Libya, the internationally recognized National Transitional Council (NTC), which took control of government affairs in 2011 after the fall of the Gaddafi regime,[245] announced the formation of an interim government headed by Prime Minister El-Keib on 22 November 2011.[246] Following elections on 7 June 2012 with

www.qil-qdi.org/lintervention-de-la-russie-en-syrie-que-reste-t-il-du-principe-de-non-intervention-dans-les-guerres-civiles/.

[240] As suggested by Bannelier-Christakis (n 5) 764, who noted that the perceived effort of Russia to take sides with the Syrian government met with criticism.

[241] Council of the EU, 'Council Conclusion on Syria' (12 October 2015) para 10 http://www.consilium.europa.eu/en/press/press-releases/2015/10/12-fac-conclusions-syria/.

[242] UNGA, Situation of Human Rights in the Syrian Arab Republic UN Doc A/RES/71/203 (1 February 2017) para 25. See also Corten (n 239) para 3.1.

[243] 'Putin is Fanning Syrian Civil War, Britain's Hammond Says' *Reuters* (1 February 2016) http://www.reuters.com/article/us-mideast-crisis-britain-idUSKCN0VA3RQ; Bannelier-Christakis (n 5) 764.

[244] See UN Doc S/PV.7777 (25 September 2016) 5–7 (United States); ibid 9 (United Kingdom); UN Doc S/PV.8171 (30 January 2018) 6 (France); ibid 7 (Netherlands); ibid 7–8 (United States). See also Corten (n 239) para 3.1. See also Chapter 4, section 2.

[245] See Chapter 2, section 3.3.2.

[246] Report of the Secretary-General on the United Nations Support Mission in Libya UN Doc S/2012/129 (1 March 2012) para 5.

a 62 per cent turnout, the NTC handed over its functions to the democratically elected General National Congress on 8 August 2012, after which the NTC was dissolved.[247] From the start the new Libyan government faced security challenges. Already in early December 2011 (when the TNC was still the *de jure* government), so-called revolutionary brigades with unclear lines of command were responsible for security incidents in Tripoli.[248] Throughout 2012 and 2013 fighting also erupted between different brigades and tribes in the south and east of the country.[249] The situation continued to deteriorate during 2014, escalating into the most serious outbreak of armed conflict in Tripoli, Benghazi, and other areas of the country since 2011. The fighting was characterized by serious violations of international human rights and humanitarian law, including the indiscriminate firing of heavy weaponry by all sides in densely populated areas.[250]

On 25 June 2014 a new Parliament was elected (the House of Representatives) which was to replace the General National Congress that had been elected in 2012.[251] In September 2014 the House of Representatives confirmed Mr Abdullah al-Thinni as Prime Minister, who had replaced Mr Ali Zeidan after a vote of no confidence in March 2014. However, certain members of the General National Congress, supported by the Muslim Brotherhood and the Islamist Libya Dawn, refused to relinquish power to the new legislative body and challenged the government.[252] At the time of his confirmation in September 2014, Mr al-Thinni had already left Tripoli for Tobruk as his government had no control over the capital.[253] The security situation was further aggravated by the presence of various tribal and *jihadist* groups, including a growing IS presence in central Libya and around Sirte.[254]

The acts of brutality by IS against civilians continued to escalate, and in February 2015 included the beheading of twenty-one Egyptian Christians.[255] This incident

[247] Report of the Secretary-General on the United Nations Support Mission in Libya UN Doc S/2012/675 (30 August 2012) paras 2, 3, 9.

[248] UN Doc S/2012/129 (1 March 2012) (n 246) paras 6, 9.

[249] UN Doc S/2012/675 (30 August 2012) (n 247) para 14; Report of the Secretary-General on the United Nations Support Mission in Libya UN Doc S/2013/104 (21 February 2013) paras 4, 7; Report of the Secretary-General on the United Nations Support Mission in Libya UN Doc S/2013/516 (5 September 2013) para 21.

[250] Report of the Secretary-General on the United Nations Support Mission in Libya UN Doc S/2014/653 (5 September 2014) para 2. See also UN Doc S/2014/131 (21 February 2013) (n 221) paras 2, 16, 19, 23. It *inter alia* drew attention to the fact that there was no meaningful progress in attempts to integrate members of the various brigades into an effective national army, or subsiding in tribal conflicts.

[251] UN Doc S/2014/653 (5 September 2014) (n 249) paras 7–8. The voter turnout was a mere 42%.

[252] UN Doc S/2014/653 (n 249) paras 12 ff; Bannelier-Christakis (n 5) 756–57.

[253] Report of the Secretary-General on the United Nations Support Mission to Libya UN Doc S/2015/144 (26 February 2015) para 7.

[254] Report of the Secretary-General on the United Nations Support Mission in Libya UN Doc S/2015/624 (13 August 2015) paras 2, 29 ff; Report of the Secretary-General on the United Nations Support Mission in Libya UN Doc S/2016/182 (25 February 2016) para 24; Report of the Secretary-General on the United Nations Support Mission in Libya UN Doc S/2016/452 (16 May 2016) para 21; Bannelier-Christakis (n 5) 757.

[255] UN Doc S/PV.7387 (18 February 2015) 2 (United Nations Support Mission in Libya); Bannelier-Christakis (n 5) 756.

resulted in a request by the internationally recognized Libyan government to Egypt for military support against terrorism.[256] In response, Egypt agreed to engage in airstrikes, in coordination with and with the approval of the Libyan government, in order to counter terrorism and enforce security.[257] The UNSC took no decision pertaining to the use of force in Libya at the time, nor did it criticize the consensual military intervention.[258] Criticism did come from Qatar, a member of the Arab League, which claimed that the Egyptian aerial attacks could give an unfair advantage to one side in the Libyan conflict.[259] Egypt rejected this argument, accusing Qatar of supporting terrorism due to its support for the Muslim Brotherhood.[260] The Arab League as a whole expressed its 'complete understanding' over the Egyptian military action.[261] The United States declared its respect for the right of countries to make their own decisions about their own self-defence,[262] thereby suggesting that Egypt's action was based on the right to individual self-defence rather than military assistance on request.

Parallel to these military developments, the UN-supported attempts to find a negotiated settlement between rivalling factions that would bring political stability to Libya resulted in the signing of the Libyan Political Agreement of 17 December 2015 in Skhirat, Morocco (Agreement). The Agreement established a nine-member Presidency Council of the Government of National Accord, headed by the Prime Minister-designate, Fayiz al-Sarraj.[263] The Agreement was subsequently endorsed by the UNSC in Resolution 2259 of 23 December 2015,[264] which also expressed support for the Government of National Accord as the sole legitimate government of Libya.[265] The Resolution, while acknowledging that the situation in Libya constituted a threat to international peace and security, did not adopt any measures under Chapter VII of the Charter. Instead, it urged member states to

[256] UN Doc S/PV.7387 (18 February 2015) 5 (Libya).

[257] UN Doc S/PV.7387 (18 February 2015) 7 (Egypt); Bannelier-Christakis (n 5) 756–57.

[258] Bannelier-Christakis (n 5) 757.

[259] 'CORRECTED UPDATE-4-Egypt, Qatar Trade Barbs in Dispute Over Libya Strikes' *Reuters* (19 February 2015) https://projects.zawya.com/UPDATE_1Qatar says_recalls_ambassador_to_Egypt_amid_dispute_over_air_strikes_in_Libya/story/TR20150219nL5N0VT06CX2/. See also Bannelier-Christakis (n 5) 758.

[260] 'CORRECTED UPDATE-4-Egypt (n 259).

[261] ibid; Bannelier-Christakis (n 5) 757.

[262] 'US "Respects Egypt's Right to Self-Defence" After Libya Airstrikes' *Egyptian Streets* (18 February 2015) http://egyptianstreets.com/2015/02/18/u-s-respects-egypts-right-to-self-defence-after-libya-airstrikes. On 13 November 2015, the United States exercised an airstrike on a compound in the city of Derna, during which a senior IS member was killed. It seems that this attack was exercised on the basis of self-defence, as the Pentagon stated that the measures were a sign of their resolve to go after IS leaders wherever they operate. See United States Department of Defence, 'Statement from Pentagon Press Secretary Peter Cook on US Strike in Libya' Press Operations Release No NR-436-15 (14 February 2015) https://www.defense.gov/News/News-Releases/News-Release-View/Article/628954/statement-from-pentagon-press-secretary-peter-cook-on-us-strike-in-libya. See also Bannelier-Christakis (n 5) 758.

[263] UN Doc S/2016/182 (25 February 2016) (n 254) para 3.

[264] UN Doc S/RES/2259 (23 December 2015) paras 1, 2.

[265] ibid para 3. See also UN Doc S/PRST/2017/26 (14 December 2017).

assist the Government of National Accord in 'responding to threats to Libyan security and to actively support the new government in defeating ISIL, groups that have pledged allegiance to ISIL, Ansar Al Sharia, and all other individuals, groups, undertakings and entities associated with al-Qaeda operating in Libya, *upon its request*'.[266] Thereafter the United States, in response to such requests, repeatedly engaged in airstrikes against IS and Al Qaida and also placed a small contingent of soldiers in Libya for this purpose.[267]

In the period since its international endorsement, the Government of National Accord has not yet succeeded in bringing political stability to Libya. While many armed groups that controlled Western Libya claimed to support the Agreement, it remains challenged by others.[268] Clashes between government forces and armed groups continued in Tripoli and throughout the country, while IS also remained active.[269] Following clashes in Tripoli between various armed groups from the region, the UN oversaw the negotiation of a ceasefire agreement in early September 2018.[270] However, in April 2019 the capital Tripoli was under siege by the forces of Khalifa Haftar's self-styled Libyan National Army, which had control over parts of Eastern Libya and enjoyed the alleged military support of Egypt, the United Arab Emirates, and Saudi Arabia.[271] In the wake of the deteriorating security situation, the United States also withdrew its contingent of soldiers based in Libya.[272]

[266] UN Doc S/RES/2259 (23 December 2015) para 12. In February 2016, NATO and twenty-three states participating in a meeting on Libya in Rome declared that it would only intervene in Libya after the formation of a government of national unity and a request from this government to NATIO to intervene. See Statement by NATO Secretary-General, Jens Stoltenberg, cited by N Guibert and G Paris, 'L'OTAN n'Interviendra Pas Sans Accord Politique National en Libye' *Le Monde* (2 February 2016) http://www.lemonde.fr/international/article/2016/02/01/libye-l-otan-n-interviendra-pas-sans-accord-politique-national_4857166_3210.html; see also Bannelier-Christakis (n 5) 758–59.

[267] United States Department of Defence, 'US Airstrikes Support Government of National Accord in Libya' *DoD News* (4 August 2016) https://www.defense.gov/News/Article/Article/905197/us-airstrikes-support-government-of-national-accord-in-libya/; France 24, AFP, AP and Reuters, 'Haftar's Forces Continue Push Into Tripoli as Libya Crisis Escalates' *France 24* (9 April 2019) https://www.france24.com/en/20190407-libya-haftar-forces-air-strike-tripoli-gaddafi-usa.

[268] UN Doc S/2016/182 (25 February 2016) (n 254) para 15; UN Doc S/2016/452 (16 May 2016) (n 254) para 8; Report of the Secretary-General on the United Nations Support Mission in Libya UN Doc S/2016/1011 (1 December 2016) para 5; C Ehrhardt and F Schmidt, 'Welche Rolle Spielt Russland im Libyschen Chaos?' *Frankfurter Allgemeine Zeitung* (4 February 2017) http://www.faz.net/aktuell/politik/ausland/unterstuetzt-putin-general-haftar-in-libyen-14835324.html.

[269] Report of the Secretary-General on the United Nations Support Mission in Libya UN Doc S/2016/182 (25 February 2016) paras 15 ff; UN Doc S/2016/452 (16 May 2016) (n 226) paras 13, 15 ff; UN Doc S/2016/1011 (1 December 2016) (n 268) paras 12 ff; Report of the Secretary-General on the United Nations Support Mission in Libya UN Doc S/2017/726 (22 August 2017) paras 2 ff.

[270] Report of the Secretary General United Nations Support Mission in Libya UN Doc S/2019/19 (7 January 2019) paras 2–3. See also UN Doc S/PV.8488 (20 March 2019) 2 (UNSG Special Representative).

[271] See P Wintour and C Stephen, 'Battle for Tripoli Escalates as Fighting Nears Libyan Capital' *Guardian* (7 April 2019) https://www.theguardian.com/world/2019/apr/07/libya-us-forces-evacuated-haftar-seeks-military-control; P Wintour 'Libya Crisis: Egypt's Sisi Backs Haftar Assault on Tripoli' *Guardian* (14 April 2019) https://www.theguardian.com/world/2019/apr/14/libya-crisis-egypt-sisi-backs-haftar-assault-on-tripoli.

[272] Wintour and Stephen (n 271).

5. Implications for the existence of a prohibition of military assistance during a civil war

The above practice of regional organizations and states reveals that military assistance on request in civil wars/NIACs since the end of the Cold War were undertaken predominantly by individual states or coalitions of individual states. In sharp contrast to the interventions by (sub)-regional organizations illuminated in section 3, those conducted by (coalitions of) individual states on the side of the government all occurred in situations where the recognized government itself was involved in a protracted civil war/NIAC. Furthermore, in the case of the CAR, Libya, Somalia, and Mali they occurred at the bequest of transitional (negotiated) governments, the representativeness of which may be as questionable as that of a beleaguered recognized government.[273] Yet, this did not deter the intervening states from accepting the respective requests for military assistance. This would also apply to France, despite its proclaimed post-Cold War policy of non-intervention in former African colonies.[274] Moreover, hardly any third state or international organization suggested that any of the forcible interventions illuminated in section 4 violated the negative equality principle or the right to self-determination, nor questioned the competence of transitional government to extend a request for military assistance.[275] The only exception was Qatar in relation to Libya, which expressed concerns about the tilting of the conflict in favour of one of the parties.[276]

[273] See Nolte (n 6) 159–60, who argues that such a transitional regime should not be engaging in decisions that would undermine or pre-empt the future, elected government.

[274] See Mitterrand (n 120).

[275] Ruys and Ferro (n 5) 82–83 find support for the negative equality principle in United Nations practice relating to Somalia in 1992 and Albania in 1997. In the case of Somalia, the UNSG, referring to the collapse of the state structures in Somalia at the time, noted that there was no government in Somalia that could request forcible intervention (Letter dated 29 November 1992 from the Secretary-General addressed to the President of the Security Council UN Doc S/24868 (30 November 1992) 3). In Albania, the country spiralled into civil turmoil in 1997, after the collapse of the pyramid investment systems. The government requested military and police assistance from a group of countries for the purpose of protecting humanitarian activities. In a letter addressed to the UNSC in March 1997, it stated that '[t]aking into consideration the situation in Albania, we feel that such a force must also have the necessary support and authorization of the Security Council of the United Nations' (Letter dated 28 March 1997 from the Permanent Representative of Albania to the UNSC Addressed to the President of the Security Council UN Doc S/1997/259 (28 March 1997) 1). On 28 March 1997 the government determined that the situation in Albania constituted a threat to international peace and security and authorized limited use of force in order to facilitate the distribution of humanitarian aid (UN Doc S/RES/1101 (28 March 1997) para 4). However, it is not clear how either of these examples would support the negative equality principle. In Somalia there was no government at all in place at the time which could extend an invitation (see UN/ Doc S/24868, 3 (30 November 1992) 3, 6.) In the case of Albania, the statement does not explain why the Albanian government regarded that UNSC involvement was deemed necessary, ie whether it was deemed necessary for legal rather than political reasons. In particular, there was no explicit reference to the negative equality principle, nor the right to self-determination.

[276] The Independent International Fact-Finding Mission on the Conflict in Georgia in 2009 also raised the negative equality principle, claiming that neither the Georgian government nor the rebels were allowed to invite outside assistance during the conflict. See Report of the Independent International Fact-Finding Mission on the Conflict in Georgia Vol II (2 September 2009) 277–78.

While Iran also objected to the legality of the military intervention in Yemen, it referred to the UN Charter in broad terms, without any explicit reference to either the negative equality principle or the right to self-determination.

This virtual absence of any explicit reliance on the negative equality principle or the right to self-determination in UNSC debates or the reactions of states and international organizations to military assistance on request of the recognized government suggests that there is no rule in general international law prohibiting such assistance during a civil war (NIAC). At this juncture it is worth recalling that the reactions of third states to practice, including inaction (in addition to oral and written statements) can amount to *opinio juris*.[277] Whether such inaction or toleration on the part of third states is an indication of their acceptance that the practice engaged in by (an)other state(s) was in accordance with rights and obligations under customary international law will depend on the circumstances of the case.[278] Factors to be taken into account in making this determination will include whether a reaction was called for under the circumstances, as well as whether the silent state(s) was/were deemed to have had knowledge of the conduct at the time and had reasonable time and ability to react.[279]

The extent to which these factors are present will in turn be influenced by others. These notably include the frequency of the disputed practice, the extent to which it was publicized, as well as whether it (adversely) affected the interests of third states.[280] If a particular practice is engaged in by several states on a regular or ongoing basis, it will become more likely that such practice affects the legal interests of other states, thereby also increasing the expectation that they should react.[281] This would be the case even more so where the practice in question was well publicized through letters addressed to UN organs or in statements adopted by these organs.[282] Where in such instances the practice in question is met with the resounding silence of third states, it is fair to conclude that this lack

However, the mission was made up by independent experts and its findings cannot outweigh state practice and *opinio juris*.

[277] That is, conduct 'undertaken with a sense of legal right or obligation', for the purpose of identifying customary international law. See ILC Report of the Work of the 68th Session UN Doc A/71/10 (2016), Chapter V, Conclusion 9(1).

[278] See also ILC Report of the Work of the 68th Session (n 277), Chapter V, Commentary to Conclusion 10(1), para 7; P Starski, 'Silence Within the Process of Normative Change and Evolution of the Prohibition on the Use of Force: Normative Volatility and Legislative Responsibility' (2017) 4 Journal on the Use of Force and International Law 26.

[279] See also ILC Report of the Work of the 68th Session (n 277), Chapter V, Commentary to Conclusion 10(1) para 7; Starski (n 278) 31.

[280] See also ILC Report of the Work of the 68th Session (n 277), Chapter V, Commentary to Conclusion 10(1) para 7; Starski (n 278) 31–32.

[281] Starski (n 278) 31; see also ILC Report of the Work of the 68th Session (n 277), Chapter V, Commentary to Conclusion 10(1) para 7.

[282] Starski (n 278) 36, 38.

of protest expresses their acceptance of the practice as being in accordance with customary international law.[283]

As far as the military interventions on invitation illuminated here are concerned, they were conducted by an increasing number of state actors across regions. In addition, these interventions were of a protracted nature and *inter alia* were announced in letters to and/or statements by the UNSC, as well as press statements. It would therefore be difficult to claim that one is dealing with isolated state practice that could have gone unnoticed by other states. If one further considers that the right to self-determination has *erga omnes* effect,[284] as a result of which the legal interests of all states were potentially affected by these interventions on request,[285] it is reasonable to conclude that third states were expected to react to these incidents of military assistance on request. The fact that states nonetheless refrained from doing so (and in particular did not express any concerns for the consequences of such assistance for right to self-determination) justifies the conclusion that they did not regard this right as legally relevant in the circumstances. Stated differently, the virtual absence of protest suggests that there is no rule in customary international law that requires states to observe negative equality during a civil war/NIAC.

Yet, several scholars submit that the tolerance by states of these interventions does not evince support for the non-existence of the negative equality requirement as such. They point out that states have never claimed a general right to extend military assistance to a recognized government during a civil war/NIAC but rather justified such assistance with reference to specific exceptions.[286] According to this line of reasoning states (implicitly) support the existence of a general prohibition to intervene in a NIAC, while recognizing that in certain exceptional instances military assistance to the recognized government is permissible, as it is not intended to influence the outcome of the conflict.[287] In relation to the interventions described in this chapter, these exceptions would notably include military assistance for the purpose of counter-terrorism and counter-intervention (ie where armed groups on a state's territory have received prior, external military assistance).[288]

At first sight, the narrative used by states and international organizations when invoking or applauding direct military assistance on request does provide some support for this reasoning. For example, the AU's Initiative against

[283] ibid 38.

[284] See Separation of the Chagos Archipelago from Mauritius, Advisory Opinion (n 6) para 180.

[285] See ILC Report of the Work of the 68th Session (n 277), Chapter V, Commentary to Conclusion 10(1) para 7, fn 316, which underscores that certain practices could be regarded as impacting almost all states.

[286] Ruys and Ferro (n 5) 88; Bannelier-Christakis (n 5) 748.

[287] Ruys and Ferro (n 5) 90, 92; Bannelier-Christakis (n 5) 745, 748. See also De Wet (n 65) 309.

[288] Ruys and Ferro (n 5) 88, 90, 92; Bannelier-Christakis (n 5) 745, 748; O Corten, 'Intervention by Invitation: The Expanding Role of the UN Security Council' 4 Max Planck Trialogues on the Law of Peace and War (forthcoming, on file with author) 9; Christakis and Bannelier (n 10) 124 ff.

the LRA concerned the elimination of an AU-classified terrorist organization.[289] Similarly, the BSA between the United States and Afghanistan explicitly mentioned the countering of terrorism as one of its purposes.[290] When Iraq requested military assistance from the international community in 2014, its letter to the UNSC specifically referred to 'the need for support in order to defeat ISIL and protect our territory and people'.[291] The Kenyan military action in Somalia was directed at countering the al-Shabaab terrorist militia attacks emanating from Somalia,[292] while France invoked counter-terrorism rhetoric in responding to the request for military assistance by Mali.[293] Subsequently, ECOWAS expressed its gratitude to France 'for having successfully launched operations, while observing Malian sovereignty and international legality, that contained the advance of terrorist and extremist groups'.[294] Also in Libya, the UNSC endorsed military support at the request of the Government of National Accord in order to counter (groups and individuals associated with) ISIL, Ansar al-Sharia, and Al Qaida.[295]

In other instances, the narrative referred to external interference on the side of armed groups, thereby alluding to counter-intervention. For example, in the case of Yemen this notably concerned references to Iranian support for the Houthi rebels.[296] In Syria several Western and Middle Eastern states have openly conceded military support to so-called moderate rebels, as illuminated in Chapter 2.[297] The claim that states therefore are 'merely' intervening in order to counter terrorism and/or for the purpose of counter-intervention—without any intention

289 AUPSC, Communiqué of the 299th Meeting, PSC/PR/COMMM (CCXCIX) (22 November 2011) paras 5, 10 http://archives.au.int/bitstream/handle/123456789/5511/2011_299_COMM_C2E.pdf?sequence=1andisAllowed=y; Report of the Chairperson of the Commission on Terrorism and Violent Extremism in Africa PSC/AHG/2(CDLV) (2 September 2014) (n 103) para 60.

290 Bilateral Security Agreement (n 123) art 2.1.

291 Letter dated 25 June 2014 from the Permanent Representative of Iraq to the United Nations Addressed to the Secretary-General UN Doc S/2014/440 (24 June 2014). See Corten (n 288) 26, who interprets this statement as an implicit reference to protection of the right to self-determination.

292 Letter dated 17 October 2011 from the Permanent Representative of Kenya to the United Nations Addressed to the President of the Security Council UN Doc S/2011/646 (18 October 2011).

293 See Identical Letters dated 11 January 2013 from the Permanent Representative of France to the UN Addressed to the Secretary-General and the President of the Security Council UN Doc S/1013/17 (11 January 2013) UN Doc S/1013/17. See also Corten (n 288) 42; Ruys and Ferro (n 5) 90.

294 Extraordinary Session of the Authority of ECOWAS Heads of State and Government 19 January 2013 http://www.ecowas.int/wp-content/uploads/2015/02/2013-Extra-Jan-Mali.pdf; for a similar response by the UNSC see UN Doc S/RES/2013 (25 April 2013). See also Corten (n 288) 45.

295 UN Doc S/RES/2259 (23 December 2015) para 12. In February 2016, NATO and twenty-three states participating in a meeting on Libya in Rome declared that it would intervene in Libya only after the formation of a government of national unity and a request from this government to NATO to intervene. See Statement by NATO Secretary-General, Jens Stoltenberg, cited by N Guibert and G Paris, 'L'OTAN n'Interviendra Pas Sans Accord Politique National en Libye' *Le Monde* (2 February 2016) http://www.lemonde.fr/international/article/2016/02/01/libye-l-otan-n-interviendra-pas-sans-accord-politique-national_4857166_3210.html; see also Bannelier-Christakis (n 5) 758–59.

296 See Statement Issued by the Kingdom of Saudi Arabia, the United Arab Emirates, the Kingdom of Bahrain, the State of Quarter and the State of Kuwait (n 213) 4. See also Chapter 6, section 2.

297 See Chapter 2, section 2.

of upsetting the negative equality principle—can come across as credible at first sight.[298]

However, closer scrutiny reveals that claims that these references to counter-terrorism and counter-intervention would merely confirm the existence of certain exceptions to a general prohibition to intervene in a NIAC is open to question. First, general international law does not oblige states to make legal claims explicitly. Instead, their right to engage in a particular conduct, such as to provide military assistance to a recognized government on request, can also be implied by or inferred from the context.[299] In this context it is noteworthy that the above-mentioned 'purposive rhetoric' has been embedded in statements that tend to recognize the rights of governments to request military assistance in rather broad terms. For example, the United States justified the French intervention in Mali in 2013 with reference to the right of the Malian authorities to seek 'what assistance they can receive'.[300] Also, in relation to Iraq's request for military assistance in 2014, Australia, France, and the United Kingdom argued that the prohibition of the use of force does not apply where a state is using force on the territory of another, if this was requested by the territorial state.[301] These justifications were not qualified by any reference to a general prohibition against military intervention on the side of the government during a NIAC, nor the need to protect the right to self-determination.

Seen in this light, the invocation of the 'purposive rhetoric' by states and the UNSC may be interpreted as having a political purpose rather than a legal one. Instead of affirming any *legal* limitations on the right of a recognized government to request military assistance during a NIAC (or the right of third states to provide such assistance), the purposive rhetoric underscores the *political* urgency for the need to provide military assistance to a recognized government in a certain context.[302] The submission that the 'purpose rhetoric' is merely of political

[298] Regarding Yemen, Corten (n 288) 15 ff finds implicit recognition of the importance of the right to self-determination in the UNSC's recognition of the Hadi government and its endorsement of a political transition process culminating in free and fair elections. See UN Doc S/RES/2140 (26 February 2014) paras 1, 10, 17 ff; UN Doc S/RES/2216 (14 April 2015) Preamble. See also UN Doc S/PV.7999 (12 July 2017) 9 (Bolivia), for a statement that the political transition must be led by the 'people of Yemen'. Bolivia also called on all parties to respect the sovereignty, independence and territorial integrity of the Republic of Yemen. See also ibid 8 (Uruguay); UN Doc S/PV.8027 (18 August 2017) 9 (Bolivia); UN Doc S/PV.8066 (10 October 2017) 6 (Bolivia).

[299] See also Starski (n 278) 32.

[300] Rice (n 194). During France's intervention in Chad in 2019, it made use of military equipment of Operation Barkhane, which can be understood as implying that the rebels from the north constituted a terrorist threat. It also referred to Chad as an ally in the fight against terrorism in the region. However, in its official justification, France primarily relied on the invitation by the Chadian government and the need to stabilize the country in broad terms. See R Moncrieff and T Lesueur, 'Rebel Incursion Exposes Chad's Weaknesses' *International Crisis Group* (13 February 2019) https://www.crisisgroup.org/africa/central-africa/chad/au-tchad-lincursion-des-rebelles-devoile-les-fragilites-du-pouvoir.

[301] (United Kingdom) Prime Minister's Office (n 153); T Abbott (Australian Prime Minister) (n 154); JY le Drian (French Minister of Defence) (n 154); Akande and Vermeer (n 41).

[302] Similarly, it is arguable that the 1990 statement by former President Mitterrand (n 120) that France is not to interfere in internal conflicts of former African colonies was of a political rather than legal nature.

relevance is also supported by the fact that there are hardly any statements by third states condemning the legality of forcible intervention on the side of a recognized government during a NIAC in situations where counter-terrorism or counter-intervention were not at issue. The most prominent example in this regard is that of the Ugandan military assistance to the government of South Sudan at the latter's request. In this instance, the Ugandan forces were first and foremost fighting political rivals of the recognized South Sudanese government that formerly formed part of the government. Yet, no state (or international organization) objected on the basis that the Ugandan intervention was as such illegal and/or that it violated the right of the South Sudanese people to self-determination.

Second, even if one accepted for the sake of argument that states (implicitly) supported a general prohibition of intervention on the side of the government during a NIAC, the application of the counter-terrorism and counter-intervention exceptions is likely to entirely erode the prohibition in practice. As far as the counter-terrorism exception is concerned, this first and foremost exception is due to the non-viability of any distinction between terrorist and 'other' opposition groups. A viable distinction in this regard depends on the existence of an agreed definition of terrorism, as well as a minimum consensus on how to apply the benchmarks of such a definition in practice. However, such consensus has yet to emerge in a decentralized international order where it first and foremost is up to states (represented by their recognized governments) to determine what constitutes terrorism.[303] As a result, it is highly likely that the recognized government of the state requesting military assistance and its allies will regard all opposition groups as terrorist movements.[304] In the absence of clear criteria of why this classification is inaccurate, it becomes very difficult to counter from a legal perspective.

This reality is particularly visible in Syria, where the Syrian government (supported by Russia) seems to consider all groups opposing government forces as terrorists.[305] Western countries for their part have been opposed to classifying moderate rebel groups as terrorists.[306] However, thus far they have been unable to

[303] A fact conceded by Ruys and Ferro (n 5) 91.

[304] Also conceded by Bannelier-Christakis (n 5) 747.

[305] See Identical Letters dated 26 January 2016 from the Chargé d'Affaires of the Permanent Mission of the Syrian Arab Republic to the United Nations Addressed to the Secretary-General and the President of the Security Council UN Doc /S2016/80 (28 January 2016). In this letter IS, the Nusrah Front, the Army of Islam, the Islamic Front, the Army of Conquest, Ahrar al-Sham, and the Free Army were all described as armed terrorist groups. See also 'Syria Crisis: Vladimir Putin Insists Russia is Only Bombing IS' *Independent* (12 October 2015) http://www.independent.co.uk/news/world/middle-east/syria-crisis-vladimir-putin-says-russia-only-wants-to-bomb-isis-as-critics-say-he-is-becoming-a6690346.html; 'Russia Rejects Criticism of Air Strikes in Syria' *Al Jazeera* (1 October 2015) http://www.aljazeera.com/news/2015/10/russia-rejects-criticism-air-strikes-syria-151001173827826.html; Bannelier-Christakis (n 5) 764, 747.

[306] See eg Council of the EU, 'Council Conclusion on Syria' (12 October 2015) para 10 http://www.consilium.europa.eu/en/press/press-releases/2015/10/12-fac-conclusions-syria/; 'Putin is Fanning Syrian Civil War, Britain's Hammond Says' *Reuters* (1 February 2016) http://www.reuters.com/article/us-mideast-crisis-britain-idUSKCN0VA3RQ.

explain how the notion of 'moderate' is defined and which particular group would fulfil these criteria at any given point in time. For example, the FSA (the military wing of the Syrian Opposition Coalition which has been supported by states opposing the Assad regime) have worked with the al-Nusrah which was subsequently designated as an Al Qaida affiliate by the UNSC.[307] Would this collaboration not justify elevating all members of the FSA to terrorists and if not, why not? Such uncertainties make it difficult, if not impossible, to classify a particular opposition group as 'legitimate' or 'moderate' in the sense of being non-terrorist.[308]

Furthermore, even in situations where the UNSC has provided certainty by classifying groups such as Al Qaida, IS, or the al-Nusrah Front as terrorist movements, this is not the end of the matter.[309] None of these resolutions granted the UNSC the exclusive right to identify terrorist groups in relation to the conflict in question. Stated differently, it has not denied the respective recognized government or third states the right to identify additional terrorist groups as a manifestation of their sovereignty. In fact, Resolution 2259 (2015) pertaining to Libya may even be read as encouraging states to do so, when urging them to assist 'the Government of National Accord in responding to threats to Libyan security and to support the new government in defeating IS, *groups that have pledged allegiance to IS, Ansar al-Sharia and all other individuals, groups, undertakings and entities associated* with al-Qaeda operating in Libya, upon its request'.[310] The sweeping references to groups and/or individuals in alliance with terrorist groups gives the Libyan government and its allies a very broad discretion in identifying terrorist groups which may effectively result in classifying all opposition groups as such.[311] As a result, any recognition of a counter-terrorism exception to the prohibition of military intervention on the side of the government in a NIAC effectively amounts to an erosion and, therefore, de facto abolition of the general prohibition (to the extent that it indeed existed).[312]

If one now turns to the counter-intervention exception, it transpires that it is equally likely to erode any general prohibition of military intervention on the side of the recognized government. Those supporting this exception claim that where armed groups on a state's territory have received prior, external military assistance during a NIAC, this undermines the ability of the people of the state to determine their political future without external interference. In consequence, the recognized government may request military assistance in an attempt to uphold or restore the

[307] UNSC Press Release, UN Doc SC/11010 (30 May 2013); Gray (n 121) 165.

[308] De Wet (n 65) 310.

[309] See Bannelier-Christakis (n 5) 748 who emphasized that during the French intervention in Mali in 2013, all groups targeted by France were classified as terrorist by the UNSC. Similarly, in the case of Syria, Iraq, and Libya, the UNSC had identified IS, the Al-Nusrah Front, and Al Qaida as terrorist organizations.

[310] UN Doc S/RES/2259 (23 December 2015) para 12 (emphasis added).

[311] De Wet (n 65) 310–11.

[312] De Wet (n 65) 311.

right to self-determination by requesting military assistance from third states.[313] Supporters of the counter-intervention exception further distinguish between external military assistance to armed groups that would trigger the right to individual or collective self-defence in article 51 of the UN Charter, on the one hand, and foreign support to such groups that remains below this threshold, on the other.[314] In the latter instance (so the argument goes), the external support to armed opposition groups may nonetheless justify a request by the recognized government for military assistance in order to restore the rights of the people to determine their political future without external interference.[315]

As will be illuminated in Chapter 6, the extent of foreign involvement required for triggering article 51 of the UN Charter seems to have been lowered significantly in recent years. As a result, the right to collective self-defence could be invoked as a parallel, separate ground for requesting the military assistance of third states in an increasing range of situations. This development in and of itself casts doubt on the relevance of the right to self-determination in the context of counter-intervention. If one accepts that it is increasingly difficult to identify any type of foreign support to armed groups that would remain below the threshold of an armed attack, it becomes equally difficult to identify situations in which counter-intervention for the purpose of upholding or restoring self-determination remains relevant. Moreover, even if one accepted that there still is an identifiable category of foreign support to armed groups that remains below the threshold of article 51 of the UN Charter, it is highly unlikely that any request by the recognized government for military assistance to counter such assistance will have the effect of upholding or restoring the right to self-determination of the people of that state.

First, it is very difficult to verify whether claims of prior intervention on the side of armed groups is accurate or fabricated by governments in order to justify requests for military assistance.[316] Recognized governments could therefore easily abuse the counter-intervention argument to gain the upper hand in a NIAC. Second, if the purpose of the counter-intervention is to restore the rights of the people within a state to determine their political future without external interference, the extent of the military support provided to the recognized government arguably has to remain proportionate to external support received by the armed groups.[317] Stated differently, in order for counter-intervention to uphold or restore the right to self-determination, it should not go beyond neutralizing the impact of the prior external intervention on the side of the armed opposition groups.[318]

313 Corten (n 288), 9; Ruys and Ferro (n 5) 93. See also the United Kingdom Foreign Policy Document No 148 (n 1) para II. 7, 616.
314 Ruys and Ferro (n 5) 92.
315 Corten (n 7) 301; Ruys and Ferro (n 5) 92–93.
316 Ruys and Ferro (n 5) 93.
317 ibid.
318 ibid.

Anything else would facilitate the shifting of the balance of the conflict towards the recognized government, thereby eroding the general prohibition of intervention in a NIAC of all meaning.[319]

Yet, in practice it will be very difficult to identify any limits to the permissible (proportionate) assistance to the recognized government, as the extent of the prior, external assistance to armed groups is likely to remain covert and very difficult to measure. This in turn makes it very difficult to determine whether the scope of military assistance provided to the recognized government has become disproportionate, in the sense that it has upset the balance of the conflict. In consequence, governments would be provided with an open door to abuse the counter-intervention exception in a manner that erodes any general prohibition to receive military assistance during a NIAC.

6. Conclusion

This analysis has shown that post-Cold War state and organizational practice does not convincingly support the claim that direct military assistance at the request of a recognized government is prohibited during a civil war, otherwise known as a NIAC. Attempts to explain current state practice by means of counter-terrorism and counter-intervention exceptions to a general prohibition of such assistance also is not grounded in state or organizational practice, nor are such exceptions viable in practice. Instead, state and organizational practice seem to confirm the right of recognized governments to request military assistance from third states, also during civil wars/NIACs, as long as they retain their recognized, *de jure* status. The potential lack of 'representativeness' in such a situation does not seem to limit the extent to which the *de jure* government can act on behalf of the state (and its people) in matters pertaining to the use of force.

This in turn suggests that the right to self-determination does not pose any meaningful limitation to the right of the recognized government to request military assistance as such, nor to third states for providing such assistance. From a policy perspective, this reality is a source of concern as it may serve as an encouragement for befriended, authoritarian governments to sustain one another militarily and quell any form of resistance for as long as they are able to generate military support from one another. In addition, a right of beleaguered governments to request military assistance—without any need for consideration of the right to self-determination—may facilitate neo-colonization. States weakened by years of armed conflict are unlikely to be in a position to decline any 'offers' of military assistance from (comparatively) strong states with hegemonic ambitions. This

[319] Ruys and Ferro (n 5) 94.

in turn may result in an extended, foreign military presence that exercises decisive influence over decisions of the *de jure* government. This risk is further enhanced by the fact that, as will be illuminated in Chapter 5, it is very difficult to establish in practice whether the consent underpinning a request for military assistance was not given freely (ie was coerced).

4

Direct Military Assistance to Incumbent Governments Implicated in Violations of International Humanitarian and/or Human Rights Law

1. Introduction

A further question meriting exploration is whether the 'international law pedigree' of the requesting (territorial) state potentially affects the validity of such request. Notably, the question arises as to whether third states are prohibited from sending their armed forces to requesting states implicated in widespread violations of international humanitarian and human rights law. If the answer were no, it would essentially imply that the validity of the consent extended by an incumbent government for such military assistance would depend on whether it honoured its international obligations in terms of international humanitarian and human rights law. Article 3 of the Resolution on Military Assistance by Request of the Institut de Droit International (IDI) 2011[1] has stimulated this debate, in as far as it claims that the 'sending of armed forces by one state to another state upon the latter's request' is prohibited if it is in violation of 'generally accepted standards of human rights'.[2] This statement may be read in various ways. First, it can be understood as meaning that the troops of the intervening (assisting) state themselves must adhere to international human rights standards when exercising force at the request of the territorial (recipient) state. Stated differently, the intervening state must refrain from conduct that will directly trigger state responsibility under international human rights law. This, for example, would include the wilful killing of civilians or the commission of torture during military operations in the assisted state.[3]

[1] *Institut de Droit International* (IDI), Resolution on Military Assistance on Request (8 September 2011) arts 1(a) and (b) http://www.idi-iil.org/idiE/navig_res_chon.html. For its earlier work on the same topic, see IDI, Resolution on the Principle of Non-Intervention in Civil Wars (14 August 1975) art 1 http://www.idi-iil.org/idiE/resolutionsE/1975_wies_03_en.pdf. This chapter builds on the article by E de Wet, 'Complicity in the Violations of Human Rights and Humanitarian Law by Incumbent Governments through Direct Military Assistance on Request' (2018) 67 International and Comparative Law Quarterly (2018) 287–314.

[2] IDI (n 1) art 3.

[3] V Lanovoy, *Complicity and Its Limits in the Law of International Responsibility* (Hart Publishing 2016) 6. Examples of direct violations of international humanitarian law by the intervening state would

However, article 3 of the IDI 2011 Resolution could also be interpreted as prohibiting direct military assistance that would result in the aiding or assisting of human rights violations by the recipient state. In situations of forcible assistance on request, such derivative responsibility would be incurred where the intervening state aids or assists any of the above-mentioned acts (or other violations of international human rights law by the assisted state).[4] The drafting history of the IDI 2011 Resolution does not clarify whether article 3 indeed also encompasses this second interpretation, as the issue of state responsibility did not feature during the debates.[5] Yet, the possibility of aiding and assisting gross violations of international human rights and humanitarian law in the context of direct military assistance on request is real, as the provision of direct military support by one state to another implies close cooperation on various levels. In the interests of a coherent military strategy within the same geographical space, such support is very likely to be accompanied also by the sharing of intelligence, coordination of military operations, and the provision of other operational support. Therefore, regardless of the scope of applicability of article 3 of the 2011 IDI Resolution,[6] the question of whether an intervening state can incur responsibility for the international human rights and humanitarian law violations of the territorial state merits attention. Furthermore, the consequences of the incurrence of state responsibility under such circumstances need to be assessed. In particular, the question arises as to whether an intervening (assisting) state will have to withdraw its troops and/or military air power from the inviting (territorial) state in order to avoid any further derivative state responsibility for violations of human rights and/or humanitarian law by the latter.

The current chapter will explore these questions pertaining to the incurrence and consequences of derivative state responsibility of an intervening state for the violations of international human rights and humanitarian law of the territorial

include the indiscriminate targeting of civilians by the assisting state during military operations, which can occur either through the use of weapons, which in themselves are indiscriminate, or by the indiscriminate use of lawful weapons. See Protocol Additional to the Geneva Conventions of 12 August 1949, and Relating to the Protection of Victims of International Armed Conflicts (adopted 8 June 1977) 1125 UNTS art 51(2). See B Finucane, 'Partners and Legal Pitfalls' (2016) 92 International Law Studies 412.

[4] G Nolte and HP Aust, 'Equivocal Helpers—Complicit States, Mixed Messages and International Law' (2009) 58 International and Comparative Law Quarterly 5. In addition, there may be individual criminal responsibility for state agents under international criminal law. See H Moynihan, 'Aiding and Assisting: Challenges in Armed Conflict and Counterterrorism' (November 2016) Chatham House Research Paper, 7 https://www.chathamhouse.org/sites/files/chathamhouse/publications/research/2016-11-11-aiding-assisting-challenges-armed-conflict-moynihan.pdf. See also C Gray, 'The Limits of Force' (2016) 367 Collective Courses of The Hague Academy of International Law 175.

[5] See G Nolte, 'The Resolution of the *Institut de Droit International* on Military Assistance on Request' (2012) 45 Revue Belge de Droit International 253, 260.

[6] According to IDI (n 1) art 2, the Resolution does not apply to situations of non-international armed conflicts (NIACs). If the Resolution indeed were not to apply to NIACs, most current situations of direct military assistance on request of incumbent governments would fall outside of its scope.

state. In so doing, the analysis will be informed by case law and doctrine relating to derivative responsibility for such violations through conduct stopping short of direct military support. For example, derivative responsibility for international human rights and humanitarian law violations may arise as a result of the supply of arms, intelligence, financial resources, or training provided to an incumbent government embroiled in an armed conflict.[7] This was vividly illustrated in the recent case of *The Queen (on the Application of the Campaign Against Arms Trade) v the Secretary of State for International Trade* (*CAAT* case) in the United Kingdom.[8] Moreover, the general framework of the principles of complicity (as the aiding and assisting of internationally wrongful acts are often referred to),[9] as well as the implications of this framework for direct military assistance on request will constitute the point of departure for the analysis. Central to this framework is article 16 of the 2001 Articles on Responsibility of States for Internationally Wrongful Acts (ASR) of the International Law Commission (ILC),[10] which represents the customary international law standard pertaining to responsibility for aiding and assisting an internationally wrongful act.[11]

The responsibility regime comprised by article 16 ASR is of a residual nature and becomes applicable in the absence of more specific obligations (*lex specialis*).[12]

[7] For example, the transfer of conventional weapons from one state to another could trigger state responsibility if the assisting state was aware that the arms would be used to attack civilians or civilian objects. See Arms Trade Treaty (adopted 2 April 2013) 52 International Legal Materials 988 art 6; see also Finucane (n 3) 419.

[8] *The Queen (on the Application of the Campaign Against Arms Trade) v the Secretary of State for International Trade* (*CAAT* case) [2019] EWCA Civ 1020. This was an appeal against the High Court's decision in *The Queen on the Application of Campaign Against Arms Trade v The Secretary of State for International Trade* [2017] EWHC 1726 (QB) (hereinafter the *CAAT High Court* case). See also *L'association sans but lucratif Coordination Nationale D'action Pour La Paix et la démocratie and l'association sans but lucratif Ligue des Droits Humains v la Région wallonne*, Belgian Council of State, Administrative Section, 15th Chamber, Decision No 244.804 (June 2019).

[9] See Lanovoy (n 3) 41–42.

[10] 'ILC Draft Articles on Responsibility of States for Internationally Wrongful Acts with Commentaries' (ASR) (2001) II Yearbook of the International Law Commission ILC; and UN Doc A/Res/56/83 (28 January 2002) art 16.

[11] The customary status of art 16 ASR (n 10) has been confirmed in the *Case Concerning Application of the Convention on the Prevention and Punishment of the Crime of Genocide (Bosnia and Herzegovina v Serbia and Montenegro)* (Merits) [2007] ICJ Rep 43 para 420. In *Al-M* (5 November 2003) 2 BVerfGE 1506/3 [47], the German Federal Constitutional Court was confronted with a case where Germany was accused of aiding the United States in luring a Yemeni citizen to Germany by trickery, after which the person faced an extradition request to the United States. The Court determined that if there indeed were an international rule against trickery, Germany would be liable in accordance with art 16 ARS. See M Jackson, *Complicity in International Law* (OUP 2015) 151; ILC ASR (n 10) para (7); Moynihan (n 4) 6; Nolte and Aust (n 4) 7. See also HP Aust, *Complicity and the Law of State Responsibility* (CUP 2011) 113 ff for a discussion of situations in which states buttressed their argumentation with art 16 ASR.

[12] This remains the case regardless of whether one regards art 16 ASR as a primary or secondary rule of international law (a distinction which in itself is controversial). On the one hand, art 16 ASR resembles a primary rule as it does not merely address the consequences of a wrongful act, but extends responsibility for that act to the assisting state. On the other hand, it has the characteristics of a secondary rule as the wrongfulness of the assisting state's conduct is derived from the wrongfulness of the conduct of the receiving state. See Nolte and Aust (n 4) 8; Moynihan (n 4) 2, 7. See also Jackson (n 11) 149–50 who argues that art 16 ASR is a primary rule.

As in the case of direct responsibility, the requirements for derivative state responsibility for aiding and assisting an internationally wrongful act is determined first and foremost by any applicable, specialized treaty obligations binding on the states in question.[13] The regime contained in article 16 ASR also implies a higher threshold for incurring responsibility through aiding or assisting an internationally wrongful act than most obligations under international humanitarian or human rights law treaties.[14] As a result, it is unlikely that it will be the decisive rule determining whether state responsibility is incurred by an intervening state for aiding or assisting an illegal act of the inviting state. Instead, the more far-reaching specialized rules stemming from widely ratified international humanitarian or human rights law treaties are more likely to be decisive in this regard.[15]

For example, the due diligence obligations in human rights treaties often impose far-reaching precautionary measures, as can be illustrated by the case of *El-Masri v The Former Yugoslav Republic of Macedonia*.[16] The European Court of Human Rights (ECtHR) determined that the Macedonian authorities actively facilitated the detention of the applicant by handing him over to the US Central Intelligence Agency, although they ought to have been aware of the risk of maltreatment that might result from this transfer.[17] While the ECtHR also referred to article 16 ASR,[18] its decision first and foremost turned on the specialized obligations in the European Convention on Human Rights (ECHR), such as those relating to the prohibition of torture.[19] Such facilitation of detention and transfer of prisoners can also occur during forcible military assistance on request, where the intervening state assists in the arrest and detention of members of opposition groups and subsequently hands them over to the inviting state. This, in turn, could

[13] Aust (n 11) 383; Moynihan (n 4) 28; NHB Jørgensen, 'Complicity in Torture in a Time of Terror: Interpreting the European Court of Human Rights Extraordinary Rendition Cases' (2017) 16 Chinese Journal of International Law 22.

[14] See Aust (n 11) 383, 417, who describes art 16 ASR as the 'red line' for incurring responsibility for aiding or assisting the 'point of no return'.

[15] Aust (n 11) 390–91, 417.

[16] Lanovoy (n 3) 211.

[17] *El-Masri v The Former Yugoslav Republic of Macedonia*, App No 39630/09, ECtHR Judgment of 13 December 2012 (GC) paras 180–223; Lanovoy (n 7) 2011. Similarly, art III(e) of the Convention on the Prevention and Punishment of Genocide (adopted 9 December 1948) 278 UNTS 1021 (Genocide Convention) constitutes an example of a specialized regime. Although this provision focuses on the punishing of individuals who were involved in genocide, the ICJ has concluded that the acts enumerated in art III (which include complicity to genocide) could also trigger state responsibility.

[18] *El Masri* decision (n 17) para 97.

[19] See also *Al Nashiri v Poland*, App No 28761/11, ECtHR Judgment of 24 July 2014 (Former Fourth Section); *Husayn (Abu Zubaydah) v Poland*, App No 7511/13, ECtHR Judgment of 24 July 2014 (Former Fourth Section); and *Nasr and Ghali v Italy*, App No 44883/09, ECtHR, Judgment of 23 February 2016 (Fourth Section). While the ECtHR did make general references to art 16 ASR, it did not integrate its benchmarks into its analysis. Therefore, it is difficult to ascertain whether and to what extent art 16 ASR informed the ECtHR's decision. See Jørgensen (n 13) 31. See *Bosnia Genocide* decision (n 11) para 166. See also Aust (n 11) 383; Lanovoy (n 3) 225-26; Moynihan (n 4) 28.

trigger due diligence and other specialized obligations contained in human rights treaties binding on the intervening state, leaving little room for a central role for article 16 ASR.[20]

Even so, article 16 ASR remains a useful analytical tool as it can serve as a vehicle to inform the interpretation of any specialized regime on international responsibility, including that of international human rights and humanitarian law.[21] Furthermore, the high threshold requirements contained in article 16 ASR as such underscore the relevance of the questions addressed in this chapter. If even these high threshold requirements for derivative responsibility can be triggered by the type of military assistance rendered during forcible interventions by invitation, intervening states will have to consider what measures to take in order to prevent any further derivative responsibility under such circumstances.

An additional relevance lies in the fact that the principles underpinning article 16 ASR have also influenced the responsibility framework applicable to international organizations, as article 14 of the 2011 Draft Articles on the Responsibility of International Organizations (DARIO)[22] effectively mirrors the content of article 16 ASR.[23] The ILC Commentary underscored that the rules applicable between states in relation to responsibility for aiding and assisting should also apply where international organizations aid or assist a state[24] or another international organization in the commission of an internationally wrongful act, despite the limited practice specifically relating to international organizations.[25] The importance of

[20] See B Oswald, 'Interplay as Regards Dealing with Detainees in International Military Operations' in E de Wet and JK Kleffner (eds), *Convergence and Conflicts of Human Rights and International Humanitarian Law in Military Operations* (Pretoria University Law Press 2014) 76 ff.

[21] Lanovoy (n 3) 204.

[22] ILC, 'Draft Articles on the Responsibility of International Organizations, with Commentaries 2011' (2011) II Yearbook of the International Law Commission (DARIO).

[23] Art 14 DARIO (n 22) determines: 'An international organization which aids or assists a state or another international organization in the commission of an internationally wrongful act by the state or the latter organization is internationally responsible for doing so if (a) the organization does so with knowledge of the circumstances of the internationally wrongful act; and (b) the act would be internationally wrongful if committed by that organization.'

[24] ILC, Commentary to art 14 (n 22) paras (1) and (6). In 2009 the United Nations Legal Council raised concerns about the military support which the United Nations Organization Mission in the Democratic Republic of the Congo (MONUC) provided to the *Forces armées de la République démocratique du Congo* (FARDC), as the latter was suspected of involvement in violations of international humanitarian, human rights law and refugee law. According to the United Nations Legal Council, it would be illegal for MONUC under customary international law to provide logistical support to any FARDC operation, if MONUC had reason to believe that the FARDC was involved in such violations.

[25] Art 58 DARIO (n 22) determines: '1. A state which aids or assists an international organization in the commission of an internationally wrongful act by the latter is internationally responsible for doing so if (a) the state does so with knowledge of the circumstances of the internationally wrongful act; and (b) the act would be internationally wrongful if committed by that state. 2. An act by a state member of an international organization done in accordance with the rules of the organization does not as such engage the international responsibility of that state under the terms of this article.' Art 58(2) protects member states of an organization against responsibility for merely following the rules of the organization, for example, if a state exercises voting rights in accordance with the rules of the organization that would not as such amount to responsibility for aiding and assisting an unlawful act of the organization. The member state nonetheless remains responsible for its own actions that aid and assist in an

this 'spill-over effect' of article 16 ASR *inter alia* lies in the fact that international organizations such as the United Nations (UN), the African Union (AU), and the European Union (EU) are not (yet) bound by treaty obligations pertaining to international humanitarian and human rights law.[26] As a result, the general (customary) framework for derivative international responsibility may in future prove to be highly relevant in situations where either the international organization provides aid or assistance in the commission of an internationally wrongful act, or receives aid or assistance for such purpose.[27]

In order to provide context to an assessment of the threshold requirements pertaining to article 16 ASR and the consequences of its triggering, section 2 will first give a cursory overview of recent situations where invited states were rendering direct military assistance to incumbent governments implicated in widespread international human rights and humanitarian law violations. Section 3 for its part examines the benchmarks of article 16, as well as questions of whether its requirements equally apply in situations of serious violations of peremptory obligations of international law. Thereafter, section 4 assesses the legal consequences in case the responsibility framework of article 16 ASR is triggered. It questions in particular whether this would require the withdrawal of direct military support by the intervening (assisting) state.

2. Recipient governments implicated in widespread violations of human rights and humanitarian law

Chapter 3 elaborated on the various requests by incumbent governments for direct military assistance on request since the end of the Cold War. Closer scrutiny reveals that in those instances where the requests were extended during an armed conflict, the requesting government has almost always been implicated in widespread violations of humanitarian and/or human rights law. These typically (although by no means exclusively) include the wilful killing or indiscriminate targeting of civilians, torture, and conflict-related sexual violence. For example, in Afghanistan, government forces are currently receiving military support from the United States in their battle against the Taliban and Islamic State in Iraq and the Levant (IS) on the basis of a bilateral security agreement (BSA) signed on 30 September 2014.[28]

internationally wrongful act of an organization. This could, for example, be the case where a state provided operational support to an international organization that led a military operation resulting in the violation of international humanitarian law. See Lanovoy (n 3) 123–24.

[26] Lanovoy (n 3) 6.

[27] ibid. According to J Crawford, *State Responsibility: The General Part* (CUP 2013) 411–12, art 58 DARIO represents progressive development and minimal practices exist in relation to this article.

[28] See Chapter 3, section 4.1. See also the *Security and Defence Co-operation Agreement between the Islamic Republic of Afghanistan and the United States of America of 30 September 2014* (Bilateral

The Afghan forces have been criticized for an escalation in civilian casualties since 2015 due to the indiscriminate use of mortars and rockets during ground operations in civilian-populated areas.[29] In addition, approximately one-third of detainees in Afghan detention centres have reportedly been subjected to torture, while unofficial detention centres also continue to function.[30]

In Iraq, since August 2014 a US-led coalition has been undertaking airstrikes against the IS at the request of the Iraqi government.[31] Throughout this period, the UN and human rights organizations have expressed concern about continued reports of human rights violations perpetrated by armed groups associated with the Iraqi security forces, as well as elements of the Peshmerga and affiliated groups.[32] Iraqi forces and paramilitary groups have *inter alia* been accused of torture and unlawful killings of Sunni Arab men as a form of reprisal in their battles to free cities such as Falluja and Tikrit from IS.[33] In Somalia, Kenyan airstrikes against al-Shabaab between October 2011 and February 2012 took place at the invitation of the Somali government, in accordance with a joint Communiqué adopted by the two countries on 18 October 2011.[34] Subsequent to the adoption of UN Security Council (UNSC) Resolution 2036 of 22 February 2012, the Kenyan military

Security Agreement/BSA) http://mfa.gov.af/Content/files/BSA%20ENGLISH%20AFG.pdf. Aerial attacks by the United States at the request of the Afghan government at times have directly resulted in civilian casualties. For example, in October 2015 an erroneous aerial attack on a hospital run by *Médecins Sans Frontières* resulted in sixty-seven casualties. See Report of the Secretary-General, The Situation in Afghanistan and its Implications for International Peace and Security, UN Doc A/70/601–S/2015/942 (10 December 2015) paras 29–30. See also Report of the Secretary-General, The Situation in Afghanistan and its Implications for International Peace and Security, UN Doc A/71/616–S/2016/768 (7 September 2016) para 19.

29 Report of the Secretary-General, The Situation in Afghanistan and its Implications for International Peace and Security, UN Doc A/70/601-S/2015/942 (10 December 2015) para 29; Report of the Secretary-General, The Situation in Afghanistan and its Implications for International Peace and Security, UN Doc S/2016/1049 (13 December 2016) para 29. See also Human Rights Watch, 'Afghanistan events of 2015' *World Report: Afghanistan* (2016) https://www.hrw.org/world-report/2016/country-chapters/afghanistan. In August 2015 President Ghani issued orders to assess operational procedures and to take steps to reduce civilian casualties.

30 The National Directorate of Security (NDS) reaffirmed an order prohibiting torture in June 2015. However, it remains unclear whether and to what extent any of these cases was investigated and prosecuted. See Human Rights Watch (Afghanistan) (n 29).

31 See Chapter 3, section 4.2. See also the White House, 'Statement of the President' (7 August 2014) http://www.whitehouse.gov/the-press-office/2014/08/07/statement-president; see also K Bannelier-Christakis, 'Military Interventions Against ISIL in Iraq, Syria and Libya, and the Legal Basis of Consent' (2016) 29 Leiden Journal of International Law 751.

32 Report of the Secretary-General Pursuant to Resolution 2299 (2016) UN Doc S/2016/897 (25 October 2016) para 46; A Dewan, 'Amnesty International: Iraqi Forces Must Not Repeat "War Crimes" in Mosul Offensive' *CNN* (18 October 2016) http://edition.cnn.com/2016/10/18/middleeast/iraq-mosul-amnesty-international/.

33 Dewan (n 32). The Iraqi Prime Minister, Haider al Abadi, as well as the Kurdistan Regional Government (KRG) have stated that they have established procedures to investigate the allegations. A KRG spokesman further submitted that some officials had been punished for human rights violations.

34 See Chapter 3, section 4.3. See also Joint Communiqué issued at the Conclusion of a Meeting between the Government of Kenya and the Transitional Federal Government of Somalia of 18 October 2011, paras 1 and 2 http://graphics8.nytimes.com/packages/pdf/world/joint-communique-kenya-somalia.pdf.

operations were formally integrated into the African Union Mission in Somalia (AMISOM) under Chapter VII of the UN Charter.[35] Large-scale human rights violations, including those by government forces and AMISOM, were reported in the period before the Kenyan forces were integrated into AMISOM, as well as thereafter. These included continuous reports of rape and sexual violence against internally displaced women and girls, including those acts committed by transitional federal government soldiers.[36]

In January 2013 France intervened militarily in Mali in response to a request for assistance by the interim President of the Republic of Mali, Dioncoundra Traoré, in order to counter terrorist elements that had taken control over the northern part of the country.[37] During the time of the French intervention in Mali, the UN continued to receive allegations of serious human rights violations in the north in which the Malian armed forces were also implicated.[38] In their campaign to retake the north, Malian soldiers engaged in summary executions, enforced disappearances, and torture against suspect Islamist rebels and alleged collaborators, as well as arbitrary arrests and looting of private property.[39]

As far as the armed conflict in South Sudan is concerned, the Ugandan People's Defence Force (UPDF) was almost from the outset assisting the government of South Sudan militarily at the latter's request.[40] This presence continued until after the conclusion of the Agreement on the Resolution of the Conflict in the Republic of South Sudan on 17 August 2015.[41] The conflict has been marked by human rights abuses on all sides. For example, government and opposition forces have targeted and killed hundreds of civilians, often because of their ethnicity, and have pillaged

[35] See African Union Mission to Somalia (AMISOM) http://amisom-au.org/kenya-kdf/.

[36] Military operations by Kenyan and Ethiopian forces in late 2011 and early 2012 also directly resulted in civilian casualties. See Secretary-General, Report of the Secretary-General on Somalia, UN Doc S/2012/283 (1 May 2012) paras 68 and 70.

[37] See Chapter 3, section 4.5. See also Identical Letters dated 11 January 2013 from the Permanent Representative of France to the United Nations addressed to the Secretary-General and the President of the Security Council, UN Doc S/2013/17 (14 January 2013); see also Bannelier-Christakis (n 31) 859.

[38] Human Rights Watch, 'Mali: Events of 2013' *World Report* (2014) https://www.hrw.org/world-report/2014/country-chapters/mali.

[39] Report of the Secretary-General, Report of the Secretary-General on the Situation in Mali, UN Doc S/2013/338 (10 June 2013) para 35; Report of the Secretary-General, Report of the Secretary-General on the Situation in Mali, UN Doc S/2013/582 (1 October 2013) paras 36 ff; Human Rights Watch (Mali) (n 38).

[40] See Chapter 3, section 4.4. President Museveni of Uganda, at the invitation of President Salva Kiir, sent troops across the border shortly after fighting had broken out between forces loyal to President Kiir and rebels in December 2013. The countries signed a Status of Forces Agreement between the Government of the Republic of Uganda and the Government of the Republic of South Sudan of 10 January 2014 http://www.sudantribune.com/IMG/pdf/status_of_forces_agreement-2.pdf.

[41] The Agreement on the Resolution of the Conflict in the Republic of South Sudan of 17 August 2015 http://www.gurtong.net/LinkClick.aspx?fileticket=CytVwytJdyM%3Dandtabid=124. This Agreement was steered by the Intergovernmental Authority on Development (IGAD) and signed by the two warring parties and another breakaway SPLM faction, the G10. See F Nicolaisen, T Heggli Sagmo, and O Rolandsen, 'South Sudan—Ugandan Relations. The Cost of Peace' African Centre for the Constructive Resolution of Disputes (ACCORD) (23 December 2015) http://www.accord.org.za/conflict-trends/south-sudan-uganda-relations/.

and destroyed civilian property as well as engaged in torture.[42] Government forces were also accused of conflict-related sexual violence in areas under their control.[43] These violations have continued despite the adoption of the ceasefire in 2015.[44]

The pervasive violations of humanitarian and human rights law by all parties in the Syrian conflict have ranged from torture, extra-judicial killings, sexual violence, and the indiscriminate targeting of civilians to the use of barrel bombs and chemical weapons and attacks on medical and educational facilities.[45] Since 30 September 2015, Russia has been engaged in airstrikes in support of the Syrian government that were directed against IS as well as other anti-government forces.[46] Similarly, Iran has reportedly sent up to 3,000 troops to Syria in support of the Assad regime.[47] Both Russia and Iran have justified their military presence in Syria with a request by President Assad to assist in combating IS and other terrorist groups in Syria.[48] The United Kingdom and the United States have openly accused Russia of complicity in the Assad regime's aerial attacks on hospitals and civilian targets.[49]

In Libya, successive governments have requested military assistance against IS and other groups that have since 2015 been posing a threat to security.[50] Violations

[42] Human Rights Watch, 'South Sudan: Events of 2014' World Report (2015), https://www.hrw.org/world-report/2015/country-chapters/south-sudan. In one incident, government forces rounded up between 200 and 400 Nuer men and a day later massacred all but 13.

[43] Secretary-General, Report of the Secretary-General on South Sudan, UN Doc S/2014/821 (18 November 2014) para 43.

[44] Special Report of the Secretary-General on the Review of the Mandate of the United Nations Mission in South Sudan, UN Doc S/2016/951 (10 November 2016) paras 14 ff; S Jones, 'UN Report: South Sudan Allowed Soldiers to Rape Civilians in Civil War' *Guardian* (11 March 2016) https://www.theguardian.com/global-development/2016/mar/11/south-sudans-soldiers-allowed-to-rape-civilians-civil-war-says-un-government-torture. See also UN Doc S/RES/2206 (3 March 2015) Preamble; UN Doc S/RES/2223 (28 May 2015) paras 22 ff; UN Doc S/RES/2252 (15 December 2015) para 25; UN Doc S/RES/2327 (16 December 2016) paras 22 ff.

[45] See eg UN Human Rights Council, First Report of the Independent International Commission of Inquiry on the Syrian Arab Republic, UN Doc A/HRC/S-27/2/Add.1 (23 November 2011) paras 51 ff; Seventh Report of the Independent International Commission of Inquiry on the Syrian Arab Republic, UN Doc A/HRC/25/65 (12 February 2014) paras 21 ff; Report if the Secretary-General, Implementation of Security Council resolutions 2139 (2014), 2165 (2014), 2191 (2014), 2258 (2015), 2332 (2016), 2393 (2017), 2401 (2018) and 2449 (2018) UN Doc S/2019/508 (19 June 2019) paras 12 ff.

[46] UN Doc A/HRC/31/68 (Advanced Edited Version) (11 February 2016) paras 19 and 28. See also Human Rights Council, 'They Came to Destroy: ISIS Crimes Against the Yazidis' UN Doc A HRC/32/CRP.2 (15 June 2016) para 191.

[47] Bannelier-Christakis (n 31) 760.

[48] See Chapter 3, section 4.7. See also Letter dated 15 October 2015 from the Permanent Representative of the Russian Federation to the United Nations Addressed to the President of the Security Council, UN Doc S/2015/792 (15 October 2015) 2; H Rohani, 'La lutte contre le terrorisme doit être la base de tout en Syrie' *Le Monde* (29 January 2016) http://www.lemonde.fr/international/article/2016/01/29/hassan-rohani-la-lutte-contre-le-terrorisme-doit-etre-la-base-de-tout-en-syrie_4855748_3210.html; see also Bannelier-Christakis (n 31) 760-61.

[49] Record of UNSC Meeting 7777 (25 September 2016), UN Doc S/PV.7777, 5–7 (United States); ibid 9 (United Kingdom); J Algot, 'Boris Johnson: Russian Complicity in War Crimes Precludes Syria Talks' *Guardian* (20 October 2016).

[50] See Chapter 3, section 4.8. See also Record of UNSC Meeting 7387 (18 February 2015), UN Doc S/PV.7387, 5 (Libya); UN Doc S/RES/2259 (23 December 2015) para 12. In February 2016 NATO and twenty-three states participating in a meeting on Libya in Rome declared that it would only intervene in Libya after the formation of a government of national unity and a request from this government to

of international humanitarian and human rights law by all sides and groups have been reported before and after these requests.[51] All sides have been accused of abductions and the unlawful killing of civilians who were targeted for their political opinions, affiliations, and family or tribal identity.[52] Arbitrary detention and torture reportedly occurred across the country in official detention centres as well as in one centre run by armed groups.[53]

Noteworthy is also the case of Yemen, where since 26 March 2015 Saudi Arabia has been leading an intensive aerial campaign against the Houthi insurrection at the invitation of the Hadi government.[54] In this instance, the allegations of direct violations of international human rights and humanitarian law by the intervening states have attracted extensive international attention. These *inter alia* included aerial attacks on a civilian market, a civilian funeral hall, hospitals, and water facilities.[55] The military coalition was criticized for failing to take all precautions to minimize civilian targets as required by international humanitarian law, causing disproportionate harm to civilian objects, and failing to distinguish between military and civilian targets.[56] In addition, ground operations in Yemen under the effective control of the United Arab Emirates resulted in forced disappearances of (suspected) members of terrorist groups.[57]

It is striking that in none of the above-mentioned cases did the human rights track record of the inviting state prevent the invited states from accepting the request for military assistance. In addition, criticism by third states relating to such military assistance was limited to the manner in which the military assistance was exercised and/or its implications for a political settlement. This is exemplified

NATO to intervene. See statement by NATO Secretary-General, Jens Stoltenberg, cited by N Guibert and G Paris, 'L'OTAN n'interviendra pas sans accord politique national en Libye' *Le Monde* (2 February 2016) http://www.lemonde.fr/international/article/2016/02/01/libye-l-otan-n-interviendra-pas-sans-accord-politique-national_4857166_3210.html; See also Bannelier-Christakis (n 31) 758–59.

[51] Report of the Secretary-General, Report of the Secretary-General on the United Nations Support Mission in Libya, UN Doc S/2016/1011 (1 December 2016) para 33. For human rights violations during 2014 and 2015, see Office of the United Nations High Commissioner for Human Rights, Investigation by the Office of the United Nations High Commissioner for Human Rights on Libya, UN Doc A/HRC/31/47 (15 February 2016) paras 16 ff.

[52] Report of the Secretary-General on the United Nations Support Mission in Libya (n 46) paras 37 and 43.

[53] ibid paras 39 ff.

[54] See Chapter 3, section 4.6. See also M Nichols, 'UPDATE 1—Yemen Asks UN to Back Military Action by "Willing Countries"' *Reuters* (24 March 2015) http://uk.reuters.com/article/yemen-security-un-idUKL2N0WQ29620150324.

[55] Final Report of the Panel of Experts on Yemen, S/2017/81 (31 January 2017) paras 119 and 126 ff; *CAAT High Court* case (n 8) paras 64 ff.

[56] European Parliament, Resolution on the Situation in Yemen (2015/2760(RSP), 9 July 2015 (AB B(EP)1-B(EP) 6).

[57] Final Report of the Panel of Experts on Yemen (n 55) para 132 ff; EM Lederer, 'UN Experts Say Saudi Coalition Violated International Humanitarian Law in Yemen Attack' *Independent* (21 October 2016) http://www.independent.co.uk/news/world/middle-east/un-saudi-arabia-yemen-air-strikes-violated-international-law-a7372936.html.

by the reaction of Western states to Russia's intervention in Syria, which accused Russia of direct violations of international humanitarian law, as well as aiding and assisting such violations by the Syrian government.[58] Even so, the criticism stopped short of suggesting that the invitation for direct military support (or the acceptance of the invitation) as such was illegal under international law.[59] Stated differently, state practice at first sight does not support the conclusion that the human rights record of the inviting government (or that of the invited state) would in and of itself form a legal barrier under international law to extending or accepting an invitation for forcible intervention.[60]

However, this is not the end of the matter. As indicated at the outset of this chapter, there is also the question of whether an intervening state can incur derivative responsibility for aiding or assisting internationally wrongful acts by the territorial state, as well as which consequences would result from such responsibility. The analysis now turns to these questions.

3. Threshold requirements of article 16 ASR

Article 16 ASR determines:

> A state which aids or assists another state in the commission of an internationally wrongful act by the latter is internationally responsible for doing so if—
> (a) the state does so with knowledge of the circumstances of the internationally wrongful act; and
> (b) the act would be internationally wrongful if committed by that state.[61]

In order for the responsibility regime of article 16 ASR to be triggered, several requirements need to be fulfilled. The first is that the responsibility of the assisting

[58] See Record of UNSC Meeting 7777 (25 September 2016) UN Doc S/PV.7777, 5–7 (United States); ibid 9 (United Kingdom); Algot (n 49). See Record of UNSC Meeting 8055 (25 September 2017) UN Doc S/PV.8055 9 (Russia) for criticism of the political wisdom of the United States military strategy in Afghanistan.

[59] See also Chapter 3, section 4.7.

[60] An exception would arguably exist where a requesting state was committing genocide against a group on its territory and requested a third state for direct military assistance for this purpose. In such an instance any acceptance of the request would amount to a treaty conflicting with a peremptory norm of general international law, in the sense of art 53 of Vienna Convention on the Law of Treaties, 23 May 1969, 1155 UNTS 331 (VCLT). In consequence, such a treaty would be null and void. For example, had the Hutu government requested another state for direct military assistance during the Rwandan genocide of 1994, any acceptance of such a request would have been in contravention of art 53 VCLT. See G Nolte, *Zur völkerrechtlichen Zulässigkeit des Einsatzes fremder Truppen im internen Konflikt auf Einladung der Regierung* (Springer 1999) 359. Regarding art 53 of VCLT, see generally K Schmalenbach, 'Article 53. Treaties Conflicting with a Peremptory Norm of General International Law ("*Jus Cogens*")' in O Dürr and K Schmalenbach (eds), *Vienna Convention on the Law of Treaties. A Commentary* (2nd edn, Springer 2018) 965 ff.

[61] ILC, art 16 ASR (n 10).

state cannot be engaged independently from the illegal conduct of the recipient state. The second is that such conduct must also be wrongful under international law had it been committed by the assisting state itself. Third, the assisting state must have provided actual assistance. Fourth, there has to be some causal link (nexus) between the aid and assistance rendered and the internationally wrongful act. Finally, the assisting state must have provided the aid or assistance with the knowledge of the (pending) internationally wrongful conduct and must have had the intention to facilitate it.

Article 16 ASR is not concerned with the responsibility incurred by the recipient state for an internationally wrongful act but with the responsibility for assisting that state to commit an internationally wrongful act.[62] It concerns ancillary responsibility arising from the fact that a state facilitated a wrongfully committed act by another state. Under article 16 ASR, state responsibility turns on collaborative conduct and cannot be engaged independently of the breach of international law by the recipient state.[63] Therefore, it is only engaged once the illegal act of the recipient state has occurred. If the assisted act either does not occur or does not amount to an internationally wrongful act, no responsibility arises for the assisting state.[64]

Moreover, as reflected by article 16(b) ASR, the assisting state's responsibility will only become relevant if the act performed by the recipient state would also have been illegal if performed by the assisting state.[65] This requirement protects assisting states against independent responsibility for breaches of obligations resulting from treaties to which they are not party. In essence, it is a reaffirmation of the third party principle in treaty law (*pacta tertiis*), in accordance with which a treaty does not create rights or obligations for third states without their consent.[66] However, many of the illegal acts that recipient governments are typically accused of during non-international armed conflicts (NIACs), such as torture, the wilful killing of civilians, and indiscriminate targeting, *inter alia*, are prohibited by Common Article 3 of the four Geneva Conventions of 1949, which have been ratified almost universally.[67] Therefore, it is unlikely that the *pacta tertiis* principle would pose a major hurdle for triggering article 16 ASR in the context of military assistance on request.

As far as the actual assistance provided is concerned, most authors seem to agree (although grudgingly) that the assistance provided has to be undertaken through actions attributable to the assisting state and that it does not include the aiding of

[62] Moynihan (n 4) 7; V Lowe, 'Responsibility for the Conduct of Other States' (2002) 101 Journal of International Law and Diplomacy 5.
[63] Moynihan (n 4) 29.
[64] ibid.
[65] ILC Commentary to art 16 ASR (n 10) para (6); Moynihan (n 4) 10; Jackson (n 11) 162.
[66] Moynihan (n 4) 10; Jackson (n 11) 162.
[67] The status of ratifications of the four Geneva Conventions of 1949 on the laws and customs of war are available at https://ihl-databases.icrc.org/applic/ihl/ihl.nsf/vwTreaties1949.xsp.

omissions.[68] This may be inferred from the ILC Commentary to article 16 ASR which contains no reference to an example where responsibility for complicity is incurred on the basis of an omission.[69] Also, the International Court of Justice (ICJ) in the *Bosnia Genocide* decision determined that complicity always requires that positive action has been taken to furnish aid or assistance to the perpetrators.[70] Authors have cautioned against reading too much into this statement, as it first and foremost concerns article III of the Genocide Convention which establishes the grounds for individual criminal liability in the case of genocide. It does not necessarily have to apply to article 16 ASR which embodies customary international law in relation to complicity by states.[71] Moreover, including omission in the scope of the responsibility regime of article 16 ASR would improve the coherence of the ASR, since their definitions of internationally wrongful acts include both acts and omissions.[72]

Nevertheless, despite these criticisms it is fair to conclude that the assistance contemplated by article 16 ASR does not (yet) extend to omissions. The type of acts to be provided is not defined in article 16 ASR and can include a broad range of activities of varying gravity.[73] In instances of forcible assistance on request, the sending of troops and/or air power is likely to be accompanied by tactical, technical, and operational assistance, the provision of military equipment or arms, as well as the sharing of intelligence with the inviting state's military. Depending on the circumstances, any combination of these acts could trigger the ancillary responsibility of the intervening state.

3.1 Nexus between the aid or assistance provided and the internationally wrongful act

The responsibility regime foreseen in article 16 ASR requires a link between the aid or assistance provided by the assisting state and the internationally wrongful act subsequently committed by the recipient state. However, there is considerable uncertainty in international law as to the required proximity of this link.[74] The ILC Commentary to article 16 ASR notes that the assistance need not be essential to the

[68] J Crawford, *State Responsibility: The General Part* (CUP 2013) 404–05. Both Aust (n 12) 209 and 226 and Jackson (n 11) 155–56 are critical of the dominant position and suggest that complicity through omission is plausible.

[69] Aust (n 11) 226–27.

[70] *Bosnia Genocide* decision (n 11) para 432.

[71] Jackson (n 11) 155; Aust (n 11) 226. It is also worth mentioning that in *Prosecutor v Jean Paul Akayesu*, Case No ICTR-96-4-T (2 September 1998) para 548, Trial Chamber I of the International Criminal Tribunal for Rwanda suggested that aiding and abetting in international criminal law can consist of an omission.

[72] Lanovoy (n 3) 97.

[73] Lanovoy (n 3) 95; Moynihan (n 4) 7; Jackson (n 11) 153; Aust (n 11) 129.

[74] Moynihan (n 4) 9; Aust (n 11) 195, 217.

performance of the internationally wrongful act but that it has to contribute 'significantly' to the act.[75] On the one hand, it seems clear that aid or assistance that is indeed essential for the performance of the internationally wrongful act would effectively amount to co-responsibility for the internationally wrongful act.[76] For example, the supply of combat units for military patrols that results in the targeting of civilians or medical facilities may amount to co-responsibility for internationally wrongful acts, rather than mere aid or assistance in the commitment thereof.[77] This may particularly be the case where an assisting partner emphasizes the jointness of a particular military operation that results in internationally wrongful acts, as it thereby acknowledges the operation as its own and assumes responsibility for its consequences.[78]

On the other hand, the challenge remains to identify the non-essential aid or assistance that would be sufficiently 'significant', that is, to overcome the *de minimis* threshold implied by this requirement.[79] The case of *Rasheed Haje Tugar v Italy* before the former European Commission of Human Rights illustrates the difficulties that arise in this context.[80] The applicant was injured by an anti-personnel mine of Italian origin while participating in a mine-clearing operation in Iraq in an area that was heavily mined during the Iran–Iraq war in 1985. According to the applicant, the export of anti-personnel mines by Italy to Iraq in the absence (at the time) of an effective arms transfer licensing system in Italy violated article 2 of the ECHR. He submitted that such export had exposed him to harm by 'indiscriminate' weapons that did not contain any self-detonating or self-neutralizing system, as well as the 'indiscriminate' use of such weapons by Iraq, a country with a notoriously poor human rights record.[81] However, the European Commission of Human Rights held that there was no 'immediate relationship between the mere supply, even if not properly regulated, and the possible indiscriminate use thereof by a third state'.[82]

While this decision turned on the specific obligations contained in article 2 of the ECHR, it can also illuminate the challenges in determining the content of a 'significant contribution' to an internationally wrongful act in terms of article 16

[75] ILC Commentary to art 16 ASR (n 10) paras (1) and (5). See also Jackson (n 11) 158; Moynihan (n 4) 8; Aust (n 11) 197, 210; Lanovoy (n 3) 97.

[76] Moynihan (n 4) 9; Aust (n 11) 195, 217. A further consequence of the *sine qua non* test would be to absolve the main actor from any responsibility for the international wrongful act, as the emphasis on the causal impact could shift most of the responsibility to the assisting state.

[77] Aust (n 11) 220.

[78] ibid; S Talmon, 'A Plurality of Responsible Actors – International Responsibility for Acts of the Coalition Provision Authority in Iraq' in P Shiner and A Williams (eds), *The Iraq War and International Law* (Hart Publishing 2008) 220.

[79] Lowe (n 62) 5; Lanovoy (n 3) 184, 185.

[80] *Rasheed Haje Tugar v Italy* (Admissibility) [1995] ECHR (First Chamber), App No 22869/93 Ser 83-A 26; Lanovoy (n 3) 173.

[81] *Rasheed Haje Tugar* decision (n 80).

[82] ibid 29; Lanovoy (n 3) 173.

ASR.[83] It raises the question of whether a 'significant contribution' implies that a particular act of assistance has to have a direct (ie immediate) causal link with a specific wrongful act.[84] More specifically in the context of the use of direct military force on request, the question arises as to whether the mere presence of the troops of the intervening state in certain parts of the conflict-ridden territorial state would establish a direct causal link. After all, it does provide the government troops with the opportunity to concentrate their capacity on, for example, reprisals against civilians in other parts of the country. Alternatively, would the intervening troops have to provide more concrete assistance, such as the sharing of intelligence which the territorial state then uses in reprisals against civilians who are (ethnically) related or politically sympathetic to members of rebel movements?[85] If so, how close should the relationship between the concrete assistance and the principal wrongful act be? If the provision of intelligence had been essential for identifying the relatives or sympathizers, one arguably would be dealing with a situation of co-responsibility. If the information was not essential for the identification but nonetheless accelerated it, would this constitute a significant contribution to (or even an immediate relationship with) the internationally wrongful act of the principal actor? Furthermore, how—if it all—does the fact that various other actors, such as armed groups, were also involved in the reprisals affect the nexus between the aid and assistance and the internationally wrongful conduct of the assisted state?[86]

There is support in literature for the position that a clear factual link between the aid or assistance and the principal wrongdoing should suffice to engage article 16 ASR, as any other test would make the nexus requirement in article 16(a) unworkable.[87] However, given the limited state practice as well as decisions by international courts and tribunals in this regard, the nature of the nexus between the aid or assistance and the wrongful conduct of the principal actor remains unsettled.[88]

3.2 Knowledge of the circumstances

Article 16(a) requires that the assisting (intervening) state must have had knowledge of the circumstances of the internationally wrongful act. This requires the presence of the mental elements of knowledge and intent (discussed separately in

[83] Lanovoy (n 3) 173.
[84] ibid 174.
[85] Aust (n 11) 130.
[86] Lanovoy (n 3) 174.
[87] ibid 174, 218.
[88] In *R (Al-Haq) v Secretary of State for Foreign and Commonwealth Affairs* (Judgment) [2009] EWHC 1910 (Admin) para 7, a court in the United Kingdom dismissed a claim pertaining to art 16 ASR as non-justiciable. The organization al-Haq, based in Ramallah, brought a claim for judicial review of the UK's arms trade policy with Israel, in light of the January 2009 human rights violations committed in Palestine. Al-Haq claimed that the UK's continued trading of military equipment with Israel violated the former's customary obligations under art 16 ASR. See also Lanovoy (n 3) 175.

the sections below).[89] As far as the knowledge requirement is concerned, the text of article 16(a) ASR explicitly refers to knowledge as a component of the mental element.[90] The type of knowledge at issue concerns specific illegality in the sense that the assisting state must be aware that the assistance it is providing will contribute to the commission of (a) specific internationally wrongful act(s).[91] This raises questions as to the level of specificity of the knowledge that is required as well as when this knowledge has to become known to the assisting state or an entity whose conduct is legally attributable to it.[92] For example, it is not clear whether the specificity requirement would be satisfied if the intervening state merely knows that its military assistance will lead to reprisals against civilians by the territorial state or, in the alternative, whether the intervening state also has to have knowledge of the particular (group of) individuals that will be targeted, and whether it even has be familiar with the modalities of the execution.[93]

Also, the assisting state must have advance knowledge of the likely consequences of its assistance.[94] Where an intervening state had actual prior knowledge of the fact that the territorial state intended to use the military assistance for acts such as wilful killing of or reprisals against (a specific group of) civilians, the knowledge requirement in article 16 ASR will clearly have been fulfilled.[95] However, it is more difficult to determine whether the knowledge requirement has been fulfilled in situations where the factual situation is uncertain or disputed, as article 16 ASR does not contain a constructive knowledge component.[96] It does not determine that an assisting state should have inquired—prior to providing any assistance—into the specific purposes for which the recipient state intends to use it.[97]

As a general rule, the principle of good faith in international law implies that a state may provide aid or assistance to another in the belief that it would be used for legal purposes.[98] States may assume that other subjects of international law

[89] Moynihan (n 4) 8.
[90] ILC Commentary to art 16 ASR (n 10) para (4); Moynihan (n 4) 11.
[91] Moynihan (n 4) 11; Crawford (n 61) 407. In the *Bosnia Genocide* decision (n 11) para 421, the ICJ referred to art 16 ASR when considering the complicity provision in the Genocide Convention (n 17). The Court noted that Serbia had not known that genocide was being committed by the Bosnian Serb army, since Serbia was not aware of the specific intent of the forces concerned.
[92] Moynihan (n 6) 11, 24.
[93] Lanovoy (n 3) 227.
[94] Moynihan (n 4) 11.
[95] ibid 13.
[96] ibid 12; Lanovoy (n 3) 100.
[97] Moynihan (n 4) 13, 15; Aust (n 11) 235–36; Lanovoy (n 3) 22. This point was reaffirmed during debates pertaining to art 14 of the DARIO (n 22), where it was emphasized that 'actual' and not presumed knowledge was required. See ILC, 'Responsibility of International Organizations, Comments and Observations Received from International Organizations' (14 February 2011) UN Doc A/CN.4/637, 28 (World Bank); see also ILC, 'Comments and Observations Received from Governments' (2001) UN Doc A/C.6/54/SR.22, 52 (United Kingdom; United States). See also the *Bosnia Genocide* decision (n 11) para 421. The ICJ determined that in the case of genocide, complicity at least required knowledge of the specific intent of the principal perpetrator. This suggests actual knowledge, which is a stricter requirement than 'should have known'. See also Jørgensen (n 13) 31.
[98] ILC, Commentary to art 16 ASR (n 10) para (4); Lowe (n 62) 10; Lanovoy (n 3) 99–100.

with whom they interact in the course of events will act in accordance with good faith.[99] Accordingly, there is no general obligation on states to keep themselves informed of legislative and constitutional developments in other states with which they have dealings,[100] nor does a state have to stay abreast of the international obligations of other states with which it maintains relations (something which in practice also would be very difficult to do).[101] As a result, it is unlikely that the knowledge requirement would be fulfilled if an intervening state is unaware that intelligence or operational support provided to the territorial state in the course of the military intervention will be abused to target innocent civilians who, for example, happen to be related to or acquainted with members of the rebel group.[102]

Commentators nonetheless support the view that the knowledge requirement would be met by virtual certainty that a particular wrongful conduct will occur in the ordinary course of events.[103] For example, long-standing prior cooperation between the assisting and recipient states can have an impact on the knowledge of the assisting state of any wrongful intentions of the recipient state,[104] as does geographical proximity.[105] In addition, the knowledge may be assessed in light of public statements, diplomatic exchanges, official policies of the relevant organs of the recipient state, as well as its general patterns of conduct.[106] Information about a state's record regarding human rights and humanitarian law may also be available in the public domain via media reports and the investigations of international organizations and non-governmental organizations (NGOs).[107] If credible and readily available reports of fact-finding commissions, independent monitors or international organizations such as the UN draw attention to systematic violations of international humanitarian or human rights law by the recipient states, actual knowledge on the part of the assisting state can be assumed.[108] Under these circumstances, the assisting state will have to make prior inquiries into the specific purposes for which its assistance will be used by the recipient state.[109] Anything else would amount to wilful blindness; that is, 'a deliberate effort by the assisting state to avoid knowledge of illegality on the part

99 Lanovoy (n 3) 174, 234.
100 ibid 253.
101 ibid.
102 Moynihan (n 4) 12. See also Lowe (n 62) 6 who noted that the mere possibility that assistance will be used for unlawful acts does not suffice as such a possibility always exists in principle.
103 Statement of the Netherlands (2001) II Yearbook of the International Law Commission 52; Crawford (n 61) 406; Lowe (n 62) 8; Moynihan (n 4) 13; Aust (n 11) 233–35; Lanovoy (n 3) 100.
104 Lanovoy (n 3) 227.
105 *Bosnia Genocide* decision (n 11) para 430; Lanovoy (n 3) 238.
106 Lanovoy (n 3) 100, 227.
107 ibid 101, 238. See also *The Temple of Preah Vihear (Cambodia v Thailand)* (Merits) [1962] ICJ Rep 6, 22–23, which emphasized the relevance of the publicity and communication of information (in this instance maps).
108 Moynihan (n 4) 14; Jackson (n 11) 162.
109 Moynihan (n 4) 15; Jackson (n 11) 162.

of the state being assisted, in the face of credible evidence of present or future illegality'.[110]

However, the difficulty in determining the threshold for virtual certainty or wilful blindness (which may be seen as two sides of the same coin) is illustrated by the recent *CAAT* case in the United Kingdom concerning arms exports to Saudi Arabia.[111] While the decision dealt with the domestic application of specialized rules under international law pertaining to the arms trade, it may also be instructive for interpreting the knowledge criterion (in the form of virtual certainty or wilful blindness) in article 16 ASR. At issue was whether the UK government had to cease the granting of new arms export licences to Saudi Arabia. This was due to 'a clear risk that the arms might be used in the commission of serious violations of international humanitarian law' by the Saudi-led coalition in Yemen.[112] In addition to exporting arms, the United Kingdom also provided military training and liaison to the Saudis and had considerable insight into the military systems and practices of Saudi Arabia.[113] Having become aware of concerns about Saudi Arabia's approach to international humanitarian law in Yemen, the UK government had engaged extensively with Saudi Arabia in order to improve its military processes and approach in Yemen.[114] It further monitored developments in Yemen on an ongoing basis through a variety of sources.[115] The UK government ultimately concluded that a clear risk had not (yet) been established that the exported arms would be used for serious violations of international humanitarian law.[116]

The High Court, which in the first instance decided the case, accepted that the UK's conclusion was 'rational' (reasonable), which was the public law yardstick it had to apply.[117] More precisely, the High Court accepted that it was rational for

[110] Moynihan (n 4) 13; Lanovoy (n 3) 253. The longer the violations of international law by the recipient states continue, the more likely it is that the assisting state is aware of the wrongful conduct and is turning a blind eye. See also Jackson (n 11) 162.

[111] *CAAT High Court* case (n 8) paras 64 ff; E Wilmshurt, 'Testing Jackson's Discussion of State Responsibility in the Context of Government Assistance. Book Discussion' *EJIL:Talk!* (13 April 2017) https://www.ejiltalk.org/author/elizabethwilmshurst/.

[112] *CAAT High Court* case (n 8) paras 1, 4, 6. The applicable law concerned secs 8 and 9(3) of the Export Control Act 2002. Sec 9, in particular, incorporated European Council Common Position 2008/944/CFSP (The Common Rules Governing the Control of Exports of Military Technology and Equipment), as well as obligations under the Arms Trade Treaty (n 8).

[113] Some UK staff members are located in the Saudi Arabian military headquarters in a liaison capacity, in order to obtain information about targeting procedures. However, they were not involved in any direct way in selecting targets, although they have advised the Saudi Arabian government on targeting. The United Kingdom has also trained the Saudi Arabian military personnel on compliance with international humanitarian law, and provided logistical and technical support. See also *CAAT High Court* case (n 8) para 121; Wilmshurt (n 111). See First Joint Report of the Business Innovation and Skills and International Development Committees of Session 2016–17, The Use of UK-Manufactured Arms in Yemen. Response of the Secretaries of State for International Trade, Defence and International Development (November 2016).

[114] *CAAT High Court* case (n 8) paras 126 ff.

[115] ibid paras 150 ff.

[116] ibid paras 208(7)–(8).

[117] ibid para 25.

the UK government to conclude that the Saudi-led coalition was not deliberately targeting civilians; that Saudi Arabia had put in place procedures to secure respect for international humanitarian law; that Saudi Arabia was investigating instances of alleged violations; and that it had remained highly constructive in its dialogue with the United Kingdom.[118] In reaching its conclusion, the High Court underscored the complex nature of the assessment which required specialized diplomatic and military expertise.[119] It also regarded the involvement of senior UK officials (such as the Secretary of State) in the decision-making process as evidence of a rigorous assessment process.[120] The High Court further emphasized the qualitative difference between the risk analysis undertaken by government agencies and that of third parties, such as NGOs. Whereas government agencies can draw on highly sophisticated intelligence that is often confidential, NGOs and other independent experts have to rely on much more limited, often second-hand sources.[121]

However, the conclusion that the Secretary of State had acted rationally was subsequently overturned on appeal. Specifically, the Court of Appeal regarded the Secretary of State's process relating to future risk assessment as irrational for not having sufficiently considered Saudi Arabia's past and present respect for international humanitarian law.[122] In so doing, the Court of Appeal took cognizance of the wealth of available information and evidence, on the basis of which bodies such as the UN have determined the commission of systematic violations of international humanitarian law by the Saudi-led coalition.[123] The Court of Appeal acknowledged that the UK government did consider the evidence in each case where a concern about the violation of international humanitarian law was raised.[124] It also did not doubt that the UK's assessment of Saudi Arabia's observance of international humanitarian law was rigorous and multi-layered.[125] Yet, this assessment stopped short of determining (or attempting to determine) whether a pattern of breaches of international humanitarian law had been established.[126] In the absence of such an assessment (or at least an attempt thereto), the Secretary of State was not in a position to reach a rational conclusion as to whether the training and other support provided by the United Kingdom or the high-level assurances by the Saudi Arabian authorities would have any effect on the latter's future observance of international humanitarian law.[127] Also, if the assessment confirmed that systematic

[118] ibid paras 129, 135.
[119] ibid para 31.
[120] ibid paras 209, 210.
[121] ibid para 180.
[122] ibid paras 49, 57, 145.
[123] ibid para 62.
[124] ibid para 136.
[125] ibid.
[126] ibid paras 138, 141. According to the Court of Appeal, it was clear from the facts that the question could have been answered in respect of many, if not most, of the incidents that had featured in the arguments before it.
[127] *CAAT Court of Appeal* case (n 8) 144.

violations of international humanitarian law continued despite these efforts, this would constitute a major consideration when determining whether Saudi Arabia had the genuine intent and capacity to live up to its international humanitarian law commitments in future.[128]

That being said, the Court of Appeal was also at pains to state that it was not concerned with the merits of the position taken by the United Kingdom in undertaking the risk assessment, but by the process.[129] In particular, it was not suggesting that a finding of 'historic' (ie systematic) violations of international humanitarian law necessarily implied a clear risk that exported military technology or equipment would in future be implicated in serious violations of international humanitarian law. Whether this was the case remains within the (considerable) discretion of the executive branch.[130] It can therefore not be excluded that the Secretary of State in future will again reach the conclusion that no clear risk had been established that exported military technology and equipment would be used for serious violations of international humanitarian law. Even if it were found that such violations had been committed in the recent past, there might be factual circumstances that support the conclusion that a repetition of such violations in future is unlikely.

If one by analogy applied the reasoning of the Court of Appeal to article 16 ASR, one can conclude that virtual certainty or wilful blindness implies a high level of certainty about the factual situation of each case. This certainty is not in and of itself provided by credible allegations available in the public domain pertaining to violations of international humanitarian and/or human rights law by the recipient government. Such allegations on the one hand would oblige the assisting state to assess whether systematic violations of international and/or human rights law had been committed by the recipient state. In addition, the assisting state will have to take any affirmative findings into consideration when assessing the likeliness that the recipient state will in future live up to its international humanitarian and/or human rights obligations. On the other hand, depending on the facts of the case, the assisting state might still come to the conclusion that any further systematic violations by the recipient state would be unlikely. In particular, it might still be able to conclude that, due to a range of circumstances (such as additional oversight measures), no clear risk has been established that any military assistance provided to the recipient state would be used for the commission of such violations. Stated differently, neither the fact that information in the public domain necessitates an investigation (risk assessment) into the use of its aid or assistance by the recipient

[128] ibid. The decision of the Belgian Council of State (n 8), which annulled arms export licences by the Walloon government to Saudi Arabia, also turned on the manner in which the government came to its decision. In particular, the decision of the Walloon government did not formally motivate whether it had carefully considered the attitude of Saudi Arabia towards international terrorism, the nature of its international alliances and its respect for international law.

[129] *CAAT Court of Appeal* case (n 8) para 56.

[130] ibid paras 144, 145.

state, nor a finding that it is implicated in systematic violations of international humanitarian and/or human rights law, would necessarily imply 'actual knowledge' on the part of the assisting state.

3.3 Intent

In addition to the knowledge requirement, article 16 ASR also requires wrongful intent on the part of the assisting state.[131] Although the text of article 16(a) does not refer to intent, the ILC Commentary claims that a state is not responsible for aid or assistance under article 16 unless the relevant state organ intended to facilitate the occurrence of the wrongful conduct.[132] The ILC Commentary thus clearly supports an element of intent in order to trigger article 16 ASR,[133] even though the general approach of the ASR is opposed to requiring fault or wrongful intent as a criterion for engaging state responsibility.[134] This deviation from the objective responsibility regime by introducing a subjective (cognitive) element may be regarded as necessary to prevent too broad a responsibility for complicity.[135] However, this in turn raises the question of what the benchmarks of this subjective element are and what the relationship is between intent and knowledge.

According to one line of reasoning, the intent requirement requires a desire to reach a particular outcome.[136] This argument is based on the ICJ's interpretation of complicity in accordance with article III(e) of the Genocide Convention,[137] combined with the assumption that this reasoning is equally applicable to the notion of complicity in article 16 ASR.[138] According to the ICJ, conduct can only be treated as aid or assistance to genocide if the person or organ, at the very least, had acted knowingly in the sense that it had to be aware of the specific intent of the principal wrongdoer.[139] The ICJ found a lack of intent on the part of Serbia, because of the fact that the resources in possession of the principal perpetrators of genocide resulted from a general policy of aid or assistance which was not specifically addressed towards facilitating the crime of genocide.[140] The ICJ also took cognizance

131 Lanovoy (n 3) 101.
132 ILC Commentary to art 16 ASR (n 10) para (5); Finucane (n 4) 417; Lanovoy (n 3) 101.
133 Aust (n 11) 172; Moynihan (n 4) 18; Crawford (n 61) 407–08.
134 See Aust (n 11) 235–36, 241 ff, who notes some of the criticisms against the intent requirement in the context of state responsibility. These, *inter alia*, include the difficulty in attributing psychological requirements to states that in the abstract do not have a will of their own. Also, where the assisting state's intent is inferred from its conduct, this state would bear the onus of proving that it did not have any intent to aid or assist an internationally wrongful act. Proving 'a negative' may be very difficult to do. Similarly, Lanovoy (n 3) 101.
135 Lanovoy (n 3) 221.
136 ibid 230; see *Bosnia Genocide* decision (n 11) para 419.
137 Genocide Convention (n 17).
138 Lanovoy (n 3) 230.
139 *Bosnia Genocide* decision (n 11) para 421; Lanovoy (n 3) 231.
140 *Bosnia Genocide* decision (n 11) para 422; Lanovoy (n 3) 232.

of the fact that the decision of the Bosnian Serb leaders to commit genocide had been taken only shortly before it was carried out. Even if Serbia had known that mass atrocities were about to be committed, it was not aware of the specific intent (*dolus specialis*) of the principal perpetrator of genocide at the time the assistance was rendered.[141]

Whether this high threshold attached to intent is also applicable to article 16 ASR is debatable. The ICJ was first and foremost interpreting the notion of complicity in relation to a specialized regime, namely, that of genocide.[142] The high burden of proof required in this instance is a result of the gravity of the internationally wrongful act in question. It does not necessarily mean that the customary notion of complicity in article 16 ASR contains a similarly high threshold in relation to the specificity of the intent and the temporal proximity between the assistance given and the commission of the wrongful act.[143] If this stringent threshold were to apply to article 16 ASR, this would imply that its intent requirement would not have been fulfilled where a state committed an internationally wrongful act with aid from another state that was aware of the specific pending wrongful act by the principal actor, but did not desire this outcome. This, in turn, would make article 16 ASR almost unworkable, as proving that a desired outcome indeed was intended by an assisting state could be very difficult. For example, where it depended on information that is exclusively controlled by the assisting state and which it will not disclose, it would not be possible to prove intent.[144]

As a result, there is support in scholarship for interpreting intent as the flipside of knowledge.[145] In line with this reasoning, actual knowledge of the fact that the recipient state will act illegally in the ordinary course of events will amount to intent.[146] This would further imply that knowledge in the form of virtual certainty or wilful blindness would simultaneously establish intent.[147] The fact that the assisting state did not desire a particular outcome (in the form of an internationally wrongful act) would not be decisive for establishing intent, but rather whether it knew that its assistance would be used for illegal purposes.[148] However, if the

[141] At the crucial time, it could not be established that the FRY supplied aid or assistance to the forces of Republika Srpska knowing that such assistance would be used to commit genocide. *Bosnia Genocide* decision (n 11) para 423; Lanovoy (n 3) 232.

[142] Lanovoy (n 3) 231.

[143] ibid 231, 232.

[144] ibid 229, 232; see also *Corfu Channel* (*United Kingdom v Albania*) (Merits) [1949] ICJ Rep 4, 18.

[145] Lanovoy (n 3) 221.

[146] See Moynihan (n 4) 19 who draws an analogy between individual criminal responsibility under international criminal law and state responsibility under art 16 ASR. While such analogies need to be handled with care, a logic similar to that of art 16 ASR is displayed in art 30(2) of the Statute of the International Criminal Court (adopted 17 July 1998) 2187 UNTS 38544. It determines that 'a person has intent where (a) in relation to conduct, that person means to engage in the conduct; (b) in relation to a consequence, that person means to cause that consequence or is aware that it will occur in the ordinary course of events'.

[147] Jackson (n 11) 160.

[148] Moynihan (n 4) 21; Lanovoy (n 3) 232.

reasoning of the recent *CAAT* case is anything to go by,[149] the determination of virtual certainty (and by extension intent) in complex military situations where the factual situation is likely to be disputed is highly challenging.

3.4 Knowledge and intent in the case of serious violations of peremptory obligations

At first sight it seems that the stringent requirements pertaining to knowledge and intent in accordance with article 16 ASR can be overcome more easily where the violations of international humanitarian and/or human rights law qualify as 'a serious breach by a state of an obligation arising under a peremptory norm of general international law'.[150] In accordance with article 40(2) ASR, '[a] breach of such an obligation is serious if it involves a gross or systematic failure by the responsible state to fulfil the obligation'.[151] While the list of recognized peremptory norms in international law remains limited, the prohibition of torture and the core obligations under international humanitarian law (such as the prohibition of indiscriminate targeting or the wilful killing of civilians) are recognized as constituting such obligations.[152] In order for a violation of a peremptory obligation under international law to be 'serious' or 'gross', a certain scale of intensity is required.[153] Sporadic incidents of torture in state prisons, for example, would not be covered.[154] For the purposes of the current analysis it is assumed that the type of alleged violations of humanitarian and human rights law outlined in section 2 can amount to serious violations of peremptory obligations.

Sub-articles 41(1) and (2) ASR are specifically aimed at prohibiting complicity in (the continuation of) serious breaches of international law and constitute a concretization (*lex specialis*) of article 16 ASR.[155] Article 41(1) determines that states have to cooperate to bring to an end through lawful means any serious breaches of international law.[156] In addition, sub-article 41(2) ASR determines that '[n]o state shall recognize as lawful a situation created by a serious breach within the meaning of article 40, *nor render aid or assistance in maintaining that situation*'.[157] The duty of non-cooperation in sub-article 41(1) ASR is aimed at the general (political) isolation of the state that committed a serious breach of peremptory norms.[158] The duty

[149] *CAAT Court of Appeal* case (n 8).
[150] Art 40(1) ASR (n 10).
[151] ibid art 40(2).
[152] ILC Commentary to art 40 ASR (n 10) para (5).
[153] ibid para (7); Lanovoy (n 3) 111.
[154] See Lanovoy (n 3) 112 who criticizes this limitation.
[155] Lanovoy (n 3) 106; Aust (n 11) 336.
[156] Art 41 ASR (n 10).
[157] ibid art 42 (emphasis added). See also *Legal Consequences of the Construction of a Wall in the Occupied Palestinian Territory, Advisory Opinion* [2004] ICJ Rep 136 para 159.
[158] For a discussion, see Aust (n 11) 336–37.

of non-assistance in sub-article 41(2) concerns concrete measures that can impact the wrongful conduct.[159] The specific obligations in sub-article 41(2), therefore, are an extension of the general obligation not to cooperate in sub-article 41(1).[160]

Both these articles are triggered only once serious breaches of peremptory norms have already taken place and regardless of whether the breach itself is an ongoing one.[161] Once such a wrongful situation has been brought about, states have to refrain from acts that contribute to maintaining the wrongful situation.[162] The obligations in sub-articles 41(1) and 41(2) are not dependent on evidence that the assisting state had knowledge of the circumstances of the internationally wrongful act, nor whether it had the desire to bring about the wrongful situation.[163] Instead, states aiding or assisting the principal actor are assumed to have the knowledge and the intention to provide assistance with a view to facilitating the maintenance of a situation that resulted from gross violations of peremptory norms.[164] This relates to the fact that the nature and scope of the violations of the international obligations at stake are such that they are unlikely to go unnoticed by other states.[165]

That being said, the added value of sub-article 41(2) ASR in practice, including in situations of forcible measures on request, is questionable.[166] First, the fact that an alleged serious breach of international law is unlikely to go unnoticed by states implies that credible sources will also have reported widely on it. As a result, an assisting state would be in the same situation as in the case of article 16 ASR, namely, under an obligation to engage in prior investigations before committing future aid or assistance to the government allegedly responsible for the serious breaches.[167] However, as illustrated above in section 3.2, the outcome of these investigations may not necessarily yield the factual certainty that is necessary to determine whether aid or assistance by the assisting state will in future contribute to maintaining the situation brought about by such violations. As in the case of article 16 ASR, such factual certainty may be difficult to obtain even where an assessment by the assisting state has revealed that a recipient government had indeed been responsible for (in this instance) serious breaches of peremptory norms. The result is that the assisting state's knowledge of gross violations of peremptory norms and (by extension) its intention to provide assistance that will maintain the situation brought about by these violations cannot necessarily be assumed. Finally, it also

[159] Aust (n 11) 337; Lanovoy (n 3) 108.
[160] ILC Commentary to art 41 ASR (n 10) para (4); Lanovoy (n 3) 108.
[161] ILC Commentary to art 41(2) ASR (n 10) para (11); Lanovoy (n 3) 106, 115.
[162] ILC Commentary to art 41(2) ASR (n 10) para (11); Aust (n 11) 381; Lanovoy (n 3) 107–08.
[163] ILC Commentary to art 41(2) ASR (n 10) para (11); Lanovoy (n 3) 115.
[164] ibid.
[165] ILC Commentary to art 41(2) ASR (n 10) para (11); Moynihan (n 4) 22–23; Nolte and Aust (n 11) 16; Lanovoy (n 3) 115, 238.
[166] Aust (n 11) 417.
[167] ibid 336, 343 ff. See also Lanovoy (n 3) 115. The serious breaches are also likely to be of a continuous nature and, therefore, would in any case also fall under art 16 ASR (n 10).

remains disputed whether sub-article 41(2) ASR has acquired customary international law status, which may in practice weaken its application.[168]

4. Legal consequences of complicity under article 16 ASR for direct military support

The foregoing analysis suggests that whether an intervening state risks derivative responsibility for violations of humanitarian and/or human rights law by the inviting government in terms of article 16 ASR depends on various, as of yet unclear, criteria. These include the factual and temporal proximity (nexus) between the assisting and principal act, the specificity (and certainty) of the knowledge requirement, as well as the specificity of the intent requirement and its relationship with the knowledge requirement. If one applies these criteria to the situations of forcible measures on request outlined in section 2, one would first have to assess on a case-by-case basis whether the military assistance of the intervening state in any significant manner facilitated or contributed to the principal wrongful conduct of the territorial state. This in itself can be a difficult hurdle to overcome.

As far as the knowledge requirement is concerned, it is arguable that any assumption of knowledge on the part of the assisting state must be based on a high level of factual certainty about the role of the recipient government in committing violations of humanitarian and/or human rights law and its use of military assistance for this purpose. Where the factual context remains disputed, knowledge cannot necessarily be assumed. If one were to regard knowledge and intent as two sides of the same coin, such factual uncertainty would further imply that intent also could not be assumed. Furthermore, even if one were to assume that the alleged wrongful conduct constituted serious breaches of peremptory obligations in terms of article 40 ASR, this would not make much practical difference, given the effective overlap in consequences between sub-article 41(2) and article 16 ASR.

In essence, therefore, the answer to whether the conduct of any of the intervening states in the situations outlined in section 2 triggered derivative responsibility would require a close scrutiny of the facts of each specific case. However, if one were to assume for the sake of argument that the threshold requirements for article 16 ASR have been met in the above-mentioned scenarios, general international law requires the state responsible for the internationally wrongful act 'to cease that act, if it is continuing'.[169] For the purposes of the current analysis, this raises the

[168] Moynihan (n 4) 22; Aust (n 11) 336, 343 ff. According to Lanovoy (n 3) 116–17, art 41(2) ASR and art 42 DARIO (n 22) may have a certain added value in relation to the nexus requirement, as the aid or assistance need not significantly contribute to the maintenance of the situation flowing from the serious breach of a peremptory norm. A lower degree of significance in relation to the link with the wrongful act would be acceptable, as one is dealing with the maintenance of a serious breach which has already occurred and not a situation pertaining to a wrongful act that still has to be committed.

[169] Art 30(a) ASR (n 10); Lanovoy (n 3) 109.

question of how exactly to cease the wrongful assistance and, in particular, whether this would require the intervening state to withdraw direct military support.[170] If the assisting state has agreed with the recipient state that the military assistance must be used in accordance with international humanitarian and human rights law and then becomes aware that its assistance is used in contravention of this condition, this could eventually amount to a material breach that suspends further obligations to provide military assistance.[171] However, where no such or any other agreement regarding the termination of military assistance in case of violations of humanitarian and human rights law by the recipient state is in place, it is unclear if and under which conditions general international law would so require.

In considering this question, the 2013 Human Rights Due Diligence Policy (HRDPP) of the UN, which serves as a guideline to the UN when engaging in military operations, can be instructive.[172] Its aim is to prevent the UN from rendering assistance in situations where there is credible evidence that the entities receiving such assistance are likely to commit grave violations of international humanitarian, human rights, or refugee law, and where the relevant authorities fail to take the necessary corrective or mitigating measures.[173] The type of military assistance affected may range from financial support to strategic, tactical, logistical, and operational support. It further includes field action and joint operations conducted by the UN and other forces.[174]

In accordance with this document, the threshold for withdrawal of UN military assistance is crossed only once there is a likelihood of 'grave violations' of humanitarian, human rights, and refugee law.[175] This, for example, would include war crimes or crimes against humanity as referred to in the Statute of the International Criminal Court,[176] or large-scale, repeated (patterns of) human rights violations.[177] Furthermore, the withdrawal of military support would occur only if such grave violations by the recipient government persist, despite precautionary measures that the UN may have taken.[178] If one applies the logic of this policy to (coalitions of) states engaged in forcible assistance on request, the threshold for troop withdrawal would only be crossed in cases of serious violations of peremptory obligations of international law within the meaning of article 40 ASR. Moreover,

[170] Lanovoy (n 3) 229.

[171] ibid 174.

[172] Human Rights Due Diligence Policy on United Nations Support to Non-United Nations Security Forces UN Doc A/67/775-S/2013/110 Annex (5 March 2013) paras 1, 14(d); see also HP Aust, 'The UN Human Rights Due Diligence Policy: An Effective Mechanism Against Complicity of Peacekeeping Forces?' (2015) 20 Journal of Conflict and Security Law 66.

[173] UN Doc A/67/775-S/2013/110 Annex (n 172) para 1; Aust (n 172) 64.

[174] UN Doc A/67/775-S/2013/110 Annex (n 172) paras 8(c)–8(f), 10; Aust (n 172) 64–65.

[175] Aust 71.

[176] The Rome Statute of the International Criminal Court (adopted 17 July 1998) 2187 UNTS 90, arts 7 and 8.

[177] For a list of actions that qualify as 'gross violations', see UN Doc A/67/775-S/2013/110 Annex (n 172) paras 12(a)(i), (ii), and (iii); Aust (n 172) 65–66.

[178] UN Doc A/67/775-S/2013/110 Annex (n 172) para 16; Aust (n 172) 71.

it would only become necessary after it has become clear that any precautionary measures taken have proved to be unsuccessful. In drawing this analogy, one has to keep in mind that the purpose of the HRDDP is not to determine the scope and consequences of responsibility of the UN for (complicity in) violations of international humanitarian, human rights, and refugee law. Instead, its aim is to prevent such violations from occurring.[179] The document, therefore, does not directly address the question of cessation and its implications. Even so, the issue of troop withdrawal implicitly touches on these questions. Also, the fact that troop withdrawal is to be considered only as a last resort implicitly suggests that cessation can also be achieved by lesser means.[180]

An obvious 'lesser step' would be to request concrete assurances from the territorial state about its adherence to international humanitarian and human rights law. For example, it would need to indicate the steps it is taking to improve targeting and other operational practices, as well as that it is undertaking investigations into allegations of violations of international humanitarian and/or human rights law.[181] The intervening state may also have to intensify its monitoring of and involvement in the military operations of the territorial state.[182] For example, it may need to engage in advance screening of commanding officers of the territorial state and those making up their units, the placing of operational and legal expertise within the forces of the territorial state, as well as embedding personnel in the units of the territorial state that decide on targeting practices.[183] If such measures (or any combination thereof) do not succeed in preventing gross violations of humanitarian and human rights law by the recipient state, the intervening state may ultimately be obliged to withdraw its troops. However, the point at which this obligation would arise under general international law has yet to be determined by state practice.

5. Conclusion

In light of the foregoing analysis it is fair to conclude that any claim according to which direct military assistance is prohibited if it aids or assists violations of international human rights and humanitarian law by the incumbent government does not (yet) find support in general international law. Therefore, if the statement in

[179] Aust (n 172) 71.

[180] See Final Report of the Panel of Experts on Yemen (n 55) 129 which *inter alia* stated: 'All coalition member states and their allies also have an obligation to take appropriate measures to ensure respect for international humanitarian law by the coalition. This obligation is especially incumbent upon the government of Yemen, upon whose request and with those consent the air strikes are being conducted.'

[181] As was the case with Saudi Arabia in the *CAAT High Court* case (n 8) paras 129, 135. See also Finucane (n 3) 425.

[182] Finucane (n 3) 426, 430.

[183] ibid 425, 426.

article 3 of the IDI 2011 Resolution, according to which direct military support on request would be prohibited if it violated 'generally accepted standards of human rights',[184] also encompasses direct military support that aided and assisted such violations by the requesting government,[185] it would be merely aspirational. First, the triggering of the responsibility framework in article 16 ASR in situations where direct military assistance is provided to incumbent governments accused of continued violations of international humanitarian and human rights law is fraught with uncertainty. Moreover, even if it can be assumed that article 16 ASR was triggered in all the situations of forcible assistance on request outlined in section 2, this does not in and of itself imply that the assisting states have to terminate their direct military support. State practice does not yet support the conclusion that such withdrawal is required by general international law. This remains the case even where such violations amounted to serious violations of peremptory norms of international law in terms of article 40 ASR.

If and to the extent to which an assisting state does decide to withdraw its troops and/or air power from the territorial state, this would more likely have to do with policy reasons. Intervening states may find the nature and scope of the precautionary measures necessary to prevent their implication in violations of international humanitarian and human rights law too time-consuming and costly. However, in the absence of such measures the intervening states (in addition to potentially incurring derivate state responsibility) risk significant reputational loss and credibility in terms of its own respect for international law. This risk is particularly high where the institutional shortcomings of an inviting state may be such that no amount of training or technical assistance would, within a foreseeable time, bring about the expertise and discipline required for ensuring that the governmental military forces act in accordance with international humanitarian and human rights law.[186] In such an instance, the intervening state may conclude that the withdrawal of direct military assistance would be the most prudent option.

[184] IDI (n 1) art 3.
[185] Assuming for the sake of argument that the Resolution would also apply during a NIAC.
[186] Finucane (n 3) 430.

5

Formal Requirements for Valid Consent to Direct Military Assistance

1. Introduction

Prior chapters have illuminated that the consent underpinning a request for military assistance has to be given by the internationally recognized government of the territorial state and can also be extended during a non-international armed conflict (NIAC).[1] In addition, the fact that the requesting government is responsible for widespread and systematic human rights violations does not as such prevent it from requesting direct military assistance, nor does it prevent the invited government from accepting such a request.[2] The current chapter examines potential formal requirements that may affect the validity of consent. First, section 2 raises the question as to the specific entity or entities in government that would have the competence to issue and terminate consent on behalf of the requesting (territorial) state. Second, section 3 examines the applicable benchmarks for freely given consent. A third issue, examined in section 4, is whether consent needs to be expressed explicitly or whether it can be given tacitly, that is, implied by the circumstances. Similar questions arise in relation to the revocation of consent.

Finally, section 5 explores the issue of the timing of consent. Under customary international law, consent has to be present at the time of the conduct in question, which means that it has to be given in advance or at the time of the occurrence of the conduct.[3] This raises the question of the legal implications of *ex post facto* consent, notably for the wrongfulness of the intervening state's conduct at the time of the intervention.[4] At the other end of the scale, questions also arise as to the need for temporal proximity between the prior consent issued by the requesting government and the actual military intervention by the assisting state(s). Specifically, the question arises as to whether the consent has to be given ad hoc (ie directly prior) to the specific intervention, or whether general *ex ante* consent in the form of a pro-invasion clause would suffice. In the post-Cold War era this question has gained

[1] See Chapters 2 and 3.

[2] See Chapter 4.

[3] ILC, Draft Articles on Responsibility of States for Internationally Wrongful Acts with Commentaries' (ASR) (2001) II Yearbook of the International Law Commission; UN Doc A/Res/56/83 (12 December 2001) Commentary to art 20, para (3).

[4] ASR (n 3) Commentary to art 13, para (1); *Island of Palmas (Netherlands/United States of America)* UNRIAA [1928] vol II 845.

prominence in Africa since the adoption of extensive regional security frameworks by the African Union (AU) and the Economic Community of West African States (ECOWAS) at the beginning of the twenty-first century. Both these regimes at first sight seem to provide *ex ante* consent to military intervention by the organization under specified circumstances.

2. The state organs competent to issue and withdraw consent

In accordance with general principles of treaty law, valid consent implies that the entity consenting on behalf of the state was authorized to do so. These would include, by virtue of their functions, the head of state, the head of government, and the Minister of Foreign affairs.[5] It therefore is arguable that consent to direct military assistance issued by any of these officials would validly bind the state.[6] If and to the extent to which the domestic law of the state limits the capacity of any of these officials to bind the state in this regard, it needs to be determined whether this was known or ought to have been known to those who relied on such consent.[7] General principles of treaty law further allow other state officials to express consent to be bound on behalf of a state where duly authorized to do so in accordance with their national law. These officials would either have to produce full power to this effect, or it must appear from state practice or the particular circumstances of the case that they had the capacity to bind the state.[8]

However, in doctrine there is support for the position that as far as consent to direct military assistance is concerned, it has to emanate only from the highest officials of a state, given the impact of forcible measures on a state's territorial integrity.[9] This would imply that consent has to emanate from the head of state and/or government. The post-Cold War state practice analysed in Chapter 3 provides support for this view. In all the situations analysed, the consent to forcible

[5] See Vienna Convention on the Law of Treaties 23 May 1969, 1155 UNTS 331 (VCLT) art 7(2)(a). This article also constitutes customary international law, as *inter alia* confirmed by the ICJ in *Maritime Delimitation in the Indian Ocean (Somalia v Kenya)* (Preliminary Objections) [2017] ICJ Rep 3 para 43. See also IDI (Rapporteur Gerhard Hafner), 'Final Report: Intervention by Invitation' (2009) 73 Annuaire de l'Institut de droit international 402. See Generally F Hoffmeister, 'Article 7' in O Dörr and S Schmalenbach (eds), *Vienna Convention on the Law of Treaties. A Commentary* (2nd edn, Springer 2018) 129 ff.

[6] M Byrne, 'Consent and the Use of Force: An Examination of Intervention by Invitation as a Basis for US Drone Strikes in Pakistan, Somalia and Yemen' (2016) 3 Journal on the Use of Force and International Law 117.

[7] This in turn may depend on whether such limitation was duly publicized under the circumstances. See *Somalia v Kenya* (n 5) para 48; ASR (n 3) Commentary to art 20 ASR para (4).

[8] See VCLT (n 5) arts 7(1)(a) and (b); *Somalia v Kenya* (n 5) para 43; Hoffmeister n (5) 133.

[9] O Corten, *The Law Against War: The Prohibition on the Use of Force in Contemporary International Law* (Hart Publishing 2010) 263; T Ruys and L Ferro, 'Weathering the Storm: Legality and Legal implications of the Saudi-Led Military Intervention in Yemen' (2016) 65 International and Comparative Law Quarterly 82; G Nolte, *Eingreifen auf Einladung: Zur völkerrechtlichen Zulässigkeit des Einsatzes fremder Truppen im internen Konflikt auf Einladung der Regierung* (Springer 1999) 582.

measures have consistently been issued by heads of state and/or government, regardless of whether it was extended to regional organizations, individual (groups of) states, and/or whether it was in a situation that had escalated into a NIAC. This suggests that in international law there is a strong presumption that consent to direct military assistance has to be issued by the highest officials of a state. This presumption can only be rebutted by clear evidence of a lower-ranked official's competence to consent to forcible measures, for example in the form of domestic legislation to this effect.[10]

It would follow from this that consent to forcible measures that emanated exclusively from a lower-ranked official, such as the Foreign Minister, the Minister of Defence, or the head of the military, can only suffice where the domestic law of the inviting state allows for this. Similarly, where the consent issued by a lower-ranked official is subsequently contradicted by the head of state and/or government, the latter's opinion will prevail, unless the domestic law clearly stipulates the lower-ranked official's competence to override in matters pertaining to the use of force.[11] A further logical conclusion would be that the revocation or withdrawal of consent also has to emanate from the head of state, unless the domestic law clearly dictates otherwise.[12] For example, in 2008 the chief of the Pakistani army, General Kayani, criticized the United States for sending commandos into Pakistan for a raid against the Taliban.[13] Yet, the newly elected President Zardari at the time refused to condemn the raid during a press briefing.[14] To the extent that the President's lack of protest evinced tacit consent,[15] it would override the objection of the head of the army, as there was nothing to suggest that Pakistani law allowed him to overrule the President.[16]

[10] The domestic law of the consenting state will also determine who should act on behalf of the President, where he is incapacitated. This might for example become necessary where he or she was arrested by rebels and prevented from requesting military assistance. See Hafner Report (n 5) 402; Byrne (n 6) 118–19; SD Murphy, 'The International Legality of US Military Cross-Border Operations from Afghanistan into Pakistan' (2008) 84 International Legal Studies 118.

[11] International Law Association (Committee on the Use of Force), Final Report on Aggression and the Use of Force (2018) 19 http://www.ila-hq.org/images/ILA/DraftReports/DraftReport_UseOfForce.pdf. See C Heyns, 'Report of the Special Rapporteur on Extrajudicial, Summary or Arbitrary Executions' UN Doc A/68/382 (13 September 2013) para 81. Heyns noted that in case of a difference in view between the highest authorities and lower-level officials in government, the view of the higher-level officials should be decisive. See also Byrne (n 6) 118.

[12] When the DRC revoked its consent to the military presence of Rwanda and Uganda in its territory in July 1998, this was announced by President Kabila. While his view was also shared by the Supreme Commander of the Congolese National Armed Forces and the Minister of National Defence, the revocation of consent was executed by the President. See *Armed Activities on the Territory of the Congo (Democratic Republic of the Congo v Uganda)* (Judgment) [2005] ICJ Rep 168, para 49.

[13] J Perlez, 'Pakistan's Military Chief Criticizes US Over a Raid' *New York Times* (10 September 2008) https://www.nytimes.com/2008/09/11/world/asia/11pstan.html; Murphy (n 10) 118.

[14] ibid.

[15] The issue of determining the expression of consent and its eventual withdrawal is taken up in section 4.

[16] See also Murphy (n 10) 119.

3. Freely expressed consent

The point of departure for determining whether a state's consent has been expressed freely are articles 51 and 52 of the Vienna Convention on the Law of Treaties 1969 (VCLT). These articles, both of which constitute customary international law,[17] protect the freedom of consent of the represented state(s) by denying legal effect to consent by coercion.[18] Article 51 of the VCLT concerns the coercion of the representative of the state, while article 52 encompasses the coercion of the state itself.[19] Article 51 determines that '[t]he expression of a state's consent to be bound by a treaty that has been procured by the coercion of its representative through acts or threats directed against him shall be without any legal effect'.[20] Article 52 for its part states that '[a] treaty is void if its conclusion has been procured by the threat or use of force in violation of the principles of international law embodied in the Charter of the United Nations'.[21]

The coercion against the state representative in accordance with article 51 concerns fear-inducing acts or threats as a result of which the state representative expresses consent to be bound by a treaty which, in the absence of such acts or threats, would not have been expressed.[22] The acts or threats of coercion are not limited to physical force against the representative's person, but can include emotional pressure of various kinds, for example threatening to ruin someone's career by disclosing compromising information.[23] These acts or threats also need not be directed against the person of the state representative. They can also concern acts or threats against his or her family members or dependents that have a compelling effect, as if they were directed against the representative's person.[24] However, the coercive acts or threats must be directed against the representative in his or her private capacity rather than against the official function as an agent or organ of state.[25] In the latter instance one may nonetheless be confronted with coercion in terms of article 52 of VCLT. [26]

[17] *Fisheries Jurisdiction (UK v Iceland)* (Jurisdiction of the Court) [1973] ICJ Rep 3, para 24. See also O Corten 'Article 52. Coercion of a State or of an International Organization by the Threat or Use of Force' in O Corten and P Klein (eds), *The Vienna Convention on the Law of Treaties. A Commentary* (OUP 2011) para 5.

[18] T Rensmann, 'Article 51. Coercion of a Representative of a State' in Dörr and Schmalenbach (n 5) 923; ME Villiger, *Commentary on the 1969 Convention on the Law of Treaties* (Martinus Nijhoff Publishers 2008) 634; K Schmalenbach, 'Article 52: Coercion of a State by the Threat or Use of Force' in Dörr and Schmalenbach (n 5) 938, 947, 949.

[19] Rensmann (n 18) 923.

[20] VCLT (n 5) art 51; see also ASR (n 3) Commentary to art 20 ASR paras (5) and (6); Byrne (n 6) 104; Ruys and Ferro (n 9) 82. See also Rensmann (n 18) 923; Villiger (n 18) 634.

[21] Art 52 VCLT (n 5).

[22] Rensmann (n 18) 927–28.

[23] Villiger (n 18) 633 Rensmann (n 18) 929.

[24] Rensmann (n 18) 930.

[25] ibid; Villiger (n 18) 633.

[26] The two forms of coercion provided for in arts 51 and 52 may coincide, where the acts or threats against the state simultaneously procure fear in the state representative regarding his or her own person or well-being or that of his or her family. A frequently-cited example is that of the conclusion of the

The wording of article 52 of VCLT reflects its close connection with the prohibition of the threat or use of force in article 2(4) of the UN Charter.[27] These two articles may be regarded as two sides of the same coin, as article 52 of VCLT determines the legal consequence from a violation of article 2(4) of the UN Charter in the treaty context, namely, the invalidity of a treaty imposed upon one of the parties through an act or threat of force.[28] As is the case with article 2(4) of the UN Charter, the type of force envisaged by article 52 of VCLT includes only military force.[29] At the time of the drafting of the VCLT, attempts to broaden the notion of force in order to include economic measures, such as blockades, remained unsuccessful.[30] Instead, statements to this effect were included only in the legally non-binding Declaration on the Prohibition of Military, Political or Economic Coercion in the Conclusion of Treaties,[31] which supplemented article 52 of VCLT as an authentic instrument of interpretation.[32] In accordance with the Declaration,

> the United Nations condemns the threat or use of pressure in any form whether military, political or economic, by any state, in order to coerce another state to perform any act relation got the conclusion of a treaty in violation of the principle of the sovereign equality of states and freedom of consent.[33]

While the Declaration can inform the interpretation of the term 'force' in article 52 of VCLT, as yet there has been no state practice supporting a conclusion that it has succeeded in broadening its interpretation.[34]

Treaty of 15 March 1939 between the German Reich and Czechoslovakia, establishing the 'Protectorate of Bohemia and Moravia'. In this instance the threat of destroying the country induced the President and Foreign Minister of Czechoslovakia to sign the agreement. See Rensmann (n 18) 930–31; Villiger (n 18) 633.

[27] United Nations, Charter of the United Nations (24 October 1945) 1 NTS XVI https://treaties.un.org/doc/source/docs/charter-all-lang.pdf.

[28] Schmalenbach (n 18) 938. See also *Military and Paramilitary Activities in an against Nicaragua (Nicaragua v United States)* (Merits) [1986] ICJ Rep 14 para 205.

[29] Schmalenbach (n 18) 950, ME Villiger, 'Article 52: Coercion of a State by the Threat or Use of Force' in Villiger (n 18) 642.

[30] Schmalenbach (n 18) 950. See also Villiger (n 29) 644. It was feared that an extended notion of coercion would encourage states to circumvent their obligations in burdensome treaties by invoking coercion. It could also lead to the undermining of legal certainty and *pacta sunt servanda*. For different opinions within the ILC, see (1963) I Yearbook of the International Law Commission 52–53. Corten (n 17) paras 9 ff submits that this area of international law remains unclear since neither interpretation has prevailed over the other.

[31] See Declaration on the Prohibition of Military, Political or Economic Coercion in the Conclusion of Treaties para 1, reprinted in Villiger (n 18) 651.

[32] ME Villiger 'Article 52: Declaration on the Prohibition of Military, Political or Economic Coercion in the Conclusion of Treaties' in Villiger (n 18) 657.

[33] Declaration on the Prohibition of Military, Political or Economic Coercion in the Conclusion of Treaties (n 31) para 1; Schmalenbach (n 18) 951.

[34] See Corten (n 17) para 21, who concedes that there is no precedent on invalidation due to economic pressure. Schmalenbach (n 18) 951. At 961 she notes that the Declaration (n 31) para 1 nonetheless affirms the customary international law principle that the exercise of military, economic, or political pressure in order to coerce another state into the conclusion of a treaty can violate the principle

The threshold of coercion set in articles 51 and 52 is very high, in light of the stringent causality requirements underpinning both articles.[35] The fact that the consent of the state (or its representative) had to be 'procured' means that it had to be obtained intentionally and the (threats of) pressure or force must have been directly responsible for the conclusion of the treaty.[36] Accordingly, the consent to be bound by the treaty would not have been expressed by the state (or its representative) had it not been for the coercive pressure vis-à-vis the state representative or the act or threat of force against the state.[37] From this it also follows that the intensity of the pressure exercised on a state representative must qualify as undue pressure, that is that it must extend beyond persuasion, influence, or advice.[38] Similarly, the degree of force or threat thereof has to be such that the coerced state 'has been reduced to such a degree of impotence as to be unable to resist the pressure to become a party to a treaty'.[39] In addition, any evidence presented in relation to coercion has to be precise, to the point, and credible. General or vague allegations regarding acts of threats of force will not suffice.[40] In the same vein, the mere fact that one state had previously illegally used force on the territory of another does not in and of itself prove that any subsequent treaty between them was concluded as a result of coercion.[41]

In essence, therefore, the state invoking coercion will have its work cut out when attempting to meet the causality and evidentiary requirements underpinning articles 51 and 52 of VCLT.[42] While these stringent requirements serve to protect the principle of *pacta sunt servanda* and legal certainty,[43] they can effectively place

of sovereign equality of states. This principle, contained in art 2(1) of the UN Charter (n 27), is closely intertwined with the notion of freely given consent. In consequence, where the degree of pressure was such that the state had no alternative but to conclude the desired treaty, it would trigger the state responsibility of the pressuring state. While this would imply the making of reparations and may require the termination of the treaty in question, it would not imply invalidity *ab initio*.

35 Schmalenbach (n 18) 946, 949; Corten (n 17) para 39.

36 Villiger (n 32) 645.

37 Rensmann (n 18) 932; Villiger (n 32) 645.

38 Villiger (n 18) 633.

39 Schmalenbach (n 18) 948. She further notes that while any threat or use of force in violation of art 2(4) of the UN Charter would be illegal—irrespective of its intensity—the degree of force is nonetheless an important factor when determining whether a treaty was procured through coercion. See also *Kuwait v Aminoil* (1982) 66 International Law Reports 518, 570. As Aminoil was able to make a choice, the pressure it was under did not impair its capacity to choose.

40 See ICJ *Fisheries Jurisdiction* decision (n 17) para 24. According to Iceland a '1961 Exchange of Notes took place under extremely difficult circumstances when the British Royal Navy had been using force to oppose the 12-mile fishery limit established by the Icelandic Government in 1958'. In referring to art 52 of VCLT (n 5), the ICJ refused to consider this 'vague general charge unfortified by evidence in its support'. See also Schmalenbach (n 18) 949.

41 Corten (n 17) para 24; Villiger (n 32) 645.

42 Schmalenbach (n 18) 949; Corten (n 17) para 39. At para 27 he pleads for a more lenient interpretation of art 52 of VCLT (n 5), as its text can be read as requiring a causal link in the broad sense. It could, therefore, suffice to establish a decisive influence of the alleged coercion, without the necessity to demonstrate a total absence of choice of the victim.

43 Schmalenbach (n 18) 958; See also the *Fisheries Jurisdiction* decision (n 17) para 24.

weak and fragile states at the mercy of economic and militarily powerful states. After all, strong states can use various economic or political pressures (including covert threats of force) to procure what will formally amount to freely expressed consent for the purposes of articles 51 and/or 52.[44] This risk is likely to be very pertinent in the context of direct military assistance on request, given that the requesting states typically tend to be in a fragile situation, while the assisting states are militarily strong—even overwhelmingly so. In fact, this was the case in all the military interventions illuminated in Chapter 3, including in those instances where the conflict had escalated beyond the threshold of a NIAC and the military assistance spanned several years. Yet, in none of these instances did either the consenting state or third states claim that the consent had been coerced, or that a lower causality or evidentiary threshold for coercion would apply in the specific context of military assistance on request.

In theory, one could argue that the intrusive nature of forcible assistance on request justifies a lower causal and probative threshold. For example, some scholars have suggested that when the assisting state dominates or directs the military operations, this would be indicative of coercion, reducing the consenting state to a puppet regime.[45] However, states have remained reluctant to endorse such reasoning ever since the Cold War era. This can be exemplified by the Syrian military presence in Lebanon between 1976 and 2005.[46] During this period the military presence was formalized in several agreements between the two countries.[47] These *inter alia* foresaw the deployment of Syrian forces throughout Lebanon and their use for maintaining internal law and order.[48] Israel remained highly critical of the Syrian presence, describing Lebanon as being controlled by Syria.[49] Yet, other states were cautious to depict the Lebanese government as a puppet regime that was coerced by Syria.[50] The Syrian troops ultimately withdrew from Lebanon in 2005, subsequent to the adoption of United Nations (UN) Security Council (UNSC) Resolution 1559 of 2 September 2004. The Resolution called for the withdrawal of all remaining foreign forces from Lebanon, thereby giving the impression that the

[44] See Schmalenbach (n 18) 953. Proving coercion may be particularly difficult in instances where consent was allegedly procured by means of a threat to force. The more covert or indirect a state goes about conveying to another state its intentions to use force, the more difficult it would be for the latter to make a convincing case of coercive intent. See also *Fisheries Jurisdiction* decision (n 17), dissenting opinion of Judge Padilla Nervo, 46–47.

[45] Nolte (n 9) 459.

[46] Al Jazeera, 'Syria's Role in Lebanon' *Al Jazeera* (14 October 2007) https://www.aljazeera.com/focus/lebanon/2007/07/2008525173065995l7.html.

[47] See Taif Agreement of September 1989 http://www.presidency.gov.lb/Arabic/LebaneseSystem/Documents/TaefAgreementEn.pdf; Treaty of Brotherhood, Cooperation and Coordination between the Syrian Arab Republic and the Lebanese Republic 22 May 1991, 1992 UNTS 154.

[48] See Treaty of Brotherhood (n 27) para 4; Nolte (n 9) 512.

[49] See *inter alia* UN Doc S/PV.2640 (13 January 1986) 18–19. See C Gray, *International Law and the Use of Force* (4th edn, OUP 2018) 103. See also E Lieblich, *International Law and Civil Wars. Intervention and Consent* (Routledge 2013) 19.

[50] Nolte (n 9) 513.

majority of the UNSC may have had concerns about the continued validity of the consent by the Lebanese government.[51] Even so, the Resolution did not criticize Syria outright for controlling Lebanon, nor was it adopted under Chapter VII of the UN Charter. Lebanon, for its part, consistently maintained that Syria had assisted it in maintaining stability and security within its borders.[52] The same reluctance to interpret the dominance of the assisting state(s) during military operations on request as evidence of coercion of the inviting state persists in the post-Cold War era. Even in protracted conflicts with overwhelming military involvement by states, such as Russia (in Syria), Saudi Arabia (in Yemen), and the United States (in Afghanistan), the validity of the consent issued by the recognized government has not been questioned.[53]

Finally, the *Armed Activities in the Congo* decision indicates that also in the context of military assistance on request the prior illegal use of force by the invited state against the inviting state does not in and of itself prove that the request was coerced. For this to be the case, it would have to be proven that no request or invitation would have been forthcoming had it not been for the prior, illegal use of force. Where this has not been convincingly established, the invitation would be presumed to have been freely extended.[54] In this case the invitation extended by the government of the Democratic Republic of the Congo (DRC) to Rwanda and Uganda (during the time it existed) occurred after these two states had participated in the overthrow through forcible means of the previous Congolese government.[55] Yet, the argument of coercion (due to prior use of illegal force) was not invoked to invalidate the consent that was subsequently issued by the new DRC government, nor did the International Court of Justice (ICJ) dwell on the matter.[56] In essence, therefore, there is nothing in current state practice to suggest that the requirements pertaining to coercion in the context of military assistance on request would deviate from those generally applicable in accordance with customary international law.

4. Clearly established (withdrawal of) consent

The interpretation by the International Law Commission (ILC) of validly given consent underscores the fact that it needs to 'be actually expressed by the state rather than merely presumed on the basis that the state would have consented if it

[51] UN Doc S/RES/1559 (2 September 2004) para 2.
[52] See Gray (n 49) 103. See also UN Doc S/PV.5028 (2004) 3 (Lebanon). The Resolution was adopted with six votes in favour and six abstentions.
[53] See Byrne (n 6) 107, who makes this point in relation to Yemen.
[54] Corten (n 9) 271–72.
[55] Corten (n 9) 272.
[56] Corten (n 9) 271.

had been asked'.[57] In the context of military assistance on request, the need for a clear expression of the intention of the territorial state is of particular significance, given the very intrusive nature of the use of force.[58] This raises the question of whether customary international law would attach any particular requirements to the manner in which consent is expressed by the territorial state. In particular, the question arises as to whether its consent has to be explicit (as opposed to implicit or tacit), whether it has to been in writing, and whether the consent has to be publicized. Similar questions also arise about the withdrawal of consent once extended.

Post-Cold War state practice as well as doctrine suggests that these (often closely intertwined) questions are to be answered in the negative. Consent to forcible measures can be expressed tacitly,[59] that is, it can be inferred from a failure to act where the situation calls for reaction.[60] To the extent that there has been explicit consent, it can be either written or verbal and it need not be made public.[61] Chapter 3 illustrated that in the post-Cold War era, governments consenting to direct military assistance often explicate their consent in letters to the UNSC or UN Secretary-General, or via a public (press) statement.[62] These publicized statements, therefore, clearly establish their consent as such. That being said, these statements, whether written or oral, rarely contain the details regarding the scope and the duration of the military mandate agreed to between the countries in question.[63]

[57] ASR (n 3) Commentary to art 20 ASR para 6; Byrne (n 6) 104; Hafner Report (n 5) 403.

[58] See also Hafner Report (n 5) 390.

[59] Murphy (n 10) 109, 118; Byrne (n 6) 104; O Flasch, 'The Legality of the Air Strikes Against ISIL in Syria: New Insights on the Extraterritorial Use of Force Against Non-State Actors' (2016) 3 Journal on the Use of Force and International Law 41–42.

[60] For the existence of tacit consent in general, see *Case Concerning the Temple of Preah Vihear (Cambodia v Thailand)* (Merits) [1962] ICJ Rep 6, 31; *Russian Claim for Interests on Indemnities (Damages Claimed by Russia for Delay in Payment of Compensation Owed to Russians Injured During the War of 1877–1878 (Russia v Turkey)* (192) 11 UNRIAA 1912) 431, 446.

[61] Judicial support for this position can be found in *Armed Activities in the Congo* (n 12) paras 46–47. By confirming that the DRC's consent to Ugandan troops in its territory pre-dated any written agreement to this effect between the two countries, the ICJ affirmed that consent to direct military assistance can be given orally. The Institut de Droit International (IDI), Resolution on Military Assistance on Request (8 September 2011) http://www.idi-iil.org/idiE/navig_res_chon.html in art 4(2) does not use the term 'explicit' but instead refers to 'specific' consent. See also Corten (n 9) 272; G Nolte, 'The Resolution of the *Institut de Droit International* on Military Assistance on Request' (2012) 45 Revue belge de droit international (2012) 254, 261.

[62] This approach is also supported by the IDI, 2011 Resolution (n 61) art 4(3) according to which '[a]ny request that is followed by military assistance shall be notified to the Secretary-General of the United Nations'.

[63] The military assistance by South Africa to the Central African Republic (CAR) between February 2007 and February 2013 constitutes an example of consent based on a combination of written and oral agreements that were not widely publicized. In February 2007 the two countries concluded a written Memorandum of Understanding concerning defence cooperation for the duration of five years. This resulted in the sending of several hundred South African troops, ostensibly assisting with the training of the CAR military. After the expiration of the Memorandum, the then Presidents Zuma (South Africa) and Bozize (CAR) concluded an oral agreement in accordance with which the South African troops would remain in the CAR. However, by April 2013 South Africa decided to withdraw the troops in the wake of Bozize's ousting by rebel groups. See Memorandum of Understanding between the Government of the Republic of South Africa and the Government of the Central African Republic Concerning Defence Cooperation (11 February 2007) http://www.politicsweb.co.za/politicsweb/view/politicsweb/

For example, in the case of Yemen, the letters to the UNSC that confirmed President Hadi's request for military assistance disclosed no details about the scope and modalities of the military mandate.[64] Similarly, the October 2015 Syrian letter to the UNSC indicating the Russian military measures in response to the Syrian government's request to 'cooperate in countering terrorism' did so in broad terms. It referred to 'providing air support for ground operations conducted by the Syrian Arab Army in its war against Islamic state in Iraq and the Levant (ISIL), the Nusrah Front and other terrorist organizations'.[65] It further mentioned that the Russian Federation was 'striking the bases, camps, munitions depots and command posts of armed terrorist groups that are in the territory of the Syrian Arab Republic'.[66] However, the letter remained very general and, for example, did not indicate whether Russia was expected to liaise with the Syrian government before each and every airstrike, nor did it elaborate on the Russian ground offensives in Syria which also commenced at around the same time.[67]

The lack of detail could be explained by the reluctance of states to disclose details of operations that are politically and militarily highly sensitive. Any additional written or oral agreements that elaborate on the scope and modalities of the military mandate are unlikely to reach the public domain. While the confidentiality does not as such affect the legality of the agreements, it can make it difficult to evince the limits of the mandate and to affirm whether specific acts were actually covered by the consent given.[68] In such a situation, the reaction of the consenting (territorial) state to the particular military conduct by the assisting state on its territory will be decisive for determining whether the assisting state has remained

en/page71656?oid=367938andsn=Detailandpid=71656; BBC, 'South African troops to withdraw from CAR' *BBC News* (4 April 2013) https://www.bbc.com/news/world-africa-22025593. See also Chapter 2, section 3.2.1.

[64] See *inter alia* Statement Issued by the Kingdom of Saudi Arabia, the United Arab Emirates, the Kingdom of Bahrain, the State of Quarter and the State of Kuwait, Enclosure to Annex of Identical Letters dated 26 March 2015 from the Permanent Representative of Qatar to the United Nations Addressed to the Secretary-General and the President of the Security Council UN Doc S/2015/217 (27 March 2015) 5. See also B Nußberger, 'Military Strikes in Yemen in 2015: Intervention by Invitation and Self-Defence in the Course of Yemen's "Model Transitional Process"' (2017) 4 Journal on the Use of Force and International Law 128. He notes that the addressees were also to some extent identified only implicitly. The request for military assistance addressed referred to the Gulf States and the 'allied states' they represented.

[65] Identical Letters dated 14 October 2015 from the Permanent Representative of the Syrian Arab Republic to the United Nations Addressed to the Secretary-General and the President of the Security Council UN Doc A/70/429-S/2015/789 (16 October 2015).

[66] ibid; see also Letter dated 15 October 2015 from the Permanent Representative of the Russian Federation to the United Nations Addressed to the President of the Security Council UN Doc S/2015/792 (15 October 2015) 2.

[67] See *inter alia* UN Doc A/HRC/31/68 (Advanced Edited Version) (11 February 2016) paras 19, 28; United Nations Human Rights Council, '"They came to destroy": ISIS Crimes Against the Yazidis' UN Doc A HRC/32/CRP.2 (15 June 2016) para 191. See also Chapter 3, section 7.

[68] See ASR (n 3) art 20, which determines that '[v]alid consent by a state to the commission of a given act by another state precludes the wrongfulness of that act in relation to the former state *to the extent that the act remains within the limits of that consent*' (emphasis added). See also Murphy (n 10) 119; International Law Association (n 11) 19.

within the mandate.[69] If the territorial state does not publicly object to the military conduct, it would be fair to assume that it was tacitly or implicitly consenting to it.[70] This position finds support in the decision of the International Court of Justice (ICJ) in *Armed Activities in the Congo*.[71] The DRC *inter alia* claimed that the references in the August 1998 Protocol to control of the common border between the DRC and Uganda and the elimination of rebel groups did not mention the sending of Ugandan troops across the DRC border. The ICJ rejected this argument, underscoring the fact that the lack of protest by the DRC to the presence of the Ugandan soldiers both prior and subsequent to the adoption of the Protocol amounted to consent.[72]

Where there is no explicit, public statement confirming a state's consent to military assistance as such, its subsequent reaction to the forcible measures on its territory will not only be indicative of whether the assisting state remained within its mandate. Instead, it will also determine whether the territorial state had tacitly consented to begin with. A case in point is Pakistan, where the United States has, since 2004, been engaged in drone strikes against foreign fighters crossing the border from Afghanistan. According to newspaper reports, the Pakistani government had in secret consented to these drone strikes.[73] While the Pakistani government did not issue any public statement that confirmed its consent to the drone strikes, for several years it also refrained from public condemnation of the drone strikes. This lack of protest in a situation in which a response was called for does seem to evince tacit consent.[74]

However, Pakistan's tacit consent visibly began to wane during 2011, in the face of growing Pakistani civilian and military casualties resulting from the drone

[69] In accordance with the UNGA's definition of aggression, the overstepping of the boundaries of consent can amount to an act of aggression. UN Doc A/RES/3314/ (XXIX) (14 December 1974) para 3(e) determines that '[t]he "use of armed forces of one state which are within the territory of another state with the agreement of the receiving state, in contravention of the conditions provided for in the agreement or any extension of their presence in such territory beyond the termination of the agreement" qualifies an act of aggression'. See also Flasch (n 59) 36; Ruys and Ferro (n 9) 82; PE Harrell, 'Modern Day "Guarantee Clauses" and the Legal Authority of Multinational Organizations to Authorize the Use of Force' (2008) 33 Yale Journal of International Law 429.

[70] Corten (n 9) 273; K Bannelier-Christakis, 'Military Interventions against ISIL in Iraq, Syria and Libya, and the Legal Basis of Consent' (2016) 29 Leiden Journal of International Law 769.

[71] *Armed Activities in the Congo* (n 12); Corten (n 9) 273.

[72] *Armed Activities in the Congo* (n 12) paras 45–46; E Lieblich, 'Intervention and Consent: Consensual Forcible Intervention in Internal Armed Conflict as International Agreement' (2011) 29 Boston University International Law Journal 358.

[73] Murphy (n 10) 116; see also G Miller and B Woodward, 'Secret Memos Reveal Explicit Nature of US, Pakistan Agreement on Drones' *Washington Post* (24 October 2013) https://www.washingtonpost.com. It has further been reported that until 2011, the US Central Intelligence Agency (CIA) regularly faxed to the Pakistani intelligence services information about the air space that their drones would use. The Pakistani intelligence services from their side confirmed receipt of this information. If these reports were true, it would provide strong evidence of tacit consent. See A Entous, S Gorman, and E Perez, 'US Unease Over Drone Strikes' *Wall Street Journal* (26 September 2012) https://www.wsj.com/articles/SB10000872396390444100404577641520858011452.

[74] Byrne (n 6) 104, 106; Flasch (n 59) 42.

strikes.[75] This was poignantly illustrated by the contradicting reactions of the Foreign Minister and the Prime Minister to the killing of Osama bin Laden in May 2011. The former expressed 'deep concerns and reservations' that the United States unilaterally carried out the mission in the city of Abbottabad, without Pakistan's knowledge or permission. Prime Minister Gillani, on the other hand, described the killing as a 'victory'.[76] Also, in late 2011, following strikes that resulted in Pakistani military casualties, US forces were expelled from the Pakistani Shamsi air base from where it flew drone strikes.[77] In June 2012 the Foreign Minister again condemned the drone strikes as a violation of Pakistan's sovereignty,[78] a position also reiterated by the new Prime Minister Sharif in June 2013.[79] In addition, these statements were not contradicted by the then President Zardari,[80] raising the question as to whether the combined effect of these condemnations and lack of rebuttals constituted a withdrawal of consent by the Pakistani government from future drone attacks.[81]

At this juncture it is worth recalling the decision of the ICJ in the *Armed Activities in the Congo* decision, which suggests that the withdrawal of consent to the presence of a foreign military in a state's territory can occur at any time, without any particular formalities, and also by inference.[82] In this instance, DRC President Kabila made a statement on 28 July 1998 in which he noted that the Rwandan military presence in the DRC, which had assisted the DRC during its liberation, had been terminated. He thereafter concluded by stating that '[t]his marks the end of the presence of *all* foreign military forces in the Congo'.[83] Uganda for its part

[75] See K Brulliard, 'Military Warns Against US Raids' *Boston Globe* (6 May 2011) http://archive.boston.com/news/world/asia/articles/2011/05/06/pakistans_powerful_army_warns_against_us_raids/.

[76] ibid. Subsequent to the killing of Osama bin Laden, the Pakistani intelligence services reportedly also stopped to acknowledge receipt of US faxes regarding the air space required for drone strikes, although it continued to clear air space and did not interfere with the drone strikes as such. See Entous, Gorman, and Perez (n 73).

[77] S Shah, 'Pakistan Orders US to Leave Airbase in Row Over Deadly NATO Assault' *Guardian* (27 November 2011) https://www.theguardian.com/world/2011/nov/27/pakistan-orders-us-leave-shamsi-airbase. See also Q Nauman, 'Pakistan Condemns US Drone Strikes' *Reuters* (4 June 2012) https://www.reuters.com/article/us-pakistan-usa-drones/pakistan-condemns-u-s-drone-strikes-idUSBRE8530MS20120604.

[78] Nauman (n 77).

[79] Associated Press, 'Pakistan Summons US Ambassador to Protest Against the Latest Drone Killing' *Guardian* (8 June 2013) https://www.theguardian.com/world/2013/jun/08/pakistan-us-drone-killings; Secret Memos Show Pakistan Endorsed Drone Strikes' *BBC News* (24 October 2013) https://www.bbc.com/news/world-asia-24649840. See also Byrne (n 6) 107; Flasch (n 59) 42; Bannelier-Christakis (n 70) 769.

[80] As indicated in section 2, the power to issue and withdraw consent to forcible measures first and foremost lies with the head of state.

[81] The fact that Pakistan may still secretly continue to clear air space for the drone strikes arguably would not weigh up against these public protests. See Flasch (n 59) 43; Byrne (n 6) 107. See also Murphy (n 10) 118–19, who underscores that claims that the Pakistani government was tacitly consenting by 'looking the other way' would not hold up in light of the public protests.

[82] *Armed Activities in the Congo* (n 12) paras 47, 51; Byrne (n 6) 104; Corten (n 9) 273–74.

[83] *Armed activities in the Congo* (n 12) para 49 (emphasis added).

claimed that this statement only concerned Rwandan troops and that any withdrawal of consent regarding the presence of Ugandan troops required a formal denunciation by the DRC of the 1998 Protocol to control of the common border between the DRC and Uganda.[84] The ICJ conceded that the text as such was ambiguous.[85] Nonetheless, from the context it inferred that the withdrawal of consent vis-à-vis all foreign troops had occurred at the latest by 8 August 1998, when the DRC accused both Uganda and Rwanda of 'invading its territory'.[86]

Particularly noteworthy is the fact that the ICJ did not dwell on the question of whether the 1998 Protocol between the DRC and Uganda (or any other agreement) required any procedures or time lines to be observed when consent was withdrawn. Instead, it stated rather categorically that 'no particular formalities would have been required for the DRC to withdraw its consent to the presence of Ugandan troops on its soil'.[87] This reasoning suggests that due to its intrusive nature, a state's consent to direct military assistance on request is always accompanied by an (implicit) right of revocation of such consent.[88] Moreover, such consent can be withdrawn at any time and in any manner, as long as the withdrawal is clear from the context.[89] Thereafter, any continued exercise of forcible measures by the formerly invited state in the territorial state would no longer be justifiable on the basis of the legal construct of military assistance on request.[90] If one now applies this reasoning to the above-mentioned developments in Pakistan, it is fair to conclude that the country had by June 2013 withdrawn any remaining support for the US drone strikes. Thereafter, the United States could only (if at all) justify its continued airstrikes in Pakistan on the basis of the right to individual or collective self-defence.[91]

[84] ibid para 50.

[85] ibid para 51.

[86] ibid (n 12) para 53; Byrne (n 6) 104.

[87] *Armed activities in the Congo* (n 12) para 51; see also Lieblich (n 72) 353, 363; Gray (n 49) 87.

[88] Corten (n 9) 274. See also D Wippman, 'Treaty-Based Intervention: Who can Say No?' (1995) 62 University of Chicago Law Review 647; Hafner Report (n 5) 395–96; Lieblich (n 49) 19. However, see Murphy (n 10) 119, who suggests that if consent had been given for a specific time, it cannot be withdrawn within that period.

[89] This position also finds resonance in UN Doc A/RES/3314/ (XXIX) (n 69) para 33. It determines that an act of aggression can result from 'the use of armed forces of one state which are within the territory of another state with the agreement of the receiving state, in contravention of the conditions provided for in the agreement *or any extension of their presence in such territory beyond the termination of the agreement*' (emphasis added). See also Hafner Report (n 5) paras 73–74.

[90] Subsequent to the withdrawal of consent by the DRC, the UNSC repeatedly described the presence of Ugandan and Rwandan troops in the country as a violation of the DRC's territorial integrity and sovereignty and called for their immediate withdrawal. See *inter alia* UN Doc S/RES/3004 (16 June 2000) paras 2, 3, 4(a); UN Doc S/RES/1332 (14 December 2000) para 10; UN Doc S/RES/1341 (22 February 2001) para 2; UN Doc S/RES/ 1355 (15 June 2002) para 3. See also International Law Association (n 11) 20.

[91] In late October 2011 some ambivalence also existed about the possible revocation by Somalia of its consent to Kenyan military action in Somalia against al-Shabaab, based on a Joint Communiqué Issued at the Conclusion of a Meeting Between the Government of Kenya and the Transitional Federal Government of Somalia of 18 October 2011 http://graphics8.nytimes.com/packages/pdf/world/joint-communique-kenya-somalia.pdf. By November 2011 the Somali

This evolution from tacit (if reluctant) consent to open protest by Pakistan against US airstrikes in its territory can be contrasted with the much clearer Syrian protest prior and subsequent to US military airstrikes in Syria against IS. Chapter 3 already brought to light that when the United States commenced these strikes in September 2014, it did not seek Syria's consent, although it did give the Syrian regime advance notice of its impending military operation against IS.[92] Syria for its part stated in August 2014, that is, prior to the initiation of the airstrikes, that any airstrikes without the consent of the Syrian government would be a violation of Syrian sovereignty and would be considered an act of aggression.[93] For almost a year thereafter the Assad regime did not express further outright objections against the airstrikes.[94]

This only changed on 17 September 2015 when Syria explicitly objected to the fact that the military action by the United States and its allies had not occurred in coordination with the Syrian government.[95] However, it is submitted that Syria's initial lack of protest subsequent to the commencement of the airstrikes did not amount to a form of tacit consent.[96] First, shortly before the commencement of the airstrikes in August 2014, Syria expressed clear opposition to any future airstrikes carried out without its consent. Second, the United States for its part explicitly denied having sought the consent of Syria and any willingness to cooperate with it

President reportedly expressed objections to the Kenyan military action, while the Prime Minister supported the forcible measures. However, the objection did not seem to have the effect of revoking the Joint Communiqué and the Kenyan military operations were subsequently integrated into AMISON by UN Doc S/RES/2036 (22 February 2012). See Lieblich (n 49) 16. See also Chapter 3, section 4.3.

[92] See B Ki-Moon (UNSG), Remarks at the Climate Summit Press Conference (Including Comments on Syria) (23 September 2014) https://www.un.org/sg/en/content/sg/speeches/2014-09-23/remarks-climate-summit-press-conference-including-comments-syria; Flasch (n 59) 44. See also Chapter 3, section 4.7.

[93] Associated Press, 'US Air Strikes on Syrian ISIS Targets Need Permission: Syria' *CBC News* (25 August 2014) https://www.cbc.ca/news/world/u-s-airstrikes-on-syrian-isis-targets-need-permission-syria-1.2745775; Flasch (n 59) 43; Bannelier-Christakis (n 70) 770.

[94] Flasch (n 59) 44.

[95] See *inter alia* Identical Letters dated 16 September 2015 from the Permanent Representative of the Syrian Arab Republic to the United Nations Addressed to the Secretary-General and the President of the Security Council UN Doc S/2015/718 (17 September 2015); Identical Letters dated 17 September 2015 from the Permanent Representative of the Syrian Arab Republic to the United Nations Addressed to the Secretary-General and the President of the Security Council UN Doc S/2015/719 (21 September 2015); Bannelier-Christakis (n 70) 767. See also Chapter 6, section 3.

[96] See also R van Steenberghe, 'From Passive Consent to Self-Defence after the Syrian Protest Against the US-Led Coalition' *EJIL:Talk!* (23 October 2015) https://www.ejiltalk.org/13758-2/. He contrasts the initial Syrian passivity with its strong protests during the same time against Israeli air strikes of Dimas and Damascus airport, as well as against Turkish military incursion directed at relocating the Tomb of Sulayman Shah, without the consent of Syria. See respectively the Identical Letters dated 8 December 2014 from the Permanent Representative of the Syrian Arab Republic to the United Nations Addressed to the Secretary-General and the President of the Security Council UN Doc S/2014/874 (8 December 2014); Identical Letters dated 23 February 2015 from the Permanent Representative of the Syrian Araba Republic to the United Nations Addressed to the Secretary-General and the President of the Security Council UN Doc S/2015/132 (25 February 2015).

militarily.[97] The combined effect of these facts would militate against inferring tacit consent by Syria in the period leading up to 17 September 2015.[98] Moreover, even if one were to argue that Syria initially tacitly consented to the airstrikes, this consent was subsequently clearly revoked by its unambivalent protest.[99]

In the final analysis, the challenges posed by the evincing of (continued) tacit consent, notably in the case of Pakistan, underscore the practical importance of publicizing consent to direct military assistance, as well as the revocation of such consent. Even though general international law requires neither the expression of such consent nor its revocation to be explicit or made in public, public statements by the territorial state clarifying its position on the forcible measures in question go some way towards providing legal certainty. Furthermore, any reluctance of the territorial state to express its consent to forcible measures in public is likely to be a sign that the consent is fragile and that its revocation is a real possibility. Were this to happen in a situation where the consent of the territorial state constituted the exclusive legal basis for the forcible measures of the assisting state, any continuation thereof would be in violation of article 2(4) of the UN Charter.[100]

5. The implications of the timing of consent

As the legal construct of direct military assistance on request hinges on the presence of valid consent, it logically follows that the consent must be given at the latest at the time that the forcible intervention commences.[101] Where the recognized government had not given its consent, the forcible measures will be in violation of article 2(4) of the UN Charter[102] unless it could be justified on the basis of the right to self-defence or a chapter VII authorization of the UNSC.[103] Consent

[97] See Bannelier-Christakis (n 70) 676; Flasch (n 59) 46; A Gearen, 'US Rules Out Coordinating With Assad on Airstrikes Against Islamists in Syria' *Washington Post* (26 August 2014) https://www.washingtonpost.com/world/national-security/us-rules-out-coordinating-with-assad-on-airstrikes-against-islamists-in-syria/2014/08/26/cda02e0e-2d2e-11e4-9b98-848790384093_story.html?utm_term=.08a440dc60d4.

[98] The United States consistently ruled out any military cooperation with the Assad regime. See Bannelier-Christakis (n 70) 676; Flasch (n 59) 46; Gearen (n 70).

[99] Flasch (n 59) 43–44; Bannelier-Christakis (n 79) 771; Van Steenberghe (n 96). See also UN Doc S/PV.7527 (30 September 2015) 30 for Syria's protest against the air strikes by members of the United States-led coalition.

[100] See UN Doc A/RES/3314/ (XXIX) (n 69) art 3(e).

[101] See ASR (n 3) Commentary to art 20 ASR para (3): 'Consent to the commission of otherwise wrongful conduct may be given by a state in advance or even at the time it is occurring.' See also Corten (n 9) 269.

[102] UN Charter (n 27).

[103] A well-known example from the Cold War era, where no consent was present at the time of the military intervention, is that of the Soviet invasion of Afghanistan on 25 December 1979. Only on 28 December 1979 did the Soviet Union declare that the military assistance followed on a request by the Afghan government. However, at the time of the intervention no consent by the recognized government existed (as a result of which it was overthrown two days after the invasion). See extensively CJ le Mon, 'Unilateral Intervention by Invitation in Civil Wars: the Effective Control Test Tested' (2003) 35 New York University Journal of International Law and Politics 778 ff; see also Corten (n 9) 2.

issued by the recognized government only after the commencement of the forcible measures in its territory cannot retroactively remedy any wrongfulness of the forcible measures that were commenced on its territory prior to its issuing of consent.[104] This follows from the customary international law rule that the lawfulness of conduct has to be assessed at the time of its occurrence.[105]

Any consent after the perpetration of a wrongful act (*ex post facto* consent), whether it be explicit or through acquiescence, nonetheless can cause the loss of the right to invoke state responsibility.[106] In consequence, the wronged state would become procedurally barred from invoking a claim against the perpetrating state, although the wrongfulness of the prior conduct remains intact.[107] This, for example, could be the case where the territorial state fails to protest against wrongful forcible measures on its territory within a reasonable time after its occurrence and such failure under the circumstances amounts to acquiescence.[108] A pertinent example would be the January 2017 border crossing by Senegalese soldiers into The Gambia. Chapter 3 showed that on 19 January 2017, immediately after having been sworn in as President of The Gambia, President Barrow extended a request for military assistance to ECOWAS.[109] However, according to some reports, some of the ECOWAS soldiers had already (unintentionally) crossed the border between Senegal and The Gambia shortly after midnight on 19 January 2019.[110] Had this indeed been the case, this military presence would have been in violation of the prohibition of the use of force, for having occurred before the issuing of the invitation for direct assistance.[111] However, the absence of any protest by President Barrow in relation to this prior military presence could be interpreted as acquiescence.

[104] K Kreß and B Nußberger, 'Pro-Democratic Intervention in Current International Law: The Case of The Gambia in January 2017' (2017) 4 Journal on the Use of Force in International Law 251; Ruys and Ferro (n 9) 81; Corten (n 9) 269.

[105] ASR (n 3) art 13 determines that '[a]n act of a state does not constitute a breach of an international obligation unless the state is bound by the obligation in question at the time the act occurs'. See also *Island of Palmas (Netherlands v United States of America)* UNRIAA [1928] Vol II 845; *Certain Phosphate Lands in Nauru (Nauru v Australia)* Preliminary Objections Judgment [1992] ICJ Rep 240 paras 31 ff.

[106] ASR (n 3) art 45 determines that '[t]he responsibility of a state may not be invoked if (a) the injured state has validly waived the claim; (b) the injured state is to be considered as having, by reason of its conduct, validly acquiesced in the lapse of the claim'. See also ASR (n 3) Comment to art 20 para (3): Corten (n 9) 269.

[107] Corten (n 9) 269.

[108] No specific time lapse is required and all the circumstances of the case have to be taken into account to determine whether the delay in protest constitutes acquiescence. See ASR (n 3) Commentary to art 45 paras (6), (9), (11). See also *Nauru v Australia* (n 105) para 32. See also Bannelier-Christakis (n 70) 767.

[109] 'Inaugural Address of A Barrow, President of the Republic of The Gambia' *Fatunetwork* (20 January 2017) http://fatunetwork.net/inaugural-address-adama-barrow-president-republic-gambia/. See also Chapter 3, section 3.2.

[110] See Kreß and Nußberger (n 104) 241; D Searcey, 'Why Democracy Prevailed in Gambia' *New York Times* (30 January 2017) https://www.nytimes.com/2017/01/30/world/africa/gambia-barrow-democracy-africa.html.

[111] See also Kreß and Nußberger (n 104) 251.

Another example could be the US drone strikes in Pakistan, referred to in section 4 in connection with tacit consent. In the alternative to claiming that Pakistan tacitly consented to the drone strikes during the period 2004 to 2011, it is arguable that its lack of public protest during this period amounted to acquiescence. As the existence of both tacit consent and acquiescence hinges on the lack of protest in a situation for which a response was called for, it may be difficult to distinguish between these two concepts. In consequence, the distinction between *ex post facto* consent as a mere procedural bar to the invocation of state responsibility versus the preclusion of wrongfulness of the forcible measures through tacit consent could be very difficult to sustain in practice.

That being said, the analysis in Chapter 3 revealed that in the overwhelming majority of post-Cold War situations in which direct military assistance on request occurred, the consent was issued explicitly and prior to the specific intervention in question. The challenges posed by determining and eventually distinguishing between (prior) tacit consent and (*ex post facto*) acquiescence to forcible measures have therefore not frequently arisen. Instead, a more pertinent question seems to be whether general international law requires a temporal proximity between the consent issued by the inviting state and the direct military assistance provided by the invited state. Stated differently, the question arises of whether the prior consent has to be ad hoc to the specific intervention, or whether it may also be given *ex ante* and in general terms. A typical example of the latter would be a pro-invasion treaty or treaty clause, in accordance with which (a) state(s) agree(s) in advance that (an)other state(s) or multilateral organization has the right to engage in forcible measures on its territory on the future occurrence of certain events.[112]

A key controversy pertaining to *ex ante* pro-invasion treaty clauses is that the consent to forcible measures does not only intend to bind the actual government that is concluding the treaty but also future governments.[113] At first sight this might seem unproblematic, as it is a well-established principle of international law that a state's international treaty obligations continues despite a change of government.[114] However, in view of the impact of the use of force on a state's sovereignty and territorial integrity, there is strong support in doctrine for the position that any *ex ante* consent expressed through bilateral or multilateral pro-invasion clauses has to be supplemented by specific, ad hoc consent by the recognized government at the time of the military intervention.[115] This argument seems to constitute the flipside

[112] Lieblich (n 72) 366; Lieblich (n 49) 194–95; Harrell (n 69) 429; GH Fox, 'Intervention by Invitation' in M Weller (ed), *The Oxford Handbook of the Use of Force in International Law* (OUP 2015) 831.

[113] Lieblich (n 49) 194–95.

[114] ibid.

[115] See IDI, 2011 Resolution (n 61) para 4(3) according to which '[i]f military assistance is based on a treaty, an ad hoc request is required for the specific case'. For a more stringent view from the Cold War era, see L Doswald-Beck, 'The Legal Validity of Military Intervention by Invitation of the Government' (1986) 56 British Yearbook of International Law 246 ff. She regarded treaties authorizing intervention in an *ex ante* fashion as a violation of the principle of non-intervention. In line with this reasoning, the

of the claim that the right of a state to withdraw its consent to forcible measures would prevail over any conflicting treaty formalities.[116] Seen in this light, the ad hoc consent becomes necessary to determine whether the *ex ante* consent issued at the time of treaty ratification or accession is still intact at the time of the pending military intervention.[117]

Post-Cold War and organizational practice provides some support for the position that *ex ante* consent to forcible measures in the form of pro-invasion treaty clauses has to be complemented by additional, ad hoc consent. This is most prominent in Africa, where pro-invasion clauses have found their way into article 4(h) of the Constitutive Act of the African Union (AU) of 2002,[118] as well as article 25 the Protocol Relating to the Mechanism for Conflict Prevention, Management, Resolution, Peace-Keeping and Security of 1999 of ECOWAS.[119] A reluctance to embrace *ex ante* consent to military invasion is also reflected by the Protocol on Politics, Defence and Security Operation of 2001 of the Southern African Development Community (SADC).

5.1 *Ex ante* consent within the AU security framework

The more pro-interventionist stance reflected by the current security framework of the AU forms a contrast with the non-interventionist approach of the AU's predecessor, the Organization of African Unity (OAU), which remained reluctant to engage militarily in member states.[120] By 1993, the member states had merely committed to a non-binding Declaration of the Assembly of Heads of State and Government on the Establishment within the OAU of a Mechanism for Conflict

only permissible exception would be where the treaty regulated intervention in reaction to third party involvement (ie counter-intervention).

[116] As indicated in section 4, this position finds support in the *Armed Activities in the Congo* decision (n 12) para 51. See also Corten (n 9) 274; Kreß and Nußberger (n 104) 247. However, see Fox (n 112) 832, who is reluctant to accept that incumbent governments embroiled in a non-international armed conflict can withdraw consent extended under a pro-invasion treaty, without the other parties to the conflict also consenting to such withdrawal. This argument is inspired by the lack of representativeness of the recognized government (from the perspective of self-determination) for the purpose of consenting or withdrawing consent to forcible measures. Similarly, see Harrel (n 69) 429. However, as indicated in Chapter 3, section 5, the right to self-determination hardly seems to be of any significance in post-Cold War state practice pertaining to the use of force.

[117] Corten (n 9) 274; Nolte (n 61) 254–55; Lieblich (n 72) 102, Hafner Report (n 5) 392-93.

[118] Constitutive Act of the African Union of 11 July 2000 (2158 UNTS 3) http://www.peaceau.org/uploads/au-act-en.pdf.

[119] Protocol Relating to the Mechanism for Conflict Prevention, Management, Resolution, Peace-Keeping and Security of 10 December 1999 https://www.zif-berlin.org/fileadmin/uploads/analyse/dokumente/ECOWAS_Protocol_ConflictPrevention.pdf.

[120] See N Wilen and PD Williams, 'The African Union and Coercive Diplomacy: The Case of Burundi' (2018) 4 Journal of Modern African Studies 677–768. For an analysis of the unsuccessful attempt by the OAU to intervene militarily in Chad in the late 1970s and early 1980s, see Nolte (n 9) 383 ff. See also AHG/Res 102 (XVIII) http://www.peaceau.org/uploads/ahg-res-102-xviii-e.pdf.

Prevention, Management and Resolution of 30 June 1993.[121] However, in the wake of the OAU's inability to respond to a series of atrocities in the 1990s in *inter alia* the DRC, Liberia, Rwanda, and Sierra Leone, article 4(h) found its way into the Constitutive Act of the AU in 2000.[122]

Whereas article 4(j) of the AU Constitutive Act affirms the right of member states to request military assistance from the AU to restore peace and security,[123] article 4(h) articulates the right of the AU to intervene in its member states on its own accord in specified circumstances. It determines that the AU has the right 'to intervene in a member state pursuant to a decision of the Assembly in respect of grave circumstances, namely, war crimes, genocide and crimes against humanity'.[124] If one takes the decision-making procedures for triggering an intervention in accordance with article 4(h) at face value, it seems to suggest that the soliciting of specific, ad hoc consent of the target state would not necessarily be required. In accordance with article 7(1) of the AU Constitutive Act, the Assembly of Heads of State and Government takes such a decision on the basis of consensus 'or, failing which, by a two-thirds majority of the member states of the Union'.[125]

In practice any decision to invoke article 4(h) will first be preceded by a recommendation by the AU Peace and Security Council to this effect, which was established by the Protocol Relating to the Establishment of the Peace and Security Council of the African Union of 2002.[126] This standing decision-making organ of the AU for the prevention, management, and resolution of conflicts is composed of fifteen member states that are elected on the basis of regional representation for terms of two to three years.[127] The AU Peace and Security Council *inter alia* has the competence to 'recommend to the Assembly, pursuant to article 4(h) of

[121] The Mechanism was to evolve around a Central Organ with the Secretary-General and the Secretariat as its operational arm. See AHG/DECL.3 (XXIX) para 7 http://www.peaceau.org/uploads/ahg-decl-3-xxix-e.pdf; See also Nolte (n 9) 389; G Nolte, 'Restoring Peace by Regional Action' (1993) 53 Zeitschrift für ausländisches öffentliches Recht und Völkerrecht 635 ff.

[122] G Amvane, 'Intervention Pursuant to Article 4(h) of the Constitutive Act of the African Union Without United Nations Security Council Authorisation' (2015) 15 African Human Rights Law Journal 294–95; Harrell (n 69) 442.

[123] AU Constitutive Act (n 118) art 4(j) confirms '[t]he right of member states to request intervention from the Union in order to restore peace and security'.

[124] AU Constitutive Act (n 118) art 4(h). It is further worth noting that when the Protocol on Amendments to the Constitutive Act of the African Union of 11 July 2003 enters into force, it will expand the grounds for intervention in art 4(h) to also include 'a serious threat to legitimate order to restore peace and security to the member state of the Union upon the recommendation of the Peace and Security Council'. The text of the Protocol is available at https://au.int/en/treaties/protocol-amendments-constitutive-act-african-union. However, the Protocol has not yet been ratified by the two-thirds majority required for entry into force. For the status of ratifications, see https://au.int/sites/default/files/treaties/35423-sl-PROTOCOL-3.pdf.

[125] AU Constitutive Act (n 118) art 97(1).

[126] The Protocol Relating to the Establishment of the Peace and Security Council of the African Union of 9 July 2002 art 2(1) https://au.int/en/treaties/protocol-relating-establishment-peace-and-security-council-african-union. The establishment of the AU Peace and Security Council was also foreseen in the AU Constitutive Act (n 118) art 5(2).

[127] See AU Peace and Security Protocol (n 126) art 5. In accordance with art 8(2), it can meet at the level of permanent representatives, ministers, or heads of state.

the Constitutive Act, intervention, on behalf of the Union, in a member state in respect of grave circumstances, namely war crimes, genocide and crimes against humanity, as defined in relevant international conventions and instruments'.[128] While the AU Peace and Security Council also strives to take decisions by consensus, it can take decisions by simple majority on procedural matters and by a two-thirds majority on all other matters.[129] The fact that both the AU Peace and Security Council and the AU Assembly of Heads of State and Government can take decisions regarding the invocation of article 4(h) on the basis of a qualified majority suggests that the ad hoc consent of the target state would not be legally required under the AU security framework.

A further, related point concerns the fact that the AU Constitutive Act makes no reference to the need for prior authorization by the UNSC in terms of article 53(1) of the UN Charter when invoking article 4(h). The AU Peace and Security Protocol for its part acknowledges the primacy of the UNSC in the maintenance of international peace and security, and pledges close cooperation with the UNSC in promoting and maintaining peace, security, and stability in Africa and in keeping with Chapter VIII of the UN Charter.[130] Yet, it also stops short of explicitly requiring the AU Assembly of Heads of State and Government to obtain prior UNSC authorization under Chapter VIII of the UN Charter before invoking article 4(h). This suggests that while the AU regards a UNSC authorization as politically desirable when invoking article 4(h), it is not regarded as a legal requirement.[131] This in turn can be interpreted as implying that the *ex ante* consent that the AU member states expressed vis-à-vis article 4(h) by becoming a party to the AU Constitutive Act placed any subsequent forcible measures based on article 4(h) beyond the scope of 'enforcement measures' in terms of article 53(1) of the UN Charter.[132]

However, the still embryonic practice of the AU in relation to the invocation of article 4(h) of the AU Constitutive Act reveals that member states are reluctant to bypass the ad hoc consent of the target state by relying on qualified majority decision making, or to assume that *ex ante* consent would suffice for the purposes of article 53(1) of the UN Charter. At the time of writing the AU has only on one occasion attempted to intervene militarily on the basis of article 4(h) of its Constitutive Act. This was in the wake of widespread conflict in Burundi in 2015, after President Pierre Nkurunziza had announced that he would seek a third term in office.[133]

[128] AU Peace and Security Protocol (n 126) art 7(e).

[129] ibid art 8(13).

[130] ibid arts 17(1) and (2).

[131] See also A Ferreira-Snyman, 'Intervention with Specific Reference to the Relationship Between the United Nations Security Council and the African Union' (2010) 63 Comparative and International Law Journal of Southern Africa 160.

[132] See also Chapter 1, section 1.

[133] The only other time that the AU resorted to the AU Constitutive Act (n 118) art 4(h) was to support the internationalized trial of the former Chadian President Habré, who *inter alia* was charged with widespread and systematic torture. See Wilen and Williams (n 120) 678.

On 17 December 2015 the AU Peace and Security Council authorized the deployment of a 5,000-troop African Prevention and Protection Mission in Burundi (MAPROBU).[134] In addition, it recommended to the Assembly of Heads of State and Government to implement article 4(h) of the AU Constitutive Act, should Burundi not accept to deploy MAPROBU within ninety-six hours.[135] However, parallel to this decision the AU Peace and Security Council also appealed to the UNSC to adopt a resolution under Chapter VII of the UN Charter to support a decision to resort to article 4(h).[136]

The fact that the AU Peace and Security Council combined its invocation of article 4(h) with an appeal to the UNSC to endorse the deployment of MAPROBU may be interpreted as implying that any deployment of MAPROBU in the absence of specific, ad hoc consent by Burundi would constitute 'enforcement action' in terms of article 53(1) of the UN Charter. This view finds support in the fact that Burundi rejected the deployment of MAPROBU,[137] with its Foreign Minister and President respectively comparing the deployment to an 'invasion of' and 'attack on' the country.[138] Furthermore, at an AU Summit meeting in January 2016, the (then) Gambian President Jammeh noted that in the absence of the Burundian government's consent to the deployment of the military mission, the situation in Burundi was an internal matter.[139] The President of Chad was also reported as stating that Burundi could not be forced to accept the deployment of MAPBROBU.[140]

Further reservations about the MAPROBU operation were expressed by Equatorial Guinea, Tanzania, and Uganda. These were of a political rather than legal nature, emphasizing a preference for political dialogue and expressing concerns that the military operation may aggravate the peace process.[141] Be that as it may, in its official Communiqué of the meeting, the AU Peace and Security Council reconsidered its decision to deploy MAPROBU, claiming that such deployment would be premature.[142] In consequence, the non-materialization of the

[134] AU Peace and Security Council, Communiqué, 565th Meeting, PSC/PR/COMM (DLXV) (17 December 2015) para 13(a)(i) http://www.peaceau.org/uploads/psc-565-comm-burundi-17-12-2015.pdf.

[135] ibid paras 13(c)(ii) and 13(c)(iv).

[136] ibid para 15.

[137] See also AU Peace and Security Council, Communiqué, 571st Meeting PSC/AHG/COMM.3(DLXXI) (29 January 2016) para 11.

[138] Wilen and Williams (n 120) 687.

[139] ibid; S Dersso, 'To Intervene or Not to Intervene? An Inside View of the AU's Decision-Making on Article 4(h) and Burundi' *World Peace Foundation* (26 February 2016) 7 https://sites.tufts.edu/wpf/files/2017/05/AU-Decision-Making-on-Burundi_Dersso.pdf; Wilen and Williams (n 120) 686.

[140] Dersso (n 139) 9.

[141] Dersso (n 139) 7–8.

[142] See AU Peace and Security Council, Communiqué, 571st Meeting at the Level of Heads of State and Government PSC/AHG/COMM.3(DLXXI) (29 January 2016) para 11 http://www.peaceau.org/uploads/571-psc-com-burundi-29-1-2016.pdf. See also Dersso (n 97) 7. See also Wilen and Williams (n 120) 685, who noted additional concerns about the logistical and financial feasibility of the operation.

military operation in Burundi means that as yet there is as no practice supporting the invocation of article 4(h) of the AU Constitutive Act in the absence of either additional ad hoc consent, or an authorization by the UNSC under Chapter VII or VIII (which in this instance never materialized).[143]

5.2 *Ex ante* consent within the ECOWAS security framework

As far as ECOWAS is concerned, pro-invasion clauses found their way into the security framework in 1999. While initially founded in 1975 with the purpose of enhancing economic cooperation and integration among member states,[144] the organization has systematically expanded its regional security mandate.[145] The founding treaty was first complemented by the Protocol on Non-Aggression of 22 April 1978. Although this Protocol contained a clause on the peaceful settlement of disputes,[146] it also reaffirmed the principles of non-interference and state sovereignty. Next, the ECOWAS states adopted the Protocol Relating to the Mutual Assistance on Defence of 29 May 1981.[147] This collective self-defence agreement applied in cases of external aggression or conflict between member states that could not be settled in terms of the non-aggression Protocol, or internal armed conflict engineered and supported actively from outside that would be likely to endanger security and peace in the whole region.[148] It also provided for a multinational ECOWAS defence force with an elaborate command structure.[149] However, the 1981 Protocol explicitly determined that in case a member state faced external aggression or internal aggression maintained and sustained from the outside, its head of state had to send a written request for (military) assistance to the ECOWAS authority and member states.[150] The treaty itself thus required specific, ad hoc consent of the territorial state before military force could be deployed. It also did not

143 See also Wilen and Williams (n 120) 691.

144 The fifteen members include Benin, Burkina Faso, Cape Verde, Côte d'Ivoire, The Gambia, Ghana, Guinea, Guinea Bissau, Liberia, Mali, Niger, Nigeria, Senegal, Sierra Leone, and Togo. See Treaty of the Economic Community of West African States of May 1975 art 2, reprinted in (1975) 14 International Legal Materials 1200. See, generally, I Sampson, 'The Responsibility to Protect and ECOWAS Mechanisms on Peace and Security: Assessing their Convergence and Divergence on Intervention' (2011) 16 Journal of Conflict and Security Law 507.

145 Sampson (n 144) 507–08.

146 Protocol on Non-Aggression of ECOWAS of 22 April 1978, reprinted in P Gonidec, *Les Organisations Internationales Africaines* (L'Harmattan 1987) 275–76; see also Nolte (n 121) 613.

147 Protocol Relating to the Mutual Assistance on Defence of 29 May 1981 A/SP3/5/81 (1970–1990) http://www.operationspaix.net/DATA/DOCUMENT/3827~v~Protocole_d_Assistance_Mutuelle_en_matiere_de_Defense.pdf.

148 1981 ECOWAS Protocol (n 147) arts 2–4.

149 ibid art 13.

150 ibid arts 16 and 18(1). In case of a conflict between ECOWAS member states, art 17 merely allowed for the stationing of troops between the countries. In addition, art 18(2) did not allow for military intervention in case of purely internal conflicts.

allow for military intervention in case of purely internal conflicts,[151] which was in keeping with the non-interventionist approach on the continent at the time.

The revised Treaty of ECOWAS of 1993 consolidated the regional security framework, reflecting a shift towards a more comprehensive approach towards regional security. Its fundamental principles *inter alia* reaffirmed the commitment of member states to good neighbourliness through non-aggression between member states, as well as the maintenance of regional peace and security.[152] Article 58(2) of the revised 1993 Treaty further contains the commitment by member states to cooperate with ECOWAS in establishing and strengthening appropriate mechanisms for the timely prevention and resolution of intra-state and inter-state conflicts.[153] This commitment was concretized through the adoption of the Protocol Relating to the Mechanism for Conflict Prevention, Management, Resolution, Peace-Keeping and Security of 1999 that established an elaborate regional peace and security mechanism, including a military component (ECOWAS Ceasefire Monitoring Group/ECOMOG).[154]

The ECOWAS Mechanism was designed to function in a range of situations, including inter-state and intra-state conflicts. According to article 25 of the 1999 Protocol, these range from external (threats of) aggression, to inter-state conflict, situations of serious and massive violations of human rights and the rule of law, as well as the overthrow or attempted overthrow of a democratically elected government.[155] It can further be deployed in domestic conflicts that threaten to trigger a humanitarian disaster, or that pose a serious threat to peace and security in the sub-region.[156] While the ECOWAS Mechanism can be initiated at the request of a member state, it can also be initiated on the initiative of organs of ECOWAS.[157] Decisions about whether to deploy military troops from ECOMOG in any of the broad-ranging situations mentioned in article 25 rest with the organization's Mediation and Security Council,[158] which decides on the basis of a two-thirds majority vote of members present and voting.[159] The ECOWAS Mechanism is thus set up in a way that that can in principle facilitate the deployment of ECOMOG

[151] 1981 ECOWAS Protocol (n 147) art 18(2).

[152] See Economic Community of West African States (ECOWAS) Revised Treaty of 24 July 1993 arts 4(d) and 4(e) http://www.ecowas.int/wp-content/uploads/2015/01/Revised-treaty.pdf.

[153] Economic Community of West African States (ECOWAS) Revised Treaty of 24 July 1993 art 58(2), reprinted in S Ebobrah and A Tanoh (eds), *Compendium of African Sub-Regional Human Rights Documents* (Pretoria University Law Press 2010) 184; see also E Birikorang, 'Lessons Learned and Best Practice From a Troubled Region: ECOWAS and the Development of the ECOWAS Standby Force', in U Engel and J Gomes Porto (eds), *Towards an African Peace and Security Regime* (Ashgate 2013) 89.

[154] ECOWAS Mechanism Protocol (n 119) arts 3, 10(c), 21, and 22; Sampson (n 144) 508; Harrell (n 69) 438.

[155] ECOWAS Mechanism Protocol (n 119) art 25.

[156] ibid art 25.

[157] ibid art 26.

[158] ibid arts 10(a)-(f); see also arts 6 and 7.

[159] ECOWAS Mechanism Protocol (n 119) art 9.

troops in a member state without the specific, ad hoc consent of the recognized government.

The formal relationship of the ECOWAS Mechanism with the UNSC reflects an ambivalence that is similar to that between the AU security framework and the UNSC. The ECOWAS revised 1993 Treaty merely states that the organization will 'cooperate' with the UN system in the pursuit of its objectives.[160] The 1999 Protocol for its part states that in accordance with Chapters VII and VIII of the UN Charter, it will inform the UN of any military intervention undertaken in accordance with the Protocol.[161] The term 'inform' suggests that ECOWAS does not necessarily regard a prior UNSC authorization as a legal requirement when adopting military measures in accordance with its own security framework. Once again (as in the case of the AU), there seems to be an implication that by ratifying the revised ECOWAS security framework (notably the 1999 Protocol), member states have given *ex ante* consent to any forcible measures based on this treaty framework and do not regard any such measures as falling under 'enforcement measures' in terms of article 53(1) of the UN Charter.

However, since the adoption of the 1999 Protocol, ECOWAS has consistently deployed ECOMOG forces only after having obtained the additional, ad hoc consent of the recognized government, or with prior UNSC authorization under Chapter VII or VIII of the UN Charter (or both). This is poignantly illustrated by the January 2017 deployment of ECOMOG forces in The Gambia. As shown earlier, these forces only (intentionally) entered The Gambia from Senegal after the new, democratically elected and internationally recognized President was sworn in and requested military assistance.[162] The ECOWAS member states thus did not invoke any *ex ante* treaty-based consent emanating from the 1999 Protocol as the legal basis for the military deployment in The Gambia.[163]

At this juncture it is worth reminding that also in the era before the adoption of the 1999 Protocol, the deployment of ECOMOG (in the absence of prior UNSC authorization under Chapter VII or VIII of the UN Charter) occurred with ad hoc consent of the respective internationally recognized governments. This was notably the case in Liberia in August 1990,[164] Sierra Leone in 1997,[165] as well as Guinea-Bissau in 1998.[166] However, in the latter instance the military operation resembled

[160] ECOWAS revised 1993 Treaty (n 153) art 83(2).

[161] ECOWAS Mechanism Protocol (n 119) art 52.

[162] See also Chapter 3, section 3.2.

[163] See also Kreß and Nußberger (n 104) 247, who note that states such as Senegal did not raise any such claims in the UNSC debates pertaining to UN Doc S/RES2377 (19 January (2017).

[164] See Letter Addressed by President Samuel K Doe to the Chairman and Members of the Ministerial Meeting of ECOWAS Standing Mediation Committee, Doc No 39 (14 July 1990) in M Weller (ed), *Regional Peace-Keeping and International Enforcement: The Liberian Crisis* (CUP 1994) 61. See also Chapter 3, section 3.2.

[165] See the ECOWAS Final Communiqué of the Meeting of 26 June 1997, annexed to UN Doc S/1997/499 (27 June 1997); Lieblich (n 72) 367. See also Chapter 2, section 3.

[166] UN Doc S/RES/1216 (21 December 1998) paras 4 ff; see also Chapter 3, section 3.2.

a classic peace-keeping operation. In the cases of Liberia and Sierra Leone, the doctrines of humanitarian intervention and *ex post facto* UNSC authorization have also been forwarded as legal justification for the ECOMOG military.[167] As a result, none of these instances would serve as a convincing example of military assistance to the government based on ad hoc consent. Even so, the fact remains that there is yet to be an ECOWAS military operation exclusively based on *ex ante* consent as articulated in article 25 of the 1999 Protocol.

5.3 The absence of *ex ante* consent within the SADC security framework

The (at first sight) permissive approach of the AU and ECOWAS security frameworks to pro-invasion treaty clauses may be contrasted with that of the SADC. This sub-regional economic community was established in 1992, in the wake of the formal abolition of apartheid in South Africa.[168] The 1992 SADC Treaty only contained general references to regional peace and security issues. Article 5(1)(c) determined that it was an objective of SADC to promote and defend peace and security. Article 21 further determined that politics, diplomacy, international relations, and peace and security were areas of cooperation.[169] In 1996 the security framework was complemented by the adoption of the Botswana Communiqué by the SADC Heads of State and Government. The Communiqué added the principle that military intervention of whatever nature shall be decided only after all possible political remedies have been exhausted in accordance with the Charter of the (then still existing) OAU and the UN. It further established the SADC Organ of Politics, Defence and Security (SADC Organ), which *inter alia* had the aim of protecting the people of the region against instability arising from the breakdown of law and order, inter-state conflict, and external aggression. [170]

Internal differences of opinion about the extent to which the SADC Organ operated independently from other SADC structures continued until 2001, when a revised legal framework was introduced. The Consolidated Text of the Treaty of

167 See Chapter 2, section 3 and Chapter 3, section 3.2. See also E de Wet 'The Evolving Role of ECOWAS and the SADC in Peace Operations: A Challenge to the Primacy of the United Nations Security Council in Matters of Peace and Security?' (2014) 27 Leiden Journal of International Law 360 ff.

168 Treaty of the Southern African Development Community of 17 August 1992 http://www.iss.co.za/AF/RegOrg/unity_to_union/pdfs/sadc/8SADC_Treaty.pdf. The members include Angola, Botswana, the DRC, Lesotho, Madagascar, Malawi, Mauritius, Mozambique, Namibia, South Africa, Swaziland, Tanzania, Zambia, and Zimbabwe.

169 1992 SADC Treaty (n 168).

170 Communiqué, Summit of Heads of State and Government of the Southern African Development Community of 28 June 1996, cited in Institute for Security Studies (ed), *Building Security in Southern Africa* (1999) https://www.sadc.int/files/3913/5292/8384/SADC_SUMMIT_COMMUNIQUES_1980-2006.pdf.

the Southern African Development Community of 2001 (the revised SADC treaty) confirmed that consolidating, defending, and maintaining democracy, peace, security, and stability was a SADC objective.[171] Article 9 further established the Organ on Politics, Defence and Security Cooperation,[172] leaving its detailed regulation to the Protocol on Politics, Defence and Security Cooperation of 14 August 2001. This instrument integrated the former SADC Organ into the main structure of SADC, reducing the possibility of contentious deployment of troops in future.[173]

The SADC Protocol on Politics, Defence and Security Operation *inter alia* made concrete the jurisdiction and competencies of the organization in relation to security matters.[174] Article 11(2) granted the organization jurisdiction over inter-state conflicts (where at least one of the parties to the conflict is a member state); intra-state conflicts concerning large-scale violence between sections of the population or between the state and sections of the population, including genocide, ethnic cleansing, and gross violations of human rights; a military coup or other threat to the legitimate authority of a state; and a condition of civil war or insurgency.[175] However, article 11(3)(c), read together with articles 11(3)(d) and 11(4)(a) of the Protocol on Politics, Defence and Security Operation suggests that this broad jurisdiction is not to be understood as including *ex ante* consent to forcible measures. According to article 11(3)(c), the Chairperson of the SADC Organ may suggest to the Summit of Heads of State and Government 'enforcement action' against disputing parties where peaceful means of resolving a conflict are unsuccessful. Article 11(3)(d) continues by stating that the Summit 'shall resort to enforcement action only as a last resort, and in accordance with Article 53 of the United Nations Charter, only with the authorization of the United Nations Security Council'.[176] Article 11(4)(a) for its part determines that '[i]n respect of both inter- and intra-state conflicts, the Organ shall seek to obtain the consent of the disputant parties to its peacemaking efforts'.

The combined effect of these explicit references to 'enforcement action' and article 53(1) of the UN Charter, on the one hand, and the consent of the disputing (state) parties, on the other, is that forcible measures in the absence of ad hoc consent by the target state would amount to coercive military action for which UNSC authorization is required.[177] This conclusion is also supported by the recent albeit

[171] Consolidated Text of the Treaty of the Southern African Development Community, as Amended August 2001, art 5(1) https://www.sadc.int/files/5314/4559/5701/Consolidated_Text_of_the_SADC_Treaty_-_scanned_21_October_2015.pdf.

[172] ibid art 9(1)b).

[173] De Wet (n 167) 365–66.

[174] Protocol on Politics, Defence and Security Co-operation of 14 August 2001 https://www.sadc.int/files/3613/5292/8367/Protocol_on_Politics_Defence_and_Security20001.pdf.

[175] Protocol on Politics, Defence and Security Cooperation (n 174) arts 11(2)(a)–(2)(b). See also art 11(1) which reaffirms the right to self-defence in accordance with the UN Charter.

[176] According to the SADC 2001 Treaty (n 171) art 10(9), decisions by the Summit are taken by consensus.

[177] See Chapter 1, section 1.

very limited practice of SADC. As illuminated in Chapter 3, the SADC has only authorized one military operation since the adoption of the 2001 Protocol on Politics, Defence and Security Operation. This operation, in Lesotho in November 2017, was conducted with the ad hoc consent of the recognized government.[178]

6. Conclusion

From the above analysis it may be concluded that customary international law only imposes two specific, formal limitations on the legal construct of military assistance on request. The first would be that the request for or consent to military assistance must be issued (and withdrawn) by the highest officials of a state, namely, the head of state and/or government. Where these two positions are not combined within the same person and there is disagreement between them as to whether consent (still) exists, the domestic law of the country in question may be decisive in determining who has the final say in the matter. However, such disagreement between the two highest state officials is likely to be an indication of the fragility of the consent which (at least as a matter of policy, if not law) should caution against relying exclusively on consent as the legal basis for the forcible measures.

The second constraint imposed by customary international law concerns the requirement that *ex ante* consent as expressed in pro-invasion treaty clauses must be complemented by ad hoc consent at the time of the forcible measures. While the post-Cold War practice in this regard is limited, current (African) state and organizational practice suggests that the pro-invasion clauses in article 4(h) of the AU Constitutive Act and article 25 of the 1999 ECOWAS Protocol have in practice been interpreted and applied in line with this customary right of states to withdraw prior consent to forcible measures at any time. In consequence, the ad hoc consent serves to verify that the prior consent has not since been (implicitly) withdrawn. This restrictive interpretation of article 4(h) of the AU Constitutive Act and article 25 of the 1999 ECOWAS Protocol reflects a reluctance on the part of member states to deploy decision-making by a qualified majority in a way that presumes the target state's actual consent to the pending forcible measures, based on its *ex ante* consent expressed through treaty ratification or accession. Simultaneously there is a reluctance on their part to accept that such *ex ante* consent places the forcible measures resulting from the respective pro-invasion clauses beyond the scope of

[178] Subsequent to the second operation, the AU underscored the fact that the SADC mission was 'in line with the United Nations (UN) Charter, Chapter VI, the Protocol Relating to the Establishment of the Peace and Security Council of the AU and the relevant provisions contained in the SADC Treaty, Protocol on Politics, Defence and Security Cooperation, including the Memorandum of Understanding (MoU) establishing the SADC Standby Brigade of 2007'. See AU Peace and Security Council 748th Meeting, Communiqué, PSC/AHG/COM.(DCCXLIX) (27 January 2018) para 3 http://www.peaceau.org/uploads/psc.summit.749.com.ahg.terrorism.27.01.2018.pdf. See also Chapter 3, section 3.1.

'enforcement measures' in terms of article 53(1) of the UN Charter. Instead, any such forcible measures in the absence of additional, ad hoc consent of the target state are still perceived by some member states as coercive action that requires the authorization of the UNSC under Chapter VII or VIII of the UN Charter.

Apart from these two constraints, customary international law does not seem to impose any particular formal requirements on states expressing consent to forcible measures on its territory. States enjoy considerable freedom in relation to the manner in which their consent is expressed or withdrawn. While it is preferable for the purposes of legal certainty that any consent to military assistance be issued expressly, it can also be done tacitly. Whether this was the case will depend on the circumstances and, in particular, on the conduct of the territorial state subsequent to any military intervention. Similarly, the conduct of the territorial state will be decisive for determining whether particular military action falls within the scope of the consent issued, as well as whether consent has been withdrawn.

Problematic from a policy perspective are the very high customary thresholds attached to coercion, as a result of which any established consent by the recognized government is effectively presumed to have been freely given. This can facilitate coercive military intervention in all but name, as the states 'requesting' direct military assistance are likely to be politically and militarily fragile. They may therefore not be in a position to resist pressure from militarily strong states with hegemonic motives to accept 'offers' of military assistance. Similarly, the territorial state may refrain from withdrawing any consent to military assistance, due to covert pressure from a militarily strong 'assisting' state. The risk of covert coercion would be particularly acute where the request for direct assistance is issued to a single, strong state or states outside the legal framework of a regional organization. The deliberative decision-making processes existing within regional organizations can go some way towards countering potentially coercive influences of the regional powers.[179] However, the vast majority of requests for direct military assistance on the side of the recognized government since the end of the Cold War have occurred outside the checks and balances provided by regional organizations. In these situations, the high bar attached to establishing coercion bears the risk of reducing the requirement of freely given consent to a fiction.

[179] Harrell (n 69) 431.

6

The Relationship Between Military Assistance on Request and the Right to Individual or Collective Self-Defence

1. Introduction

Military assistance on request and the right to individual or collective self-defence in article 51 of the Charter of the United Nations (UN) (UN Charter)[1] constitute two separate legal constructs under international law. Whereas the former turns on the freely expressed consent of the *de jure* recognized government during the entire duration of the military intervention, the latter is triggered when a state falls victim to an armed attack.[2] Despite the different legal

[1] United Nations, Charter of the United Nations (24 October 1945) 1 NTS XVI https://treaties.un.org/doc/source/docs/charter-all-lang.pdf art 51 determines: 'Nothing in the present Charter shall impair the inherent right of individual or collective self-defence if an armed attack occurs against a member of the United Nations, until the Security Council has taken measures necessary to maintain international peace and security. Measures taken by members in the exercise of this right of self-defence shall be immediately reported to the Security Council and shall not in any way affect the authority and responsibility of the Security Council under the present Charter to take at any time such action as it deems necessary in order to maintain or restore international peace and security.' This chapter builds on the article by E de Wet 'The Invocation of the Right to Self-Defence in Response to Armed Attacks Conducted by Armed Groups: Implications for Attribution' (2019) 32 Leiden Journal of International Law 91–110.

[2] The extensive literature pertaining to the right to self-defence generated since the turn of the century include JI Charney, 'The Use of Force Against Terrorism and International Law' (2001) 95 American Journal of International Law 836 ff; T Franck, 'Terrorism and the Right to Self-Defence' (2001) 95 American Journal of International Law 839 ff; J Brunnée and S Toope, 'The Use of Force: International Law After Iraq' (2004) 53 International and Comparative Law Quarterly 785 ff; J Brunnée and S Toope, 'Self-Defence Against Non-State Actors: Are Powerful States Willing But Unable to Change the International Law?' 2018 (67) International and Comparative Law Quarterly 263 ff; S Murphy, 'Self-Defence and the Israeli Wall Advisory Opinion: An *Ipse Dixit* from the ICJ?' (2005) 99 American Journal of International Law 62 ff; GP Fletcher and JD Ohlin, *Defending Humanity. When Force is Justified and Why* (OUP 2008) 208–18; CJ Tams, 'The Use of Force Against Terrorists' (2009) 20 European Journal of International Law 359 ff; T Ruys, *'Armed Attack' and Article 51 of the UN Charter* (CUP 2010); R van Steenberghe, 'Self-Defence in Response to Attacks by Non-state Actors in the Light of Recent State Practice: A Step Forward?' (2010) 23 LJIL 183 ff; D Bethlehem, 'Principles Relevant to the Scope of a State's Right of Self-Defence Against an Imminent or Actual Armed Attack by Non-state Actors' (2012) 106 American Journal of International Law 769 ff; A Randelzhofer and G Nolte, 'Article 51' in B Simma and others (eds), *The Charter of the United Nations. A Commentary Vol II* (OUP 2012) 1397 ff; HH Koh, 'International Law in Cyberspace' *Opinio Juris* (18 September 2012) http://opiniojuris.org; A Deeks, '"Unwilling or Unable": Towards a Normative Framework for Extraterritorial Self-Defence' (2012) 52 Virginia Journal of International Law 483 ff; D Tladi, 'The Nonconsenting Innocent State: The Problem with Bethlehem's Principle 12' (2013) 107 American Journal of International Law 572 ff; M Hakimi, 'Defensive Force Against Non-State Actors: The State of Play' (2015) 91 International

criteria underpinning these two legal constructs, forcible measures in third states are sometimes justified with reference to both military assistance on request and the right to individual or collective self-defence. For example, as indicated in Chapter 3, the presence of Russia and Iran in the Syrian conflict was based on an invitation extended by the Assad regime.[3] The United States-led international coalition against Islamic State (IS), on the other hand, was based on the right to individual or collective self-defence.[4] In Yemen the Saudi-led coalition against the Houthi's invoked self-defence,[5] while the United Sates was relying on the invitation extended by President Hadi.[6] These examples suggest that the legal constructs of military intervention on request and the right to individual or collective self-defence can serve as parallel grounds for the use of force in the same state. The purpose of the current chapter is to examine the legal relationship between these constructs in such situations.

In so doing, the analysis places particular emphasis on the increasingly expansive interpretation of the right to individual or collective self-defence and the (potential) implications thereof for the notion of consent that underpins the legal construct of military assistance on request. In this context, two situations in particular come to mind, both potentially affecting the role of the consent of the state on whose territory the forcible measures are undertaken to such measures. The first concerns requests by incumbent governments for military assistance in

Law Scholarship 1 ff; K Tibori-Szabo, 'Self-Defence and the United States Policy on Drone Strikes' (2015) 20 Journal of Conflict and Security Law 381 ff; R van Steenberghe, 'The Law of Self-Defence and the New Argumentative Landscape on the Expansionists' Side (2016) 29 LJIL 43 ff; P Starski, 'Right to Self-Defence, Attribution and the Non-State Actor: Birth of the "Unable or Unwilling" Standard?' (2015) 75 Heidelberg Journal of International Law 455 ff; P Starski, 'Silence Within the Process of Normative Change and Evolution of the Prohibition on the Use of Force: Normative Volatility and Legislative Responsibility' Max Planck Institute for Comparative Public Law and International Law (MPIL) Research Paper No 2016-20 (13 October 2016); O Corten, 'The "Unwilling or Unable" Test: Has it Been and Could It Be Accepted?' (2017) 4 Journal of the Use of Force in International Law 14 ff; O Corten, 'The "Unwilling or Unable" Test: Has It Been and Could It Be Accepted?' (2016) 29 LJIL 777 ff; N Tsagourias, 'Self-Defence Against Non-State Actors: The Interaction Between Self-Defence as a Primary Rule and Self-Defence as a Secondary Rule' (2016) 29 LJIL 801 ff; V Lanovoy, 'The Use of Force by Non-State Actors and the Limits of Attribution of Conduct' (2017) 28 European Journal of International Law 563 ff.

[3] Letter dated 15 October 2015 from the Permanent Representative of the Russian Federation to the United Nations Addressed to the President of the Security Council UN Doc S/2015/792 (15 October 2015) 2.

[4] Letter dated 23 September 2014 from the Permanent Representative of the United States of America to the United Nations Addressed to the Secretary-General UN Doc S/2014/695 (23 September 2014).

[5] Identical Letters dated 26 March 2015 from the Permanent Representative of Qatar to the United Nations addressed to the Secretary-General and the President of the Security Council, Annex UN Doc S/2015/217 (27 March 2015) 4–5; see also M Zamani and M Nikouei, 'Intervention by Invitation, Collective Self-Defence and the Enigma of Effective Control' (2017) 16 Chinese Journal of International Law 24.

[6] See Letter dated 15 October 2016 from the Permanent Representative of the United States of America to the United Nations Addressed to the President of the Security Council UN Doc S/2016/869 (17 October 2016).

response to (alleged) prior foreign intervention in the respective state's territory on the side of insurrectional groups.[7] Such support by third states against an incumbent government can under certain circumstances amount to an indirect armed attack by a state. Accordingly, the incumbent government can claim a right to receive military assistance from other states on the basis of the right to collective self-defence. If this were to occur, the request for military assistance may constitute a component of the right to collective self-defence rather than a separate legal basis for the use of force. Moreover, the broader the scope of the type of third state support that would qualify as an indirect armed attack, the more leeway the territorial state and its allies will have to invoke the right to collective self-defence instead of the legal construct of military assistance on request.

Second, states increasingly rely on the right to individual or collective self-defence when retaliating against armed attacks perpetrated by non-state actors located in third states (territorial states), regardless of the extent to which such groups have received assistance from the territorial (or another) state. In these situations, the states invoking self-defence against the non-state actor do not regard the seeking of the consent of the territorial state as decisive for determining the legality of their military operations within the latter's territory. Instead, the question whether such consent was given would be merely one consideration in determining the necessity of the defensive measures in the territory of the state where the non-state actor is located.

A pertinent question that thus arises is whether the invocation of the right to self-defence in reaction to an increasing range of purported indirect armed attacks, as well as its invocation against non-state actors, have the potential to displace or usurp the legal construct of military assistance on request. However, in order to answer this question it is necessary first to examine whether the invocation of the right to self-defence in these contexts indeed are reconcilable with the threshold requirements pertaining to the right to individual or collective self-defence in article 51 of the UN Charter. If not, the question of whether the legal construct of military assistance on request risks being (legally) usurped by the right to self-defence does not arise. At first sight, the invocation of the right to self-defence in the above-mentioned scenarios can be at odds with the principles of attribution as endorsed by the International Court of Justice (ICJ) since its *Nicaragua* decision of 1986.[8] First, depicting a broad range of support by third states to insurrectional groups as an indirect armed attack seems to challenge the high threshold that the ICJ has set for the attribution of conduct of non-state actors to states within the self-defence paradigm. Second, the invocation of the right to individual or collective

[7] This is often described as counter-intervention, as also referred to in Chapter 3, section 5.

[8] *Military and Paramilitary Activities in and Against Nicaragua (Nicaragua v United States)* Merits, Judgment of 27 June 1986 [1986] ICJ Rep 14.

self-defence against non-state actors seems to challenge the ICJ's position that armed attacks can only be executed by states.[9]

As far as the authorship of armed attacks is concerned, it is worth recalling that article 51 of the UN Charter merely states that the right to self-defence is triggered by an 'armed attack' against a member state of the UN. It does not explicate who the author of such an armed attack is. Yet, states are regarded as the traditional authors of armed attacks through their land, air, and maritime forces. This is illustrated by article 3 of the 1974 UN General Assembly's Definition of Aggression,[10] which informed the ICJ's understanding of 'armed attack' in its *Nicaragua* decision, as well as in that of *Democratic Republic of the Congo (DRC) v Uganda.*[11] Article 3(g) of the Definition of Aggression also acknowledges indirect acts of aggression (ie indirect armed attacks) by states acting through non-state actors such as armed groups. It determines that an indirect act of aggression would exist in case of '[t]he sending by or on behalf of a state of armed bands, groups, irregulars or mercenaries, which carry out acts of armed force against another state of such gravity as to amount to the acts listed above, or its substantial involvement therein'.[12]

According to the ICJ in the *Nicaragua* decision, the relationship (nexus) between the state and the non-state actor had to be very close for the state to be regarded as the author of an armed attack.[13] Such a group either had to be sent and controlled by the state itself (as a de facto state organ), or had to act under its direct instruction or control.[14] Furthermore, the understanding of the majority of the ICJ of 'substantial involvement' in an armed attack also implied a high threshold for imputing such an attack to a state.[15] While violating the prohibition of the use of force, state assistance to armed bands in the form of weapons, funds, training, or logistical support would not amount to an armed attack that triggered the right of individual or collective self-defence.[16] In fact, this understanding raises the

[9] *Legal Consequences of the Construction of a Wall in the Occupied Palestinian Territory,* Advisory Opinion of 9 July 2004 [2004] ICJ Rep 136 para 129. According to the majority of the ICJ, article 51 of the UN Charter did not excuse Israel's security barrier on the Palestinian territories, in part because Israel did not claim that it had been attacked by another state. A similar logic appeared in *Armed Activities on the Territory of the Congo (Democratic Republic of the Congo v Uganda)* Judgment of 19 December 2005 [2005] ICJ Rep 168 para 146. See also Hakimi (n 2) 5; Tsagourias (n 2) 804. See Tladi (n 2) 572.

[10] UNGA, Res 3314 (XXIX), Definition of Aggression, UN Doc A/RES/29/3314 (14 December 1974); arts 3(a)–(f) give examples of the type of actions undertaken by state organs that would amount to a direct act of aggression.

[11] *Nicaragua* decision (n 8) para 195; *Armed Activities in the Congo* decision (n 9) para 146. In fact, in practice the terms 'act of aggression' and 'armed attack' may be regarded as two sides of the same coin in that both generate from states, even though the Definition of Aggression (n 10) initially was intended to clarify the term 'aggression' in art 39 of the UN Charter. See Randelzhofer and Nolte (n 2) 1407–408.

[12] Definition of Aggression (n 10) art 3.

[13] Tsagourias (n 2) 805; Council of European Union, Independent International Fact-Finding Mission on the Conflict in Georgia Vol II (2009) 260 http://www.mpil.de/files/pdf4/IIFFMCG_Volume_II1.pdf.

[14] *Nicaragua* decision (n 8) para 195; *Armed Activities in the Congo* decision (n 9) para 146; Ruys (n 2) 479 ff; Tsagourias (n 2) 814; Independent International Fact-Finding Commission (n 13) 260.

[15] *Nicaragua* decision (n 8) paras 115, 195, 226–31; Tsagourias (n 2) 815.

[16] See *Nicaragua* decision (n 8) para 205.

question as to whether any form of assistance, falling short of direct instruction, could amount to the type of 'substantial involvement' that crossed the threshold of an armed attack. After all, if the support of non-state actors by means of weapons, training, and/or intelligence did not amount to substantial involvement, it is difficult to see how the term 'substantial involvement' could in practice be anything but synonymous with direct instruction.[17]

While the restrictive interpretation of the ICJ majority was in line with the drafting history of the Definition of Aggression, dissenting judges and scholars have criticized it for not sufficiently taking into account the different ways in which states can incite forcible measures (amounting to armed attacks) against other states.[18] These can vary from the active provision of (a combination of) arms, training, financial, and logistical support to armed bands perpetrating attacks against third states, to passive support in the form of safe havens, or tolerating such groups.[19] The result is a responsibility vacuum in situations where a state that shares a common purpose with a non-state actor provides the latter with the opportunity to carry out an armed attack, without incurring responsibility for the attack as such.[20]

The subsequent analysis will first explore whether the invocation of the right to self-defence by states in recent times constitutes a response to this criticism in the sense that it lowered the threshold requirements for indirect armed attacks. It will also examine whether armed attacks at times are directly attributable to non-state actors.[21] Specifically, section 2 will provide an overview of situations in which states have invoked the right to self-defence. Section 3 for its part focuses on the reactions of other states to such invocations. While non-exhaustive, this account of the (reactions to) invocations of self-defence across regions since the 1980s provides the necessary factual (empirical) basis for assessing the threshold requirements for indirect armed attacks in section 4.1. It simultaneously also serves as factual (empirical) basis for examining whether armed attacks can be directly attributable to armed groups in section 4.2.

The analysis of the threshold requirements for indirect armed attacks focuses on the meaning of 'substantial involvement' in an armed attack, the 'harbouring' doctrine, the 'unwilling' prong of the 'unwilling or unable' doctrine, as well as the potential interrelationship of these terms. It concludes that the threshold requirements for the attribution of armed attacks to states have indeed been lowered since

17 A fact criticized in the Dissenting Opinion of Judge Sir Robert Jennings, *Nicaragua* (n 8) 543.

18 See Dissenting Opinion of Judge Sir Robert Jennings, *Nicaragua* decision (n 8); similarly the Dissenting Opinion of Judge Schwebel, *Nicaragua* decision (n 8) 268–69, 332 ff. See also Ruys (n 2) 415 ff; Randelzhofer and Nolte (n 2) 1415–16.

19 Tsagourias (n 2) 816; Starski (2015) (n 2) 472–73; and Brunnée and Toope (2018) (n 2) 267.

20 Lanovoy (n 2) 578, 580.

21 Contested aspects of self-defence that are not examined in this analysis include notably the gravity threshold that is implied by an armed attack, the temporal requirements attached to self-defence, as well as the intricacies pertaining to the relationship between the necessity and proportionality requirements.

the ICJ's *Nicaragua* decision of 1986. The assessment of the attribution of armed attacks directly to non-state actors includes an examination of the implications of the 'unable' prong of the 'unwilling or unable' doctrine for the invocation of article 51 of the UN Charter. This analysis places particular emphasis on the meaning of the necessity requirement within the self-defence paradigm and supports an interpretation of this requirement in accordance with article 25(1)(a) of the Articles on Responsibility of States for Internationally Wrongful Acts (ASR).[22] This part of the analysis concludes that the standards for the attribution of armed attacks have also evolved in the sense that armed attacks can now be attributed directly to non-state actors.

Finally, in section 5 the chapter turns to the legal implications of lowered threshold requirements for indirect armed attacks and that of the attribution of armed attacks to non-state actors for the legal construct of military assistance on request. It questions in particular whether there is a risk that this construct may be usurped or subsumed by the right to self-defence, by being reduced to a component of the necessity principle.

2. The invocation of the right to self-defence by states

As early as 1981 Israel invoked the 'unwilling or unable' doctrine in justifying the use of force in Lebanon against Hezbollah and the Palestine Liberation Organization.[23] During a debate in the United Nations Security Council (UNSC), Israel asserted that 'under international law, if a state is unwilling or unable to prevent the use of its territory to attack another state, the latter state is entitled to take all necessary measures in its own defence'. In October 2003 Israel attacked alleged Palestinian terrorist targets in Syria on the basis of self-defence.[24] In July 2006 it also retaliated in self-defence after Hezbollah kidnapped two Israeli soldiers and continued indiscriminate firing of rockets into Northern Israel.[25] Lebanon did not at the time have effective control over its territory (notably Southern Lebanon).[26] Israel *inter alia* carried out airstrikes against targets in Lebanon, including the Beirut airport, followed by extensive military operations in Lebanon that lasted a month.[27]

[22] ILC Draft Articles on Responsibility of States for Internationally Wrongful Acts with Commentaries 2001 II Yearbook of the International Law Commission (ASR); and UN Doc A/Res/56/83 (28 January 2002).

[23] See UN Doc S/PV.2292 (17 July 1981) paras 54–55 (Israel), emphasizing in particular Lebanon's inability to control the PLO. See also Deeks (n 2) 486; Ruys (n 2) 422–23.

[24] UN Doc S/PV 4836 (5 October 2003) 7 (Israel); G Myre, 'Attacks What It Calls a Terrorist Camp in Syria' *New York Times* (6 October 2003) http://www.nytimes.com/2003/10/06/world/mideast-turmoil-airstrike-israel-attacks-what-it-calls-terrorist-camp-syria.html.

[25] UN Doc S/PV.5498 (30 July 2016) 3 [UNSG].

[26] As also recognized by the UNSC in UN Doc S/RES/1701 (11 August 2006) para 3; Hakimi (n 2) 9.

[27] Ruys (2) 449 ff.

In 1985 President Reagan described the provision of 'material support for terrorist groups which attack US citizens' as 'armed aggression against the United States under established principles of international law, just as if it had used its own armed forces'.[28] The United States further relied on the harbouring doctrine after the Al Qaida bombings of its embassies in Kenya and Tanzania in 1998, when striking a pharmaceutical plant in Sudan allegedly used by Al Qaida for producing chemical weapons, as well as terrorist camps in Afghanistan.[29] The 'harbouring' and 'unwilling or unable' doctrines gained momentum subsequent to the 9/11 attacks in the United States. While these attacks were instructed by Al Qaida, the United States regarded the Taliban regime in Afghanistan as co-responsible for allowing Al Qaida to use Afghan territory as its operational base.[30] Relying explicitly on the right of individual and collective self-defence, the United States on 7 October 2001 informed the UNSC that it had initiated military measures in response to these attacks.[31] Shortly afterwards, in 2002, the Australian Prime Minister John Howard asserted his country's right to use unilateral force against terrorist threats in neighbouring countries (but without acting on this assertion).[32] In the same year Russia used force in self-defence in Georgia against Chechen rebels who, operating from Georgia, had conducted violent attacks in Russia. According to Russia, Georgia was 'unwilling or unable' to suppress the activities of the rebel groups.[33] In the wake of the Beslan school siege in 2004, Russia described the incident as an attack on the country.[34] It held Chechen rebels backed by

[28] This was subsequent to the Libyan attacks on the Rome and Vienna airports in 1985. See R Reagan, 'The President's News Conference' (7 January 1986) http://www.presidency.ucsb.edu/ws/index.php?pid=36812. See also M Jackson, *Complicity in International Law* (OUP 2015) 182; Ruys (n 2) 426; Lanovoy (n 2) 571.

[29] Letter dated 20 August 1998 from the Permanent Representative of the United States of America to the United Nations Addressed to the President of the Security Council UN Doc S/1998/780 (20 August 1998).

[30] Letter of the Permanent Representative of the United States of America to the United Nations Addressed to the President of the Security Council UN Doc S/2001/946 (7 October 2001); Tsagourias (n 2) 806.

[31] Letter of the Permanent Representative of the United States of America to the United Nations Addressed to the President of the Security Council UN Doc S/2001/946 (7 October 2001); C Gray, 'Limits to the Use of Force' 2014 (376) Collected Courses of The Hague Academy of International Law 138–39.

[32] C McGrath (Transcript of Interview with Johan Howard), 'PM Supports Action Through Pre-Emptive Strikes' *ABC Local Radio* (2 December 2006) http://www.abc.net.au/am/stories/s738657.htm; T Allard, 'Pre-Emptive Strikes: PM Weights UN Rules Change' *Sydney Morning Herald* (6 December 2002) http://www.smh.com.au/articles/2002/12/05/1038950147512.html; Jackson (n 28) 185.

[33] Letter dated 11 September 2002 from the Permanent Representative of the Russian Federation to the United Nations Addressed to the Secretary-General UN Doc S/2002/1012 Annex (12 September 2002) 2, 3. Furthermore, Russia also invoked Art 51 of the UN Charter in 1993, when engaging in extensive military action against non-state actors operating from and supported by Afghanistan. See Letter dated 15 July 1993 from the Permanent Representative of the Russian Federation Addressed to the Secretary-General UN Doc S/26110, Annex (19 July 1993) 2, 3; Jackson (n 28) 183; Deeks (n 2) 486.

[34] V Putin (translated transcript of televised remarks on 4 September 2004), 'Putin Tells the Russians: "We Shall Be Stronger"' *New York Times* (5 September 2004) http://www.nytimes.com/2004/09/05/world/europe/putin-tells-the-russians-we-shall-be-stronger.html.

Muslim militants responsible and vowed to strike terrorist bases 'anywhere in the world'.[35]

In Latin America, Colombia invoked self-defence in March 2008 when raiding a camp of the Revolutionary Armed Forces of Colombia (FARC) across the border in Ecuador.[36] Colombia implied that the bombing, which killed the FARC commander Raul Reyes, was executed in self-defence, referring to it as 'essential'.[37] The FARC maintained a strong presence in Ecuador which it used to its advantage in planning and launching attacks in Colombia in the period leading up to the bombing.[38] In Africa, states invoked the self-defence doctrine in various contexts since the 1990s, although not always explicitly. In 1992 and 1995 Senegalese war planes targeted suspected rebel bases in Guinea-Bissau, which were alleged to be safe havens for Casamance rebels.[39] In 1996 Sudan criticized Eritrea for perpetrating armed aggression by sponsoring and hosting rebel movements that aimed to overthrow the Sudanese government. However, the criticism stopped short of referring explicitly to the right to self-defence in article 51 of the UN Charter.[40]

One year later Burundi justified incursions into Tanzania with the argument that Tanzania had harboured Burundian terror groups and provided them with military training and weapons.[41] In 2006 Ethiopia undertook a military excursion into Somalia, apparently with the purpose of defending itself against Islamist groups that controlled parts of Somali territory in 2006.[42] In January of the previous year, the African Union (AU) had opted for the AU Non-Aggression and Common Defence Pact, in which it defined aggression as 'the encouragement,

[35] BBC, 'Russia to Launch Beslan Inquiry' *BBC News* (10 September 2004) http://news.bbc.co.uk/2/hi/europe/3645022.stm; Hakimi (n 2) 9.

[36] Reply of the Ministry of External Affairs to the Government of Ecuador (2 March 2008) http://www.cancilleria.gov.co/en/content/reply-ministry-external-affairs-government-ecuador. See also Deeks (n 2) 53; Jackson (n 28) 185.

[37] Reply of the Ministry of External Affairs to the Government of Ecuador (n 36). However, Colombia did not specifically articulate the basis for exercising the right to self-defence. See also Deeks (n 2) 534.

[38] Staff of the United States Senate Commission on Foreign Relations, Report to the Committee on Foreign Relations, 110th Congress, 2nd Session, 'Playing with Fire: Colombia, Ecuador and Venezuela' (28 April 2008) 5–6; Deeks (n 2) 536.

[39] Jackson (n 28) 183.

[40] Letter dated 13 May 1996 from the Chargé d'Affaires AI of the Permanent Mission of the Sudan to the United Nations addressed to the President of the Security Council UN Doc S/1996/356 Annex (21 May 1996) paras 3, 4. In para 5 reference was made to the fact that Eritrea would have to bear the full consequences of its aggressive behaviour towards Sudan, which could propel the region into full-scale confrontation. See also Ruys (n 2) 428–29; Jackson (n 28) 183.

[41] UNSG, Report of the Secretary-General on the Situation in Burundi UN Doc S/1997/547 (15 July 1997) para 9. Pan African News Agency, 'Burundi Denies Wanting to Attack Tanzania' *Reliefweb* (30 April 1997) https://reliefweb.int/report/burundi/burundi-denies-wanting-attack-tanzania. See also Ruys (n 2) 429.

[42] However, there were also indications that Somalia had consented to the Ethiopian military presence. See UN Doc S/PV.5614 (26 December 2006) 3 (Special Representative of the UNSG and head of the UN Political Office for Somali). See also Hakimi (n 2) 11; Gray (n 31) 138. However, see AAM Khayre, 'Self-Defence, Intervention by Invitation, or Proxy-War? The Legality of the 2006 Ethiopian Invasion of Somalia' (2014) 22 African Journal of International and Comparative Law 208 ff, who questions the authenticity of the consent.

support, harbouring or provision of any assistance for the commission of terrorist acts and other violent trans-nationally organized crimes against a member state'.[43] This broad definition (which is in force in respect of the twenty-two signatories)[44] suggests that any involvement in the use of force by non-state actors as described in the Friendly Relations Declaration[45] will amount to aggression, that is, an armed attack.[46]

A similarly progressive understanding of the type of assistance that amounts to an armed attack can be witnessed in the Gulf region, in relation to the current conflict in Yemen.[47] In his letter to the Cooperation Council for the Arab States of the Gulf (GCC) of 24 March 2015, President Hadi of Yemen invoked the collective self-defence provisions enshrined in article 51 of the UN Charter, in the Arab League Charter[48] and in the Arab Treaty of Joint Defence.[49] Referring to aggression by the Houthis, who were also supported by 'regional powers', he urged the six GCC countries to provide immediate support and take the necessary measures, including military intervention, to protect Yemen and its people.[50] While President Hadi's official request for military assistance in terms of article 51 of the UN Charter did not specify the regional powers supporting the Houthi rebels, other statements by himself and Yemeni officials at the time pointed to Iran.[51] With the exception of Oman, the members of the GCC engaged in military operations under the leadership of Saudi Arabia.[52] Saudi Arabia also subsequently identified Iran as the

[43] See African Union Non-Aggression and Common Defence Pact of 1 January 2005 art 1(c)(xi) https://au.int/en/treaties/african-union-non-aggression-and-common-defence-pact.

[44] Status of Ratification https://au.int/sites/default/files/treaties/7788-sl-african_union_non-aggression_and_common_defence_pact.pdf.

[45] UNGA Res 2625 (XXV) Declaration on Principles of International Law Concerning Friendly Relations and Cooperation Among States in Accordance with the Charter of the United Nations UN Doc A/RES/25/2625, Annex (25 October 1970). The customary status of the Resolution has been confirmed in the *Nicaragua* decision (n 8) para 191 and *Armed Activities in the Congo* decision (n 9) para 162.

[46] Tsagourias (n 2) 818.

[47] Lanovoy (n 2) 572.

[48] Pact of the League of Arab States of 22 March 1945, art 6, 70 UNTS 241 https://treaties.un.org/pages/showDetails.aspx?objid=080000028015a44b; Zamani and Nikouei (n 5) 24–25.

[49] Treaty of Joint Defence and Economic Co-operation Between the States of the Arab League of 17 June 1950, art 2 http://avalon.law.yale.edu/20th_century/arabjoin.asp.

[50] Identical Letters dated 26 March 2015 from the Permanent Representative of Qatar to the United Nations Addressed to the Secretary-General and the President of the Security Council, Annex UN Doc S/2015/217 (27 March 2015) 4–5; T Ruys and L Ferro, 'Weathering the Storm: Legality and Legal Implications of the Saudi-Led Military Intervention in Yemen' (2016) 65 International and Comparative Law Quarterly 71.

[51] Statement by Mr Alyemany, Permanent Representative of Yemen to the UN, noting that Iran is the promotor of the coup, as well as the instigator of the sedition in Yemen. See UN Doc S/PV.7411 (22 March 2015) 4 (Yemen). See also Letter dated 24 April 2015 from the Permanent Representative of Qatar to the United Nations Addressed to the President of the Security Council UN Doc S/2015/279 (27 April 2015) 2; Ruys and Ferro (n 50) 73.

[52] The United States justified its airstrikes on radar facilities in Houthi-held areas in October 2016 by the fact that it had been requested by President Hadi and not art 51 of the UN Charter. See Letter dated 15 October 2016 from the Permanent Representative of the United States of America to the United Nations Addressed to the President of the Security Council UN Doc S/2016/869 (17 October 2016). See also Ruys and Ferro (n 50) 71–72.

country arming the Houthi rebels. In addition, it submitted that the Houthis were engaging in cross-border attacks against Saudi Arabian territory.[53] Thus far, the military coalition has limited its operations to the territory of Yemen and has not engaged in airstrikes against Iran.

Turkey for its part has frequently invoked the right to self-defence since the 1990s to justify its incursions into Northern Iraq and the use of force against the Kurdish Workers' Party (PKK), despite strong protest from the Iraqi government.[54] Turkey emphasized that the PKK operated from areas not under the control of the Iraqi government.[55] Turkish operations *inter alia* included attacks on weapon stock piles of militants associated with the PKK in 2008, as well as incursions against the PKK subsequent to the outbreak of the Syrian conflict.[56] However, Turkey did not explicitly base these claims on article 51 of the UN Charter, nor did it consistently report its operations to the UNSC as required by this article.[57] Iran, for its part, also engaged in cross-border operations in Iraq against Kurdish fighters in the 1990s. Iran reported these incursions to the UNSC, basing them on article 51 of the UN Charter. It accused Iraq of supporting terrorist groups through military training and financial, logistical, and intelligence support, as well as providing them with a sanctuary from where they prepared their attacks.[58] On one occasion, Iran also claimed that it had been forced to take defensive measures, as Iraq did not have control over its territory.[59]

[53] Letter Sated 14 September 2016 from the Permanent Representative of Saudi Arabia to the United Nations Addressed to the President of the Security Council UN Doc S/2016/786 (16 September 2016).

[54] For example, Letter dated 2 July 1996 from the Minister for Foreign Affairs of Turkey Addressed to the Secretary-General and to the President of the Security Council UN Doc S/1996/479 (2 July 1996); Letter dated 3 January 1997 from the Minister for Foreign Affairs of Turkey Addressed to the Secretary-General and to the President of the Security Council UN Doc S/1997/7 (14 February 1997); Deeks (n 2) 487; Jackson (n 28) 183.

[55] See eg Identical Letters dated 2 July from the Chargé d'Affaires of the Permanent Mission of Turkey to the United Nations addressed to the Secretary-General and to the President of the Security Council UN Doc S/1996/479, Annex (2 July 1996) 2–3; Identical Letters dated 1997 from the Permanent Mission of Turkey to the United Nations addressed to the Secretary-General and to the President of the Security Council UN Doc S/1997/7, Annex (14 February 1997); see also Deeks (n 2) 487; Jackson (n 28) 183.

[56] I Traynor, 'Upsurge in Kurdish Attacks Raises Pressure on Turkish Prime Minister to Order Iraq Invasion' *Guardian* (9 October 2017) http://www.theguardian.com/world/2007/oct/09/turkey.iraq1; Jackson (n 28) 185.

[57] Gray (n 31) 138–39.

[58] See eg Letter dated 25 May 1993 from the Permanent Representative of the Islamic Republic of Iran to the United Nations addressed to the Secretary-General UN Doc S/25843 (25 May 1993); Letter dated 9 November 1994 from the Chargé d'Affaires of the Islamic Republic of Iran to the United Nations addressed to the Secretary General UN Doc S/1994/1273 (9 November 1994); Letter dated 29 July 1996 from the Permanent Representative of the Islamic Republic of Iran to the United Nations Addressed to the Secretary-General UN Doc S/1996/602 (29 July 1996); Letter dated 13 March 2000 from the Permanent Representative of the Islamic Republic of Iran to the United Nations Addressed to the Secretary-General UN Doc S/2000/216, Annex (14 March 2000); Letter Dated 22 March 2001 from the Permanent Representative of the Islamic Republic of Iran to the United Nations Addressed to the Secretary-General UN Doc S/2001/271, Annex (22 March 2001); Ruys (n 2) 432.

[59] Letter dated 29 July 1996 from the Permanent Representative of the Islamic Republic of Iran to the United Nations Addressed to the Secretary-General, UN Doc S/1996/602 (29 July 1996); Ruys (n 2) 432.

The United States-led airstrikes against the Islamic state (IS) in Syria commenced in September 2014. The letter by the United States to the UNSC underscored the fact that Iraq had requested the United States to lead an international coalition against attacks perpetrated by IS from Syrian territory.[60] The United States further emphasized the right to individual and collective self-defence, as IS posed a threat not only to Iraq, but also to other states, while the Syrian government was 'unwilling or unable' to prevent the use of its territory for such attacks.[61] It is worth noting that, unlike Russia and Iran, which are militarily supporting the Syrian regime with its consent,[62] the United States explicitly did not request Syria's consent to engage in airstrikes against IS,[63] although it gave the Syrian regime advance notice of its impending military operation against IS.[64]

Several other (also non-Western) states have since joined the US-led military coalition against IS in Iraq and Syria.[65] These states tend to rely on a mixture of individual and collective self-defence in justifying their respective military operations, sometimes also invoking the 'unwilling or unable' doctrine. For example, Turkey emphasized the threat posed by IS to itself, while invoking the right to individual and collective self-defence. It also emphasized that Syria was 'neither capable nor willing' to prevent attacks by IS.[66] Similar reactions were forthcoming from Australia and Canada.[67] In its 2018 cross-border military operations into

[60] Letter dated 23 September 2014 from the Permanent Representative of the United States of America to the United Nations Addressed to the Secretary-General UN Doc S/2014/695 (23 September 2014). See also Letter dated 25 June 2014 from the Permanent Representative of Iraq to the United Nations Addressed to the Secretary-General UN Doc S/2014/440, Annex (25 June 2014).

[61] Letter dated 23 September 2014 from the Permanent Representative of the United States of America to the United Nations Addressed to the Secretary-General UN Doc S/2014/695 (23 September 2014).

[62] Letter dated 15 October 2015 from the Permanent Representative of the Russian Federation to the United Nations Addressed to the President of the Security Council UN Doc S/2015/792 (15 October 2015) 2; H Rohani, 'La lutte contre le terrorisme doit être la base de tout en Syrie' *Le Monde* (29 January 2016) http://www.lemonde.fr/international/article/2016/01/29/hassan-rohani-la-lutte-contre-le-terrorisme-doit-etre-la-base-de-tout-en-syrie_4855748_3210.html.

[63] Corten (2016) (n 2) 779

[64] See B Ki-Moon (UNSG), 'Remarks at the Climate Summit Press Conference (Including Comments on Syria)' (2014) http://www.un.org/sg/en/content/sg/speeches/2014-09-23/remarks-climate-summit-press-conference-including-comments-syria; Hakimi (n 2) 27. See also Chapter 3, section 4.7 and Chapter 5, section 4.

[65] Middle Eastern states that have joined the coalition included at an early stage Bahrain, Jordan, Saudi Arabia, the United Arab Emirates, and Qatar. See Reuters Staff, 'Qatar, a Partner in US Airstrikes, says Syrian Regime Main Problem' *Reuters* (24 September 2014) http://www.reuters.com/article/us-un-assembly-qatar/qatar-a-partner-in-u-s-airstrikes-says-syrian-regime-main-problem-idUSKCN0HJ24D20140924.

[66] Letter dated 24 July 2015 from the Chargé d'Affaires of the Permanent Mission of Turkey to the United Nations Addressed to the President of the Security Council UN Doc S/2015/563 (24 July 2015).

[67] Letter dated 9 September 2015 from the Permanent Representative of Australia to the United Nations Addressed to the President of the Security Council UN Doc S/2015/693 (9 September 2015) 1; Letter dated 31 March 2015 from the Chargé d'Affaires of the Permanent Mission of Canada to the United Nations Addressed to the President of the Security Council UN Doc S/2015/221 (31 March 2015). The government of New Zealand, after having received a request for military assistance from Iraq in February 2015, stated that IS posed a significant threat to peace and security, including that of New Zealand. This suggests that it regarded military assistance to Iraq as a manifestation of individual or collective self-defence. See S Nenadic, 'Lawfulness of New Zealand's Military Deployment to Iraq: Intervention by

the Afrin region in Syria, Turkey invoked the right to self-defence under article 51 of the UN Charter (without specifying whether in its individual or collective manifestation). It described Turkey as being under direct threat from PKK-affiliate groups in Syria (Yekîneyên Parastina Gel (YPG/PYD)), as well as Daesh (IS). On this occasion, Turkey did not explicitly invoke the 'unwilling or unable' doctrine.[68] Instead, it stated that the Afrin region was under control of the YPG/PYD from where rockets were fired at Turkish provinces.[69]

Even before the Paris attacks of November 2015, France referred to the direct threat that IS also posed to itself, invoking article 51 of the UN Charter.[70] The United Kingdom in 2014 initially emphasized the right to collective self-defence, as IS was engaged in an ongoing armed attack against Iraq.[71] Since September 2015, the United Kingdom has also been invoking the right to individual self-defence in accordance with article 51 of the UN Charter, in light of planned attacks against the United Kingdom.[72] However, France and the United Kingdom have not (yet) referred to the 'unwilling or unable' doctrine in their official invocation of article 51 of the UN Charter.[73] Other states invoking article 51 of the UN Charter against

Invitation Tested' (2014) 12 New Zealand Yearbook of International Law 5–6. See also New Zealand Government, 'PM Announces Contribution to Coalition Against ISIL' Press Release (25 February 2015) https://www.beehive.govt.nz/release/pm-announces-contribution-coalition-against-isil.

68 Identical Letters dated 20 January 2018 from the Chargé d'Affaires of the Permanent Mission of Turkey to the United Nations Addressed to the Secretary-General and the President of the Security Council UN Doc S/2018/53 (22 January 2018) 1.

69 ibid. In January 2019 Israel attributed an Iranian missile attack on Northern Israel to Syria and which was launched from Syrian territory. Israel depicted the missile attack as an act of aggression and responded by targeting Iranian military infrastructure in Syria. See UN Doc S/PV.8449 (22 January 2019) 8 (Israel). As this incident involved the invocation of self-defence against infrastructure of a *state* located in another state, it could potentially be a manifestation of art 3(f) of the Definition of Aggression (n 10). This article concerns 'the action of a state in allowing its territory which it has placed at the disposal of another state, to be used by that other state for perpetrating an act of aggression against a third state'. However, Israel did not explicitly invoke this article. Syria criticized the Israeli action as an act of aggression, while Iran described it as a violation of Syrian territory. See UN Doc S/PV.8449 (22 January 2019) 31 (Syria); Al Jazeera and News Agencies, 'Iran Warns Israel of "Firm" Response to Air Raids in Syria' *Al Jazeera* (5 February 2019) https://www.aljazeera.com/news/2019/02/iran-warns-israel-firm-response-air-strikes-syria-190205133522150.html. See also B Nußberger and P Fischer, 'Justifying Self-Defence Against Assisting States: Conceptualizing Legal Consequences of Inter-state Assistance' *EJIL:Talk!* (23 May 2019) https://www.ejiltalk.org/justifying-self-defense-against-assisting-states-conceptualizing-legal-consequences-of-inter-state-assistance/.

70 Identical Letters dated 8 September 2015 from the Permanent Representative of France to the United Nations Addressed to the Secretary-General and the President of the Security Council UN Doc S/2015/745 (9 September 2015); Letter dated 24 July 2015 from the Chargé d'Affaires of the Permanent Mission of Turkey to the United Nations Addressed to the President of the Security Council UN Doc S/2015/563 (24 July 2015).

71 Letter dated 7 September 2015 from the Permanent Representative of the United Kingdom of Great Britain and Northern Ireland to the United Nations Addressed to the President of the Security Council UN Doc S/2015/688 (8 September 2015).

72 Letter dated 7 September 2015 from the Permanent Representative of the United Kingdom of Great Britain and Northern Ireland to the United Nations Addressed to the President of the Security Council UN Doc S/2015/688 (8 September 2015); Letter dated 3 December 2015 from the Permanent Representative of the United Kingdom of Great Britain and Northern Ireland to the United Nations Addressed to the President of the Security Council UN Doc S/2015/928 (3 December 2015).

73 Brunnée and Toope (2018) (n 2) 271.

IS for perpetrating attacks against third states from Syrian territory, subsequent to the Paris attacks, included Germany, Denmark, Norway, and Belgium.[74] In these instances there also was no explicit reference to the 'unwilling or unable' doctrine. Germany and Belgium instead underscored that IS occupied a certain part of Syrian territory over which the Syrian government did not at the time exercise effective control.[75]

One of the most recent series of incidents at the time of writing in which the right to self-defence was (implicitly) invoked concerned India's aerial attacks on alleged *jihadist* training camps in Pakistan. Already in 2016, India engaged in so-called surgical strikes in order to neutralize terrorist groups that executed attacks in India after allegedly infiltrating the country from Pakistan.[76] In its official statements at the time, India indicated that it expected Pakistan to cooperate in erasing terrorism as Pakistan agreed 'not to allow its soil or territory under its control for any terrorist activities against India'.[77] However, India did not explicitly invoke the right to self-defence in article 51 of the UN Charter, nor did it make any explicit references to the harbouring or 'unwilling or unable' doctrines. The same could be said of India's justifications for its February 2019 airstrikes against the Jaish-e-Mohammad training camps in Pakistan, following a suicide bombing in Indian-controlled Kashmir.[78] Notably, it stated that Pakistan has been receiving information on the training camps and they could not have functioned without Pakistan's knowledge. India also noted that 'Pakistan has taken no concrete actions to dismantle the infrastructure of terrorism on its soil'.[79] India's reliance on the right to (pre-emptive) self-defence can also be inferred from its claim that as credible evidence had been received that more suicide attacks were planned, 'in the face of imminent danger, a pre-emptive strike became absolutely necessary'.[80]

[74] Letter dated 10 December 2015 from the Chargé d'Affaires of the Permanent Mission of Germany to the United Nations Addressed to the President of the Security Council UN Doc S/2015/946 (10 December 2015); Letter dated 11 January 2016 from the Permanent Representative of Denmark to the United Nations Addressed to the President of the Security Council UN Doc S/2016/34 (13 January 2016); Letter dated 3 June 2016 from the Permanent Representative of Norway to the United Nations Addressed to the President of the Security Council UN Doc S/2016/513 (3 June 2016); Letter dated 7 June 2016 from the Permanent Representative of Belgium to the United Nations Addressed to the President of the Security Council UN Doc S/2016/523 (9 June 2016).

[75] See UN Doc S/2016/523 (9 June 2016) (Belgium); UN Doc S/2015/946 (10 December 2015) (Germany); Brunnée and Toope (2018) (n 2) 271.

[76] Government of India (Ministry of External Affairs), Transcript of Joint Briefing by MEA and MoD (29 September 2016) https://www.mea.gov.in/media-briefings.htm?dtl/27446/Transcript_of_Joint_Briefing_by_MEA_and_MoD_September_29_2016.

[77] ibid.

[78] Government of India (Ministry of External Affairs) (n 76).

[79] ibid.

[80] India's simultaneous claim that the strikes on the *jihadist* training camp were 'non-military pre-emptive action' is somewhat unconvincing and contradictory, as it is difficult to see how forcible measures undertaken by its own air force is of a non-military nature. See Government of India (Ministry of External Affairs) (n 76). See also C Henderson, 'Tit-for-Tat-for-Tit: The Indian and Pakistani Airstrikes and the *Jus ad Bellum*' *EJIL:Talk!* (28 February 2019) https://www.ejiltalk.org/author/chenderson/.

3. Reactions of other states

The reaction of other states in instances where the right to self-defence was invoked is an important consideration in assessing whether the scope of this right has evolved under article 51 of the UN Charter and under its customary counterpart. Such reaction constitutes subsequent practice which is relevant for treaty interpretation in accordance with article 31(3)(b) of the Vienna Convention on the Law of Treaties of 1969 (VCLT).[81] It can contribute to clarifying the meaning of a treaty, including the widening of its interpretation.[82] The weight of any subsequent practice will be influenced by whether and how it is repeated.[83] While no particular frequency is required, the subsequent practice must reflect a common understanding of the parties regarding the (evolution of the) meaning of the treaty terms, which is quite a high barrier.[84] Reactions of other states can further amount to *opinio juris*, that is, conduct 'undertaken with a sense of legal right or obligation' for the purpose of identifying customary international law.[85] Both in terms of subsequent practice and *opinio juris*, inaction by third states (in addition to oral and written statements) can be an indication that they accept certain conduct as law. Whether such toleration by (a) state(s) amounts to acceptance of or acquiescence in the legality of the conduct in question will depend on the circumstances of the case. In relation to subsequent practice one would have to determine whether reaction by other states was called for under what is likely to be very fact-specific circumstances.[86] For the purpose of determining *opinio juris*, the relevance of inaction would *inter alia* hinge on whether the silent state was deemed to have had knowledge of the conduct at the time, as well as whether its interests were affected.[87]

When considering the reactions of third states to the above-mentioned invocations of the right to individual or collective self-defence, it is difficult to identify an unambiguous pattern of explicit endorsement or acquiescence. In fact, the military response of the United States subsequent to the 9/11 attacks seems to be the only instance in which the invocation of the harbouring doctrine met with virtual unanimous support. At the time, it received explicit support

[81] Vienna Convention on the Law of Treaties 23 May 1969, 1155 UNTS 331, art 31(3)(b). See generally O Dörr, 'Article 31. General Rule of Interpretation' in O Dörr and K Schmalenbach (eds), *Vienna Convention o the Law of Treaties. A Commentary* (2nd edn, Springer 2018) 595 ff.

[82] ILC Report of the work of the 68th session, UN Doc A/71/10 (2 May–10 June and 4 July–12 August 2016) ch VI, Conclusion 7(1). See also Starski (2015) (n 2) 20.

[83] ILC Report (n 82) ch VI, Conclusion 9(2).

[84] ILC Report (n 82) ch VI, Commentary on Conclusion 9, paras (10)–(11). See also *The South China Sea Arbitration (The Republic of Philippines v The People's Republic of China)* (Award) PCA Case No 2013-19 (12 July 2016) para 552 https://pcacases.com/web/sendAttach/2086; *Advisory Opinion Concerning the Legality of the Use by a State of Nuclear Weapons in Armed Conflict* ICJ Reports [1996] ICJ Rep 66 paras 19, 27; *Kasikili/Sedudu Island (Botswana/Namibia)* Judgment [1999] ICJ Rep 1045 paras 48–63.

[85] ILC Report (n 82) ch V, Conclusion 9(1); Starski (2015) (n 2) 20.

[86] ILC Report (n 82) ch VI, Conclusion 10(2) and Commentary to Conclusion 10 paras (19) ff.

[87] ILC Report (n 82) ch V, Commentary to Conclusion 10(1) para (7).

from *inter alia* the United Kingdom,[88] the European Union (EU),[89] members of the North Atlantic Treaty Organization (NATO),[90] and the Organization of American States (OAS).[91] However, this response occurred against the backdrop of UNSC Resolution 1368 of 12 September 2001 and UNSC Resolution 1373 of 28 September 2001. Both Resolutions were adopted under Chapter VII of the UN Charter and referred in their Preambles to the right to individual and collective self-defence. This may have convinced some states that the UNSC endorsed the military measures against Al Qaida and the Taliban under Chapter VII of the UN Charter.[92]

No similar resolutions were adopted in relation to the other incidents of self-defence referred to above, and the reaction of third states is not as clear-cut. For example, the Australian statement of 2002 was condemned by Malaysia, Thailand, and the Philippines,[93] while explicit condemnation on the Russian invocation of article 51 of the UN Charter in relation to Georgia in 2002 came from the United States and the Council of Europe's Parliamentary Assembly,[94] yet reactions of other states remained muted. The 2008 Colombian raid of the FARC camp across the Ecuadorian border was condemned as 'a violation of the sovereignty and territorial integrity of Ecuador and of principles of international law' by an OAS Commission of Inquiry.[95] The OAS Permanent Council for its part underscored that 'the territory of a state is inviolable and may not be the object, even temporarily, of military occupation or of other measures of force taken by another state, directly or indirectly, on any grounds whatsoever'.[96] In Africa, Guinea-Bissau protested against the

[88] Letter dated 7 October 2001 from the Chargé d'Affaires of the Permanent Mission of the United Kingdom of Great Britain and Northern Ireland to the United Nations Addressed to the President of the Security Council UN Doc S/2001/947 (7 October 2001).

[89] See European Council, Conclusions and Plan of Action of the Extraordinary European Council Meeting on 21 September 2001 http://www.consilium.europa.eu/en/press/press-releases/?q=andfrDt=11%2F09%2F2001andfrDt_submit=11%2F09%2F2001andtoDt=31%2F10%2F2001andtoDt_submit=31%2F10%2F2001andent%5B%5D=600andstDt=20170930.

[90] See Statement by the North Atlantic Council, NATO Press Release (2001) 124 http://www.nato.int/docu/pr/2001/p01-124e.htm. See also Hakimi (n 2) 9.

[91] See OAS, Convocation of the 23rd Meeting of Consultation of Ministers of Foreign Affairs, OEA/Ser.G.CP/Res. 796 (1293/01) (2001).

[92] For example, the Statement of the European Council (n 89) referred to UN Doc S/RES1368 (12 September 2001). See also the *Consequences of the Construction of a Wall* decision (n 9), Declaration of Judge Buergenthal, para 6 and Separate Opinion of Judge Kooijmans, para 35; Tams (n 2) 377; Tsagourias (n 2) 806; Bethlehem (n 2) 5. However, see Tladi (n 2) 575 who cautions against reading too much into the general, preambular references to the right to self-defence in these resolutions.

[93] Ruys (n 2) 447–48; Myre (n 24); Jackson (n 28) 185.

[94] Parliamentary Assembly of the Council of Europe Recommendation, 'The Situation in Georgia and Its Consequences for the Stability of the Caucasus Region' Recommendation 1580 (2002) para 5 http://www.assembly.coe.int/nw/xml/XRef/Xref-XML2HTML-en.asp?fileid=17043andlang=en; Hakimi (n 2) 14.

[95] Organization of American States Commission, Report of the OAS Commission that Visited Ecuador and Colombia 10 OEA/Ser.F/II.25 RC.25/doc.7/08 (16 March 2008); Hakimi (n 2) 7.

[96] Organization of American States, Convocation of the Meeting of Consultation of Ministers of Foreign Affairs and Appointment of a Commission OAS/CP/RES/930 (1632/08) (5 March 2008). See also Deeks (n 2) 538: Hakimi (n 2) 7; Jackson (n 28) 185.

Senegalese incursions of 1995, underscoring that it did not support rebel incursions. Senegal apologized in response.[97] Tanzania also objected to the allegations of harbouring Burundian rebels.[98] However, the reaction of third states to these incidents remained muted. The same applied to the Ethiopian intervention in Somalia in 2006. Moreover, the broad definition of aggression in the AU Non-Aggression and Common Defence Pact,[99] while not yet invoked in practice, has not met with any protest by third states.

The Israeli airstrikes in Syria in 2003 at the time were explicitly rejected by almost all UNSC members, with the exception of Russia and the United States.[100] However, in 2006 the objection to the Israeli intervention in Lebanon was not so much directed at the invocation of the right to self-defence as to the scope (disproportionality) of the Israeli response.[101] International reaction to Turkey's incursions into Iraq received support from the United States and the United Kingdom on the basis that Iraq was 'unable or unwilling' to prevent the use of its territory for attacks against Turkey.[102] The EU expressed concern about the proportionality of the larger-scale operations but did not condemn these as illegal.[103] Nonetheless, the incursions in the mid-1990s were criticized by the League of Arab States and the Non-Aligned Movement (NAM) as a violation of Iraqi territorial integrity and the rules of international law.[104] Iraq also protested against the Turkish operations on its territory in 2008 as a violation of its sovereignty.[105] While the United States was supportive of the Turkish military incursions into Iraq, it claimed that similar incursions by Iran had no justification.[106] This statement comes across as

[97] See C Gray, *International Law and the Use of Force* (4th edn, OUP 2018) 146.

[98] See *inter alia* United Nations Office of the Coordination of Humanitarian Affairs, 'Burundi-Tanzania: Tanzania "outraged" by claims of support for rebels' *Reliefweb* (16 July 2002) https://reliefweb.int/report/burundi/burundi-tanzania-tanzania-outraged-claims-support-rebels.

[99] See African Union Non-Aggression and Common Defence Pact (n 43).

[100] For statements, see *inter alia* UN Doc S/PV.4836 (5 October 2003) 3 (Syria); 8 (Pakistan, Spain, China); 9 (United Kingdom, Russia, Germany, France); 10 (Bulgaria, Mexico, Chile); 13 (United States); and 14 (League of Arab States). See also Ruys (n 2) 447–48; Jackson (n 28) 185.

[101] UN Doc S/PV.5498 (30 July 2016) 3 (UNSG); Jackson (n 28) 185; Ruys (n 2) 449 ff.

[102] United States State Department, Daily Press Briefings of 28 March 1991, 31 March 1995, 17 April 1995, 7 July 1995, 5 September 1996, 6 November 1996, and 11 February 1998, cited in Ruys (n 2) 431. See also United Kingdom statements, cited in (1995) 66 British Yearbook of International Law 725 and (1998) 69 British Yearbook of International Law 586.

[103] EU Presidency Statement on the Military Action Undertaken by Turkey in Iraqi Territory (25 February 2008) http://www.eu2008.si/en/News_and_Documents/CFSP_statements/February/0225MZZturkey.html.

[104] Letter dated 24 September 1996 from the Permanent Observer for the League of Arab States to the United Nations Addressed to the Secretary-General UN Doc S/1996/796, Annex 1 (24 September 1996); on behalf of the Non-Aligned Movement, see Letter dated 6 June 2000 from the Permanent Representative of South Africa to the United Nations Addressed to the Secretary-General UN Doc A/54/917-S/2000/580 (16 June 2000) para 137.

[105] See eg M Karouney, 'Iraq Condemns Turkish Incursion' *Reuters* (26 February 2008) http://uk.reuters.com/article/uk-turkey-iraq/iraq-condemns-turkish-incursion-idUKL2691363520080226. See also Hakimi (n 2) 13.

[106] United States State Department, Daily Press Briefings, 30 July 1996 and 18 September 1996, cited in Ruys (n 2) 432.

contradictory, given the long-standing support of the United States for the 'harbouring' and 'willing or unable' doctrine.[107]

In the case of Yemen, Iran rejected allegations of direct involvement in the supply of arms to the Houthis. It underscored that the allegations were not corroborated by concrete evidence.[108] When Yemeni officials intercepted a shipment of arms originating from Iran and destined for Houthi rebels in January 2013, Iran emphasized the fact that Yemen had not provided evidence of actual Iranian involvement in the shipment.[109] Allegations of Iranian involvement in arms supplies nonetheless persisted, while the Houthis themselves claimed extensive financial support from Iran.[110] After the commencement of the airstrikes by the United States and its allies against IS in Syria in September 2014, the Assad regime initially did not protest against the airstrikes. At the time, its protests were primarily directed at the military support provided by Turkey, Israel, Qatar, Jordan, Saudi Arabia, and numerous Western states to (other) rebel groups in Syria.[111] However, as of 17 September 2015 this position changed.[112] Syria explicitly objected to the fact that the military action by the United States, along with that by Australia, Canada, France, and the United Kingdom, had not occurred in coordination with the Syrian government. It underscored on several occasions that it was in continuous military confrontations with armed groups, including IS, and that it was also ready to cooperate with the UN in this regard.[113]

[107] See also Ruys (n 2) 432.

[108] Ruys and Ferro (n 50) 76.

[109] Letter dated 12 February 2013 from the Permanent Representative of the Islamic Republic of Iran to the United Nations Addressed to the President of the Security Council UN Doc S/2013/88 (12 February 2013) paras 4 ff.

[110] Letter dated 14 September 2016 from the Permanent Representative of Saudi Arabia to the United Nations Addressed to the President of the Security Council UN Doc S/2016/786 (16 September 2016) paras 4 ff; Final Report of the Panel of Experts on Yemen UN Doc S/2017/81 (31 January 2017) paras 61–62; AFP, 'Houthis Sign Huge Finance Deal with Iran' *New Arab* (12 March 2015) http://www.alaraby.co.uk/english/politics/2015/3/12/houthis-sign-huge-finance-deal-with-iran; Ruys and Ferro (n 50) 75.

[111] For example, Identical Letters dated 26 September 2014 from the Permanent Representative of the Syrian Arab Republic to the United Nations Addressed to the Secretary-General and the President of the Security Council UN Doc A/69/411–S/2014/705 (1 October 2014) para 6; Identical Letters dated 25 May 2015 from the Permanent Representative of the Syrian Arab Republic to the United Nations Addressed to the Secretary-General and the President of the Security Council UN Doc A/69/912–S/2015/371 (1 June 2015) 1-2; Identical Letters dated 29 June 2015 from the Permanent Representative of the Syrian Arab Republic to the United Nations Addressed to the Secretary-General and the President of the Security Council UN Doc A/69/969-S/2015/487 (2 July 2015) 1–2. See also R Goodman, 'Is the United States Already in an "International Armed Conflict" with Syria?' *Just Security* (11 October 2016) http://www.justsecurity.org/33477/united-states-international-armed-conflict-syria/.

[112] Identical Letters dated 17 September 2015 from the Permanent Representative of the Syrian Arab Republic to the United Nations Addressed to the Secretary-General and the President of the Security Council UN Doc S/2015/719 (21 September 2015).

[113] See *inter alia* Identical Letters dated 2 June 2015 from the Permanent Representative of Jordan to the United Nations Addressed to the Secretary-General and the President of the Security Council UN Doc S/A/69/923–S/2015/403 (4 June 2015); Identical Letters dated 16 September 2015 from the Permanent Representative of the Syrian Arab Republic to the United Nations Addressed to the Secretary-General and the President of the Security Council UN Doc S/2015/718 (17 September 2015); Identical Letters dated 17 September 2015 from the Permanent Representative of the Syrian Arab

Syria rejected their invocation of article 51 of the UN Charter in relation to the fight against IS as justification, claiming that this amounted to a distortion of the UN Charter.[114] In a subsequent letter, the Syrian government repeated this position. The letter continued by stating that in order to conform to the requirements of article 51 of the UN Charter, there should be an ongoing act of aggression by an armed force against a member state, that the response should be temporary, and that it should respect the authority and responsibility of the UNSC. These conditions were not met in Syria by states such as the United Kingdom.[115] The US-led airstrikes against IS in Syria were also condemned as illegal by Russia and Iran.[116] China did not explicitly condemn the attacks. Instead, it noted that China supported counter-terrorism efforts, but that international law, sovereignty, independence, and territorial integrity of the relevant countries should be respected.[117]

Explicit support for and/or participation in the airstrikes against IS were forthcoming from five Arab states, including Saudi Arabia.[118] While these states did not explicitly link their support to the right to self-defence or to the 'unwilling or unable' doctrine,[119] they also did not criticize the invocation of these doctrines. Given their knowledge of the airstrikes and that their own (regional) security interests were also affected, it is not unreasonable to interpret this lack of criticism as acquiescence in the manner in which these doctrines were invoked.[120] Similarly,

Republic to the United Nations Addressed to the Secretary-General and the President of the Security Council UN Doc S/2015/719 (21 September 2015).

[114] Identical Letters dated 16 September 2015 from the Permanent Representative of the Syrian Arab Republic to the United Nations Addressed to the Secretary-General and the President of the Security Council UN Doc S/2015/718 (17 September 2015); Identical Letters dated 17 September 2015 from the Permanent Representative of the Syrian Arab Republic to the United Nations Addressed to the Secretary-General and the President of the Security Council UN Doc S/2015/719 (21 September 2015). See also Tsagourias (n 2) 803.

[115] Identical Letters dated 29 December 2015 from the Permanent Representative of the Syrian Arab Republic to the United Nations Addressed to the Secretary-General and the President of the Security Council UN Doc A/70/673- S/2015/1048 (4 January 2016) para 4; Corten (2016) (n 2) 787.

[116] Russia described the airstrikes against IS in Syria without the consent of the Assad government as an act of aggression. See A Anishchuk and J Irish, 'Russia Says Air Strikes in Syria Would Be an Act of Aggression Without UN Vote' *Reuters* (11 September 2014) http://uk.reuters.com/article/uk-russia-u-s-syria-airstrikes/russia-says-air-strikes-in-syria-would-be-act-of-aggression-without-u-n-vote-idUKKBN0H61BF20140911; I Black and D Roberts, 'Isis Air Strikes: Obama's Plan Condemned by Syria, Russia and Iran' *Guardian* (12 September 2014) http://www.theguardian.com/world/2014/sep/11/assad-moscow-tehran-condemn-obama-isis-air-strike-plan; Corten (2016) 788–89; Starski (2015) (n 2) 487.

[117] See Ministry of Foreign Affairs of the Peoples' Republic of China, Foreign Ministry Spokesperson Hua Chunying's Regular Press Conference on 23 September 2014, transcript available at http://www.fmprc.gov.cn/mfa_eng/xwfw_665399/s2510_665401/t1194096.shtml.

[118] P Stewart and T Perry, 'US and Arab Allies Launch First Strikes on Militants in Syria' *Reuters* (23 September 2014) http://www.reuters.com/article/us-syria-crisis-usa-strikes/u-s-and-arab-allies-launch-first-strikes-on-militants-in-syria-idUSKCN0HI03A20140923.

[119] Brunnée and Toope (2018) (n 2) 270. See also O Flasch, 'The Legality of the Air Strikes Against ISIL in Syria: New Insights on the Extraterritorial Use of Force against Non-state Actors' (2016) 3 Journal of the Use of Force and International Law 60.

[120] However, see Starski (2015) (n 2) 489, according to whom the normative value of the prohibition of the use of force in international law requires explicit approval as opposed to tacit acquiescence.

there was a muted reaction from the seventy-five states belonging to the Global Coalition against Daesh. This coalition was formed in September 2014 with the purpose of eliminating IS from Iraq and Syria, including through military means 'in accordance with the principles of international law, including the United Nations Charter'.[121] The fact that these states chose to belong to this coalition may be interpreted as an affirmation of the relevance of the military operations in Syria for their own security interests. In addition, through their membership of this coalition, they may be deemed to have knowledge of the manner in which other coalition members invoke the right to self-defence in Syria. Their lack of protest in this regard, therefore, may be interpreted as tacitly accepting such invocation to be in accordance with the UN Charter.

In 2016 the NAM vaguely stated that 'consistent with the practice of the UN and international law, as pronounced by the ICJ, article 51 of the UN Charter is restrictive and should not be rewritten or re-interpreted'.[122] It is uncertain whether this statement has any direct bearing on any of the conflicts in which self-defence was at the time invoked, given its general nature. Furthermore, several members of the NAM support a broad notion of aggression also by non-state actors. These include Jordan, Bahrain, and the United Arab Emirates which are participating in the airstrikes against IS in Syria,[123] as well as the twenty-two African states that ratified the AU Non-Aggression and Common Defence Pact. This makes it difficult to determine what is meant by a 'restrictive' interpretation of article 51 of the UN Charter, or whether the statement would constitute a criticism against the 'unwilling or unable' doctrine.[124]

As far as the 2018 Turkish incursion into Afrin was concerned, Syria repeatedly objected to the Turkish military presence, which it described respectively as an occupation, a violation of the UN Charter, and aggression towards Syria.[125] However, reaction by third states was either not forthcoming or nuanced. This can be exemplified by the German reaction only two months after the commencement of the incursion. On the one hand, it condemned the high number of civilian casualties and impact on the civilian population, and also expressed concern about the potential illegality of long-term Turkish presence in the region.[126] Germany, therefore, was critical of the disproportionality of the operation and its humanitarian

[121] See Global Coalition against Daesh, 'Guiding Principles from the Global Coalition to Defeat Daesh' (3 February 2018) http://theglobalcoalition.org/en/guiding-principles-global-coalition-defeat-daesh/.

[122] The 17th Summit of Heads of State and Government of the Non-Aligned Movement, Final Document, para 25.2, NAM 2016/CoB/DOC.1. Corr.1 (2017).

[123] Flasch (n 119) 64.

[124] As is suggested by Brunnée and Toope (2018) (n 2) 275.

[125] UN Doc S/PV.8181 (14 February 2018) 11 (Syria); UN Doc S/PV.8195 (28 February 2018) 20 (Syria).

[126] DPA, 'Merkel verurteilt erstmals türkische Syrien-Offensive' *Handelsblatt* (21 March 2018) http://www.handelsblatt.com/politik/deutschland/inakzeptabel-was-in-afrin-geschieht-merkel-verurteilt-erstmals tuerkische-syrien-offensive/21099162.html.

consequences. On the other hand, Germany acknowledged the justified security interests of Turkey and stopped short of depicting the military operation as illegal.[127] Similarly, the European Parliament criticized the humanitarian implications of the military operation as such, as well as its political repercussions for a negotiated settlement in Syria.[128]

In the same vein, the reaction of third states to the Indian airstrikes against terrorist targets in Pakistan stopped short of condemning them, despite vociferous objection by Pakistan. In 2016 and 2019 Pakistan referred to the strikes as aggression, and depicted them as being based on pretextual claims that were not backed by evidence.[129] Moreover, subsequent to the 2019 incident Pakistan undertook airstrikes along the border area (Control Line) in order to demonstrate the 'will and capability for self-defence'.[130] While these strikes did not result in human casualties or damage to infrastructure, a subsequent escalation in aerial skirmishes between the two countries *inter alia* resulted in the capture of two Indian military pilots.[131] In the wake of these developments, Australia, China, France, the United Kingdom, and the EU all called on India and Pakistan to exercise restraint and underscored the need for regional stability and dialogue.[132] However, none of these denounced the Indian airstrikes as illegal. Australia and the United States also urged Pakistan to take action against terrorist groups in its territory.[133] In fact, the US Department of State went as far as to state that it 'stood publicly and resolutely with India in its response to the attack', thereby seemingly supporting India's invocation of the right to self-defence.[134]

On the whole, it is fair to conclude that there is growing state support for applying the right to self-defence outside the narrow parameters proclaimed by

[127] ibid.

[128] European Parliament, European Parliament Resolution on the Situation in Syria 2018/2626 (RSP) (2018) para F. See also the reaction of Iran, whose criticism concerned the political ramifications of the intervention. K Sulaivany, 'Iran Latest to Condemn Turkish Military Campaign Against Kurds in Afrin' Kurdistan 24 (21 January 2018) http://www.kurdistan24.net/en/news/5ed63e9f-1483-4267-95d9-ccb90acd5e27

[129] Government of Pakistan (Ministry of Foreign Affairs), 'Pakistan Condemns LoC Violations by India, Rejects Indian Claim of Surgical Strikes' Latest Press Releases/Speeches (29 September 2019) http://www.mofa.gov.pk/pr-details.php.

[130] ibid. See also Henderson (n 80).

[131] See Henderson (n 80). See also M Safi and M Zahra-Malik, 'Pakistan Says It Has Shot Down Indian Jets After Kashmir Cross-Border Attack' *Guardian* (27 February 2019) https://www.theguardian.com/world/2019/feb/27/pakistan-india-jets-shot-down-airstrikes-kashmir.

[132] FP Staff, 'EU, Australia, China and UK Urge India-Pakistan to Exercise "Maximum Restraint" After IAF Strikes JeM Camps in Balakot' *Firspostt* (29 February 2019) https://www.firstpost.com/india/eu-australia-china-and-uk-urge-india-pakistan-to-exercise-maximum-restraint-after-iaf-strikes-jem-camps-in-balakot-6157691.html.

[133] ibid; Safi and Zahra-Malik (n 131).

[134] PTI, 'US Focused on Pressing Pakistan to Take Sustained, Irreversible Actions Against Terrorists' *Economic Times* (16 March 2019) https://economictimes.indiatimes.com/news/defence/us-focused-on-pressing-pakistan-to-take-sustained-irreversible-actions-against-terrorists/articleshow/68436570.cms?from=mdr.

the ICJ in the *Nicaragua* decision.[135] This broader application also includes support for the invocation of the 'harbouring' doctrine, as well as the 'unwilling or unable' doctrine. Whether this practice is already clear and consistent enough to reflect a widened common understanding of article 51 of the UN Charter is debatable, given the vagueness or ambiguity plaguing many invocations of the right.[136] Similarly, there may be diverging views as to whether (the acceptance of) the broader application of the right to self-defence is sufficiently widespread and consistent to reflect customary international law.[137] For example, the protests of the territorial (and thereby specifically affected) states may cast doubt in this regard.[138] In addition, it remains challenging to determine whether any lack of protest indeed intended to communicate a state's agreement that a particular practice was in line with its international rights obligations, or whether it occurred as a matter of political expediency.[139] Moreover, it is arguable that the probative value of silence should be treated with particular caution where it impacts the scope of peremptory obligations with *erga omnes* effect, such as article 2(4) of the UN Charter.[140] Assuming too readily that silence has the effect of altering the scope of such an obligation would violate the very purpose of its exceptional normative strength.[141]

That being said, the lack of protest can nonetheless have a normative impact if there was an expectation under the circumstances that states protest. This would particularly be the case where the conduct in question is repeated at frequent intervals and well-publicized, for example through letters to the UNSC.[142] This has arguably been the case with most of the instances of lack of protest in relation to the invocation of the right to self-defence referred to earlier. Furthermore, to the extent that states did protest, the weight of the protest may be reduced by the fact that they had themselves invoked the 'harbouring' or 'unwilling or unable doctrine' in connection with the right to self-defence.[143] Moreover, the criticism often was more concerned with the application of the right to self-defence in a particular

[135] See also PA Nollkaemper, 'Nader Advies Geweldgebruik Tegen ISIL in Syrie' (23 June 2015) para 14 https://www.internationaal-recht.nl/documents/20531/0/Kabinetsreactie-en-Nader-Advies-Extern-Volkenrechtelijke-advisseur-geweldgebruik-tegen-ISIS-in-Syri-.pdf/b8001b7f-9629-1010-36f0-9d31e363163c?version%3D1.0. However, see Brunnée and Toope (2018) (n 2) 266. They note that it has mainly been invoked by powerful Western states referring predominantly to their own practice.

[136] See also Starski (2016) (n 2) 63.

[137] See also ILC Report (n 82) ch V, Conclusion 8(1) and Commentary to Conclusion 9(1) para (5).

[138] ILC Report (n 82) ch V, Commentary on Conclusion 8(1), para (4), that attaches significant weight to the behaviour of particularly involved states.

[139] See Starski (2016) (n 2) 26–27, who also underscores that there is no general obligation under international law to protest actively against violations of international law.

[140] ibid 40, 43–44.

[141] ibid 40.

[142] ibid 31–32, 36.

[143] See also Hakimi (n 2) 9; C Kress, 'The Fine Line Between Collective Self-Defence and Intervention by Invitation: Reflections on the Use of Force against IS in Syria' *Just Security* (17 February 2015) https://www.justsecurity.org/20118/claus-kreb-force-isil-syria/.

context, such as the lack of the proportionality of the defensive measures, or of conclusive evidence about the author of the armed attack.[144] All in all, it is not unreasonable to argue that states are increasingly supportive of a broader invocation of the right to self-defence than the narrow concept that was proclaimed by the ICJ in the *Nicaragua* decision.

If one accepts this reasoning, the question arises as to how this impacts the principles of attribution of conduct within the self-defence paradigm. The subsequent parts argue that these developments imply a lowering of the threshold requirements for indirect armed attacks. In particular, they imply a more flexible interpretation of 'substantial involvement' in an armed attack, as well as a potential interrelationship between the notions of 'substantial involvement', 'harbouring', and the 'unwilling' prong of the 'unwilling or unable' doctrine. In addition, the above-mentioned developments support the conclusion that armed attacks may be directly attributed to non-state actors in states that are 'unable' to prevent attacks by non-state actors located in their territory.

4. Implications for attribution of conduct within the self-defence paradigm

4.1 Expansive attribution to states of armed attacks

This overview of state practice suggests that the current threshold of an indirect armed attack in terms of article 51 of the UN Charter is lower than that established in the *Nicaragua* decision.[145] Similarly, this threshold is more flexible than the customary international law standard for attribution of conduct of private actors to states, according to which a close nexus between the state and the non-state actor is required.[146] State practice indicates that third state support to armed groups, which the ICJ in the *Nicaragua* decision qualified as 'mere' violations of the prohibition of the use of force, nowadays could trigger the right of individual and collective self-defence of the victim state against the state(s) that supported the non-state actor.[147] This implies that state support in the form of weapons, finances, training,

[144] In the *Nicaragua* decision (n 8) 85 ff, as well as the *Armed Activities in the Congo* decision (n 9) paras 72 ff, the lack of evidence of [state involvement] in the alleged armed attacks was one important factor influencing the ICJ's decision. See also Ruys (n 2) 494; Charney (n 2) 836 ff; Franck (n 2).

[145] Flasch (n 119) 57.

[146] Art 8 ASR (n 22), which represents the customary standard, determines that '[c]onduct of a person or group of persons shall be considered an act of a state under international law if the person or group of persons is in fact acting on the instructions of, or under the direction or control of, that state in carrying out the conduct'. See also *Case Concerning Application of the Convention on the Prevention and Punishment of the Crime of Genocide (Bosnia and Herzegovina v Serbia and Montenegro)* Merits, Judgment of 26 February 2007, [2007] ICJ Rep 43, paras 406 and 659; Tams (n 2) 385; Tsagourias (n 2) 805; Jackson (n 28); Lanovoy (n 2) 566.

[147] Brunnée and Toope (2018) (n 2) 273.

logistical support, or any combination of these, to non-state actors attacking another state could amount to the type of 'substantial involvement' in an armed attack that would make such an attack against a state attributable to the supporting state.[148] While states are yet to describe such measures of support as constituting 'substantial involvement' in explicit terms, it is difficult to see how else to reconcile this requirement with, for example, article 1(c)(xi) of the AU Non-Aggression and Defence Pact.

Furthermore, the right to self-defence could also be triggered by a state's violation of its due diligence obligation under international law, where it failed to act against a non-state actor engaged in attacks against another state. This, in turn, suggests that the 'harbouring' doctrine and the 'unwillingness' prong of the 'unwilling or unable' doctrine constitute particular concretizations of the violation of the due diligence obligation in the *jus ad bellum* context. Both concepts may be understood as referring to the inaction of the territorial state vis-à-vis a non-state actor, despite knowledge on the part of the territorial state of the presence of the non-state actor and its activities.[149] Inaction under these circumstances can trigger the right of individual or collective self-defence of the victim state.[150] Moreover, it is also plausible to regard 'unwillingness' and/or 'harbouring' as a form of 'substantial involvement' through omission.[151] This is because of the fact that the territorial state has knowledge of the circumstance that the presence of the non-state actor on its territory will facilitate an armed attack against another state.[152] Read in this way, 'unwillingness' and/or 'harbouring' will constitute the flipside of 'substantial involvement'.

At this juncture, one has to point out that state practice is yet explicitly to endorse any interrelationship between 'unwillingness', 'harbouring', and 'substantial involvement'. In fact, it is not even certain that those states invoking the 'unwilling or unable' doctrine actually depart from a clear common denominator, as they either do not explain what they mean or use vague and, to some extent, different terminology.[153] For example, in the ongoing Syrian conflict, the United States has indicated that Syria cannot and will not confront IS safe havens in Syria

[148] Some authors nonetheless insist that the mere provision of weapons or financial support would not amount to 'substantial involvement'. They propose involvement comparable to 'overall control', as articulated in *Prosecutor v Tadic*, Judgment, Case No IT-94-1-A, Appeals Chamber, 15 July 1999 para 137. See Ruys and Ferro (n 50) 75. See also Tsagourias (n 2) 806, 818; Randelzhofer and Nolte (n 2) 1416. However, see Corten (2016) (n 2) 794 ff, who is highly critical of any expansive interpretation of an armed attack.

[149] Tsagourias (n 2) 806, 816.

[150] Tams (n 2) 384–85; Brunnée and Toope (2004) (n 2) 795.

[151] Tsagourias (n 2) 806, 818; Lanovoy (n 2) 582.

[152] Some authors prefer to describe this combination of knowledge (at the time the non-state actor was present on its territory) and the causality between such presence and the armed attack perpetrated by the non-state actor as complicity. See notably Lanovoy (n 2) 582 ff, *contra* I Plakokefalos, 'The Use of Force by Non-state Actors and the Limits of Attribution of Conduct: A Reply to Vladyslav Lanovoy' (2017) 28 European Journal of International Law 587–93.

[153] See Brunnée and Toope (2018 (n 2) 273–74; Starski (2015) (n 2) 498.

'effectively'.[154] Australia described the 'failure to constrain' attacks by IS in Iraq as a demonstration of unwillingness or inability.[155] Canada and Turkey, for their part, merely claimed that the (Syrian) government was not able (capable) or willing to 'prevent attacks emanating from its territory'.[156]

That being said, it is possible to read state practice as implicitly confirming that the 'harbouring' and 'unwillingness' doctrines are manifestations of violations of due diligence, as well as that they constitute 'substantial involvement' through omission. If state practice indeed were reflective (or to become reflective) of a close relationship between 'unwillingness', 'harbouring', and 'substantial involvement', an armed attack would be attributable to a state either through its substantial involvement in the form of active support of non-state actors attacking the victim state or in the form of passive involvement through failing to act against the presence of such a non-state actor on its territory. In these instances, the exception to the prohibition of the use of force against the territorial integrity of a state contained in article 51 of the UN Charter is triggered, allowing the victim state (and its allies) to use defensive force in the territory of (the) states(s) that is/are the author(s) of the armed attack.[157]

Where article 51 of the UN Charter is triggered in such a way, all forcible measures exercised by the victim state and its allies will have to conform to the principles of necessity and proportionality embedded in the right to self-defence.[158] The necessity requirement first of all relates to the question of whether in the circumstances less severe means of redress are available. A response in the form of self-defence, therefore, should be a last resort.[159] In making this assessment, the issue of the consent of the territorial state becomes an important consideration. The victim state will bear the onus to indicate why it did not first attempt to obtain the cooperation of the 'unwilling' territorial state, including consent for executing military measures in its territory.[160] If the victim state claimed to have concerns about the collusion between the territorial state and the non-state actor, it would have to present credible evidence to this effect.[161] The necessity

[154] Letter Dated 23 September 2014 from the Permanent Representative of the United States of America to the United Nations Addressed to the Secretary-General UN Doc S/2014/695 (23 September 2014).

[155] Letter dated 9 September 2015 from the Permanent Representative of Australia to the United Nations Addressed to the President of the Security Council UN Doc S/2015/693 (9 September 2015).

[156] Letter dated 31 March 2015 from the Chargé d'Affaires of the Permanent Mission of Canada to the United Nations Addressed to the President of the Security Council UN Doc S/2015/221 (31 March 2015); Letter dated 24 July 2015 from the Chargé d'Affaires of the Permanent Mission of Turkey to the United Nations Addressed to the President of the Security Council UN Doc S/2015/563 (24 July 2015).

[157] K Trapp, 'Back to Basics: Necessity, Proportionality, and the Right of Self-Defence Against Non-State Terrorist Actors' (2007) 56 International and Comparative Law Quarterly 146.

[158] Ruys and Ferro (n 50) 93–94.

[159] See Ruys (n 2) 434–35.

[160] Bethlehem (n 2); Trapp (n 157) 147. See also Charney (n 2) 836 ff.

[161] Presenting credible evidence to this effect is often fraught with practical challenges, as can be illustrated by the Colombian raid of the FARC camp across the Ecuadorian border in March 2008. A day after the raid, Colombia stated that computer files seized during the raid revealed that the Ecuadorian

requirement further implies that the defensive response has to target military objects that are the actual source of the attack.[162] This would include those non-state actors involved in the execution of the armed attack along with their infrastructure. It can also include those facilities and personnel of the state to which the armed attack is attributed, in as far as they directly supported or facilitated the armed attack.[163]

The issue of military targeting, however, can also have bearing on the proportionality of the defensive measures. The proportionality requirement concerns the overall scope and scale of the defensive measures. It thus concerns the relationship (ie the need for correlation) between the gravity of the armed attack and the intensity of the response.[164] This at times can have consequences for military targeting practices, suggesting a close intertwinement of necessity and proportionality.[165] For example, the targeting practices of the Saudi-led coalition against the Houthis in Yemen has faced severe criticism for lacking in both necessity and proportionality.[166] Both principles would also have to be considered before expanding the defensive operations to targets in Iran (which, according to Yemen and Saudi Arabia, sponsored the attacks). Thus far, the coalition has limited the military operation to the territory of Yemen.

4.2 Limited attribution to non-state actors of armed attacks

While this analysis illuminated the lowering of the threshold requirements for attribution of armed attacks to states, this section focuses on the attribution of armed attacks to non-state actors. One situation in which this seems to be occurring is where a state has lost effective control over the area in its territory where the non-state actor is located. As a result, the territorial state is unable to prevent the use of the respective part of its territory by non-state actors in the preparation of an armed attack against other states.[167] This, in turn, suggests that the loss of territorial

Minister of Security had been in contact with the high FARC official Reyes in the month before the raid. Ecuador for its part questioned the authenticity of the computer files and claimed that Colombia should have sought its consent for the raid. See Report to the Committee on Foreign Relations (n 38) 2, 7, 9, 12 ff. See also Deeks (n 2) 519–20, 540, 543; Hakimi (n 2) 10–11.

162 See *Case Concerning Oil Platforms (Islamic Republic of Iran v United States of America)* Judgment of 6 November 2003, [2003] ICJ Rep 161 para74. The ICJ was not convinced, in light of the evidence, that the actual platforms targeted by the United States constituted a staging base for launching small-scale attacks on neutral, commercial shipping vessels; Ruys (n 2) 109–10.

163 For example, Brunnée and Toope (2018) (n 2) 895–96. See also Bethlehem (n 2) 7.

164 Ruys (n 2) 108, 111 ff.

165 ibid; Randelzhofer and Nolte (n 2) 1427; Trapp (n 157) 146.

166 See also Final Report of the Panel of Experts on Yemen (n 110) paras 119, 126 ff.

167 See also Institut de Droit International, Present Problems of the Use of Armed Force in International Law, Resolution 10A, 27 October 2007 para 10(ii) http://www.idi-iil.org/app/uploads/2017/06/2007_san_02_en.pdf; Brunnée and Toope (2018) (n 2) 274.

control constitutes 'inability' in line with the 'unable' prong of the 'unwilling or unable' doctrine.

For example, in Syria the incumbent government did not have effective control over the areas from which IS operated, despite attempts by the government to eradicate IS militants.[168] This lack of control was also explicitly mentioned by Germany and Belgium when invoking article 51 of the UN Charter against IS.[169] Similarly, Turkey claimed that the Afrin region was under the control of the YPG/PYD, implying that the Syrian government did not have control over the region.[170] Interestingly, none of these countries explicitly invoked the 'unwilling or unable doctrine' in these respective situations. Therefore, they have not yet explicitly linked the 'unable' prong of the doctrine to a lack of territorial control. Even so, it is arguable that an inability would exist in situations where the non-state actor has gained and stabilized its control over a territory within a state.[171] Also, it seems that in such situations states have attributed the armed attack directly to the non-state actor, allowing the victim state(s) to use self-defence directly against it.[172] For example, Belgium and Germany explicitly made IS responsible for armed attacks and underscored the fact that their military measures were directed against IS only and not against the Syrian state.[173] In relation to the situation in Afrin, Turkey suggested the same by stating that its military operations would 'target only terrorists and their hideouts, shelters, emplacements, weapons, vehicles and equipment'.[174]

Furthermore, when invoking article 51 of the UN Charter in relation to IS, Germany, Belgium, Denmark, Norway, and the United Kingdom made reference to UNSC Resolution 2249 (2015) which called upon 'member states that have the

[168] See *inter alia* Report of the Secretary-General on the Implementation of Security Council Resolutions 2139 (2014) and 2165 (2014) UN Doc S/2014/756 (23 October 2014) para 59; Report of the Secretary-General on the Implementation of Security Council Resolution 2139 (2014), 2165 (2014), and 2191 (2014) UN Doc S/2015/862 (11 November 2015) para 13; Report of the Secretary-General on the implementation of Security Council Resolutions 2139 (2014), 2165 (2014), 2191 (2014 2258 (2015), and 2332 (2016) UN Doc S/2017/794 (21 September 2017) para 6. See also Corten (2016) (n 2) 792.

[169] See Letter dated 7 June 2016 from the Permanent Representative of Belgium to the United Nations Addressed to the President of the Security Council UN Doc S/2016/523 (9 June 2016); Letter dated 10 December 2015 from the Chargé d'Affaires of the Permanent Mission of Germany to the United Nations Addressed to the President of the Security Council UN Doc S/2015/946 (10 December 2015). See also Brunnée and Toope (2018) (n 2) 272.

[170] Identical Letters Dated 20 January 2018 from the Chargé d'Affaires of the Permanent Mission of Turkey to the United Nations Addressed to the Secretary-General and the President of the Security Council UN Doc S/2018/53 (23 January 2018) 1.

[171] See also Brunnée and Toope (2018) (n 2) 272.

[172] Tsagourias (n 2) 809; Jackson (n 28) 186.

[173] Letter dated 10 December 2015 from the Chargé d'Affaires of the Permanent Mission of Germany to the United Nations Addressed to the President of the Security Council UN Doc S/2015/946 (10 December 2015); Letter dated 7 June 2016 from the Permanent Representative of Belgium to the United Nations Addressed to the President of the Security Council UN Doc S/2016/523 (9 June 2016); Letter dated 3 June 2016 from the Permanent Representative of Norway to the United Nations Addressed to the President of the Security Council UN Doc S/2016/513 (3 June 2016). See Tsagourias (n 2) 811.

[174] Identical Letters dated 20 January 2018 from the Chargé d'Affaires of the Permanent Mission of Turkey to the United Nations Addressed to the Secretary-General and the President of the Security Council UN Doc S/2018/53 (22 January 2018) 1.

capacity to do so to take all necessary measures, in compliance with international law, in particular with the United Nations Charter ... on the territory under the control of ISIL ... in Syria and Iraq'.[175] This suggests that they interpreted the Resolution as allowing them to invoke the right to individual and collective self-defence directly against non-state actors. In fact, Denmark[176] and Germany[177] explicitly confirmed this interpretation. However, it is worth noting that, while UNSC Resolution 2249 (2015) refers to the use of 'all necessary means, in compliance with international law', it was not adopted under Chapter VII of the UN Charter, nor does it explicitly refer to article 51 of the UN Charter. Therefore, it does not in and of itself authorize force against IS as a non-state actor as a matter of self-defence.[178] Instead, it merely encourages states to use force within the IS-controlled areas in as far as international law allows for this in the absence of a UNSC Chapter VII authorization.[179]

Stated differently, while the Resolution may be read as implicitly encouraging states to consider whether article 51 of the UN Charter can be invoked directly in relation to IS in Syria, it would not seem to give a clear answer as to whether this indeed is the case.[180] Nonetheless, despite the vagueness of this Resolution, there does seem to be growing support among states for attributing armed attacks exclusively to non-state actors in situations where they operate from areas over which the territorial state does not have control.[181] While the current military operations in Syria may not in itself be sufficiently widespread evidence of this development, one should not overlook article 1(c)(xi) of the AU Non-Aggression and Common Defence Pact. This article, which is already in force for twenty-two signatories in Africa, explicitly acknowledges that an act of aggression can be committed by a non-state actor.[182] These developments in state practice seem to vindicate the views

[175] UN Doc S/RES/2249 (20 November 2015) para 5.

[176] Letter dated 11 January 2016 from the Permanent Representative of Denmark to the United Nations Addressed to the President of the Security Council UN Doc S/2016/34 (13 January 2016).

[177] Deutscher Bundestag (Antrag der Bundesregierung), Einsatz bewaffneter deutscher Streitkräfte zur Verhütung und Unterbindung terroristischer Handlungen durch die Terrororganisation IS auf Grundlage von Artikel 51 der Satzung der Vereinten Nationen in Verbindung mit Artikel 42 Absatz 7 des Vertrages über die Europäische Union sowie den Resolutionen 2170 (2014), 2199 (2015), 2249 (2015) des Sicherheitsrates der Vereinten Nationen, Drucksache 18/6866 (2015) 3, stating: 'Das Vorgehen gegen den IS in Wahrnehmung des kollektiven Selbstverteidigungsrechts gemäß Artikel 51 der Charta der Vereinten Nationen ist von der Resolution 2249 (2015) des Sicherheitsrates der Vereinten Nationen umfasst.'

[178] See Corten (2016) (n 2) 791, who distinguishes UN Doc S/RES/2249 (20 November 2015) from UN Doc S/RES/1368 (12 September 2001), which in the Preamble referred to the right to self-defence.

[179] Flasch (n 119) 59. See also D Akande and M Milanovic, 'The Constructive Ambiguity of the Security Council's ISIS Resolution' *EJIL:Talk!* (21 November 2015) http://www.ejiltalk.org/the-constructive-ambiguity-of-the-security-councils-isis-resolution/.

[180] See Corten (2016) (n 2) 791.

[181] However, see Corten (2016) (n 2) 798; ME O'Connell, 'Dangerous Departures' (2013) 107 American Journal of International Law 380, 383. They question whether the evolving state practice is sufficiently widespread and accepted on this point.

[182] Art 1(c) of the AU Non-Aggression and Common Defence Pact (n 43) determines: 'Aggression means the use, intentionally and knowingly, of armed force or any other hostile act by a state, a group

of individual ICJ judges in the *Armed Activities in the Congo* decision, according to which cross-border attacks carried out by irregular forces from territories which were not under governmental control, nonetheless amounted to armed attacks, despite not being attributable to the territorial state.[183]

If one accepted that an armed attack can be attributed directly to a non-state actor located in the territory of an 'unable state' that has lost control over parts of its territory, the logical consequence would be that measures of self-defence would be allowed against the non-state actor as such. This, in turn, would imply an intrusion into the territorial integrity and sovereignty of the territorial state, despite the fact that it was not responsible for the armed attack. This raises the question of whether such an intrusion could be accommodated within the UN Charter article 51 paradigm. After all, the exception to the prohibition of the use of force against the territorial integrity of a state contained in this article is only triggered as of right, where the armed attack is attributable to that state.[184]

It is arguable that defensive measures against a non-state actor on the territory of an 'unable' state can be accommodated within the article 51 paradigm through the necessity principle. Section 4.1 indicated that necessity is also applicable where self-defence is invoked in relation to armed attacks attributable to states. However, when invoked in relation to 'unable' states, the necessity principle requires the function of a circumstance precluding wrongfulness. It allows for the victim state and its allies to exercise measures in self-defence in the 'unable' state, without engaging state responsibility for violating the territorial integrity and sovereignty of the latter.[185] This reasoning essentially regards the right to self-defence as both an inherent right and a justification (or excuse). Stated differently, it supports the view that article 51 of the UN Charter functions as a primary and secondary norm.[186] Such an interpretation is likely to be opposed by those supporting a strict separation between primary and secondary norms. In line with a strict separation, the right to invoke self-defence against the perpetrator of an armed attack in article 51 of the UN Charter represents a primary norm, while justification for intrusion into

of states, an organization of states or non-state actor(s) or by any foreign or external entity, against the sovereignty, political independence, territorial integrity and human security of the population of a state party to this Pact.'

[183] See *Armed Activities in the Congo* decision (n 9) Separate Opinion of Judge Simma, para 12, and Separate Opinion of Judge Kooijmans, para 30. In their respective individual opinions in the Advisory Opinion on the *Construction of a Wall in the Occupied Territories* (n 9), Judges Buergenthal, Higgins, and Kooijmans underscored that the wording of art 51 of the UN Charter did not make the exercise of the right to self-defence dependent on an armed attack by a state. *Construction of a Wall* decision (n 9) Declaration of Judge Buergenthal, para 6, Separate Opinion of Judge Higgins, para 33, and Separate Opinion of Judge Kooijmans, para 35. See also Franck (n 2) 2 840; Hakimi (n 2) 10; Tsagourias (n 2) 811.

[184] Trapp (n 2) 146.

[185] See also Tsagourias (n 2) 804; RD Sloane, 'In the Use and Abuse of Necessity in the Law of State Responsibility' (2012) 106 American Journal of International Law 505.

[186] See also Sloane (n 185) 491–92.

the territory of an (unable) state has to be found in a secondary norm.[187] However, the propriety of such a strict separation between primary and secondary is questionable, as the ILC introduced the distinction for organizational purposes and not as a conceptual tool.[188]

Moreover, accepting a more flexible relationship between primary and secondary norms would facilitate a reading of article 51 of the UN Charter that is informed by article 25(1)(a) of the ASR.[189] This article, which allows for the invocation of the principle of necessity if it is 'the only way for the state to safeguard an essential interest against a grave and imminent peril',[190] constitutes one of the six circumstances precluding wrongfulness in chapter V of the ILC Commentary to the ASR.[191] Such a reading would be quite novel, as the state of necessity referred to in article 25 of the ASR is a separate construct from the customary principle of necessity that governs the right to self-defence in article 51 of the UN Charter. Also, there is nothing in the work of the ILC pertaining to state responsibility (nor as of yet in state practice) that explicitly refers to a link between these different manifestations of necessity.[192] On the other hand, there is nothing in the work

[187] See Tsagourias (n 2) 804 ff, who argues that the justification for the intrusion in the territory of the ('unable') state where the non-state perpetrator is located stems from art 21 of the ASR (n 22) a secondary norm. This article determines that '[t]he wrongfulness of an act of a state is precluded if the act constitutes a lawful measure of self-defence taken in conformity with the Charter of the United Nations'.

[188] See *inter alia* F Paddeu, *Justification and Excuse in International Law: Concept and Theory of General Defences* (CUP 2018) 55–56. The ASR also contains norms with both primary and secondary characteristics.

[189] Art 25(1) ASR (n 22) determines: 'Necessity may not be invoked by a state as a ground for precluding the wrongfulness of an act not in conformity with an international obligation of that state unless the act (a) is the only way for the state to safeguard an essential interest against a grave and imminent peril; and (b) does not seriously impair an essential interest of the state or states towards which the obligation exists, or of the international community as a whole.'

[190] Art 25(1)(a) ASR (n 22).

[191] While art 25 is placed in ch V of the ASR (n 2) which concerns circumstances precluding wrongfulness, it remains disputed whether necessity constitutes an excuse (that mitigates the responsibility arising from a wrongful act) or a justification (that excludes the illegality of the act). While art 25 ASR is placed in ch V of the ASR which concerns circumstances precluding wrongfulness, it remains disputed whether necessity constitutes an excuse (that mitigates the responsibility arising from a wrongful at) or a justification (that excludes the illegality of the act). The ILC Commentary does not draw a clear distinction between the two terms and seems to use them interchangeably. Several authors nonetheless suggest that necessity is an excuse, which does in principle allow for compensation (unlike a justification). However, in practice there will arguably be little difference in describing the use of force against non-state actors on the territory of a third state as an excuse rather than a justification, as a formal declaration of illegality by an international court or tribunal is unlikely to be forthcoming. See I Johnstone, 'The Plea of Necessity in International Legal Discourse: Humanitarian Intervention and Counter-Terrorism' (2005) 43 Columbia Journal of Translational Law 353–54; Sloane (n 185) 484; J Crawford, 'Revising the Draft Articles on state Responsibility' (1999) 10 European Journal of International Law 444; A Roberts, 'Legality vs Legitimacy: Can Uses of Force Be Illegal But Justified?' in P Alston and E Macdonald (eds), *Human Rights, Intervention, and the Use of Force* (OUP 2008) 20; J Vidmar, 'The Use of Force as a Plea of Necessity' (2018) 111 American Journal of International Law Unbound 302 ff; Paddeu (n 188) 414 ff.

[192] The ASR also does not apply directly to conduct that is regulated by specialized regimes such as the *jus ad bellum*. Art 55 ASR (n 22) determines that these articles 'do not apply where and to the extent that the conditions for the existence of an internationally wrongful act or the content or implementation of the international responsibility of a state are governed by special rules of international law'. See also ILC Commentary to Art 25 ASR (n 22) para (21); Sloane (n 185) 494.

of the ILC (nor in state practice) that necessarily excludes such a link. Accepting a reading of article 51 of the UN Charter that is informed by article 25(1)(a) of the ASR would infuse the imprecise customary standard of necessity in the self-defence context with more exact benchmarks.[193] This seems desirable in light of the severe impact of defensive military operations on the sovereignty of the 'unable' territorial state.[194]

According to the wording of article 25(1)(a) of the ASR, the peril must be both grave and imminent, and must be clearly established on the basis of evidence reasonably available at the time, while the measures for its eradication must be the only means available for safeguarding the interests at stake.[195] When applying this reasoning to the invocation of necessity in the context of article 51 of the UN Charter, one may argue that the inability of a state to control territory from where armed attacks by non-state actors emanate can result in a grave and imminent peril to the national security of other states, which is an essential interest.[196] However, the victim state and its allies would further have to argue that the invocation of self-defence was the only way for safeguarding the essential interest. This places a strong onus on the victim state and its allies to demonstrate why less severe measures were not feasible under the circumstances. Among others, they will have to establish why military measures were unavoidable and, if so, why this did not occur with the consent of and in coordination with the government of the 'unable' state. The states invoking self-defence will further have to limit their defensive measures very strictly to the source of the attack, which in the case of an 'unable' state would only include (the infrastructure of) the non-state actor(s) responsible for the armed attacks.[197]

If, by way of illustration, one applies this reasoning to the manner in which the right to self-defence was invoked against IS in Syria, it is questionable whether the exacting standards of article 25(1)(a) would have been met. On the one hand, the Assad regime did not at the time have effective control over the parts of its territory from which IS operated. The activities of IS also constituted a grave and imminent peril to the national security of the states invoking self-defence. On the other hand, the Assad regime was willing to coordinate its military operations against IS with those of other states.[198] The US-led coalition nonetheless insisted

[193] ILC Commentary to Art 25 ASR (n 22) para (14); Johnstone (n 191) 356.

[194] See also Starski (2015) (n 2) 491.

[195] ILC Commentary to Art 25 ASR (n 2) paras (15)–(16); Johnstone (n 191) 155, 37; Ruys (n 191) 378–79.

[196] The *Caroline* incident of 1837 is often cited as a famous example of necessity in self-defence. See *British and Foreign State Papers: 1840–1841* Vol 29 (1857) 1129; ILC Commentary to Art 25 ASR (22) para (5); Sloane (n 185) 457. See also Johnstone (n 191) 368.

[197] For example, Brunnée and Toope (2018) (n 2) 895–96; see also Bethlehem (n 2) 7.

[198] See eg Identical Letters dated 16 September 2015 from the Permanent Representative of the Syrian Arab Republic to the United Nations Addressed to the Secretary-General and the President of the Security Council UN Doc S/2015/718 (17 September 2015); Tsagourias (n 2) 809; Zamani and Nikouei (n 5) 19.

on conducting its own, separate military campaign against IS on the basis of self-defence. In line with the necessity principle as described earlier, these states would have to show that there was no other way of safeguarding their national security. One plausible argument can be that this military strategy was the only way in which to eliminate the grave threat posed by IS, without becoming complicit in the international crimes of the Syrian regime.[199] Stated differently, accepting the Assad regime's conditions for military cooperation would necessarily implicate the members of the international coalition in the widespread violations of human rights and humanitarian law by the Syrian regime.[200] At the same time, the threat emanating from IS posed a grave and imminent peril that justified a military response.

However, for this argument to meet the high threshold of article 25 ASR(1)(a), the respective states would have to present it in clear and convincing terms. In particular, they would have to explain why their justified concerns for complicity in war crimes would necessarily exclude every form of cooperation with the Syrian regime in relation to the fight against IS. Moreover, similar justifications would be required in situations in Syria where government forces had regained territorial control but could not yet entirely prevent IS from presenting a grave peril to other states. In such a situation, the inability would not so much relate to a lack of territorial control as to limited military capacity of the government forces. Thus far, such detailed explanations have not been forthcoming from the states invoking self-defence against IS in Syria. As a result, it is doubtful whether they comply with the stringent requirements of article 25(1)(a) of the ASR, assuming that one accepted the relevance of this article for the interpretation of the necessity principle within the *jus ad bellum* paradigm.

5. Implications for military assistance on request

This analysis has illustrated that the standards for attribution of armed attacks executed by non-state actors have evolved since the 1986 *Nicaragua* decision. First, the threshold requirements for attributing armed attacks to states have been lowered. Second, it seems that armed attacks can now be attributed directly to non-state actors. While these developments may have been necessitated by a responsibility vacuum that previously existed within the *jus ad bellum* paradigm, they may potentially have an eroding impact on legal certainty in relation to the principles of attribution applicable within this paradigm. In an attempt to find a balance between the need for evolution and the need for legal certainty, the analysis also

199 Kress (n 143); Tsagourias (n 2) 809; Nollkaemper (n 135).

200 See eg UN Human Rights Council, First Report of the Independent International Commission of Inquiry on the Syrian Arab Republic, UN Doc A/HRC/S-17/2/Add.1 (23 November 2011) paras 51 ff; Seventh Report of the Independent International Commission of Inquiry on the Syrian Arab Republic UN Doc A/HRC/25/65 (5 March 2014) paras 21 ff.

proposed an interpretation of the 'harbouring' and 'unwilling or unable' doctrines that would anchor them more firmly in principles of state responsibility.

As far as the threshold requirements for the attribution of armed attacks to states are concerned, the chapter makes a case for interpreting 'harbouring' and the 'unwillingness' prong of the 'unwilling or unable' doctrine as manifestations of due diligence and as the potential flipside of 'substantial involvement'. By anchoring these concepts in due diligence it becomes more difficult for states to infuse them with entirely subjective and arbitrary standards. It would further mean that even if the invocation of the 'unwilling or unable' doctrine were in time to eclipse that of 'harbouring' in practice, it need not necessarily mean that the threshold requirements for attribution were lowered even further. At least as far as the 'unwillingness' prong is concerned, the benchmarks of due diligence would remain relevant for attributing the armed attack to the state where the non-state actor was located. The attribution of armed attacks directly to non-state actors would be most plausible where non-state actors operated from an area over which the territorial state has lost control. Such a situation constitutes the clearest example of 'inability'; that is, of the 'unable' prong of the 'unwilling or unable' doctrine. However, as the invocation of self-defence in such a context has drastic consequences for the 'unable' state's sovereignty, the necessity requirement attached to the right to self-defence must be strictly interpreted. In order for this to happen, the imprecise necessity principle within the law of self-defence needs to be infused with more exacting standards. One possibility for doing so is to interpret it in line with the requirements underpinning article 25(1)(a) ASR.

Moreover, while the analysis developed this argument specifically in relation to 'unable' states, it is worth considering the application of such a stringent interpretation of necessity in all instances where the right to self-defence is invoked. Concepts such as 'harbouring', 'unwilling', and 'substantial involvement' suffer from various degrees of imprecision which can open them up to abuse. In addition, the lines between these concepts can be fluid. For example, victim states and territorial states might disagree over whether ineffective measures by the territorial state against an armed group within the territory are a result of a lack of capacity (inability) or lack of political will (unwillingness). In addition, they may also disagree as to what constitutes 'effective measures' in a particular context.[201] In such

[201] The practical challenges arising in this context can *inter alia* be illustrated by the Russian military operations against Chechen rebels in Georgia in 2002. In its correspondence to the UN, Russia described Georgia as unwilling or unable to put an end to the attacks by terrorists emanating from its territory. According to Russia, it had been trying to obtain the cooperation of the Georgian authorities in this regard since 1999. Georgia for its part submitted that Russia had been informed in detail regarding all the measures to be undertaken by the Georgian military and law enforcement agencies to mitigate the situation. It found any invocation of art 51 of the UN Charter unfounded under the circumstances. See Letter dated 11 September 2002 from the Permanent Representative of the Russian Federation to the United Nations Addressed to the Secretary-General, Annex UN Doc S/2002/1012 (12 September 2002) 2; Letter dated 31 July 2002 from the Chargé d'Affaires of the Permanent Mission of the Russian Federation to the UN, Addressed to the Secretary-General UN Doc S/2002/854, Annex (31 July 2002);

circumstances, the application of an exacting standard of necessity, along the lines of article 25 ASR, can assist in preventing an abusive or pre-textual invocation of the right to self-defence.

In light of the purpose of the current chapter, it further needs to be considered what this lowered threshold for attribution of indirect armed attacks, as well as that of the attribution of armed attacks to non-state actors, implies for the legal construct of military assistance on request. What, in particular, would the implications of these developments be for the consent of the territorial state that underpins the construct of military assistance on request? Can the lowering of the threshold for attribution of indirect armed attacks to states lead to an eclipsing of military assistance on request by the right to collective self-defence? Also, can the attribution of armed attacks to non-state actors reduce the consent of the territorial state to an element of the necessity principle, as a result of which the construct of military assistance on request becomes redundant? What role, if any, can the stringent interpretation of the necessity principle (as per article 25(1)(a) of the ASR) play in mitigating these risks?

The relevance of these questions may be illustrated by two scenarios, the first relating to collective self-defence and the second to individual self-defence. Where a victim state responds to an indirect armed attack attributable to an 'unwilling'/'harbouring'/'substantially involved' state, or to an armed attack attributable to a non-state actor in an 'unable' state, the victim state can request direct military assistance from (a) third state(s). Depending on how this request is phrased, it can either represent a manifestation of military assistance on request, or of collective self-defence. Where a victim state requests military assistance against non-state actors on its own territory, without any reference to article 51 of the UN Charter and without the victim state and its allies informing the UNSC that their action is based on collective self-defence, the request would rather be a manifestation of military assistance on request. In such an instance, the victim states and its allies will have to limit all forcible measures to the territory of the victim state.

It is possible that a victim state and its allies may prefer to follow this option when it remains uncertain whether the armed groups attacking the victim state are being supported by a third state, or whether they are operating from an 'unable' state. There may also be situations where there is certainty as to the identity and extent of a third state's support for an armed group against the victim state, or that the armed group is in operation from within a (neighbouring) unable state. However, the victim state and its allies may wish to withhold this information, in an attempt to contain the conflict. Moreover, by relying on the legal construct of

Permanent Representative of Georgia to the United Nations, Letter dated 13 September 2002 from the Permanent Representative of Georgia to the UN Addressed to the Secretary-General A/57/409–S/2002/1035, Annex (16 September 2002) 2; Permanent Representative of Georgia to the United Nations, Letter dated 13 September 2002 from the Permanent Representative of Georgia to the UN Addressed to the Secretary-General, A/57/409–S/2002/1035, Annex (16 September 2002) 2; Hakimi (n 2) 14.

military assistance on request for forcible measures within its territory, the victim state and its allies would be relieved of the burden of proving that an (indirect) armed attack has indeed been perpetrated and/or is being perpetrated repeatedly. On the other hand, the victim state and its allies may wish to keep open the option of expanding the geographical scope of the forcible measures undertaken in collective self-defence. This route would in principle be available to them if they invoked the right to collective self-defence under article 51 of the UN Charter, notwithstanding any evidentiary challenges that this may imply. The victim state and its allies would then be allowed to undertake military measures on the territory of the 'unwilling'/'harbouring'/'substantially involved' state, or in the 'unable' state where the responsible non-state actor is located.

In all these situations, the victim state and its allies have to adhere to the principles of necessity and proportionality. Where 'unwilling'/'substantially involved'/ 'harbouring' states are concerned, defensive military measures can be directed at (the infrastructure of) the non-state actor as well as those facilities and personnel of the territorial state that were directly involved in the armed attacks. In the case of 'unable' states, the defensive measures may only be directed at (the infrastructure of) the responsible non-state actor. Moreover, if one is willing to interpret the necessity principle inherent to the right to self-defence in line with article 25(1)(a) ASR, the victim states and their allies will further have to argue convincingly that the invocation of self-defence was the only way to safeguarding essential national security interest. As mentioned in section 4.2, they will have to explain why less severe measures were not feasible under the circumstances, including why military measures (to the extent that they were unavoidable) did not occur with the consent of and in cooperation with the government of the 'unwilling'/substantially involved/' harbouring or 'unable' state.

These constraints may go some way towards discouraging victim states to resort to the invocation of collective self-defence and in particular in preventing an abusive invocation of the right. Even so, the fact remains that if it is invoked in a plausible manner (which will depend on the circumstances of the case in question), the victim state and its allies will be able to resort to defensive force within a broader geographical scope than would be the case with military assistance on request. This factor, combined with the wide range of situations in which states can potentially be classified as 'unwilling'/'harbouring'/'substantially involved' or 'unable' may tempt states that fall victim to armed attacks by non-state actors to increasingly rely on the right to collective self-defence rather than the legal construct of 'military assistance on request'.

Furthermore, the lowering of the threshold for attribution of indirect armed attacks and the attribution of armed attacks to non-state actors also have potential implications for the relationship between the right to *individual* self-defence and the legal construct of military assistance on request. Where an invited state's military or air force is exercising forcible measures on the territory of another on the basis of the latter's request for military assistance, the invited state has to terminate the forcible measures if the inviting (territorial) state withdraws its invitation. Anything else would in principle be a violation of the prohibition of the use of force.[202] However, it is theoretically possible that the third state may refuse to heed the request (or perhaps attempt to circumvent it) by claiming that a non-state actor in the victim state is perpetrating armed attacks against the invited state. Stated differently, previously invited states may change the narrative by claiming that the consent of the territorial state as a legal basis for their presence has been superseded or subsumed by the right to individual self-defence. As a consequence, they would still be provided with a legal basis in international law for continuing forcible measures in the territory of the (previously) inviting state.

An illustrative (albeit controversial) example would be Pakistan, where since 2004 the United States has been engaged in drone strikes against the Taliban and Al Qaida on an ongoing basis. Chapter 5 indicated that the Pakistani government's consent to these measures visibly disintegrated subsequent to the killing of Osama bin Laden in 2011.[203] Yet, the drone strikes continued, as the United States regards itself as entitled to invoke the right to individual self-defence vis-à-vis Al Qaida and the Taliban as such.[204] This illustrates that Pakistan's consent would no longer be decisive for determining the legality of such airstrikes, as it would be superseded by the right to individual self-defence of the United States. Put differently and in line with the line of reasoning developed in this chapter, Pakistan would have become an 'unwilling'/'substantially involved'/'harbouring' or potentially 'unable' state, whose consent to defensive force can, depending on the circumstances, be discarded as a matter of necessity. In fact, various statements by the United States over the years have alluded to the fact that Pakistan was 'unwilling or unable' to suppress the threats that groups such as Al Qaida posed to the United States and that elements within its security services were colluding with some of these groups.[205]

[202] See also Chapter 5, section 4.

[203] See also Chapter 5, section 4. For recent statistics on the drone strikes, see Bureau of Investigative Journalism, 'Pakistan: Reported US Strikes 2017' https://www.thebureauinvestigates.com/drone-war/data/pakistan-covert-us-reported-actions-2017.

[204] See *inter alia* HH Koh, 'The Obama Administration and International Law' (Speech at the Annual Meeting of the American Society of International Law, Washington, DC, 25 March 2010) https://2009-2017.state.gov/s/l/releases/remarks/139119.htm. The White House, 'US Policy Standards and Procedures for the Use of Force in Counterterrorism Operations Outside the United States and Areas of Active Hostilities' (23 May 2013) https://obamawhitehouse.archives.gov/the-press-office/2013/05/23/fact-sheet-us-policy-standards-and-procedures-use-force-counterterrorism. See also Tibori-Szabo (n 2) 382–83.

[205] See Deeks (n 2) 485; N Schmidle, 'The CIA's Maddening Relationship with Pakistan' *The New Yorker* https://www.newyorker.com/news/news-desk/the-cias-maddening-relationship-with-pakistan. See also statement of the United States cited by the PTI (n 134), subsequent to the 2019 suicide bombing in India for which a Pakistan-based terrorist group claimed responsibility.

In line with the reasoning developed in section 4.2, it would nonetheless remain debatable whether the continued and protracted drone strikes on the basis of self-defence indeed were the only way to guard the essential security interests of the United States, whether the alleged untrustworthiness of elements within the Pakistani security forces necessarily justified the extent to which the United States excluded its coordination of the drone strikes with the Pakistani authorities, and whether the drone strikes were strictly limited to those non-state actors from which the security threat emanated.[206] Be that as it may, the Pakistani example nonetheless illustrates that the attribution of armed attacks to non-state actors can result in the superseding of military assistance on request by the right to individual self-defence. In such a situation, the consent of the territorial state to forcible measures against non-state actors no longer is a prerequisite for determining their legality. Instead, the consent of the territorial state becomes a potentially disposable element of the necessity principle underpinning the right to individual self-defence.

6. Conclusion

The current chapter has revealed that the evolving nature of the right to self-defence in article 51 of the UN Charter has the potential to reduce the role of consent as a mechanism for protecting state sovereignty in the *jus ad bellum* paradigm. This is due to the lowering of the threshold for attribution of indirect attacks, as well as the attribution of armed attacks to non-state actors. This diminished relevance of consent may under certain circumstances result in a decline in the reliance on the legal construct of military assistance on request as the legal basis for forcible measures in inter-state relations. In instances where armed attacks by non-state actors are attributed to 'unwilling'/'substantially involved'/'harbouring' states or to non-state actors in 'unable' states, victim states may—depending on the situation—prefer to invoke individual or collective self-defence in article 51 of the UN Charter rather than the legal construct of military assistance on request. Despite evidentiary burdens that victim states may face when doing so, the invocation of individual or collective self-defence would potentially allow them to exercise forcible measures in a broader geographical area and potentially without the consent of the state on whose territory the forcible measures are used. This possibility in principle encroaches on the relevance of the role of state consent in the *jus ad bellum* paradigm.

[206] For different perspectives on the legality of the protracted US drone strikes in *inter alia* Pakistan, see C Schaller, 'Using Force Against Terrorists "Outside Areas of Active Hostilities": The Obama Approach and the Bin Laden Raid Revisited' (2015) 20 Journal of Conflict and Security Law 195 ff: Deeks (n 2) 484 ff. See also B Emmerson, Report of the Special Rapporteur on the Promotion and Protection of Human Rights and Fundamental Freedoms While Countering Terrorism' UN Doc A/HRC/25/59 (10 March 2014) 3 ff.

At the same time, it would be premature to conclude that the legal construct of military assistance on request is likely to be displaced or eclipsed by the right to individual or collective self-defence in the near future. Instead, the specific circumstances of the situation in question will determine whether states prefer to rely on either the one legal construct or the other, or even rely on both as parallel grounds for the use of force in the pursuit of non-state actors.

7
Conclusion

1. The limited requirements for military assistance on request under customary international law

The analysis undertaken in this monograph attempted to identify the legal requirements set by contemporary customary international law for the legal construct of military assistance on request. As the notion of request in this study is synonymous with that of valid consent, the answer to this question turns on identifying the preconditions for valid consent by the requesting state to the sending of armed forces (whether by land, air, or sea) by the sending state(s) or international organization. The preceding chapters attempted to identify these conditions by exploring them in relation to the authority entitled to extend a request or invitation for military assistance; the type of situations (conflicts) during which such assistance may (or may not) be requested; the international humanitarian and human rights law pedigree of the requesting state; the formal treaty law requirements applicable to military assistance on request; and the relationship between the legal construct of military assistance on request and the right to individual or collective self-defence in article 51 of the United Nations (UN) Charter.[1]

The key requirements for valid consent to direct military assistance that have emerged from the preceding analysis can be summarized as follows. First, the extension of a request or invitation for direct military assistance remains the exclusive prerogative of the recognized, *de jure* government. Second, state and organizational practice further revealed that military assistance on request by the recognized government is permissible as long as the incumbent government remains recognized. In particular, the fact that a besieged, incumbent government has lost control over parts of its territory and population would not curb its competence to request and receive direct military assistance. Current state practice and *opinio juris*, therefore, do not support the widely shared view in scholarship that military assistance on request is not permissible during a civil war or non-international armed conflict (NIAC). Third, the pedigree of the requesting government in relation to international humanitarian and human rights law does not as such prevent it from requesting or receiving direct military assistance. Fourth, very few formal requirements apply to the issuing of valid consent, apart from the fact that it has to

[1] United Nations, Charter of the United Nations (24 October 1945) 1 NTS XVI https://treaties.un.org/doc/source/docs/charter-all-lang.pdf.

be issued (and withdrawn) by the head of state and/or government and that it must be of an ad hoc nature. Fifth and finally, the legal construct of military assistance on request and the right to individual or collective self-defence constitute separate (parallel) legal bases for military action in the territorial state. However, it is possible that the latter can be displaced by the former if the valid consent of the territorial state is reduced to an element of the necessity requirement.

As far as the first requirement for military assistance on request is concerned, the analysis in Chapter 2 revealed that beyond the confinements of the decolonization context, (any) military assistance to opposition groups still constitutes a violation of the principle of non-intervention, as well as the prohibition of the use of force. Furthermore, the effective control doctrine remains the point of departure for determining the *de jure* government, even though democratic legitimacy in the form of free and fair elections have at times been decisive in this regard. However, state and organizational practice, particularly in the Americas and Africa, indicates that coup regimes and unfree and unfair elections remain to be tolerated at regular intervals. Therefore, it would be premature to claim that democratic legitimacy of origin is a prerequisite for governmental recognition. Also, the proliferation of internationally recognized interim governments that came about through negotiated settlements suggests that in conflict situations both effective control and democratic legitimacy at times remain aspirational criteria for governmental recognition. In these situations the recognition of the interim authority as the *de jure* government is based on the hope that a government in which all major parties to the conflict are represented may ultimately yield the stability required for effective control and the holding of free and fair elections.

Once recognized as the *de jure* government, international law attaches a strong presumption of continued recognition to the incumbent government. This implies that also in instances of internal turmoil in which the incumbent government may have lost control over parts of its territory, it retains the competence to incur rights and obligations on behalf of the state. However, this exception would not apply where the incumbent regime no longer is identifiable due to implosion. It is also arguable that it would no longer be applicable where there is a competing authority (or competing authorities) that claim(s) to be the *de jure* government and the international community of states is clearly divided in terms of which authority to recognize. In such a situation, it is unlikely that any of the competing entities would have the competence to incur rights and obligations on behalf of a state in a comprehensive manner, including consenting to direct military assistance. While the current situation in Venezuela would be a case in point, situations in which the international community has been sharply divided about the identity of the *de jure* government have been rare since the end of the Cold War. On the whole, therefore, the presumption of continued recognition of the *de jure* government remains strong.

Moreover, the analysis further revealed that the loss of control over territory and population does not limit the right of the recognized government to request and receive direct military assistance. In particular, the analysis in Chapter 3 supports the conclusion that this would be the case even where the conflict in the requesting state has crossed the threshold of a civil war/non-international armed conflict (NIAC). Post-Cold War state and organizational practice and *opinio juris* do not convincingly support the widely held scholarly view that the right to self-determination prohibits any direct military assistance to a recognized government during a civil war/NIAC. Stated differently, it does not support the claim that the potential lack of 'representativeness' of the recognized government during a civil war/NIAC would limit the extent to which the *de jure* government can act on behalf of the state (and its people) in matters pertaining to the use of force. Furthermore, attempts to explain current state practice by means of counter-terrorism and counter-intervention exceptions to a general prohibition of military assistance during a civil war/NIAC encounter major practical (and potentially also conceptual) obstacles and, therefore, would not seem viable.

As far as any requirements regarding the international humanitarian and human rights law pedigree of the requesting government are concerned, Chapter 4 illuminated that customary international law does not prohibit direct military assistance to requesting governments implicated in widespread violations of international humanitarian and/or human rights law. Where it can be established that the direct military assistance has aided or assisted the requesting government in the violation of its obligations under international humanitarian and human rights law, this can trigger the derivate state responsibility of the assisting state under customary international law. However, the thresholds under customary international law for incurring derivative state responsibility remain high and fraught with uncertainty. Moreover, even where an assisting state does incur state responsibility under customary international law for aiding or assisting violations of international humanitarian and human rights law of the assisted (requesting) state, this does not in and of itself imply that the assisting state has to terminate its direct military support. As yet, state practice does not support the conclusion that such withdrawal is required by general international law. This remains the case even where such violations amount to serious violations of peremptory norms of international law in terms of article 40 of the Responsibility of States for Internationally Wrongful Acts of 2001.[2]

If and to the extent to which an assisting state decides to withdraw its troops and/or air power from a state with a problematic pedigree in the area of international humanitarian and human rights law, this would more likely have to do

[2] ILC Draft Articles on Responsibility of States for Internationally Wrongful Acts with Commentaries, 2001 II Yearbook of the International Law Commission (ASR); UN Doc A/Res/56/83 (28 January 2002).

with policy reasons. Intervening states may find the nature and scope of the precautionary measures necessary to prevent their implication in violations of international humanitarian and human rights law too time-consuming and costly. However, in the absence of such measures the intervening states (in addition to potentially incurring derivate state responsibility) risk significant reputational loss and credibility in terms of their own respect for international law. This risk is particularly high where the institutional shortcomings of an inviting state may be such that no amount of training or technical assistance would, within a foreseeable time, bring about the expertise and discipline required for ensuring that the governmental military forces act in accordance with international humanitarian and human rights law.[3] In such an instance, the intervening state may conclude that the withdrawal of direct military assistance would be the most prudent option.

In Chapter 5 it came to the fore that as far as formal treaty law requirements are concerned, customary international law currently only recognizes two requirements that are particular to direct military assistance on request. The first would be that the request for or consent to military assistance must be issued (and withdrawn) by the highest officials of a state, namely, the head of state and/or government. Where these two positions are not combined within the same person and there is disagreement between them as to whether consent (still) exists, the domestic law of the country in question may be decisive in determining who has the final say in the matter. In addition, customary international law requires that *ex ante* consent as expressed in pro-invasion treaty clauses must be complemented by ad hoc consent at the time of the forcible measures. While the post-Cold War practice in this regard is limited, current (African) state and organizational practice suggests that the pro-invasion clauses in article 4(h) of the Constitutive Act of the African Union (AU) of 2000[4] and article 25 of the Protocol Relating to the Mechanism for Conflict Prevention, Management, Resolution, Peace-Keeping and Security of 1999 of the Economic Community of West African States (the 1999 Protocol)[5] have in practice been applied in line with the customary right of states to withdraw prior consent to forcible measures at any time. Consequently, the ad hoc consent serves to verify that the prior consent has not since been (implicitly) withdrawn.

This restrictive interpretation of article 4(h) of the AU Constitutive Act and article 25 of the 1999 Protocol reflects a reluctance on the part of the member states to deploy decision making by a qualified majority in a way that presumes the target state's actual consent to the pending forcible measures, based on its *ex ante* consent

[3] B Finucane, 'Partners and Legal Pitfalls' (2016) 92 International Law Studies 430.

[4] Constitutive Act of the African Union of 11 July 2000 (2158 UNTS 3) http://www.peaceau.org/uploads/au-act-en.pdf.

[5] Protocol Relating to the Mechanism for Conflict Prevention, Management, Resolution, Peace-Keeping and Security of 10 December 1999 https://www.zif-berlin.org/fileadmin/uploads/analyse/dokumente/ECOWAS_Protocol_ConflictPrevention.pdf.

expressed through treaty ratification or accession. Simultaneously, there is a reluctance on their part to accept that such *ex ante* consent places the forcible measures resulting from the respective pro-invasion clauses beyond the scope of 'enforcement measures' in terms of article 53(1) of the UN Charter. Instead, any such forcible measures in the absence of additional, ad hoc consent of the target state are still perceived as coercive action that requires the authorization of the United Nations Security Council (UNSC) under Chapter VII and/or Chapter VIII of the United Nations Charter.

Apart from these two constraints, customary international law does not seem to impose any particular formal requirements on states expressing consent to forcible measures on its territory. Notably, the same high thresholds attached to coercion under customary international law apply, as a result of which any established consent by the recognized government is effectively presumed to have been freely given. Also, states enjoy considerable freedom in relation to the manner in which their consent is expressed or withdrawn. While it is preferable for the purposes of legal certainty that any consent to military assistance be issued expressly, it can also be done tacitly. Whether this was the case will depend on the circumstances and, in particular, on the conduct of the territorial state subsequent to any military intervention. Similarly, the conduct of the territorial state will be decisive in determining whether particular military action falls within the scope of the consent issued, as well as whether consent has been withdrawn.

Finally, Chapter 6 illuminated that the evolving nature of the right to individual or collective self-defence in article 51 of the UN Charter,[6] including the lowering of the threshold for attribution of indirect attacks to states and the attribution of armed attacks to non-state actors, has the potential to diminish the relevance of the legal construct of military assistance on request. In instances where armed attacks by non-state actors are attributed to 'unwilling'/'substantially involved'/'harbouring' states or to non-state actors in 'unable' states, victim states may—depending on the situation—prefer to invoke the right to individual or collective self-defence rather than the legal construct of military assistance on request.

Despite evidentiary burdens that victim states may face when doing so, the invocation of individual or collective self-defence potentially would allow them to exercise forcible measures in a broader geographical area and potentially without the consent of the state on whose territory the forcible measures are used. This possibility in principle encroaches on the relevance of the role of state consent in the *jus ad bellum* paradigm. At the same time, it would be premature to conclude that the legal construct of military assistance on request is likely to be displaced or eclipsed by the right to individual or collective self-defence in the near future. Instead, the specific circumstances of the situation in question will determine whether states

[6] UN Charter (n 1).

prefer to rely on either the one legal construct or the other, or even rely on both as parallel grounds for the use of force in the pursuit of non-state actors.

2. The erosion of the prohibition of the use of force and collective security?

The limited constraints placed by customary international law on the legal construct of military assistance on request can contribute to the further erosion of the prohibition of the threat or use of force in article 2(4) of the UN Charter. This is in an era where the scope of this prohibition is already under pressure due to the expansive use of the right to individual or collective self-defence in article 51 of the UN Charter. Any such erosion would simultaneously also imply a weakening of the notion of the centralization of the use of force underpinning the UN Charter. The more leeway states have to request and provide direct military assistance unilaterally, the more limited the role of the UNSC becomes in taking a collective decision on decisions pertaining to the use of force.[7]

Particularly disconcerting is the fact that due to the high customary thresholds attached to coercion, any established consent by the recognized government effectively is presumed to have been freely given. This can facilitate coercive military intervention in all but name, as the states consenting to direct military assistance are likely to be politically and militarily fragile. They may therefore not be in a position to resist undue (if covert) pressure from militarily strong states with hegemonic motives to accept 'offers' of military assistance. Similarly, the territorial state may refrain from withdrawing any consent to military assistance, due to covert pressure from a militarily strong 'assisting' state. The fact that states formally have the right to withdraw consent to forcible measures at any time and without any formal requirements, therefore, may in practice not provide meaningful protection to its sovereignty and territorial integrity. Consequently, there is a real risk that—depending on the circumstances—military assistance on request can reduce article 2(4) of the UN Charter to an empty shell. In addition, it underscores the risk of abuse of military assistance on request by powerful states for imperialistic and neo-colonial purposes.

Furthermore, the limited relevance of the right to self-determination in posing a meaningful limitation to the right to military assistance on request in practice is further evidence of the erosion of article 2(4) of the UN Charter and, by extension, the central role of the UNSC in relation to decisions pertaining to the use of

[7] See also J Brunnée and S Toope, 'Self-Defence Against Non-State Actors: Are Powerful States Willing But Unable to Change the International Law?' (2018) 67 International and Comparative Law Quarterly 280–81; see also J von Bernstorff, 'Drone Strikes, Terrorism and the Zombie: On the Construction of an Administrative Law of Transnational Executions' (2016) 5 European Society of International Law (ESIL) Reflections http://www.esil-sedi.eu/node/1368.

force. Chapter 3 referred to the fact that conceptually, direct military assistance that violates the right to self-determination by preventing a state (or its peoples) from independently determining its political future also amounts to the use of force against the political independence of a state. Stated differently, military assistance to a recognized government in a manner that violates the right to self-determination would simultaneously amount to a violation of the prohibition of the use of force 'against the territorial integrity or independence' of the state in question.[8] However, due to the fact that military assistance to a recognized government in practice never seems to reach the threshold where it violates the right to self-determination, the question of whether article 2(4) of the UN Charter has (also) been violated does not arise. On the one hand, this reality reduces the relevance of article 2(4) of the UN Charter. On the other hand, it also implies that the construct of military assistance on request can serve as an instrument by means of which befriended, authoritarian governments can sustain one another militarily and quell any form of resistance for as long as they are able to generate military support from one another.

It is arguable that these risks to article 2(4) of the UN Charter and collective security are more prominent in instances where requests for direct military assistance are issued to (an) individual state(s), than when they are extended to (sub)-regional organizations such as the African Union (AU) or ECOWAS. In the latter instances, the deliberative decision-making processes and qualified majority requirements provided for in the respective treaty framework of the organization in question can curb some of the coercive and imperialistic motives that may be present among those member states that are keen to offer military assistance.[9] In fact, the inclusion of articles 4(j) and 4(h) in the AU Constitutive Act and of article 25 in the 1999 Protocol makes it possible for these (sub)-regional organizations to deploy military assistance on request as a collective security tool on the regional level. This may particularly be the case in situations where a UNSC authorization for the use of force is prevented by a (threat of) veto by any of the five permanent members, even though a majority of UNSC members favour military intervention.

Military assistance by the (sub)-regional organization at the request of a member state can under these circumstances constitute a residual form of collective security.[10] The political (if non-binding) endorsement by the UNSC of the ECOWAS military support at the request of the new Gambian President in 2017 arguably exemplifies such a situation.[11] Similarly, and depending on the circumstances of

[8] The UN Charter (n 1) art 2(4) determines that '[a]ll members shall refrain in their international relations from the threat or use of force against the territorial integrity or political independence of any state, or in any other manner inconsistent with the purposes of the United Nations'.

[9] PE Harrell, 'Modern-Day "Guarantee Clauses" and the Legal Authority of Multinational Organizations to Authorize the Use of Force' (2008) 33 Yale Journal of International Law 431.

[10] G Nolte, *Eingreifen auf Einladung: Zur völkerrechtlichen Zulässigkeit des Einsatzes fremder Truppen im internen Konflikt auf Einladung der Regierung* (Springer 1999) 627–28.

[11] UN Doc S/RES/2337 (17 January 2017).

the case, requests to (an) individual state(s) for direct military assistance can also overlap with the collective security interests of the international community. This *inter alia* was the case in Mali, where the French military assistance to the besieged Malian government resulted from the inability of the African-led International Support Mission in Mali (AFISMA) to give effect to a UNSC authorization under Chapter VII of the UN Charter. In accordance with its mandate, AFISMA was authorized to take all necessary measures to support the Malian authorities in recovering the areas in the north of its territory under the control of terrorist, extremist, and armed groups.[12] However, when it transpired that AFISMA would not be capable of giving effect to its mandate, the Malian government extended a request for military assistance to France, whose intervention was subsequently praised by the UNSC.[13]

However, any deployment of military assistance on request as a collective (regional) security tool essentially concerns ad hoc requests for such assistance. As indicated earlier, *ex ante* consent in the form of pro-invasion clauses, such as article 4(h) of the AU Constitutive Act[14] and article 25 of the 1999 Protocol[15] is only compatible with article 53(1) of the UN Charter when complemented by ad hoc consent of the territorial state at the time of the planned military operation. Stated differently, in contemporary international law the only pro-invasion clause that does not require the additional ad hoc consent of the territorial state is article 39 of the UN Charter in combination with articles 42 and/or 53 of the UN Charter. The UNSC remains the only organ with the competence to authorize the use of force within a member state on the basis of Chapters VII and VIII of the UN Charter, regardless of whether the state in question consents to the forcible measures at the time they are occurring.

It remains to be seen whether the persistent reluctance of the UNSC to take coercive action under Chapter VII of the UN Charter in relation to the major armed conflicts of our time will trigger any significant development in relation to state practice and *opinio juris* in this regard.[16] The reluctance within the AU to follow through with the invocation of article 4(h) of the AU Constitutive Act in Burundi in 2015 (in the absence of the ad hoc consent of the Burundian government) suggests that the members of (sub)-regional organizations are not necessarily less reluctant than the UNSC to authorize military measures. Instead, these organizations are also plagued by internal divisions, which in practice makes it very difficult to reach the required majorities for triggering the respective pro-invasion clauses. Added to that, the (sub)-regional organizations under discussion rarely possess the

[12] UN Doc S/RES/ 2085 (20 December 2012) para 9(b).
[13] UN Doc S/RES/2100 (13 April 2013).
[14] AU Constitutive Art (n 4) art 4(h).
[15] See ECOWAS Mechanism Protocol (n 5) art 25.
[16] See also D Wippman, 'Treaty-Based Intervention: Who Can Say No' (1995) 62 University of Chicago Law Review 654–55, who supports legal development in this regard.

military, financial, or logistical capacity required for large-scale military assistance. As already noted, this *inter alia* was the case in Mali where AFISMA's capacity constraints impaired its ability to give effect to a military mandate authorized under Chapter VII of the UN Charter.

In light of these realities it is fair to conclude that in the immediate future, direct military assistance on request is likely to be performed by individual state(s) with a strong geopolitical interest the territorial state. Moreover, as long as the UNSC and (sub)-regional organizations remain reluctant to take collective action in relation to escalating internal conflicts, bilateral requests for direct military assistance by fragile *de jure* governments to military strong states are likely to proliferate in the immediate future. This in turn implies an increased risk of a further erosion of article 2(4) of the UN Charter and the gains of collective security since the adoption of the UN Charter.

Selected Bibliography

Alston P and Macdonald E (eds), *Human Rights, Intervention, and the Use of Force* (OUP 2008)

Amvane G, 'Intervention Pursuant to Article 4(h) of the Constitutive Act of the African Union Without United Nations Security Council Authorisation' (2015) 15 African Human Rights Law Journal 282

Arceneaux C and Pion-Berlin D, 'Issues, Threats, and Institutions: Explaining OAS Responses to Democratic Dilemmas in Latin America' (2007) 49 Latin American Politics and Society 1

Aust HP, *Complicity and the Law of State Responsibility* (CUP 2011)

Bannelier-Christakis K, 'Military Interventions Against ISIL in Iraq, Syria and Libya, and the Legal Basis of Consent' (2016) 29 Leiden Journal of International Law 743

Bannelier K and Christakis T, 'Under the UN Security Council's Watchful Eyes: Military Intervention by Invitation in the Malian Conflict' (2013) 26 Leiden Journal of International Law 861

Bennouna M, *Le Consentement à l'Ingérence Militaire dans le Conflits Interne* (Librairie Générale de Droit et de Jurisprudence 1974)

Bethlehem D, 'Principles Relevant to the Scope of a State's Right of Self-Defence Against an Imminent or Actual Armed Attack by Non-State Actors' (2012) 106 American Journal of International Law 770

Birikorang E, 'Lessons Learned and Best Practice From a Troubled Region: ECOWAS and the Development of the ECOWAS Standby Force' in Engel U and Gomes Porto J (eds), *Towards an African Peace and Security Regime* (Ashgate 2013) 89

Brunnée J and Toope S, 'The Use of Force: International Law After Iraq' (2004) 53 International and Comparative Law Quarterly 785

Brunnée J and Toope S, 'Self-Defence Against Non-State Actors: Are Powerful States Willing But Unable to Change the International Law?' (2018) 67 International and Comparative Law Quarterly 263

Byrne M, 'Consent and the Use of Force: An Examination of "Intervention by Invitation" as a Basis for US Drone Strikes in Pakistan, Somalia and Yemen' (2016) 3 Journal of the Use of Force in International Law 97

Cerna CM, 'Universal Democracy: An International Legal Right or the Pipe Dream of the West?' (1995) 27 New York University Journal of International Law and Politics 289

Cerna CM, 'Democratic Legitimacy and Respect for Human Rights: The New Gold Standard' (2015) 108 American Journal of International Law Unbound 222

Charlesworth H, 'Democracy and International Law' (2014) 37 Collected Courses of the Hague Academy of International Law 43

Charney JI, 'The Use of Force Against Terrorism and International Law' (2001) 95 American Journal of International Law 835

Christakis T and Bannelier K, '*Volenti non fit injuria*? Les effets du consentement à l'intervention militaire' (2004) 50 Annuaire Français de Droit International 102

Corten O, *The Law Against War: The Prohibition on the Use of Force in Contemporary International Law* (Hart Publishing 2010)

Corten O, 'The "Unwilling or Unable" Test: Has it Been and Could It Be Accepted?' (2016) 29 Leiden Journal of International Law 777

Corten O, 'L'intervention de la Russie en Syrie: que reste-t-il du principe de non-intervention dans les guerres civiles?' (2018) 4 Questions of International Law http://www.qil-qdi.org/lintervention-de-la-russie-en-syrie-que-reste-t-il-du-principe-de-non-intervention-dans-les-guerres-civiles/

Corten O, 'Intervention by Invitation: The Expanding Role of the UN Security Council' 4 Max Planck Trialogues on the Law of Peace and War (forthcoming in 2020, on file with author) 1

Corten O and Klein P (eds), *The Vienna Convention on the Law of Treaties. A Commentary* (OUP 2011)

Crawford J, 'Revising the Draft Articles on State Responsibility' (1999) 10 European Journal of International Law 435

Crawford J, *State Responsibility: The General Part* (CUP 2013)

David E, 'International (Non-International) Armed Conflict' in Clapham A and Gaeta P (eds), *The Oxford Handbook of International Law in Armed Conflict* (OUP 2014) 352

Dekker I and Myjer E, 'Air Strikes on Bosnian Positions: Is NATO Also Legally the Proper Instrument of the UN?' (1996) 9 Leiden Journal of International Law 411

D'Aspremont J, 'Legitimacy of Governments in the Age of Democracy' (2006) 38 New York Journal of International Law and Politics 877

Deeks A, '"Unwilling or Unable": Towards a Normative Framework for Extraterritorial Self-Defence' (2012) 52 Virginia Journal of International Law 483

Dersso SA, 'The Jurisprudence of the African Commission on Human and Peoples' Rights With Respect to Peoples' Rights' (2006) 6 African Human Rights Law Journal 358

Dersso SA, 'To Intervene or Not to Intervene? An Inside View of the AU's Decision-Making on Article 4(h) and Burundi' World Peace Foundation (26 February 2016) 1–15 https://sites.tufts.edu/wpf/files/2017/05/AU-Decision-Making-on-Burundi_Dersso.pdf

De Wet E, *The Chapter VII Powers of the United Nations Security Council* (Hart Publishing 2004)

De Wet E, 'The Evolving Role of ECOWAS and the SADC in Peace Operations: A Challenge to the Primacy of the United Nations Security Council in Matters of Peace and Security?' (2014) 27 Leiden Journal of International Law 361

De Wet E, 'The Modern Practice of Intervention by Invitation in Africa and its Implications for the Prohibition of the Use of Force' (2015) 26 European Journal of International Law 979

De Wet E, 'Reinterpreting Exceptions to the Use of Force in the Interest of Security: Forcible Intervention by Invitation and the Demise of the Negative Equality Principle' (2017) 111 American Journal of International Law Unbound 307

De Wet E, 'Complicity in the Violations of Human Rights and Humanitarian Law by Incumbent Governments through Direct Military Assistance on Request' (2018) 67 International and Comparative Law Quarterly 287

De Wet E, 'The Invocation of the Right to Self-Defence in Response to Armed Attacks Conducted by Armed Groups: Implications for Attribution' (2019) 32 Leiden Journal of International Law 91

Dinstein Y, *War, Aggression and Self-Defence* (5th edn, CUP 2011)

Dörr O and Schmalenbach K (eds), *Vienna Convention on the Law of Treaties. A Commentary* (2nd edn, Springer 2018)

Doswald-Beck L, 'The Legal Validity of Military Intervention by Invitation of the Government' (1986) 56 British Yearbook of International Law 189

Ferreira-Snyman A, 'Intervention with Specific Reference to the Relationship Between the United Nations Security Council and the African Union' (2010) 63 Comparative and International Law Journal of Southern Africa 139

Finucane B, 'Partners and Legal Pitfalls' (2016) 92 International Law Studies 408

Flasch O, 'The Legality of the Airstrikes Against ISIL in Syria: New Insights on the Extraterritorial Use of Force Against Non-State Actors' (2016) 3 Journal on the Use of Force and International Law 37

Fleck D, *The Handbook of International Humanitarian Law* (3rd edn, OUP 2013)

Fletcher GP and Ohlin JD, *Defending Humanity. When Force is Justified and Why* (OUP 2008)

Fombad CM, 'Constitutional Reforms and Constitutionalism in Africa: Reflections on Some Current Challenges and Future Prospects' (2011) 59 Buffalo Law Review 1007

Fox GH, 'Intervention by Invitation' in Weller M (ed), *The Oxford Handbook of the Use of Force in International Law* (OUP 2015) 817

Fox GH and Nolte G, 'Intolerant Democracies' (1995) 36 Harvard International Law Journal 1

Fox GH and Roth BR, *Democratic Governance and International Law* (CUP 2010) 1

Franck T, 'The Emerging Right to Democratic Governance' (1992) 86 American Journal of International Law (1992) 46

Franck T, 'Terrorism and the Right to Self-Defence' (2001) 95 American Journal of International Law 839

Franck T, 'Rethinking Collective Security' in Schmitt M and Peijc J (eds), *International Law and Armed Conflict: Exploring the Faultlines. Essays in Honour of Yoram Dinstein* (Martinus Nijhoff Publishers 2007) 21

Gray C, 'The Limits of Force' (2016) 376 Collected Courses of The Hague Academy of International Law 93

Gray C, *International Law and the Use of Force* (4th edn, OUP 2018)

Hafner G, 'Final Report: Intervention by Invitation' (2009) 73 Annuaire de l'Institut de droit international 299

Hakimi M, 'Defensive Force Against Non-State Actors: The State of Play' (2015) 91 International Law Scholarship 1

Harrell PE, 'Modern Day "Guarantee Clauses" and the Legal Authority of Multinational Organizations to Authorize the Use of Force' (2008) 33 Yale Journal of International Law 417

Jackson M, *Complicity in International Law* (OUP 2015)

Johnstone I, 'The Plea of Necessity in International Legal Discourse: Humanitarian Intervention and Counter-Terrorism' (2005) 43 Columbia Journal of Translational Law 337

Jørgensen NHB, 'Complicity in Torture in a Time of Terror: Interpreting the European Court of Human Rights Extraordinary Rendition Cases' (2017) 16 Chinese Journal of International Law 11

Khayre AAM, 'Self-Defence, Intervention by Invitation, or Proxy-War? The Legality of the 2006 Ethiopian Invasion of Somalia' (2014) 22 African Journal of International and Comparative Law 208

Kreß C and Nußberger B, 'Pro-Democratic Intervention in Current International Law: The Case of The Gambia in January 2017' (2017) 4 Journal on the Use of Force and International Law 239

Lanovoy V, *Complicity and its Limits in the Law of International Responsibility* (Hart Publishing 2016)

Lanovoy V, 'The Use of Force by Non-State Actors and the Limits of Attribution of Conduct' (2017) 28 European Journal of International Law 563

Levitt BS, 'A Desultory Defense of Democracy: OAS Resolution 1080 and the Inter-American Democratic Charter' (2006) 48 Latin American Politics and Society 93

Levitt J, 'Humanitarian Intervention by Regional Actors in Internal Conflicts: The Case of ECOWAS in Liberia and Sierra Leone' (1998) 12 Temple Journal of International and Comparative Law 333

Le Mon CJ, 'Unilateral Intervention by Invitation in Civil Wars: The Effective Control Test Tested' (2003) 35 New York University Journal of International Law and Politics 297

Liang YL, 'Recognition by the United Nations of the Representation of a Member State: Criteria and Procedure' (1951) 45 American Journal of International Law 689

Lieblich E, 'Intervention and Consent: Consensual Forcible Intervention in Internal Armed Conflict as International Agreement' (2011) 29 Boston University International Law Journal 339

Lieblich E, *International Law and Civil Wars. Intervention and Consent* (Routledge 2013) 16

Lowe V, 'Responsibility for the Conduct of Other States' (2002) 101 Journal of International Law and Diplomacy 1

Marks S, 'What has Become of the Emerging Right to Democratic Governance?' (2011) 22 European Journal of International Law 507

Moelle MP, *The International Responsibility of International Organizations: Co-operation in Peacekeeping Operations* (CUP 2017)

Moynihan H, 'Aiding and Assisting: Challenges in Armed Conflict and Counterterrorism' Chatham House Research Paper, November 2016 1 https://www.chathamhouse.org/sites/default/files/publications/research/2016-11-11-aiding-assisting-challenges-armed-conflict-moynihan.pdf

Murphy SD, *Humanitarian Intervention: The United Nations in an Evolving World Order* (University of Pennsylvania Press 1996) 342

Murphy SD, 'Democratic Legitimacy and the Recognition of States and Governments' (1999) 48 International and Comparative Law Quarterly 545

Murphy SD, 'Self-Defence and the Israeli Wall Advisory Opinion: An *Ipse Dixit* from the ICJ?' (2005) 99 American Journal of International Law 62

Murphy SD, 'The International Legality of US Military Cross-Border Operations from Afghanistan into Pakistan' (2008) 84 International Legal Studies 109

Nenadic S, 'Lawfulness of New Zealand's Military Deployment to Iraq: Intervention by Invitation Tested' (2014) 12 New Zealand Yearbook of International Law 3

Nguyen QTT, 'Rethinking the Legality of Intervention by Invitation: Toward Neutrality' (2019) [First View] Journal of Conflict and Security Law 1

Nolte G, 'Restoring Peace by Regional Action' (1993) 53 Zeitschrift für ausländisches öffentliches Recht und Völkerrecht 603

Nolte G, *Eingreifen auf Einladung Zur völkerrechtlichen Zulässigkeit des Einsatzes fremder Truppen im internen Konflikt auf Einladung der Regierung* (Springer 1999)

Nolte G, 'The Resolution of the *Institut de Droit International* on Military Assistance on Request' (2012) 45 Revue Belge de Droit International 241

Nolte G and Aust HP, 'Equivocal Helpers—Complicit States, Mixed Messages and International Law' (2009) 58 International and Comparative Law Quarterly 1

Nowrot K and Schabacker EW, 'The Use of Force to Restore Democracy: International Legal Implications of the ECOWAS Intervention in Sierra Leone' (1998) 14 American University International Law Review 312

Nußberger B, 'Military Strikes in Yemen in 2015: Intervention by Invitation and Self-Defence in the Course of Yemen's "Model Transitional Process"' (2017) 4 Journal on the Use of Force and International Law 110

O'Connell ME, 'The UN, NATO, and International Law After Kosovo' (2000) 22 Human Rights Quarterly 57

O'Connell ME, 'Dangerous Departures' (2013) 107 American Journal of International Law 380

Orakhelashvili A, 'The Legal Framework of Peace Operations by Regional Organisations' (2007) 11 Journal of International Peacekeeping 133

Österdahl I, *La France dans l'Afrique de l'Après-Guerre Froide Interventions et Justifications* (Nordiska, Afrikainstitutet 1997)

Österdahl I, 'The Continued Relevance of Collective Security Under the UN: The Security Council, Regional Organisations and the General Assembly' (1999) 10 Finnish Yearbook of International Law103

Oswald B, 'Interplay as Regards Dealing with Detainees in International Military Operations' in E de Wet and JK Kleffner (eds), *Convergence and Conflicts of Human Rights and International Humanitarian Law in Military Operations* (Pretoria University Law Press 2014) 67

Paddeu F, *Justification and Excuse in International Law* (CUP 2018)

Paliwal S, 'The Primacy of Regional Organisations in International Peacekeeping: The African Example' (2011) 51 Virginia Journal of International Law 185

Perkins JA, 'The Right to Counter-Intervention' (1987) 17 Georgia Journal of International and Comparative Law 171

Plakokefalos I, 'The Use of Force byNon-State Actors and the Limits of Attribution of Conduct: A Reply to Vladyslav Lanovoy' (2017) 28 European Journal of International Law 587

Roth BR, *Governmental Illegitimacy in International Law* (OUP 2000).

Roth BR, 'Secessions, *Coups* and the International Rule of Law: Assessing the Decline of the Effective Control Doctrine' (2010) 11 Melbourne Journal of International Law 393

Ruys T, *'Armed Attack' and Article 51 of the UN Charter* (CUP 2010)

Ruys T, 'Of Arms and "Non-lethal Assistance" – Issues Surrounding Third-State Intervention in the Syrian Civil War' (2014) 13 Chinese Journal of International Law 13

Ruys T and Ferro L, 'Weathering the Storm: Legality and Legal Implications of the Saudi-Led Military Intervention in Yemen' (2016) 15 International and Comparative Law Quarterly 61

Sampson I 'The Responsibility to Protect and ECOWAS Mechanisms on Peace and Security: Assessing their Convergence and Divergence on Intervention' (2011) 16 Journal of Conflict and Security Law 507

Saranti V, 'Pro-Democratic Intervention, Invitation, or "Responsibility to Protect"? Challenges to International Law from the "Arab Spring"' in Panara C and Wilson G (eds), *The Arab Spring: New Patterns for Democracy and International Law* (Brill 2013) 169

Sarkin J, 'The Role of the United Nations, the African Union and Africa's Sub-Regional Organisations in Dealing with Africa's Human Rights Problems: Connecting Humanitarian Intervention and the Responsibility to Protect' (2009) 53 Journal of African Law 1

Saul M, 'From Haiti to Somalia: The Assistance Model and the Paradox of State Reconstruction in International Law' (2009) 11 International Community Law Review 119

Schaller C, 'Using Force Against Terrorists "Outside Areas of Active Hostilities"—The Obama Approach and the Bin Laden Raid Revisited' (2015) 20 Journal of Conflict and Security Law 195

Scott JB, 'The Central American Peace Conference of 1907' (1907) 1 American Journal of International Law 121

Schuit A, Recognition of Governments in International Law and the Recent Conflict in Libya' (2012) 14 International Community Law Review 381.

Simma B and others (eds), *The Charter of the United Nations. A Commentary Vol II* (OUP 2012)

Sivakumaran S, *The Law of International Armed Conflict* (OUP 2012)

Slaughter AM, *A New World Order* (Princeton University Press 2004)

Sloane RD, 'In the Use and Abuse of Necessity in the Law of State Responsibility' (2012) 106 American Journal of International Law 447

Söderbaum F and Hettne B, 'Regional Security in a Global Perspective' in Engel U and Gomes Porto J (eds), *Africa's New Peace and Security Architecture* (Routledge 2011) 13

Söderbaum F and Tavares R (eds), *Regional Organizations in African Security* (Routledge 2011)

Starski P 'Right to Self-Defence, Attribution and the Non-State Actor—Birth of the "Unable or Unwilling" Standard?' (2015) 75 Heidelberg Journal of International Law 455

Starski P, 'Silence Within the Process of Normative Change and Evolution of the Prohibition on the Use of Force: Normative Volatility and Legislative Responsibility' (2017) 4 Journal on the Use of Force and International Law 14

Talmon S, *Recognition of Governments in International Law. With Particular Reference to Governments in Exile* (OUP 1998)

Talmon S, 'De-Recognition of Colonel Qaddafi as Head of State of Libya?' (2011) 60 International and Comparative Law Quarterly 759

Talmon S, 'Recognition of Opposition Groups as the Legitimate Representative of a People' (2013) 12 Chinese Journal of International Law 219

Tams CJ, 'The Use of Force Against Terrorists' (2009) 20 European Journal of International Law 359

Tibori-Szabo K, 'Self-Defence and the United States Policy on Drone Strikes' (2015) 20 Journal of Conflict and Security Law 381

Tladi D, 'Security Council, the Use of Force and Regime Change: Libya and Côte d'Ivoire' (2012) 37 South African Yearbook of International Law 22

Tladi D, 'The Nonconsenting Innocent State: The Problem with Bethlehem's Principle 12' (2013) 107 American Journal of International Law 570

Trapp K, 'Back to Basics: Necessity, Proportionality, and the Right of Self-Defence Against Non-State Terrorist Actors' (2007) 56 International and Comparative Law Quarterly 141

Tsagourias N, 'Self-Defence Against Non-State Actors: The Interaction Between Self-Defence as a Primary Rule and Self-Defence as a Secondary Rule' (2016) 29 Leiden Journal of International Law 801

Van der Vleuten A and Ribeiro Hoffmann A, 'Explaining the Enforcement of Democracy by Regional Organizations: Comparing EU, Mercosur and SADC' (2010) 3 Journal of Common Market Studies 737

Van Steenberghe R, 'Self-Defence in Response to Attacks by Non-State Actors in the Light of Recent State Practice: A Step Forward?' (2010) 23 Leiden Journal of International Law 183

Van Steenberghe, R. 'The Law of Self-Defence and the New Argumentative Landscape on the Expansionists' Side (2016) 29 Leiden Journal of International Law 43

Vidmar J, *Democratic Statehood in International Law* (Hart Publishing 2013) 15

Vidmar J, 'The Use of Force as a Plea of Necessity' (2018) 111 American Journal of International Law Unbound 302

Villiger ME, *Commentary on the 1969 Convention on the Law of Treaties* (Martinus Nijhoff Publishers 2008)
Wilen N and Williams PD, 'The African Union and Coercive Diplomacy: The Case of Burundi' (2018) 4 Journal of Modern African Studies 673
Wippman D, 'Treaty-Based Intervention: Who can Say No?' (1995) 62 University of Chicago Law Review 607
Wippman D, 'Military Intervention, Regional Organizations and Host-State Consent' (1996) 7 Duke Journal of Comparative and International Law 209
Wright Q, 'The Cuban Quarantine' (1963) 57 American Journal of International Law 546
Zamani M and Nikouei M, 'Intervention by Invitation, Collective Self-Defence and the Enigma of Effective Control' (2017) 16 Chinese Journal of International Law 663

Index

Note on index: *For the benefit of digital users, indexed terms that span two pages (e.g., 52–53) may, on occasion, appear on only one of those pages.*